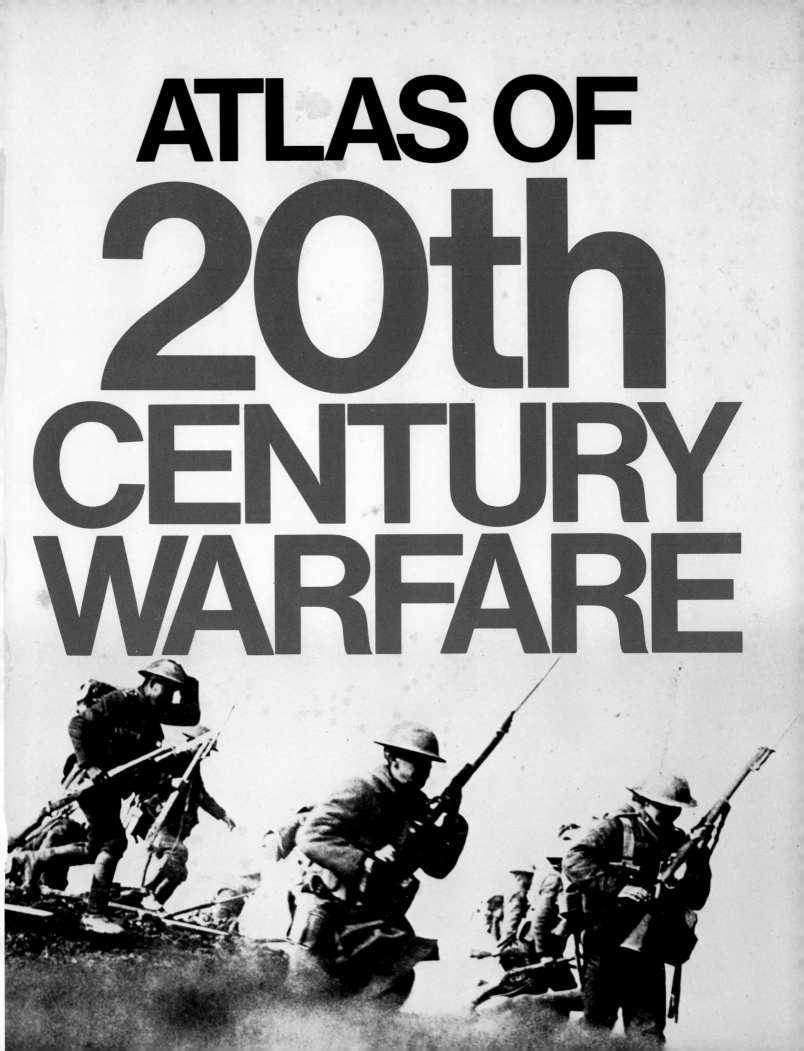

# ATLAS OF
# 20th
# CENTURY
# WARFARE

# ATLAS OF 20th CENTURY WARFARE

## RICHARD NATKIEL

**TEXT BY DONALD SOMMERVILLE & JOHN N. WESTWOOD**
**INTRODUCTION BY JOHN KEEGAN**

GALLERY BOOKS
An imprint of W.H. Smith Publishers Inc.
112 Madison Avenue
New York, New York 10016

A Bison Book

Published by
Gallery Books
A Division of W.H. Smith Publishers Inc.
112 Madison Avenue
New York, New york 10016

Produced by
Bison Books Corp.
15 Sherwood Place
Greenwich, CT. 06830 USA

Maps Copyright © Richard Natkiel
Text Copyright © 1982 Bison books Corp.

ISBN 0-8317-0489-6

2 3 4 5 6 7 8 9 10

Printed in Hong Kong

# Contents

South Vietnamese troops man a machine-gun post near Trang Bang at the height of the Vietnam War.

# Introduction

## by John Keegan

Maps are great teachers. Making a map with theodolite and plane-table was – so said officers of the old school who had been obliged to do so as cadets – the best way ever devised of imprinting the facts of landscape on a young mind. A man who had once made a map, they insisted, would never run the risk of losing himself, however bad the map off which he was trying to plot his whereabouts. Officers of a yet older generation regarded any map as a treasure trove, for maps were secret documents of state, whose loss might show an enemy the way into your territory or reveal the ground on to which he could best draw your army into unsought battle. Maps were kept under lock and key, therefore, were stolen, bought, bartered, surreptitiously copied, and valued among the richest booty which could be captured from the enemy. And their value endured, so great was their rarity. Napoleon was pleased to have a Prussian map 50 years old when planning his campaign of 1806 which was to culminate in the great victories of Jena and Auerstädt.

We have come to take maps for granted, so commonplace have they been made by modern processes of reproduction, and so various are the forms in which they are now produced. Yet the very diversity of modern cartography now makes maps better teachers than they have ever been – teachers of geography, of course, but also of economics, strategy, politics, indeed of almost any subject which the cartographer chooses to make his own.

And of no subject are maps a better teacher than history. At a glance the reader is taught or reminded of the great shifts of frontiers which mark the climacterics of the past; closer study re-creates the small but significant differences of opinion between peoples which so often precede and usually follow the major upheavals; detailed scrutiny of perhaps only a single map, if it has been drawn with care and understanding, may yield as much information as many pages of the printed word.

All this is amply borne out by Richard Natkiel's new volume of maps of the twentieth century world. How simple that world was when the century began. Three great empires – the German, Austro-Hungarian and Russian – dominated Europe east of the Rhine. Three other great empires – the British, French and Turkish – dominated the world beyond Europe. Small nationalities could find breathing space scarcely anywhere, even in Europe, which had intoxicated itself with nationalist feeling throughout the nineteenth century. Serbs, Bulgarians, Rumanians and Greeks, it is true, had achieved statehoods of their own, but only because none of the great powers could manage the shamelessness necessary to incorporate one or all after they had been helped to win their liberty from the Turks. Poles, Czechs, Croats, Irish, the submerged nationalities of the great empires, were either told that their nationalisms were invented, or ignored when they produced evidence to the contrary. Non-Europeans were simply punished as rebels when they dared invoke memory of their former freedom.

And so the world might have gone on, for a good part of the century at least, had not the sensations of dissolution from within – partly real but perhaps largely imagined – driven the empires to seek relief by an attack on each other. The result of this bizarre compulsion was the dissolution of one of the three great European empires and the diminution of the other two; a dozen small nationalities, Baltic, Balkan, Caucasian, were delivered in the process. The colonial empires, on the other hand, emerged apparently strengthened, albeit by France and Britain devouring the possessions of Turkey. Turkey shrank to the dimensions of her Anatolian heartland. France and Britain became rulers of her former Arab subjects, as well as of numbers of African tribespeople and Pacific islanders formerly under German rule. The French and British empires were never bigger than in the years after World War I.

Yet their size was not matched by real power, either at home or at the colonial extremities where the imperial idea grated against that of burgeoning local nationalism. The bitter after-taste of World War I made Germany a dangerous neighbor to France and Britain in Europe. Resentment of their patronage by Japan, which was also irked by the condescension of American foreign policy, put their Pacific empires under threat. Between them Germany and Japan, in an alliance at which no one would have guessed even ten years before it was forged, were to impose the second great transformation of twentieth century world politics.

The consequences of their bid for dominance are with us yet. Most important among them was the revival of Russia as a world power, in convulsive reaction to Germany's efforts to destroy her nationhood in 1941. But the discrediting of European rule in Asia by Japan, which brought independence to the whole of its southern and southeastern regions, was as significant. Independence was infectious. It stimulated the mood for it in the rest of the colonial world. It sapped the will to resist the demand for it among the imperial governments. The enormous multiplication of sovereign states in the world which has taken place since 1945 owes more to Japanese example than it does to the anti-imperialist sentiments of revolutionary movements and regimes.

The shape of the ex-colonial world is still to be determined, as the last wars of empire are fought out and the antagonisms of new sovereignties find their expression. In the Third World, war is still a fruitful activity. Paradoxically in the European world, which now inextricably includes the United States, a political rigidity has descended on all the member states and their inter-relationships precisely because war is no longer possible between them. The map of European politics, it seems, must remain fixed as it was left by the outcome of World War II in 1945.

Rest or change, we need a record of what has happened to our world in our century, if we are to understand both and have any glimpse of their future. It is that which this atlas provides.

# The World in 1900

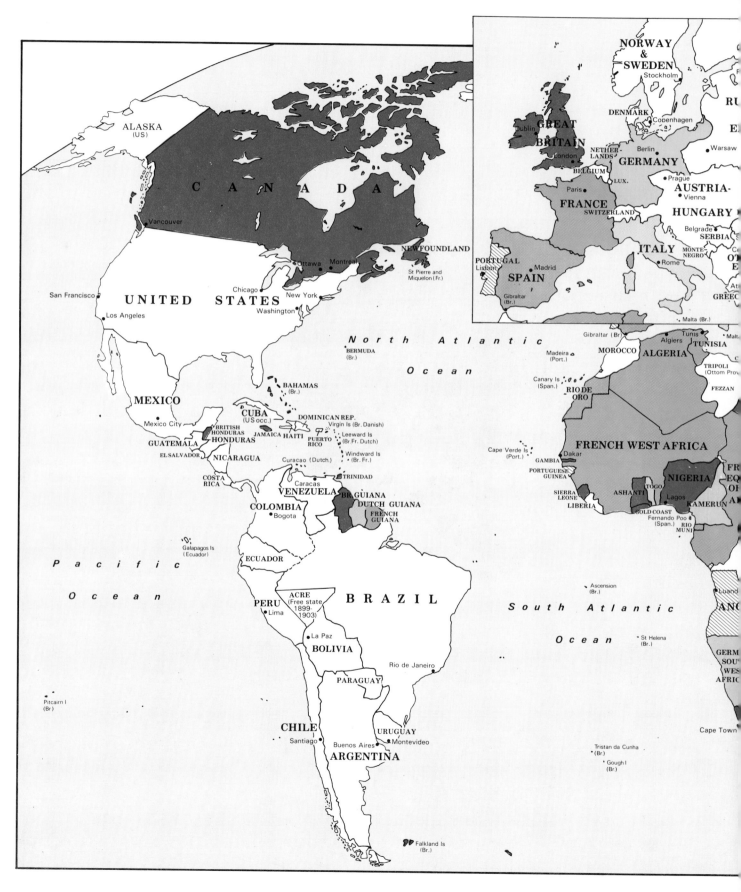

# The New Century, 1900-14

Battered Russian warships in Port Arthur
during the Russo-Japanese War.

14

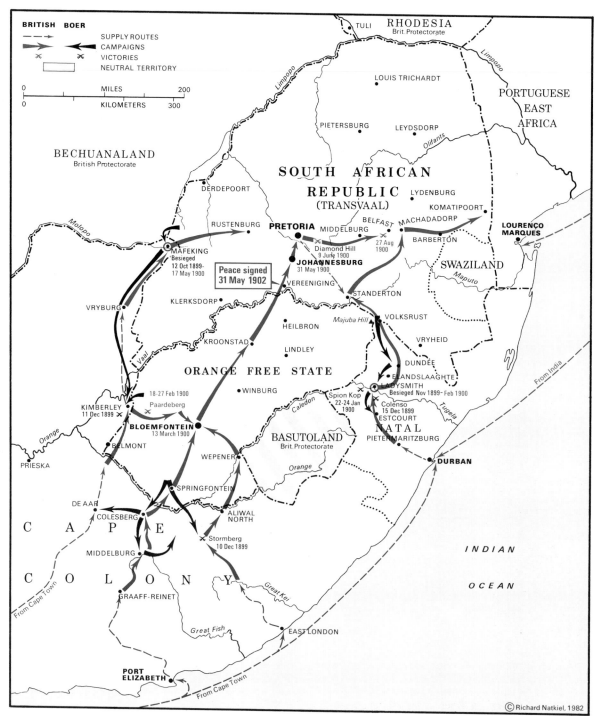

Map legend:

**BRITISH  BOER**
- SUPPLY ROUTES
- CAMPAIGNS
- VICTORIES
- NEUTRAL TERRITORY

MILES 200
KILOMETERS 300

RHODESIA
Brit. Protectorate

TULI

LOUIS TRICHARDT

PORTUGUESE
EAST
AFRICA

BECHUANALAND
British Protectorate

PIETERSBURG     LEYDSDORP

Olifants

DERDEPOORT

SOUTH AFRICAN
REPUBLIC
(TRANSVAAL)

LYDENBURG

KOMATIPOORT

RUSTENBURG     PRETORIA     MIDDELBURG     BELFAST     MACHADADORP     LOURENÇO MARQUES

MAFEKING
Besieged
12 Oct 1899-
17 May 1900

BARBERTON

Diamond Hill
9 June 1900

27 Aug
1900

Peace signed
31 May 1902

JOHANNESBURG
31 May 1900

SWAZILAND

VEREENIGING     STANDERTON     Maputo

VRYBURG     KLERKSDORP

Vaal

ORANGE FREE STATE

KROONSTAD     HEILBRON     LINDLEY

Majuba Hill     VOLKSRUST

VRYHEID

DUNDEE

ELANDSLAAGHTE
LADYSMITH
Besieged Nov 1899- Feb 1900

From India

18-27 Feb 1900

KIMBERLEY
11 Dec 1899

Paardeberg

WINBURG

Spion Kop
22-24 Jan
1900

Colenso
15 Dec 1899
ESTCOURT

BLOEMFONTEIN
13 March 1900

Orange

BELMONT

PRIESKA

WEPENER

BASUTOLAND
Brit. Protectorate

Caledon

Orange

NATAL
PIETERMARITZBURG

Tugela

DURBAN

DE AAR

COLESBERG

SPRINGFONTEIN

ALIWAL
NORTH

Stormberg
10 Dec 1899

INDIAN

OCEAN

MIDDELBURG

C A P E     C O L O N Y

GRAAFF-REINET

Great Kei

From Cape Town

Great Fish     EAST LONDON

PORT
ELIZABETH

From Cape Town

Bottom left: British irregular horse and scouts form a firing line during clearance operations in the Brandwater Basin area, 1901.
Bottom center: a British 4.7-inch naval gun in action during the Battle of Colenso, 15 December 1899.
Bottom right: men of the Highland Light Infantry on the march.
Below left: Canadian troops, armed with Long Lee-Enfield rifles, storm a kopje.

# The Boer War

Although it was the Dutch-speaking settlers, the Boers or Afrikaners, who sent the ultimatum, the Boer War was really started by the British, whose provocations of the Boers amounted to a successful attempt at a preventive war. In South Africa the Afrikaners out-numbered the British settlers, and the republic which President Kruger led, far to the north in the Transvaal, threatened to gain the allegiance of those Boers who lived in the two British colonies of Cape Colony and Natal. Moreover the Transvaal had been producing gold since the mid-1880s.

In the first phase of the war, from October 1899 to January 1900, the Boers moved into Natal and Cape Colony, encouraging the local Afrikaners to join them, or at least to revolt. Mafeking, Ladysmith and Kimberley were besieged. In one week in early December the British forces lost three battles, at Stormberg, Magersfontein and, worst of all, at Colenso. The British Commander in Chief, General Buller, had made the mistake of dividing his forces to relieve Ladysmith and Kimberley at the same time. He was soon replaced by Lord Roberts, who brought General Kitchener as his chief of staff.

Kitchener decided that the British must no longer be tied to the railroads in their advance, and this extra flexibility, together with the arrival of reinforcements, helped win the Battle of the Modder River, where a Boer army was encircled and forced to surrender. This was accompanied by the relief of Kimberley, and shortly afterward the siege of Ladysmith came to an end. The Battle of Spion Kop, which preceded the relief of Ladysmith, was the hardest-fought battle of the war for both sides. Their victories enabled the British to annex the Boer Orange Free State, Bloemfontein being captured and most of the Free State's army surrendering. After some weeks Johannesburg and Pretoria were taken, and in September 1900 the British were strong enough to annex the Transvaal formally. This brought the second stage of the war to a close.

The final stage lasted longest of all. Beaten in the field, the Boers refused to surrender. Exploiting their advantages of mobility and marksmanship, they settled down into fast small-scale warfare. Their *commandos*, a kind of mounted infantry, ensured that the British could not settle down in their conquered territories but needed to maintain a large and expensive army to defend all possible targets. It was only in 1901, after Kitchener had taken over command and introduced ruthless measures which included concentration camps, burning of farmsteads, and execution of Boer irregulars, that the Boers agreed to negotiate. The Peace of Vereeniging promised the Boers self-government, from which natives would be excluded, and the preservation of their language, in exchange for which all the Boers became British subjects. In 1906 the British did grant responsible government to the Transvaal and Orange Free State, and in 1910 the Union of South Africa was formed to unite them with Cape Colony and Natal.

# European Influence in China

From the mid-nineteenth century Britain, France and Germany forced the weak Chinese government to grant their respective nationals the right to trade, and to live in self-administered communities in the so-called treaty ports, where European control of the Chinese customs administration soon followed. Later in the century the Chinese had to accept a British-demarcated frontier with India, the acquisition of Indo-China by the French, and the establishment of 'spheres of influence' centered on one or other of the treaty ports. Britain's sphere was the Yangtze valley, while France had the south. Soon the Japanese and Russians began to carve out spheres for themselves. Japan made war against China in 1894 and won a quick victory. Among its trophies was the Manchurian harbor of Port Arthur, which was so valuable that the other powers forced Japan to hand it over to Russia. However, the Treaty of Shimonoseki which ended this war gave to Japan the island of Formosa and a dominant influence in Korea. Russia, meantime, built the Trans-Siberian Railway across Chinese Manchuria, by agreement, and established military settlements along it.

Colonial rivalry caused the Russo-Japanese War of 1904–05, fought on Chinese territory without the permission or participation of the Chinese government. The Japanese victory gave it the opportunity to annex Korea in 1910 and gradually to take control of Manchuria. However, further dismemberment of China was postponed by the Chinese revolution of 1911. There had been a previous revolt, the Boxer rebellion, in 1900, which was a popular movement directed both against the ineffective Manchu dynasty and the foreign domination. This had been quelled by a joint campaign of the great powers. However, the successful 1911 revolution was a brake on further foreign inroads.

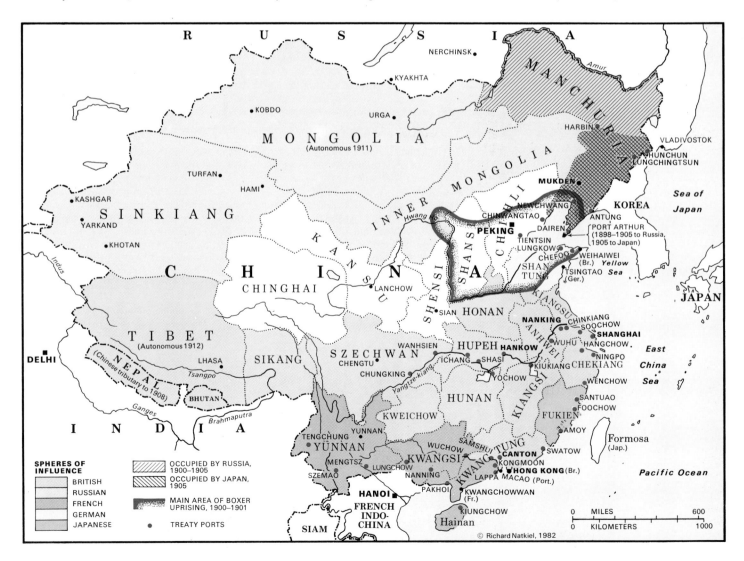

17

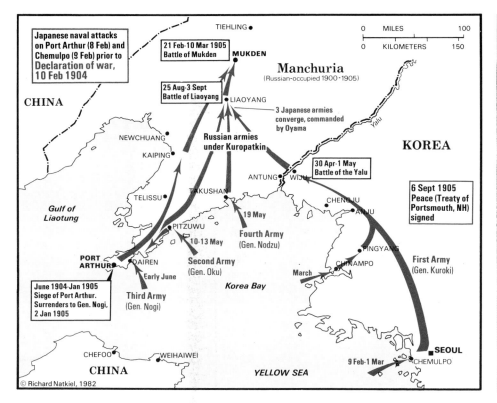

# The Russo-Japanese War

By 1900 conflicting colonial ambitions in Manchuria and Korea had convinced both the Japanese and Russian governments that a war was inevitable, but it was Japan which took the plunge at a carefully-planned moment, in February 1904. The ice was melting in the Korean ports, modern reinforcements for the Russian Pacific Squadron were expected only in 1905, and the Trans-Siberian Railway, on which the Russians would rely to transport reinforcements, was not quite finished.

The war started with what has since been described as 'a rehearsal for Pearl Harbor.' Without any declaration of war, Japanese torpedo boats made a night attack on the Russian squadron, anchored outside its base at Port Arthur. Losses were less than the Japanese had hoped, but the morale of the Russians was shattered until, some weeks later, a new admiral, Makarov, arrived. Makarov restored morale and efficiency but,

in April 1904, he was lured over a minefield by the Japanese and lost his life and his flagship within view of the Russian garrison.

Japanese troops landed at Chemulpo (Inchon) on the first day of the war and advanced to the Yalu, where they won their first battle against the Russians. Further landings were made on the south Manchurian coast and soon the Japanese had cut off Port Arthur; their Third Army was left under General Nogi to besiege this strongpoint, while their main forces advanced northward against the Russian army under Kuropatkin. In the initial battles on the latter front, at Telissu, Tashihchiao and Liaoyang, the Japanese prevailed, but the Russians might have won had they been less preoccupied with their fear of defeat. In the final big battle, outside Mukden, the Russians were again beaten, but paradoxically the Japanese now faced defeat, for whereas they had reached the end of their manpower resources the Russians were only just beginning to tap and send east their huge reserves. In the meantime, Port Arthur had surrendered, after a stubborn defense behind strong fortifications. The Tsarist regime then had to face the 1905 Revolution and

the catastrophic naval defeat of Tsushima. Both sides were therefore ready for the Treaty of Portsmouth, which gave Japan much less than she had wanted, but opportunity enough to expand her activity in Korea and Manchuria.

# The Battle of Tsushima

Because their armies depended on sea communications for supply and reinforcement, it was evident that to win the Russo-Japanese War the Japanese needed to gain command of the sea. When the war started the two sides fleets were fairly equal in numbers, but the Japanese, having fought a war with China a decade previously, were more experienced and in any case benefited from the British training of their superior officers and the British design and construction of their largest ships. Although they were to lose two of their six modern battleships to Russian mines, they had a decisive superiority in armored cruisers.

To swing the balance the Russians decided to send out their Baltic Squadron under the command of Admiral Rozhdestvensky. This set sail in October 1904, having been delayed so as to enable four new battleships to be sent too. Although they made a bad start by firing on British trawlers fishing the Dogger Bank, having mistaken them for Japanese torpedo boats, the voyage around the world was quite an achievement. With ships which had to be coaled every ten days or so, with crews which in the case of the new ships were only partly trained, and with no base facilities en route, to reach Japanese waters was in itself remarkable. By then it was already spring. Port Arthur had fallen and the original Pacific Squadron, with which Rozhdestvensky had been ordered to join, was lying on the bottom of Port Arthur harbor. So the Baltic Squadron made instead for Vladivostok.

Japanese cruisers spotted the Russian Squadron as it was passing through the Tsushima Strait. As the Japanese battleline of Admiral Togo approached, the Russian admiral arranged his ships in line ahead. First came his four new battleships, including the flagship *Suvorov*, then three older battleships and a venerable armored cruiser. Next came a quartet of little fighting value sent out late by St Petersburg to catch up with the main Squadron. This consisted of the very old battleship, in which the second-in-command, Nebogatov, flew his flag, and three coast defense ships. A cruiser squadron brought up the rear. Togo's line, of twelve ships, was led by his four modern battleships, followed by his eight armored cruisers. Togo crossed the Russians' bows and then turned, to pass ahead of their leading ships, on which he could concentrate his fire. In the exchange the Russians fared

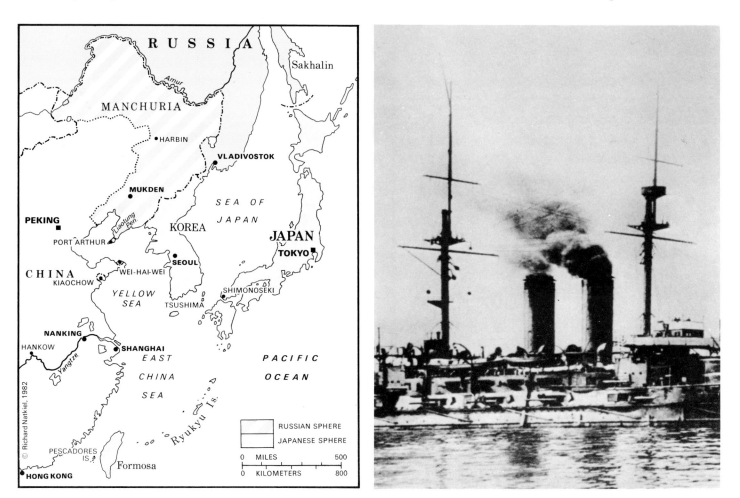

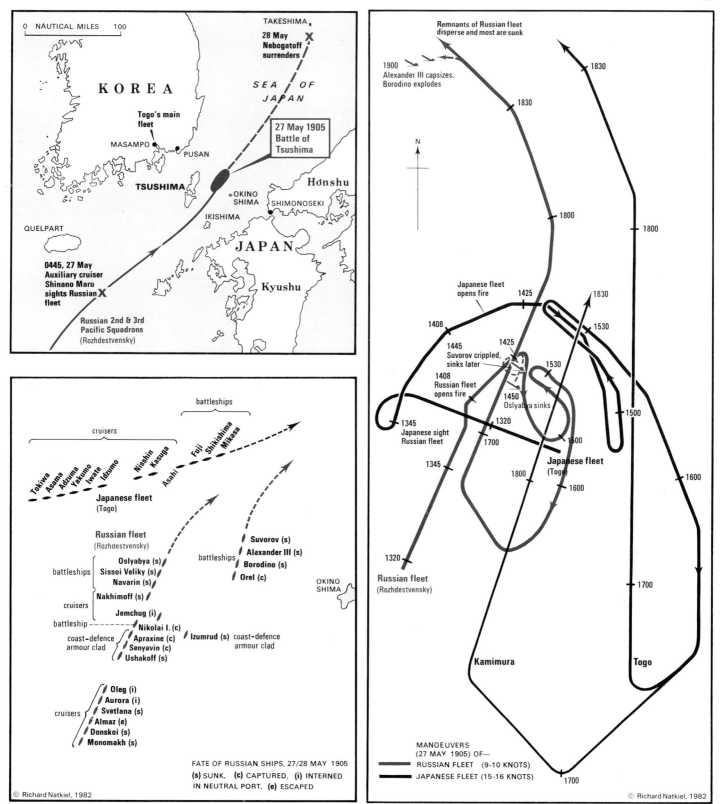

### Map 1 (top left)

0 NAUTICAL MILES 100

TAKESHIMA

**28 May
Nebogatoff
surrenders** X

**K O R E A**

*SEA
OF
JAPAN*

**Togo's main
fleet**

MASAMPO
● PUSAN

**27 May 1905
Battle of
Tsushima**

**TSUSHIMA**

○ OKINO
SHIMA

SHIMONOSEKI ●

H o n s h u

IKISHIMA

**JAPAN**

QUELPART

**0445, 27 May
Auxiliary cruiser
Shinano Maru
sights Russian** X
**fleet**

K y u s h u

**Russian 2nd & 3rd
Pacific Squadrons
(Rozhdestvensky)**

### Map 2 (bottom left)

battleships

cruisers

Tokiwa Asama Adzuma Yakumo Iwate Idzumo Nisshin Kasuga Asahi Fuji Shikishima Mikasa

**Japanese fleet
(Togo)**

**Russian fleet
(Rozhdestvensky)**

battleships
**Oslyabya (s)
Sissoi Veliky (s)
Navarin (s)**

cruisers
**Nakhimoff (s)**

**Jemchug (i)**

battleship
**Nikolai I. (c)**

coast-defence
armour clad
**Apraxine (c)
Senyavin (c)
Ushakoff (s)**

battleships
**Suvorov (s)
Alexander III (s)
Borodino (s)
Orel (c)**

**Izumrud (s)** coast-defence
armour clad

OKINO
SHIMA

cruisers
**Oleg (i)
Aurora (i)
Svetlana (s)
Almaz (e)
Donskoi (s)
Monomakh (s)**

FATE OF RUSSIAN SHIPS, 27/28 MAY 1905
**(s)** SUNK, **(c)** CAPTURED, **(i)** INTERNED
IN NEUTRAL PORT, **(e)** ESCAPED

© Richard Natkiel, 1982

### Map 3 (right)

Remnants of Russian fleet
disperse and most are sunk

1900
Alexander III capsizes,
Borodino explodes

1830 / 1830 / 1800 / 1800

N

Japanese fleet
opens fire — 1425

1408

**1445
Suvorov crippled,
sinks later** — 1425 / 1530 / 1830 / 1530

**1408
Russian fleet
opens fire**

1450
Oslyabya sinks — 1500

1345
Japanese sight
Russian fleet — 1320 / 1700 / 1500

**Japanese fleet
(Togo)** — 1600

1345 / 1800 / 1600

1320

**Russian fleet
(Rozhdestvensky)**

1700

**Kamimura**

**Togo**

MANOEUVERS
(27 MAY 1905) OF—
RUSSIAN FLEET (9-10 KNOTS)
JAPANESE FLEET (15-16 KNOTS)

© Richard Natkiel, 1982

worse, largely because their shells often failed to explode. In this preliminary gun battle the Japanese gained the initiative, which they held thereafter.

After two hours, fog separated the fleets, but the Russians had already lost one battleship, *Oslyabya*, and the flagship *Suvorov* was in a sinking condition. In the late afternoon Togo again came upon the Russians as they plodded toward Vladivostok. At a range of 2200 yards his gunfire forced the Russians to turn away into the mist, but in the early evening there was another encounter in which the two new battleships *Alexander III* and *Borodino* were sunk. As the defeated Russians plowed northward, Togo removed his heavy ships for fear of torpedo attacks, and sent in his own hordes of torpedo craft. During the night torpedoes removed three other vessels from the Rus-

sian battleline and in the morning Nebogatov, now in command, found himself with a handful of ships of negligible fighting power confronted by Togo's fleet, almost unscathed. He hauled up a white flag, and negotiations began which ended in the surrender of his ships to the Japanese. Of the squadron which had set out from the Baltic, only two destroyers and a lightly-armed yacht reached Vladivostok.

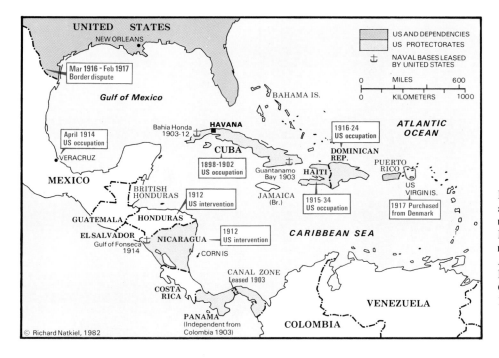

Far left: the lower, middle and upper locks at Gatun, on the Panama Canal, pictured under construction in 1912.
Below far left: US Marines on the march near Vera Cruz, Mexico, during the American expedition, 1914.
Below: the Culebra Cut on the Panama Canal during construction in December 1912.

# The USA and the Caribbean

From the end of the Civil War to the 1890s the USA had enough power, enough commercial, strategic and humanitarian motives, and also enough imperialistically-inclined leaders, to adopt an active overseas policy. The only thing lacking was the support of the general public, and this changed when Americans began to believe in their 'Manifest Destiny.' By then, the USA extended to the Pacific, which meant that a two-ocean navy was required. This in turn raised the need for a ship canal across the Central American Isthmus and the canal, once built, demanded bases in the Caribbean to defend it.

In 1898 the USA entered a war, which was enormously popular, against the Spanish Empire; the Cubans' previous attempts to eject the Spanish from their island had been watched with sympathy, but no overt help. After their easy victory the Americans occupied Cuba for a time, Americanizing its institutions and also, more heroically, eliminating yellow fever. They also occupied Puerto Rico until 1900, and remained influential in that island thereafter; in 1917 Puerto Ricans became US citizens.

The Panama Canal was started in 1904 and came into service in 1914. It was built through the territory of a new state, Panama, which was created by the revolution of a national liberation movement financed and largely imagined by the US Government. US intervention in neighboring countries, motivated mainly by a desire for an orderly backyard, was frequent in this period with troops sent, between 1912 and 1915, to Nicaragua, Mexico, Haiti, and Santo Domingo [Dominican Republic].

## The Italo-Turkish War, 1911-12

Despite being rebuffed in Abyssinia in 1889 and being treated as a poor relation at the Algeciras Conference of 1906, Italy was hungry for a place in the sun and a position like other European nations as a major colonial power. Being the weakest of the major European states, Italy had come late to the colonial supper and as a result was forced to devour the crumbs. Her positions in Eritrea and Italian Somaliland, both of questionable economic and strategic value, were insufficient to Italian pride. Successive Italian governments were determined to annex something, preferably defensible and nearby. Turkish control over Tripolitania and Cyrenaica was becoming increasingly weak in the early twentieth century, and Britain and France were not displeased to have a weak Italian buffer standing between French North Africa and British-controlled Egypt. Therefore in 1911 the Italians launched a two-pronged attack against Libya.

Surprisingly they did not have an easy victory, but by early 1912, after a naval attack against the Dardanelles, the two parts of Libya were annexed, along with the Greek-speaking Dodecanese Islands off the coast of Turkey itself. An Italian empire in the Mediterranean was born chiefly because of two factors. First, Britain and France were not interested in the territory, and these two countries felt that Italy could be pushed around even more easily than the Ottoman Turks. Secondly, the Ottoman Empire was in a state of collapse and Italy could benefit from that collapse at little cost to herself while the Italian government could appear to the public as a virile colonial power with little danger of opposition. As it was the Italo-Turkish War nearly exhausted Italy's military, naval and financial resources. The seemingly cheap Italian victory proved to be more expensive than anyone in Rome bargained for.

## The Balkan Wars

For a hundred years before 1914 the decline of the Ottoman Empire had periodically resulted in tension and war in the Balkans as the various nationalities sought to involve rival big powers in their struggle for independence from the Turks. In 1908, for example, there had developed the Bosnia crisis, which so soured the atmosphere between Russia and Austria as to make it one of the factors in the outbreak of World War I. Bosnia had been occupied by Austria since 1878, with international agreement even though it was still formally part of the Turkish Empire. In 1908 Austria annexed it, fearing Turkish resurgence there. This was resented by the Russians, who demanded compensation for Austria's gain, but the latter called upon her ally Germany to persuade the Tsar, not very amicably, to accept the situation.

This crisis was followed by the two Balkan Wars of 1912 and 1913. Normally the Balkan nations, though united in hatred of the Turk, disliked or despised each other so much that cooperation between them was impossible. But in 1912 two Russian diplomats, who thought that all Slavs should work together under the benevolent supervision of Mother Russia, persuaded Bulgaria and Serbia to forget their differences and partition, rather than fight over, neighboring Macedonia, where the Turkish rule seemed in its final stages. This diplomatic miracle was followed by another, achieved largely by *The Times* correspondent in Athens, when Bulgaria and Greece came to an agreement, despite the fact that both intended to take the port of Salonica as soon as the Turks could be ousted. In October 1912 these three, with Montenegro, attacked Turkey and won several victories; the Bulgarian Army was only a few miles from Constantinople when disease and transport difficulties halted it. The race to Salonica was won by the Greek Army, which got there a day ahead of the Bulgarians. At a conference in London a settlement was attempted in which Turkey was required to abandon most of her European territory, and a new state of Albania was to be created on the Adriatic. The Albanian idea was bitterly resented by Serbia and by King Nikita of Montenegro. Moreover, the Bulgarians realized that Greece and Serbia were conspiring to split

Below: a Bulgarian transport column
passes through a village in Serbia during
the Second Balkan War in 1913. Because
of the poor rail network throughout the
region the contending armies largely relied
on traditional methods of transport.

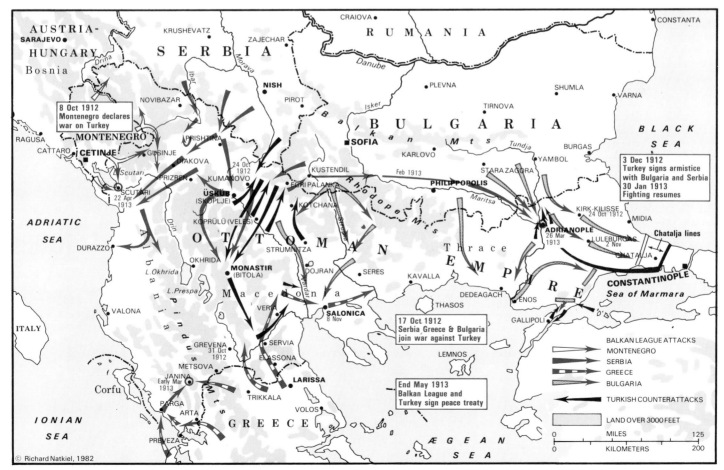

AUSTRIA-
SARAJEVO •
HUNGARY
Bosnia

SERBIA

RUMANIA

CRAIOVA •

CONSTANTA •

KRUSHEVATZ •

ZAJECHAR •

Drina

NISH

PIROT

PLEVNA

TIRNOVA

SHUMLA

VARNA

RAGUSA

NOVIBAZAR •

MONTENEGRO

CATTARO •  CETINJE

GUSINJE

8 Oct 1912
Montenegro declares
war on Turkey

PRISHTINA

DIAKOVA

Isker

BULGARIA

SOFIA

KARLOVO •

Tundja

BLACK
SEA

BURGAS

L. Scutari

SCUTARI
22 Apr
1913

PRIZREN

KUMANOVO

24 Oct
1912

KUSTENDIL

Feb 1913

STARA ZAGORA

PHILIPPOPOLIS

YAMBOL

3 Dec 1912
Turkey signs armistice
with Bulgaria and Serbia
30 Jan 1913
Fighting resumes

ADRIATIC
SEA

ÜSKÜB
(SKOPLJE)

KÖPRÜLÜ (VELES)

EGRI PALANKA

KOTCHANA

Rhodope Mts

Maritsa

KIRK-KILISSE
24 Oct 1912

MIDIA

DURAZZO

OKHRIDA

L. Okhrida

MONASTIR
(BITOLA)

STRUMNITZA

DOJRAN

Vardar

SERES

Thrace

ADRIANOPLE
26 Mar
1913

LULEBURGAS
2 Nov

CHATALJA

Chatalja lines

L. Prespa

Macedonia

VERIA

KAVALLA •

VALONA

ITALY

GREVENA
31 Oct
1912

Pindus

METSOVA

JANINA
Early Mar
1913

SERVIA

ELASSONA

SALONICA
8 Nov

THASOS

17 Oct 1912
Serbia, Greece & Bulgaria
join war against Turkey

DEDEAGACH

ENOS

CONSTANTINOPLE
Sea of Marmara

GALLIPOLI

LEMNOS

BALKAN LEAGUE ATTACKS

MONTENEGRO

Corfu

Mts

PARGA

ARTA

TRIKKALA

LARISSA

VOLOS

End May 1913
Balkan League and
Turkey sign peace treaty

SERBIA

GREECE

BULGARIA

IONIAN
SEA

PREVEZA

GREECE

ÆGEAN
SEA

TURKISH COUNTERATTACKS

LAND OVER 3000 FEET

0          MILES          125

0          KILOMETERS          200

© Richard Natkiel, 1982

24

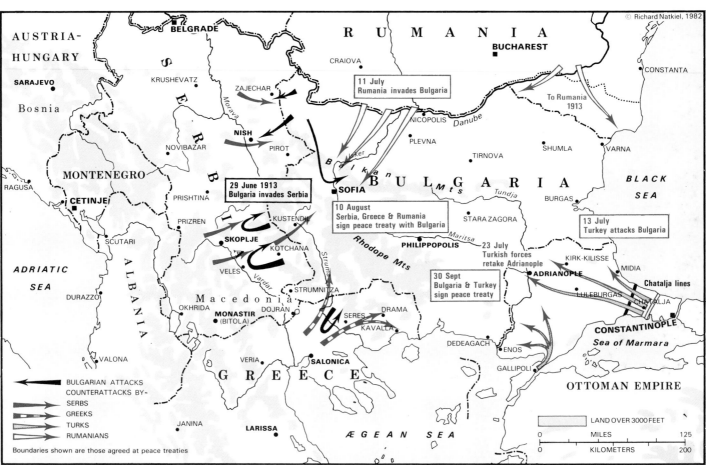

© Richard Natkiel, 1982

Map labels:

AUSTRIA-HUNGARY
BELGRADE
RUMANIA
BUCHAREST
CRAIOVA
CONSTANTA
SARAJEVO
KRUSHEVATZ
ZAJECHAR
Bosnia
NISH
NOVIBAZAR
PIROT
NICOPOLIS
Danube
PLEVNA
SHUMLA
VARNA
TIRNOVA
MONTENEGRO
RAGUSA
CETINJE
PRISHTINA
SOFIA
BULGARIA
BLACK SEA
BURGAS
STARA ZAGORA
PRIZREN
KUSTENDIL
SKOPLJE
KOTCHANA
PHILIPPOPILIS
ADRIATIC SEA
ALBANIA
VELES
Macedonia
Rhodope Mts
KIRK-KILISSE
MIDIA
ADRIANOPLE
Chatalja lines
LULEBURGAS
CHATALJA
DURAZZO
OKHRIDA
MONASTIR (BITOLA)
DOJRAN
STRUMNITZA
SERES
DRAMA
KAVALLA
CONSTANTINOPLE
Sea of Marmara
VALONA
VERIA
SALONICA
DEDEAGACH
ENOS
GALLIPOLI
OTTOMAN EMPIRE
GREECE
JANINA
LARISSA
ÆGEAN SEA

Boxes:
11 July Rumania invades Bulgaria
29 June 1913 Bulgaria invades Serbia
10 August Serbia, Greece & Rumania sign peace treaty with Bulgaria
13 July Turkey attacks Bulgaria
23 July Turkish forces retake Adrianople
30 Sept Bulgaria & Turkey sign peace treaty
To Rumania 1913

Legend:
BULGARIAN ATTACKS
COUNTERATTACKS BY-
SERBS
GREEKS
TURKS
RUMANIANS
Boundaries shown are those agreed at peace treaties
LAND OVER 3000 FEET
MILES 0 125
KILOMETERS 0 200

Macedonia between themselves, leaving out Bulgaria, which had suffered most of the casualties in the war. So, before the peace settlement was made, a new war started, with the Bulgarians attacking Greece and Serbia. The Turks and Rumanians joined in against Bulgaria, which was thoroughly defeated. The resulting Treaty of Bucharest maintained Albania, gave most of Macedonia to Greece and Serbia and part of Bulgaria's southern Dobruja to Rumania. Greece was now the dominant Balkan state, having acquired the key Aegean port of Salonica. Balkan politics remained unsettled with the competing ambitions of the Balkan states being supplemented by the influence of the great powers Austria-Hungary and Russia.

**Right: guns are emplaced in old fortifications overlooking the harbor of Durazzo in Albania in 1913.
Far right: Montenegrin troops assault a fort during their advance on Scutari in October 1912.**

German infantry on the advance in
November 1914.

# The Great War, 1914-18

# The European Alliance System, 1914

The two alliance systems of the European powers were insurance policies in case of conflict rather than a cause of war. But they did imply that once hostilities occurred between two powers, the conflict would spread.

Having defeated France in the war of 1870–71, the German chancellor, Bismarck, had sought protective alliances to isolate France and to prevent Germany having to fight a war on two fronts. His 1879 secret alliance with Austria, which had pledged the two powers to come to each other's aid in the event of attack by Russia, was supplemented in 1882 by the Triple Alliance, in which Germany, Austria, and Italy pledged mutual support in the event of an attack by

France. These alliances were still in force in 1914.

During the 1890s, to counter these agreements, France and Russia drew closer in an open alliance with secret provisions. Germany could only assume that France and Russia would come to each other's assistance in the event of either being attacked by Germany or Austria. In fact, secret conventions meant that military cooperation between France and Russia was well developed by 1914.

Britain had traditionally steered clear of continental entanglements in peacetime, but she no longer had the confidence to continue her policy of 'splendid isolation.' In 1902 came the Anglo-Japanese agreement, which offered some protection to British interests in the Far East. Then, in 1904, the *Entente Cordiale* between France and Britain settled longstanding disputes between the two countries. This was not a formal alliance and was not directed against

Germany, but in the following decade it provided the right atmosphere for Anglo-French collaboration. Such collaboration included secret military and naval understandings about which parliament and most of the British government knew little or nothing. One such understanding was Britain's agreement to send an expeditionary force to France in the event of a German attack. This meant that in the 1914 crisis Britain could no longer honorably follow her old and often advantageous strategy of holding back, in order to enter the conflict at a time and place and with a strength of her own choosing. It was an understanding, therefore, which was to cost Britain dear. Meanwhile, since Russia had an alliance with France, it was only natural that Britain and Russia should patch up their differences, which mainly centered around colonial rivalry in the east.

Russia had its own understanding with Serbia, so when the latter was threatened by

Below: in 1905 Count Alfred von Schlieffen devised a plan for Germany to fight a war on two fronts with France and Russia.

Austria in 1914, a conflict between Russia and Austria became imminent. Their alliances meant that Germany and France were drawn in. Britain and Italy were not, formally, required to step in. Italy decided that her partners Germany and Austria had not been attacked, and stayed out for the time being. Britain, because of her gentleman's agreements with France, and steeled by Germany's invasion of Belgium, did declare war.

And so, thanks to interlocking alliances, when in 1914 Austria made war on Serbia, Germany made war to help Austria and Russia made war to help Serbia. France made war for Russia, Britain made war for France, and Japan made war for Britain.

# The Schlieffen Plan

For several decades before 1914, the possibility of a war on two fronts preoccupied the German military planners. The combined strength of Russia and France was far greater than that of Germany. A solution to this problem was proposed in 1905 by the Chief of the German General Staff, Count von Schlieffen. Germany would deploy her main strength to win a quick victory over France. Then the efficient German railroads would shift the victorious armies to the Eastern Front, where the Russians, thanks to their very sparse railroads, would only just be completing their mobilization. Against France, two armies to the south of Metz, the left wing, would initially advance against the bulk of the French Army to pin it down or to lure it eastward. Meanwhile five armies to the north of Metz would cross Belgium, turn southwest, envelop Paris, attack the rear of the main French forces and rout them.

In 1906 the younger von Moltke succeeded Schlieffen, and soon modified the plan. Notably, he strengthened the left wing at the expense of the wheeling attack through Belgium. Meanwhile, with French help the Russian railroad network was so improved that the Russians expected that they would be able to mobilize two thirds of their enormous army in eighteen days, just three days longer than the Germans planned to mobilize their own. These two circumstances alone meant that in 1914 the Schlieffen Plan would not work as anticipated.

The mechanics of the Schlieffen Plan exerted an enormous influence on the German political and diplomatic leaders. The pressure of the mobilization timetable gave every incentive for an early and perhaps hasty decision to go to war while the detailed arrangements of the plan meant that a desire to help Austria against Russia virtually compelled Germany to attack France. The violation of Belgian neutrality that the plan required was also a major motivation for Britain's decision to fight Germany. Thus the effects of the Schlieffen Plan complemented the alliance system and helped make a Balkan quarrel into a world war.

Below: the younger von Moltke succeeded von Schlieffen as Chief of the German General Staff and attempted to put the Schlieffen Plan into execution in August. 1914. He is pictured second from the right with the Kaiser during maneuvers in 1913.

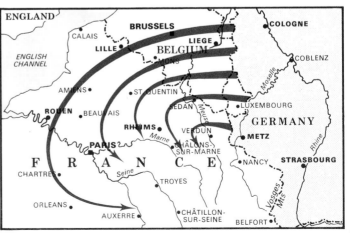

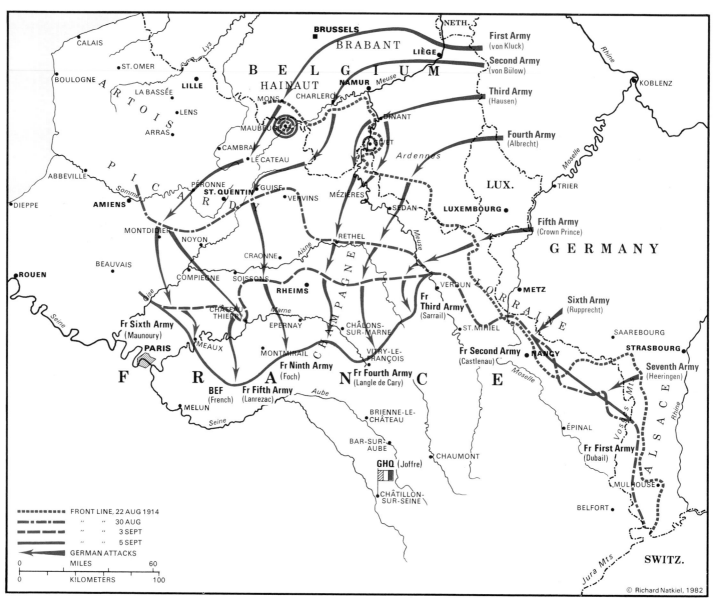

FRONT LINE, 22 AUG 1914
" " 30 AUG
" " 3 SEPT
" " 5 SEPT
GERMAN ATTACKS

MILES 60
KILOMETERS 100

© Richard Natkiel, 1982

# The Battle of the Frontiers

On 3 August 1914 German cavalry led the German formations into Belgium whose territory was essential for the passage of the armies destined to wheel through northern France in accordance with the Schlieffen Plan. The Belgian defenders of the fortified city of Liège were finally subdued on 16 August. On 8 August the French Commander in Chief, Joffre, ordered his First and Second Armies to advance into Lorraine and, in accordance with the Schlieffen Plan, the German Sixth Army withdrew under this attack. In mid-August Joffre realized that the main German forces were in Belgium.

Meanwhile, although the original Schlieffen Plan had hoped to lure the main French forces into Lorraine so as to make it easier to take them in the rear from the north, personal ambitions persuaded the com-mander of the German Sixth Army to take the offensive against the advancing French First and Second Armies. He pushed the French back out of the trap into which they had been lured, but both his Army and the supporting Seventh Army took heavy losses in this fighting. The French also suffered heavily. The Schlieffen Plan was further compromised when the German First, Second and Third Armies, advancing through Belgium, had to detach part of their strength to take care of Antwerp and Namur, and when Kluck's First Army was ordered to turn southwestward instead of taking the westward course laid down in the Plan. This latter change also meant that an opportunity to take the British Expedi-tionary Force (BEF) from the flank at Mons was lost. The BEF was able to make a fight-ing withdrawal from Mons.

As the German plan became clear, Joffre launched his Third and Fourth Armies, into the difficult Ardennes region to cut the three northern German armies from their bases. This advance was unsuccessful. More-over, it meant that the BEF and the French Fifth Army alone had to bear the brunt of the German attack as it wheeled south-westward. On 22 August the Fifth Army was mauled at Charleroi by the German Second and Third Armies, and the French left wing began to retreat toward Paris.

**Above right: a column from the 2nd Battalion Scots Guards marches through a Belgian village in 1914.**
**Right: Belgian troops man a barricade outside Louvain during the retreat to Antwerp, 1914.**

# The Battle of the Marne

As the German right wing wheeled toward Paris, the French created their Sixth Army to cover the capital. Back at his head-quarters, still in Germany, Moltke urged a rapid advance so as to allow the French no time to recover. Kluck's First Army was to advance west of the Oise and pass to the west of Paris. Bülow's Second Army was to move directly toward Paris, while the Third and Fourth Armies were to march, respectively, on Château-Thierry and Epernay. Further to the east, the Sixth and Seventh Armies were to prevent the French advancing into Lorraine and Alsace, while the Fifth Army was to besiege the key French fortress at Verdun. Kluck and Bülow, with Moltke's approval, soon modified this plan; Kluck's army was to move to the east, so as to give better support to Bülow. For some reason, both commanders took little notice of reports that the French were bringing troops by rail to places such as Amiens and Montdidier.

On 1 September Joffre ordered Maun-oury's Sixth Army to retire toward Paris, and hinted that this Army, with the Paris garrison, might be used in an offensive role. Meanwhile Kluck's and Bülow's armies moved more and more east of their intended line of advance. The German First Army, which was to have passed to the west of Paris, was now well to the east, crossing the Marne and paying little attention to the skirmishes on its right flank as Maunoury's patrols made contact. Joffre, meanwhile, strengthened his defenses by forming the Ninth Army, under Foch, to fill the gap between his Fourth and Fifth Armies, and then began to plan a counter-offensive.

This counter-offensive, known as the Battle of the Marne, consisted of numerous engagements all the way from the Parisian region to the frontier near Verdun. On 5 September fighting near the River Ourcq between the French Sixth Army and Kluck's right flank grew fiercer. When Kluck realized the seriousness of his situation, he trans-ferred two corps from his left flank. This had the effect of widening the gap between his army and Bülow's Second Army. To help Maunoury cope with this German re-action the Governor of Paris, General Galliéni, commandeered 1200 taxi-cabs to take reinforcements to him from the Paris garrison. However, Maunoury was saved when the French Fifth Army, which the Germans had thought to be in full retreat, fell upon Kluck's left wing. This French attack, in the direction of Montmirail, threatened the flank of Bülow's Second Army, forcing it to retire behind the River Petit Morin on 7 September. A further French success made Bülow retire another six or seven miles east, opening farther the gap between his army and Kluck's First Army. An attempt by the German Third Army to repair the situation by breaking through Foch's Ninth Army was hard-fought but unsuccessful.

The smaller BEF faced the gap between the German First and Second Armies. A personal appeal from Joffre to the British commander, Sir John French, had secured British cooperation in the intended French offensive. On 6 September the BEF crept forward, meeting no resistance. Its progress was slow, but it outflanked two German armies; as a French commentator later put it, 'Sir John French saved the situation even though he did not understand it.' Although it took the British three days to move for-ward 25 miles, both the German and French Commanders in Chief saw that the situation was now dramatically changed. Joffre order-ed his Fifth Army to cover the British right flank. Moltke, whose headquarters were still outside France, sent a staff officer to assess the situation and he ordered a with-drawal. The Germans withdrew to the Aisne and dug themselves in. The Battle of the Marne had lasted seven days, and marked the failure of the Schlieffen Plan.

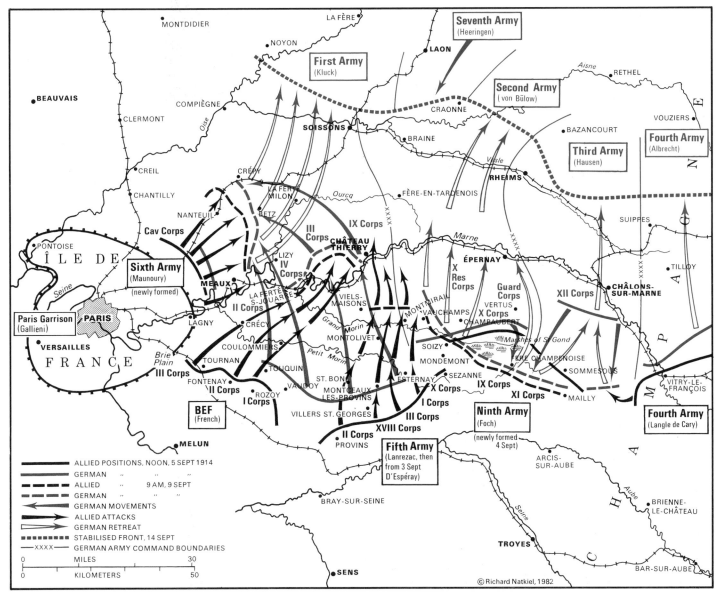

MONTDIDIER

LA FÈRE

NOYON

**Seventh Army**
(Heeringen)

**First Army**
(Kluck)

LAON

Aisne

RETHEL

BEAUVAIS

COMPIÈGNE

**Second Army**
(von Bülow)

CLERMONT

CRAONNE

VOUZIERS

Oise

SOISSONS

BRAINE

BAZANCOURT

**Fourth Army**
(Albrecht)

CREIL

Vesle

**Third Army**
(Hausen)

CHANTILLY

CRÉPY

RHEIMS

LA FERTÉ
MILON

Ourcq

FÈRE-EN-TARDENOIS

NANTEUIL

BETZ

SUIPPES

Cav Corps

III
Corps

IX Corps

Marne

TILLOY

**Sixth Army**
(Maunoury)

LIZY

CHÂTEAU
THIERRY

ÉPERNAY

XXXX

**(newly formed)**

IV
Corps

X
Res
Corps

VERTUS

XII Corps

CHÂLONS-
SUR-MARNE

Seine

MEAUX

VIELS-
MAISONS

Guard
Corps

ÎLE DE

LA FERTÉ
S-JOUARRE

X Corps

**Paris Garrison**
(Gallieni)

**PARIS**

II Corps

MONTMIRAIL

VAUCHAMPS

CHAMPAUBERT

VERSAILLES

LAGNY

CRÉCY

Grand Morin

Marshes of St Gond

**FRANCE**

COULOMMIERS

MONTOLIVET

SOIZY

FÈRE CHAMPENOISE

SOMMESOUS

Brie
Plain

Petit Morin

MONDEMENT

III Corps

TOURNAN

TOUQUIN

VITRY-LE-
FRANÇOIS

II Corps

ROZOY

VAUDOY

ST. BON

SÉZANNE

**Ninth Army**
(Foch)

MAILLY

FONTENAY

I Corps

MONTCEAUX
LES-PROVINS

ESTERNAY

X Corps

IX Corps

XI Corps

**Fourth Army**
(Langle de Cary)

VILLERS ST. GEORGES

III Corps

**BEF**
(French)

XVIII Corps

**(newly formed
4 Sept)**

MELUN

II Corps

PROVINS

**Fifth Army**
(Lanrezac, then
from 3 Sept
D'Espéray)

ARCIS-
SUR-AUBE

BRAY-SUR-SEINE

BRIENNE-
LE-CHÂTEAU

Aube

Seine

|  | ALLIED POSITIONS, NOON, 5 SEPT 1914 |
|---|---|
|  | GERMAN          "               " |
|  | ALLIED          "        9 AM, 9 SEPT |
|  | GERMAN          "               " |
|  | GERMAN MOVEMENTS |
|  | ALLIED ATTACKS |
|  | GERMAN RETREAT |
|  | STABILISED FRONT, 14 SEPT |
| XXXX | GERMAN ARMY COMMAND BOUNDARIES |

0          MILES          30

0          KILOMETERS          50

**TROYES**

**SENS**

© Richard Natkiel, 1982

BAR-SUR-AUBE

**Bottom: Russian troops prepare to camp on the German frontier in November 1914.**

Map legend:
- FRONT LINE, EVENING 25 AUG 1914
- RUSSIAN ATTACKS
- GERMAN MOVEMENTS
- GERMAN FORTIFIED POSITIONS HELD DURING RUSSIAN ADVANCE
- MAIN RAILROADS
- OTHER RAILROADS

MILES 0 — 50
KILOMETERS 0 — 80

# The Battle of Tannenberg

The German Schlieffen Plan had relied on a slow Russian mobilization, but in 1914 not only did the Russians mobilize faster than Schlieffen had envisioned, but in order to help the French they sent two armies into East Prussia even before mobilization was completed. Rennenkampf's First Army moved westward while Samsonov's Second Army moved northward from Poland. There was little liaison between these two armies, and there was personal antipathy between their commanders; Rennenkampf had let Samsonov down in the Russo-Japanese War, and had had his face publicly slapped by the latter on a Manchurian railway station. In addition, the Russian Army was poorly supplied and its communications were weak; as the Germans soon found, Russian radio messages were uncoded.

Nevertheless, so weak were the German forces in the east, and so unexpected the Russian assault, that the German Eighth Army was defeated at Gumbinnen and had to withdraw to a new defense line astride the Masurian Lakes, where it was in danger of being caught between the two Russian armies. Moltke became alarmed, dismissed its commander, Prittwitz, and sent out a retired General, Hindenburg, with Luden-

dorff as Chief of Staff. A few units were withdrawn from the Western Front and sent east.

In fact, these measures were unnecessary, because the German corps commanders on the scene, as well as the Eighth Army's director of operations, Hoffmann, were well in command of the situation. Hoffmann's plan was to hold Rennenkampf with just a single cavalry division, anticipating that the Russian general's characteristic caution would hold him back. The bulk of the forces could then be sent against Samsonov, whom it was intended to encircle. Making good use of rail transport, and benefiting from intercepted Russian radio messages, the plan succeeded. After capturing one or two towns, the Russians realized on 22 August that they were in danger of encirclement but the order to withdraw came too late. Samsonov's underfed and confused army was virtually destroyed near Tannenberg, most of its soliders being taken prisoner. Samsonov shot himself. Rennenkampf, meanwhile, had advanced toward the Masurian Lakes and, because the German forces were now tired, was able to resist their attack, withdrawing from Prussia slowly and without losing control.

**Below: a German soldier escorts captured Russian infantry, who are towing their machine guns.**

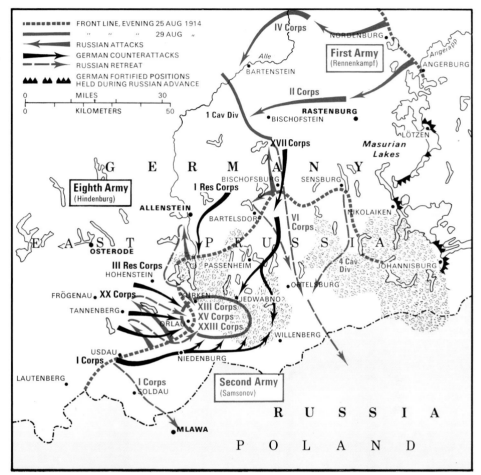

# The Race to the Sea

Apart from defeating the Germans' Schlieffen Plan, the Battle of the Marne marked the beginning of the end for mobile warfare. As soon as the German retreat began, British and French generals talked of an end to the war within a month or so but the Allied offensive was not as rapid as the German advance had been. As soon as the Germans dug themselves into defensive positions it became clear that the machine gun and other products of modern war technology had given the defense a great advantage over the attack. However, before this realization dawned, both sides sought to gain positions from which they could launch outflanking attacks. Their battle-lines ended north of the Aisne, and each tried to extend northward so as to turn his opponent's flank. This meant that they moved northward until the open flanks were closed by the sea. This short phase of the war is often called the 'race to the sea' even though it was essentially a race to the flanks; both sides, however, realized the importance of the Channel ports through which British supplies and troops had to pass. The new German Commander in Chief, Falkenhayn (who had replaced Moltke, dismissed as soon as the Battle of the Marne was lost), was the first to realize the possibilities of an outflanking movement, but he had insufficient forces to carry out his intentions. Joffre was slow to abandon his strategy of a frontal assault, and missed his chance.

One reason the Germans were short of troops was that many of their forces were engaged in Belgium, where the Belgian Army continued to resist. The siege of the fortified city of Antwerp demanded many troops. The British and French were reluctant to send help to the Belgians, although Churchill did raise a small naval division to help defend Antwerp. Even after Antwerp fell the Belgians continued their fight, which had the effect of hampering the Germans in the 'race to the sea.'

**Far right top: German gunners manhandle a field piece.**
**Far right: troops of the British Expeditionary Force rest in a Belgian village, October 1914.**

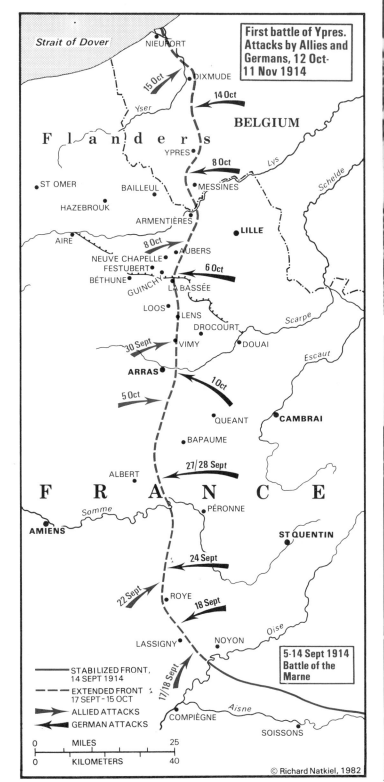

First battle of Ypres. Attacks by Allies and Germans, 12 Oct-11 Nov 1914

Strait of Dover

NIEUPORT
15 Oct
DIXMUDE
14 Oct
Yser
BELGIUM
Flanders
YPRES
8 Oct
Lys
Schelde
ST OMER
BAILLEUL
MESSINES
HAZEBROUK
ARMENTIÈRES
LILLE
AIRE
8 Oct
AUBERS
NEUVE CHAPELLE
FESTUBERT
6 Oct
BÉTHUNE
GUINCHY
LA BASSÉE
LOOS
LENS
Scarpe
DROCOURT
30 Sept
VIMY
DOUAI
Escaut
ARRAS
10 Oct
5 Oct
QUEANT
CAMBRAI
BAPAUME
27/28 Sept
ALBERT
FRANCE
Somme
PÉRONNE
AMIENS
ST QUENTIN
24 Sept
22 Sept
ROYE
18 Sept
LASSIGNY
NOYON
Oise
17/18 Sept
5-14 Sept 1914 Battle of the Marne
Aisne
COMPIÈGNE
SOISSONS

STABILIZED FRONT, 14 SEPT 1914
EXTENDED FRONT 17 SEPT-15 OCT
ALLIED ATTACKS
GERMAN ATTACKS

0  MILES  25
0  KILOMETERS  40

© Richard Natkiel, 1982

36

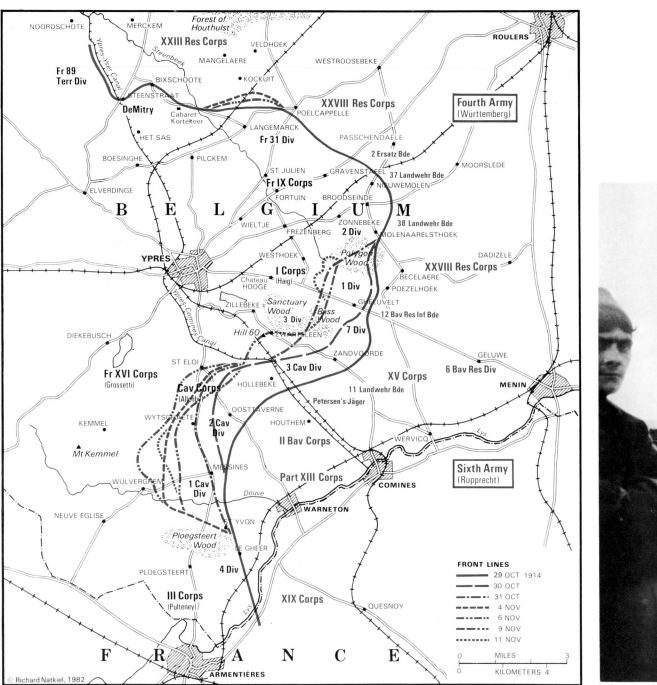

Map showing the First Battle of Ypres, with front lines dated 29 Oct 1914 through 11 Nov. © Richard Natkiel, 1982.

# The First Battle of Ypres

Toward the end of the 'race to the sea' both sides made a last and almost simultaneous effort to turn their opponent's flank. The BEF moved north by train from the Aisne to La Bassée, aiming to outflank the Germans near Ypres. The Germans were moving to the same town from the other direction, in the hope of outflanking the Allies. The two attacks collided. Although the British troops were fresh, not having been required to fight very hard in the Battle of the Marne, they were smaller in numbers, the Germans having brought up a new reserve corps, largely composed of student volunteers who had been given little military training.

On 20 October the Germans attacked with great spirit, in mass formations. The British infantry, whose rapid rifle fire had long been well rehearsed in training, took a fearsome toll. However, at one point the Germans did breach the British lines, but the defenders were able to bring up reinforcements sufficiently fast to hold the attackers. Outnumbered and dug in, the British continued to conduct a solid defense, though at the expense of heavy casualties. The fighting front was quite narrow, and with each side being reinforced daily it was possible to feed in thousands of men to replace the losses. After their lack of success on 20 October, the Germans attacked again on 31 October, but could not dislodge the British. Finally, just outside Ypres, at Nun's Wood, the Prussian Guard was committed to the battle on 11 November. Again there was much slaughter and little movement. In all, the Germans lost about 135,000 killed and wounded. The BEF losses were smaller, but meant that that force, which was the best part of Britain's professional army, was shattered.

Below: men of the 2nd Battalion, the
Warwickshire Regiment, are transported
to the front by bus during the First Battle
of Ypres.
Bottom: a cavalry trooper of the British
Expeditionary Force pauses for refreshment.

Below: a German 5.9-inch howitzer battery in action on the Western Front, November 1914. This weapon was perhaps the most effective artillery piece employed during World War I.

# The Western Front at the End of 1914

The 'race to the sea' came to a natural end when both armies extended their lines to Nieuport, on the North Sea just inside Belgium. The Western Front now stretched hundreds of miles from there down to the Swiss frontier. Only a small part of Belgium was unoccupied by the Germans, but the Belgian Army was still fighting. The German line also enclosed much of north-western France, which was the site of the French coal industry and much of her steel industry and engineering. The Channel ports, so important for the movement of British supplies and troops, seemed secure.

It was now realized that entrenchment rendered warfare static, yet no troops could survive against modern weapons without entrenchment. Later, the machine gun was singled out as the decisive instrument of mass slaughter. But in the early part of the war, at least, the magazine rifle was enough to dampen an assault. As the Germans had discovered at Mons and at Ypres, British infantry could manage fifteen rounds per minute; this was considerably less than a machine gun, but as the numbers of rifles was as large as the number of infantrymen and, as rifles were usually better-aimed than machine guns, the lethal effects were not dissimilar.

It was thought that heavy bombardment might enable attacks to break through. But at the end of 1914 the artillery was not yet sufficiently organized nor were the munitions industries ready to deliver shells at the rate needed. In this way, and in others, trench warfare meant that the war had become a conflict between industries as well as between soldiers. Britain and Germany were well placed to increase their output of munitions and weapons, but Austria and Russia were not so fortunate. France had much to do to recover from the loss of the industrial areas near the Belgian border.

The advantage given to the defender by trench warfare enabled the Germans to transfer troops to the east, where their Austrian allies were retreating before the Russians. The first such reinforcements were sent just as the Battle of Ypres was ending, and helped to turn the tide of war against the Russians.

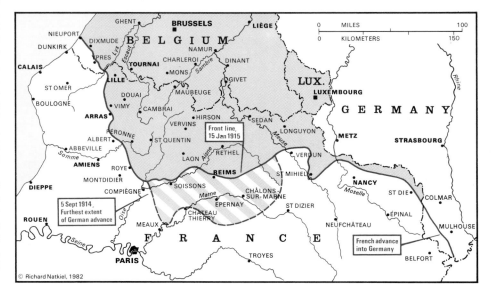

© Richard Natkiel, 1982

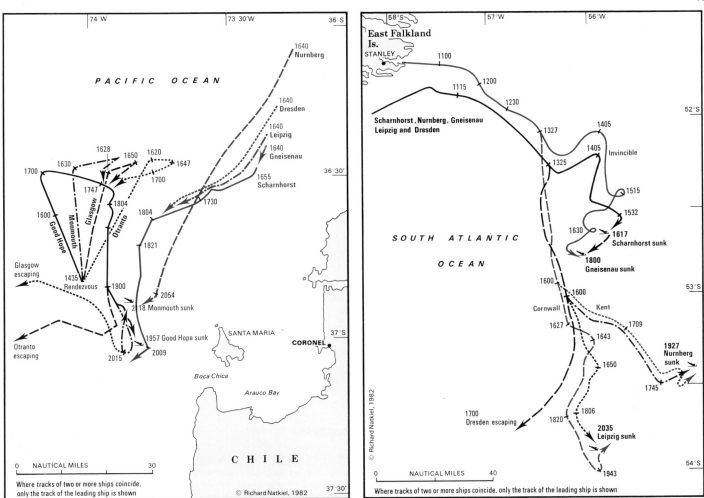

**Left map labels:**

PACIFIC OCEAN

74°W    73°30'W    36°S

1640 Nurnberg
1640 Dresden
1640 Leipzig
1640 Gneisenau
1655 Scharnhorst
36°30'

1628   1650   1620
1630    1647
1700   1747   1700
1804
1600   1730
1821
1804
Good Hope   Monmouth   Glasgow   Otranto

Glasgow escaping
1435 Rendezvous   1900
Otranto escaping
2054
2118 Monmouth sunk
1957 Good Hope sunk
2015   2009

SANTA MARIA
37°S
CORONEL
Boca Chica
Arauco Bay

CHILE

0   NAUTICAL MILES   30

Where tracks of two or more ships coincide, only the track of the leading ship is shown

© Richard Natkiel, 1982   37°30'

**Right map labels:**

58°S    57°W    56°W

East Falkland Is.
STANLEY
1100
1115   1200
1230
52°S
Scharnhorst, Nurnberg, Gneisenau Leipzig and Dresden
1327
1405
1325   1405 Invincible
1515
1532
1630   **1617 Scharnhorst sunk**
**1800 Gneisenau sunk**
SOUTH ATLANTIC OCEAN
1600
1600
Cornwall   Kent
1627
1709
1643
53°S
**1927 Nurnberg sunk**
1650
1745
1700 Dresden escaping
1820   1806
**2035 Leipzig sunk**
1943
54°S

© Richard Natkiel, 1982

0   NAUTICAL MILES   40

Where tracks of two or more ships coincide, only the track of the leading ship is shown

# Coronel and the Falklands

One of the underlying causes of the First World War was German colonial and naval expansion, which the British regarded as a threat to their own interests. One feature of this expansion had been the establishment by the Germans of a Far Eastern naval squadron, with its base at Tsingtao, in China. The entry of Japan into the war on Britain's side made the German position here untenable but, when Japanese forces attacked Tsingtao, Admiral Graf von Spee had already taken his squadron across the Pacific to prey on British shipping. The British Admiralty, through agents in foreign ports and through intercepted signals, succeeded in finding the approximate location of the Germans, and sent its South American squadron against them. The Germans had two armored cruisers, *Gneisenau* and *Scharnhorst*, and three lighter cruisers. Admiral Cradock, the British commander, had two armored cruisers, *Monmouth* and *Good Hope*, which were slower and less powerfully gunned and armored than the German armored cruisers, together with a cruiser and an armed merchant cruiser. On 1 November 1914, off the Chilean coast near Coronel, Cradock sighted the German squadron and attacked immediately. To the physical disparity between the two forces was added the disadvantage that in this evening battle the direction of both wind and sun were against the British. Only if the German ships had been fought incompetently could this battle have resulted in a British victory. Two hours after battle was joined, the British armored cruisers had been sunk, not having harmed the Germans, and the two smaller British ships had fled. Later, the Admiralty implied that this disaster was the fault of Cradock, even though the latter had been complying with the Admiralty's instructions.

The reputation of the First Lord of the Admiralty, Churchill, seemed to be at stake. Unknown to the public but increasingly obvious to the admirals, Churchill had been interfering in the day-to-day conduct of operations and was held responsible by several high naval officers for the Coronel defeat. Taking rapid measures, Churchill arranged for the dispatch of two battlecruisers, *Inflexible* and *Invincible*, to the South Pacific. These ships were prepared very quickly and arrived for coaling at the Falkland Islands before the Germans knew of their departure from England. On 8 December, as the battlecruisers were preparing for sea, the German squadron appeared, intending to raid this British colony and signal station. Spee retired immediately he saw the tripod masts of the battlecruisers, but after a day-long pursuit the British admiral, Sturdee, got within range. Exploiting his superior speed, Sturdee stayed beyond the reach of the German guns, and bombarded his opponent at leisure. British gunnery was not especially accurate but, having almost exhausted his ammunition, Sturdee sent the German armored cruisers to the bottom. Meanwhile his three cruisers dealt with the German cruisers, sinking *Leipzig* and *Nurnberg*. *Dresden* escaped, to continue commerce raiding for a few more months before being hunted down in the same area. The Battle of the Falklands restored British naval prestige, which had been seriously diminished by the Coronel disaster.

# Gallipoli

When the Western Front became static British ministers began to seek ways of livening up the war to reach a quick victory. Turkey had entered the war on the German side in October 1914, and this had raised problems for Russia. Some British ministers, including Kitchener, the War Minister, and Churchill, the First Lord of the Admiralty, favored an attack on the Dardanelles. This, it was claimed, would obtain the capture of Constantinople, the surrender of Turkey, and a supply route by which munitions could be passed to the enormous but poorly-equipped Russian Army. Churchill initially proposed that ships alone could do the job; when this incentive had swung ministers in favor of the project, he decided that troops would, after all, be needed.

Nevertheless Churchill authorized the Royal Navy to bombard the Turkish guns defending the Dardanelles. After two bombardments, on 26 February sailors and marines were landed to inspect the damage and blow up some of the remaining gun emplacements. In March there were more bombardments, one of whose effects was that the Turks were warned that an attack was impending. Their precautions not only took the form of reinforcing the land defenses but also of more sophisticated methods of mining. In the last and most important bombardment on 18 March three old battleships were destroyed by mines, and this persuaded the commanding admiral not to risk any more close bombardments. In fact, if the naval bombardment had been pressed home in its initial stages, the navy might indeed have been able to force the Dardanelles.

About 75,000 troops were in the initial landings on 25 April 1915. Of these 30,000 were Australians and New Zealanders and 17,000 were French. The landings, at five points on the tip of the Gallipoli Peninsula, were well-planned. Except in one place, resistance was slight and casualties were few. However, there was delay and confusion once the men were ashore. A supplementary landing to the north, at a place later called Anzac Cove, was also successful, but was soon assailed by strong Turkish forces. In general, the advantage of the successful landings was dissipated by un-adventurous leadership, and the troops settled down to a long hot summer of bloody attacks and counterattacks. Both sides dispatched more troops to the Peninsula. Rather than abandon the project, Churchill and Kitchener persuaded ministers to send even more troops. On 6 August new landings were made at Suvla Bay, five miles to the north of Anzac Cove. The intention was to advance inland to capture the vital high ground, thereby disorganizing the Turkish dispositions and enabling the Allies to capture the entire Peninsula and open the way to Constantinople. The landings were again very successful but, once ashore, officers made no effort to press on; they intended to 'consolidate' first. Thus, the advantage of surprise was lost once again. When the high ground was finally attacked, the Turks were ready. August was a month of costly battles which brought no great gains. It was clear that the project could no longer succeed, but it was not until the winter that the British Cabinet could steel itself to order a withdrawal. The evacuation was very successful, with no lives lost, and ended in January 1916.

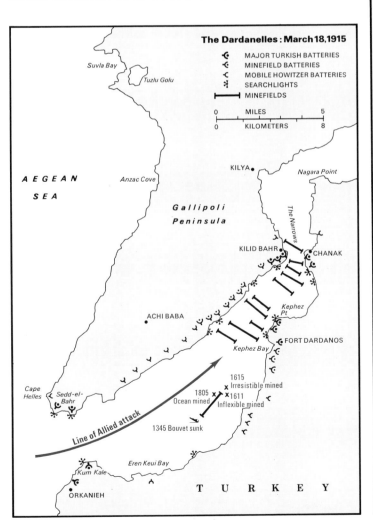

## The Dardanelles : March 18, 1915

MAJOR TURKISH BATTERIES
MINEFIELD BATTERIES
MOBILE HOWITZER BATTERIES
SEARCHLIGHTS
MINEFIELDS

0 MILES 5
0 KILOMETERS 8

*Suvla Bay*

*Tuzlu Golu*

**A E G E A N
S E A**

*Anzac Cove*

KILYA •

*Nagara Point*

*Gallipoli
Peninsula*

*The Narrows*

KILID BAHR ● CHANAK

● ACHI BABA

*Kephez
Pt.*

*Kephez Bay* ● FORT DARDANOS

*Cape
Helles* *Sedd-el-
Bahr*

1615
x Irresistible mined
1805 x x1611
Ocean mined Inflexible mined

1345 Bouvet sunk

*Eren Keui Bay*

*Line of Allied attack*

Kum Kale

● ORKANIEH

**T U R K E Y**

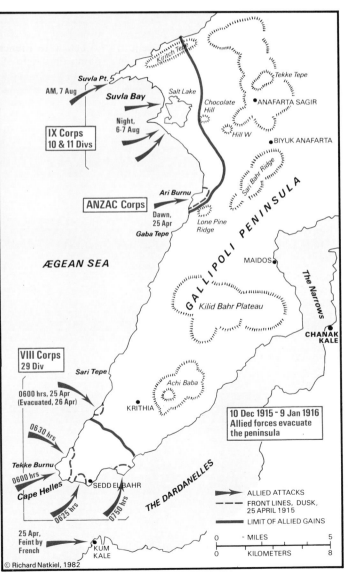

*Kiritch Tepe*

AM, 7 Aug *Suvla Pt.*

*Suvla Bay* *Salt Lake* *Tekke Tepe*

*Chocolate
Hill* ● ANAFARTA SAGIR

Night,
6-7 Aug

**IX Corps
10 & 11 Divs** *Hill W* ● BIYUK ANAFARTA

*Sari Bahr Ridge*

**ANZAC Corps** *Ari Burnu*

Dawn,
25 Apr *Lone Pine
Ridge*

*Gaba Tepe*

**A E G E A N   S E A** MAIDOS ●

*Kilid Bahr Plateau* *The Narrows*

CHANAK
KALE

**VIII Corps
29 Div** *Sari Tepe*

*Achi Baba*

0600 hrs, 25 Apr
(Evacuated, 26 Apr) **10 Dec 1915 - 9 Jan 1916
Allied forces evacuate
the peninsula**

0630 hrs ● KRITHIA

*Tekke Burnu*

0600 hrs *Cape Helles* SEDD EL BAHR

0625 hrs 0750 hrs *THE DARDANELLES*

ALLIED ATTACKS
FRONT LINES, DUSK,
25 APRIL 1915
LIMIT OF ALLIED GAINS

25 Apr,
Feint by
French KUM
KALE

0 MILES 5
0 KILOMETERS 8

© Richard Natkiel, 1982

**G A L L I P O L I   P E N I N S U L A**

44

# The Second Battle of Ypres

As the Western Front settled down into static positional warfare, with little prospect of either side making a really decisive breakthrough, commanders began to seek locations where a minor victory might be possible. In early 1915 the French and British on the Western Front undertook several offensives. In February there was a French offensive in Champagne which cost the attackers 50,000 casualties and gained only a few hundred yards of ground. In March the British attacked at Neuve Chapelle and because they were short of shells, did not make a preliminary bombardment. In this way, by accident, they achieved surprise and a breakthrough, but were unable to make use of the temporary gap in the German line. Further French and British offensives were similarly costly and unsuccessful. The Germans were content to stay on the defensive, inflicting heavy casualties on the attackers. But at Ypres they did launch an attack of their own. This began on 22 April with a poison gas emission which drifted over the French and British trenches. This was the first time poison gas was used on the Western Front, although the Germans had previously tried it out on the Russians. At Ypres it was spectacularly successful. The French and British defenders fled from their trenches, gasping. The Germans were able to capture the trenches with almost no loss, and by evening there was a gap of four miles in the Allied front. It was only by desperately combing the rear area for reserves that the British were able to plug the gap the following day.

Although the use of gas took the defenders by surprise and made a wide gap in their line, German forces had not been assembled in sufficient numbers to burst through the gap decisively. Not for the last time in this war, a technological surprise had been wasted. There were renewed Allied offensives later in 1915, at Festubert and Vimy Ridge in May-June and at Loos and in Champagne in September-October. Despite heavy casualties there were only minor gains.

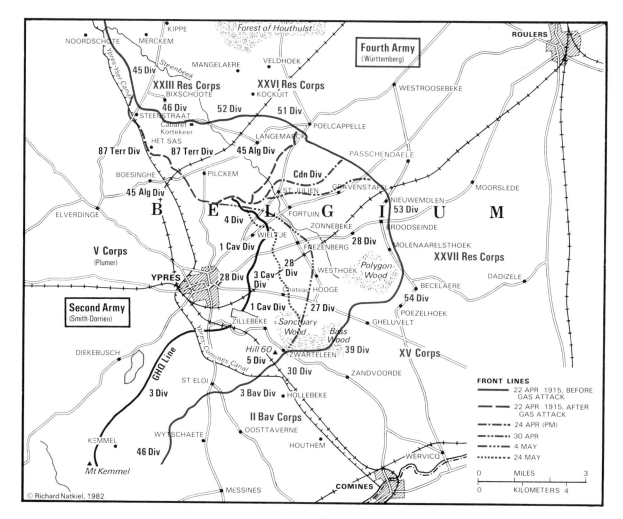

© Richard Natkiel, 1982

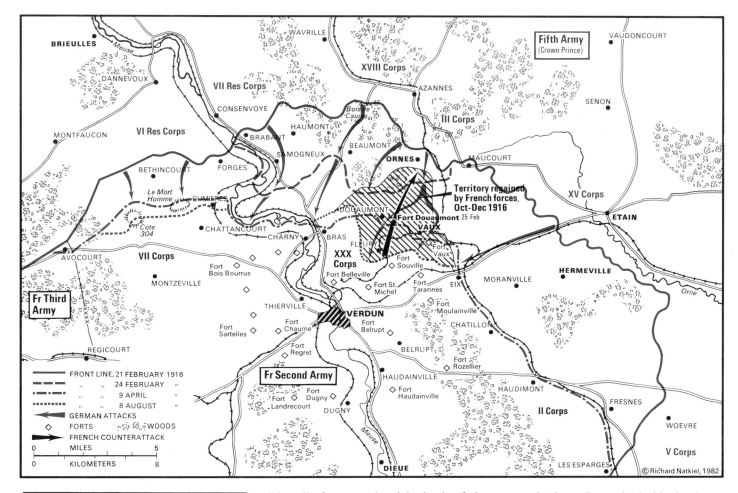

The following labels appear on the map:

Fifth Army (Crown Prince)

VAUDONCOURT
BRIEULLES — Meuse
WAVRILLE
XVIII Corps
DANNEVOUX
VII Res Corps
AZANNES
SENON
CONSENVOYE
VI Res Corps
III Corps
MONTFAUCON
HAUMONT
Bois de Caures
BRABANT
MAUCOURT
BEAUMONT
SAMOGNEUX
ORNES
XV Corps
BETHINCOURT
FORGES
Territory regained by French forces, Oct-Dec 1916
ETAIN
Le Mort Homme — GUMIERES
DOUAUMONT
Cote 304
CHATTANCOURT
Fort Douaumont 25 Feb
AVOCOURT
CHARNY
BRAS
FLEURY
VAUX
Fort Vaux
HERMEVILLE
VII Corps
XXX Corps
Fort Souville
Orne
Fort Bois Bourrus
Fort Belleville
EIX
MORANVILLE
MONTZEVILLE
Fort St. Michel
Fort Tarannes
Fr Third Army
THIERVILLE
VERDUN
Fort Moulainville
Fort Sartelles
Fort Chaume
Fort Belrupt
CHATILLON
REGICOURT
Fort Regret
BELRUPT
Fort Rozellier
Fr Second Army
HAUDAINVILLE
HAUDIMONT
FRESNES
Fort Landrecourt
Fort Dugny
Fort Haudainville
WOEVRE
DUGNY
II Corps
DIEUE
LES ESPARGES
V Corps
© Richard Natkiel, 1982

Legend:
FRONT LINE, 21 FEBRUARY 1916
" " 24 FEBRUARY "
" " 9 APRIL "
" " 8 AUGUST "
GERMAN ATTACKS
FORTS  WOODS
FRENCH COUNTERATTACK
MILES 0 — 5
KILOMETERS 0 — 8

# Verdun

By 1916 both sides saw that the war might be won by exhausting the enemy's man-power reserves and the German commander, Falkenhayn, decided that Verdun would be an advantageous site for a battle in which French infantry could be drawn under the destructive power of German artillery. Verdun was one of France's great fortresses, situated by the frontier on the River Meuse. There had been little fighting in this area, so the French defenses could be assumed to be slack. Moreover, the Germans had numerous railways leading toward Verdun, whereas the French had not.

The German attack opened on 21 February with a bombardment heavier than any hitherto seen. It was concentrated on a couple of French divisions holding an eight-mile front on the right bank of the Meuse. Resisting doggedly, the French began to withdraw from this first line of defense the next day. Meanwhile, as Falkenhayn had expected, the French began to send fresh infantry divisions to Verdun. On 24 February the second French line was broken and the Germans advanced to the third. This, four miles from Verdun, was a line of trenches joining two strong forts, Douaumont and Vaux. The former was not properly garrisoned, and the Germans captured it without any trouble. Pétain, who by this time had been appointed to command the French defense, called for more artillery, and insisted on full use being made of it. He also widened the highway leading to Verdun; this carried a dense traffic of supplies and reinforcements in, and thousands of wounded out, and soon became known as the *Voie Sacrée*. On 6 March a new German assault on both sides of the river captured new ground at heavy loss to both sides but it was not until 6 June, after a heroic defense, that the fort at Vaux was captured. There were further attacks and French counterattacks, but the German effort at Verdun was weakened by new Allied offensives elsewhere. It was not until December that the attack could be regarded as abandoned. Verdun did not fall, but the French army suffered about 360,000 casualties in defending it. Falkenhayn's intention had been to inflict totally disproportionate losses on the French but he had been drawn into a far longer and more costly battle than he originally envisioned.

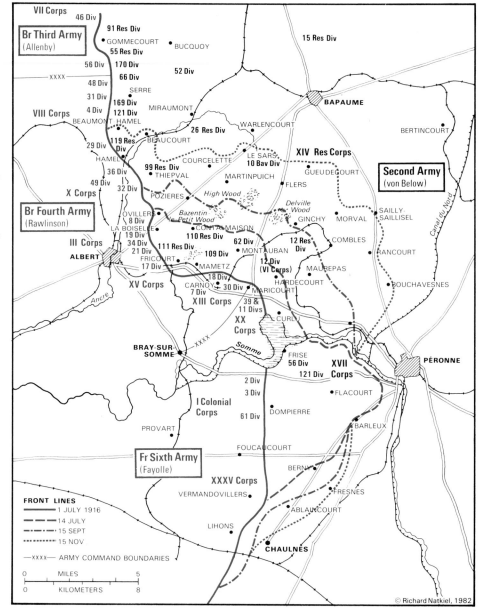

# The Battle of the Somme

By mid-1916 the British share of the Western Front had been extended south to the River Somme, and it was here that the Anglo-French command planned a great offensive for the summer. In the final plan the French were to contribute eight divisions, attacking on an eight-mile front and the British were to attack along 18 miles with 14 divisions, with a further eight in reserve.

The preliminary artillery barrage lasted almost a week, with over a million shells being dispatched to the German trenches. At 0730 on 1 July it ceased. On the German side men began to pour upward from their deep dugouts bringing their machine guns, to take up station in the fresh shell holes and the ruins of their trenches. On the British side, men rapidly began to assemble in front of their own trenches, and then move off in dense extended lines across a No Man's Land which became progressively more impassable as they entered the shell-churned belt in front of the German lines. In the French sector of the line, comparative peace and quiet prevailed. The French, at the last minute, had postponed their advance for a couple of hours; when they did advance, therefore, they took the Germans by surprise and won considerable ground for few casualties. The British had expected the German resistance to be negligible, after so much bombardment. As it turned out, with No Man's Land being about a quarter of a mile wide, the Germans had time to install themselves before the British could reach their trenches. The first British line was laid low by rifle and machine-gun fire, and so then was the second. German artillery pounded the British side of No Man's Land. But still the lines of khaki-clad men came on. Not since the Japanese assaults of the Russo-Japanese War had so many men been sacrificed for so little gain of ground. By the end of the first day 20,000 British soldiers had been killed and 40,000 wounded. The attacks by the 32nd Division on Thiepval Wood were particularly bloody.

Here and there, part of the German first line was taken, and the French did well. A night advance then secured the German second line. But an attempt by three reserve cavalry divisions to exploit the gap was crushed by machine-gun fire, and the Allied command settled down to a battle of attrition which lasted until November, when a last big battle, on the Ancre, was called off when the battlefield mud became impassable. There had also been a renewed offensive in September, the Battle of Flers Courcelette, notable because for the first time a few tanks were used. They made a deep penetration, but were too few and too slow to exploit it. In all, the Battle of the Somme cost more than 600,000 Allied casualties. German casualties were also heavy. Although the British generals' conduct of the battle has been much criticized, with considerable justice, for its lack of imagination and sophistication, German accounts of the battle say that it wrecked the German Army because of the heavy losses in the senior NCO and junior officer grades.

Below: men of the Border Regiment rest in a trench near Thiepval during the bitter fighting on the Somme.
Bottom: Indian cavalry fought as dismounted troops in July 1916.

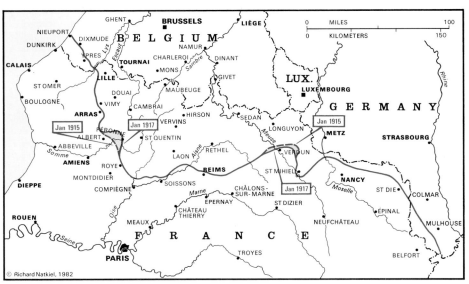

© Richard Natkiel, 1982

# The Western Front at the End of 1916

Despite the heavy fighting and the enormous number of casualties, the most arresting feature of the front line of December 1916 was its similarity to that of a year previously. Only around the sites of the two great 1916 battles, the Somme and Verdun, was there perceptible change. Around the Somme, where British casualties had amounted to a number no less than one per cent of the entire British population, the Western Front had been pushed forward for just about six miles over an 18-mile length. At Verdun, which had shattered both the French and German Armies, the Germans had gained a mile or two, but had already begun to fall back under French counter-pressure.

The technical reasons for this lethal stalemate were by now accepted by both generals and politicians. Entrenchment, plus the new weapons of mass destruction, meant that troops either stayed in their trenches and lived, or advanced from their trenches and died. Of the new weapons, it was the machine gun which both then and thereafter struck the human imagination as the most dramatic and death-dealing weapon on the Western Front. This was only partly true, although the survivors of the Battle of the Somme, who had seen lines of advancing British infantry thrashed down by well-sited defen-

sive machine guns, would never have doubted it. In fact it was the artillery which claimed the most victims. The role of the artillery in this slaughter was perhaps underrated because the number of shells which exploded harmlessly far outnumbered those doing any damage. At Verdun, for example, the opposing sides fired off 37 million shells, whereas the total French and German casualties were well under one million, and these were from all causes. But well-placed shrapnel shells could wreak mass destruction on troops in their forming-up areas, while intense bombardment of entrenchments could sometimes take a serious toll of troops lacking overhead cover.

On the Western Front, therefore, 1916 had presented a horrifying picture, and it was not only the front-line infantry who were asking how much longer this could be allowed to go on. But President Wilson's suggestion of a negotiated peace was politely ignored by the belligerent governments. In Britain, moreover, Lloyd George's ostentatious determination to fight the war to a finish brought him enough support to enable him to replace the less bloodthirsty Asquith as prime minister.

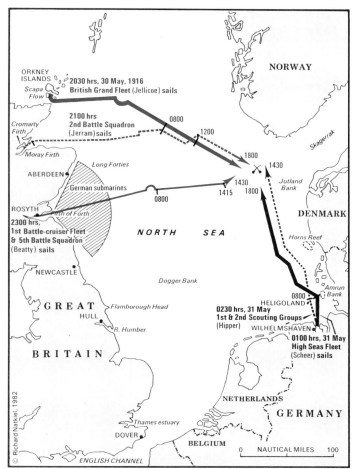

Far left: Admiral Jellicoe, Commander in Chief of the British Grand Fleet.
Left: Admiral Hood commanded a battlecruiser squadron and was killed in the *Invincible* at Jutland.
Below right: a German shell explodes amidships on the *Queen Mary* just before she blew up in the early stages of the battle.
Bottom: a squadron of German predreadnought battleships in line ahead. Second in the line is the *Pommern*, sunk at Jutland.

# The Battle of Jutland

Up to 1916 the German High Seas Fleet had evaded a full-scale battle against the larger British Grand Fleet, hoping eventually to maneuver the latter into a battle with only part of its strength facing the whole German battlefleet.

On 30 May 1916 intercepted radio messages indicated that the German fleet was preparing to leave harbor. Admiral Jellicoe, the British Commander in Chief, took his Grand Fleet on an intercepting course, with Admiral Beatty's battlecruiser squadrons and four new fast battleships scouting ahead. Cruisers from Beatty's squadron made contact off Jutland with German cruisers and soon the British battlecruisers sighted the German battlecruisers, which were screening the advance of the German battleships. Battle was joined between these scouting groups in the afternoon. German gunnery and German armor protection proved superior to British and in this preliminary engagement two of Beatty's battlecruisers

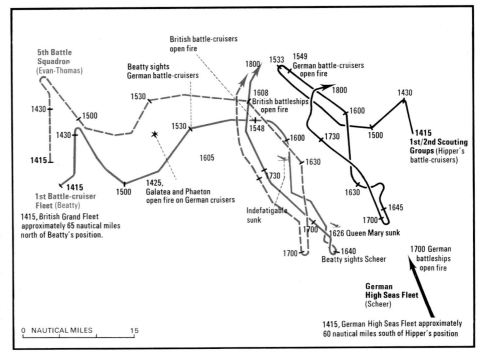

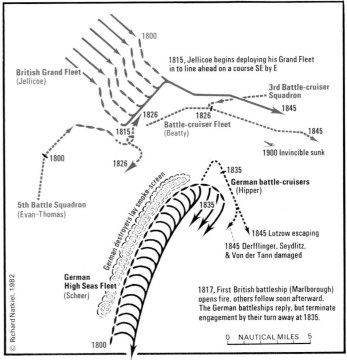

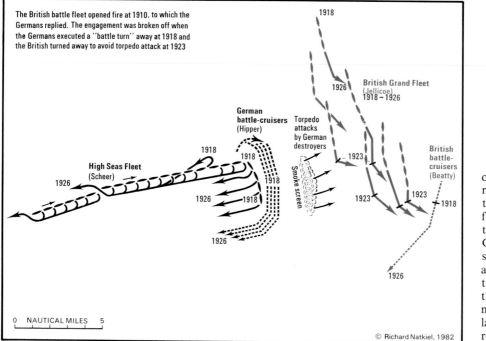

The British battle fleet opened fire at 1910, to which the Germans replied. The engagement was broken off when the Germans executed a ''battle turn'' away at 1918 and the British turned away to avoid torpedo attack at 1923

© Richard Natkiel, 1982

blew up. Beatty, who had caught sight of the German battleships approaching from the south, continued to maneuver so as to draw the Germans to the main British force.

Beatty, however, was not keeping Jellicoe well-informed of the enemy's position and course. Jellicoe's problem was to choose the best possible moment for deploying his battlefleet of 24 Dreadnoughts, which were moving in six parallel columns, a formation suitable for cruising in search of the enemy but less suitable for fighting a battle. In battle, line ahead gave all ships a chance to use their guns, and Jellicoe had to deploy into line ahead before the enemy was in

range but not before he knew the enemy's position and bearing. At 1815 the German battlecruisers encountered the three battlecruisers which had remained to screen Jellicoe. One more British battlecruiser blew up, but Jellicoe was now able to calculate the likely position of the main German forces. He started his deployment into line ahead and 20 minutes later the unsuspecting German admiral, Scheer, with his battleships in line ahead, was confronted by the British battlefleet passing ahead of him at right angles. With all the British battleships able to concentrate their fire on his leading ships, Scheer was in a perilous situation, and he

ordered his ships to do an 'all-together' reversal of course, a very difficult maneuver to perform. Half an hour later Scheer again found himself in this situation. Once more there was a brief exchange of fire while the Germans withdrew under cover of a smokescreen. This time, German destroyers made a torpedo attack on the British. Jellicoe turned away and thereby lost contact with the Germans. He was later criticized for this move, but Churchill was probably right, later, when he emphasized the enormous responsibility carried by Jellicoe.

During the night Jellicoe tried to interpose his ships between the fleeing Germans and their bases. Thanks to a muddle in the Admiralty, which failed to pass vital intercepted German radio messages and to negligent British commanders, who failed to report their ships' actions with the enemy during the night, the Germans were able to slip back to their ports. Thus the long-awaited encounter between the two fleets had ended unsatisfactorily for the British. They had lost three battlecruisers and three armored cruisers against a German loss of one battlecruiser, one old battleship, and three armored cruisers. But it was the Germans who had fled; Britain was still mistress of the seas.

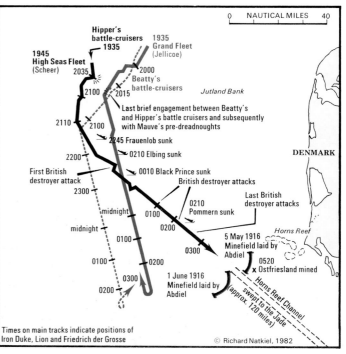

Times on main tracks indicate positions of Iron Duke, Lion and Friedrich der Grosse

© Richard Natkiel, 1982

Bottom left: the broken hull of
HMS *Invincible* at Jutland.
Below: a column of Russian prisoners-of-
war march to the rear under escort.
Although the Russians had overcome many
of their equipment shortages by 1916 the
casualty rate remained high.

# The Brusilov Offensive

On the Eastern Front the Russian Army had been forced back in a retreat during 1915, but in 1916 it began to attack. Early drives against the Germans around Lake Narosh were unsuccessful, but the Russians soon began to plan a great offensive. However, before this was ready an urgent appeal for a diversionary attack came from the Italians, whose army had been heavily attacked by the Austrians in the Trentino district. General Brusilov, the new commander of the Southern Front defending the Ukraine, was thereupon given unusual liberty of action to attack the Austrians at short notice. In fact, Brusilov was well prepared.

He had earlier instructed his commanders to dig their trenches closer to the Austrian lines; on the Eastern Front, No Man's Land was sometimes up to several miles wide, and Brusilov believed that 100 yards was more appropriate where an attack was envisioned. Secondly, Brusilov had abandoned the concept of massing reserves before an attack. Knowing his enemy had more railroad lines serving the front, he realized that for every Russian reserve division moved up, the enemy, alerted by the Russian movement, could bring up three.

The attack, soon called the Brusilov Offensive, began on 4 June. Opposing the Russians were the Austrian Fourth and Seventh Armies on the flanks, with the Second and Southern Armies in the center. Only the Southern Army included German divisions. A powerful artillery bombardment demoralized the Austrians, and their

front, when assaulted, began to dissolve in headlong retreat. So fast was the Russian breakthrough that the commander of the Fourth Army, Archduke Joseph Ferdinand, had his birthday ruined by Russian fire.

Eventually, lack of reserves caused Brusilov's advance to falter. Meanwhile the Germans had collected forces around Kovel, threatening his salient from the north. When the Germans struck, he had to retreat, and by the time he had got back to his original line he had suffered about one million casualties. But his offensive had cheered the Allies at a difficult time, probably weakened the German attack at Verdun, and had shattered what morale the polyglot Austrian army had retained up to that time. Although it was the most successful Russian operation of the war to that time the continued high Russian casualties helped pave the way for revolution in 1917.

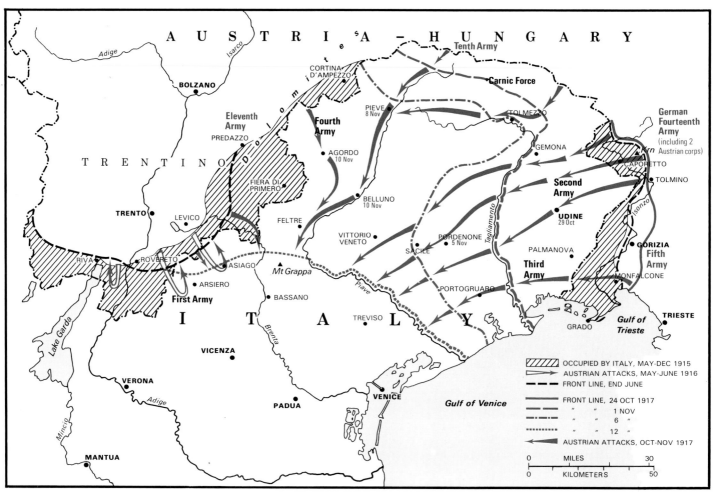

OCCUPIED BY ITALY, MAY-DEC 1915
AUSTRIAN ATTACKS, MAY-JUNE 1916
FRONT LINE, END JUNE
FRONT LINE, 24 OCT 1917
"      "    1 NOV
"      "    6  "
"      "    12 "
AUSTRIAN ATTACKS, OCT-NOV 1917

MILES    0 ——— 30
KILOMETERS 0 ——— 50

# Battles of the Isonzo

Italy declared war on the side of Britain and France on 23 May 1915, mainly in the hope of conquering the South Tyrol and Trieste, which were Austrian territory although largely Italian-speaking.

Still feeling the effects of the Libyan War of 1912, the Italian Army was ill-prepared. The expected drive northward into the Trentino was blocked by the Austrians in their strong mountain defenses and, so long as the Austrians held out here, they could threaten the rear of any Italian excursion eastward toward Trieste and Istria. In the Italian attempts to get within striking distance of Trieste the River Isonzo, backed by mountains, was the scene of eleven major battles and numerous skirmishes. In the first 10 of these battles the Italians suffered over half a million casualties but gained little significant ground. Meanwhile the Italian Army grew bigger, even including many returned Italian-Americans in its ranks. On 18 August 1917 the Italian commander, General Cadorna, launched an attack destined to be known as the Eleventh Battle of the Isonzo. This lasted almost a month, and was more successful, breaking the defense line and rolling back the demoralized Austrian troops. The Austrians

appealed for German assistance to be sent.

As Russia was already practically out of the war, the German command had seasoned troops available for transfer, and it decided to send to Austria six divisions, four of which were experienced in mountain warfare.

These six German divisions, with nine Austrian, began a massive attack on the Italian line near Caporetto on 24 October. Thanks partly to the unprecedented artillery bombardment, which included shells filled with a new type of poison gas, the Austro-German Fourteenth Army took the Italian positions with very few casualties. The capture of key positions at Caporetto and Tolmino gave the attackers the opportunity to sweep down on the disorganized Italians and cut off many of their columns. By the following day the Italians found that they were engaged in a military disaster, later known as the Battle of Caporetto. The attacking mountain troops, rapidly advancing over the high ground, were not only able to outflank the retiring Italian troops, but also the reserves moving up the valleys to restore the situation. That same day, therefore, the Italian General Cadorna ordered his shattered Second Army to retire as far as the Tagliamento.

The Italians finally established a defensive line on the Piave. This was 70 miles back, and only about 15 miles north of Venice at its closest point.

# The Third Battle of Ypres (Passchendaele)

Following the dismissal of Joffre late in 1916 General Nivelle took command of the French armies. Nivelle promised that, using methods tried out on a small scale in French attacks during the Verdun battle, he would prepare a grand offensive which would destroy the German forces. The Germans had decided in any case to shorten their line on the Western Front by a withdrawal, completed in April 1917, to an elaborately prepared defensive position, the Hindenburg Line. Despite this withdrawal Nivelle began his attack on 16 April but it quickly ended in failure. After having suffered terrible casualties during the first years of the war, the spirit of the French Army was broken and units began to mutiny. Eventually soldiers of 54 divisions were involved. There was, therefore, no prospect of significant French attacks for the rest of the year and even after Pétain had taken over from Nivelle and done much to restore morale it was uncertain if the French would withstand a serious German offensive.

Field Marshal Haig, the British com-

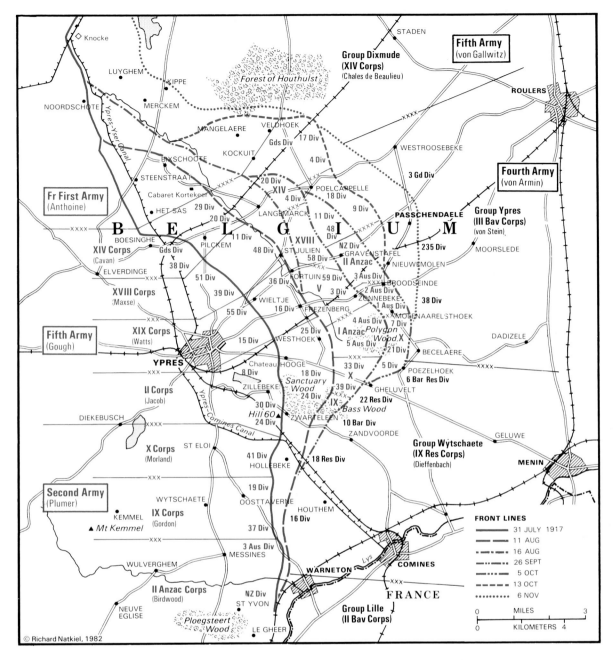

| FRONT LINES | |
|---|---|
| ——————— | 31 JULY 1917 |
| — · — · — | 11 AUG |
| — ·· — ·· — | 16 AUG |
| — ··· — ··· — | 26 SEPT |
| ——————— | 5 OCT |
| – – – – – | 13 OCT |
| ·············· | 6 NOV |

© Richard Natkiel, 1982

mander in France, had already planned attacks in the Ypres area which he hoped would turn the tide of the war. The Royal Navy supported this effort in the hope that German submarine bases in Belgium would be taken. The mutinies made the offensive seem even more necessary in order to distract the Germans from attempting to exploit French problems.

At Ypres the British salient was narrow, and its defenders were under fire from two sides. Haig intended to attack here, first to widen the salient and then to advance to Ostend and beyond. As a preliminary, at the beginning of June, mines beneath the German-held Messines Ridge (high ground dominating the Ypres salient) were detonated by British sappers, who had been burrowing beneath it for months. The ridge was then captured in a short sharp attack.

Then, on 31 July, after a week of bombardment, the main battle began. The first stage lasted until 4 August, by which time, under heavy rain, the British had won just two miles at the expense of 32,000 casualties. Two days later the struggle recommenced, but only a little ground near Langemarck was captured and the Germans remained unworried. In late September, a few days of sunshine helped meticulously prepared attacks by Plumer's Second Army to make gains in the Menin Road and Polygon Wood sectors on the right of the salient. The rain resumed early in October and the mud which had hampered the initial stages of the battle, was even thicker by November, often being at least waist deep. Nevertheless, although the army commanders wished to call a halt Haig ordered a final drive toward the village of Passchendaele. The final bloody and muddy attack came to an end on 10 November after nearly 250,000 casualties on each side and the offensive was then terminated.

# Germany's 1918 Offensives

In early 1918 the German High Command would still accept peace only on its own terms. The Russian Revolution had enabled 70 German divisions to be transferred from the Eastern to the Western Front. With these, the generals believed, it would be possible to win a crushing victory over the demoralized French and exhausted British before American forces could be ready in France in large numbers.

General Ludendorff, effectively in command of the German armies, planned to attack the British Fifth and Third Armies, breaking through north and south of Peronne, and then advancing northward with the right wing so as to drive the British farther away from the French. New tactics and specially trained storm troops were prepared for the attack. The artillery was to bombard the British rear areas using a large proportion of gas shells to disrupt communications rather than destroy defenses while the storm troops infiltrated through the front line, avoiding the strongpoints.

On 21 March the so-called *Kaiserschlacht*

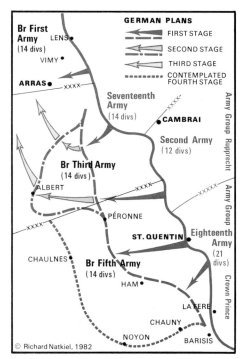

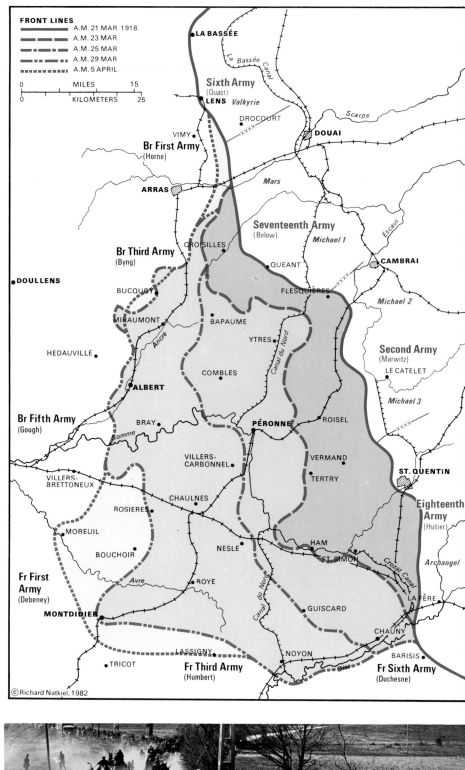

**Bottom left: a British eighteen-pounder battery moves up to the front during the March 1918 German offensive. Bottom: German troops bring a flamethrower into action.**

(Emperor's Battle) began. The gas shell bombardment was very effective and fog helped the initial infantry attacks. By 24 March the Germans had broken through the British line on a wide front and advanced 14 miles. This, in terms of the Western Front, was an enormous success. The British and French generals, Haig and Pétain, could not reach agreement; Pétain was pessimistic and envisioned a retreat toward Paris, while Haig was more optimistic and felt Pétain was too reluctant to send French reserves to help the British. To settle this discord, General Foch was appointed as grand coordinator.

By 5 April the initial momentum of the attack was exhausted, leaving the Germans in possession of a wide salient reaching to nine miles east of Amiens. To maintain the initiative, the Germans then attacked the British First Army from 9–30 April. This advance was also brought to a halt after desperate defense had limited the German gains to another salient.

The Germans then decided to turn against the French. Just before dawn on 27 May the Chemins des Dames ridge was taken by assault and by 3 June Château Thierry was reached. But this drive, too, died out. There were two more offensives, but the German reserves were becoming exhausted and casualties among the best units were high. German morale was declining whereas the Allied forces were being augmented by more and more fresh American units. On 18 July Foch began his counter-offensive eastward from Villers Cotterêts. He pushed back the Germans until, in early August, a massive and decisive Anglo-French attack completely changed the situation.

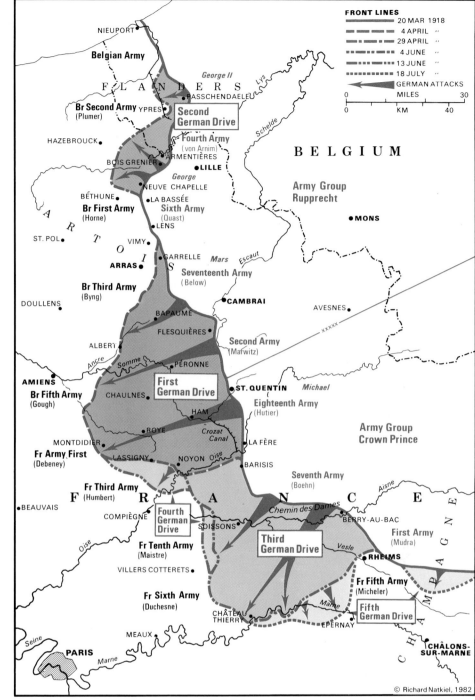

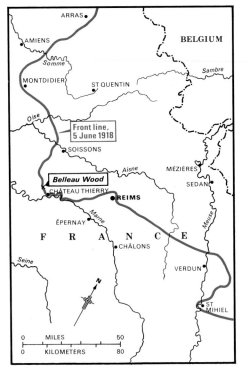

# The Battle of Belleau Wood

Lundendorff had counted on defeating the Allies in his final 1918 offensive before American troops were ready to fight in large numbers in France. Five German divisions had defeated the French in fighting on the Aisne and by 3 June were approaching Château Thierry, which was almost un-

defended by the French. The latter did scrape together some reserves, and these were joined by the US 2nd and 3rd Divisions, fresh infantrymen and marines. The 85,000 American troops made a counterattack near Belleau Wood, their riflemen advancing against the trenches through wheatfields. The battle, known also as the Battle of Château Thierry, lasted six days and prevented the Germans from gaining a foothold on the south bank of the River Marne.

That some units of the US Army were already in position and ready to fight was a triumph of organization which surprised the German High Command by its rapidity. Assembling the expeditionary forces, sending them across the Atlantic, keeping them supplied and giving them final training on arrival, was a huge task carried out very smoothly, thanks in part to the enormous resources devoted to the undertaking. In France the Americans had their own supply dumps, warehouses and recreation camps. Supplies and troops were carried by railroads manned by US railwaymen using US rolling stock. By these means the Americans were able to bring their forces into the final stage of the war, taking up a long sector of front on both sides of Verdun.

# 'The Black Day of the German Army'

The series of final Allied offensives was launched on 8 August 1918. Known by the British as the Battle of Amiens and by the French as the Battle of Montdidier, the first attack was to clear the Germans from the Paris-Amiens railroad. Tanks, which had proved themselves already in the Battle of Cambrai (November 1917) were used decisively in this battle. The British had no fewer than 554 of these weapons. Although easily knocked out by artillery, and having no great firepower themselves, their effect on morale was shattering. The German infantry was already demoralized by the apparent lack of success of the arduous offensives which it had been fighting. The soldiers' morale was further sapped by the knowledge that back home their families were starving.

The attack began at dawn in a dense fog. It had been well planned, and the assembly of 14 infantry divisions, more than 2000 guns, with cavalry and tanks, in a small area close to the Germans east of Amiens was a smooth operation conducted in effective secrecy. Much of the infantry force was Australian and Canadian. A creeping artillery barrage, tanks looming out of the fog, and a spirited infantry assault, were too much for the Germans, who fled or surrendered quite readily. By the end of the day six German divisions had been shattered, and the Allies had advanced seven miles on a wide front. The demoralization of the German Army had, after four years, finally set in. Ludendendorff called this the black day of the German Army.

However on 9 August only 145 of the British tanks were still in service, while German reinforcements were arriving. Progress was therefore slower; the French on the right wing were especially slow. On the 10th the French Third Army joined in. On the 11th the Australians and Canadians were ordered to advance to the Somme between Péronne and Ham, while the French First Army which had its own French-built tanks and had recaptured Montdidier, was to occupy Ham. However, stiffening resistance, and lack of tanks and guns, persuaded the commander of the British Fourth Army to postpone further attacks.

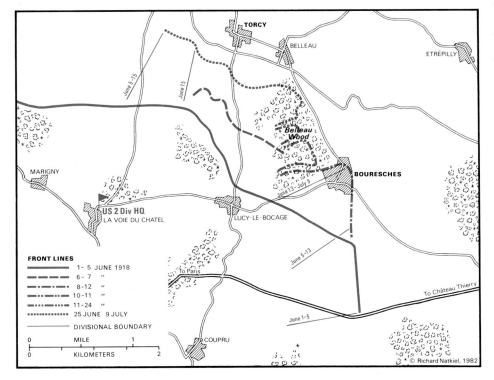

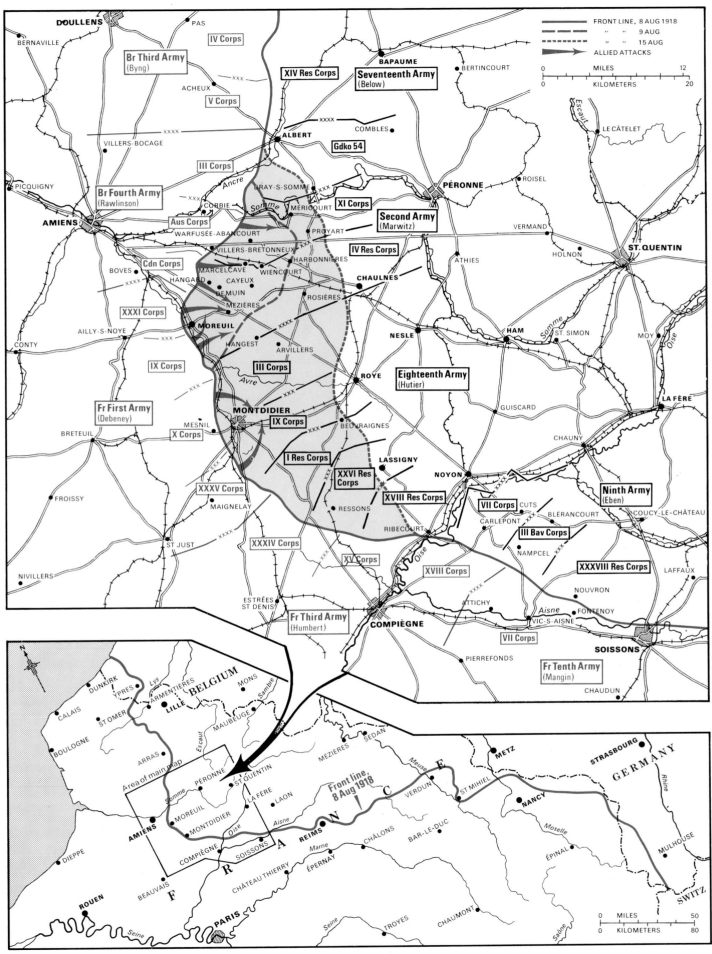

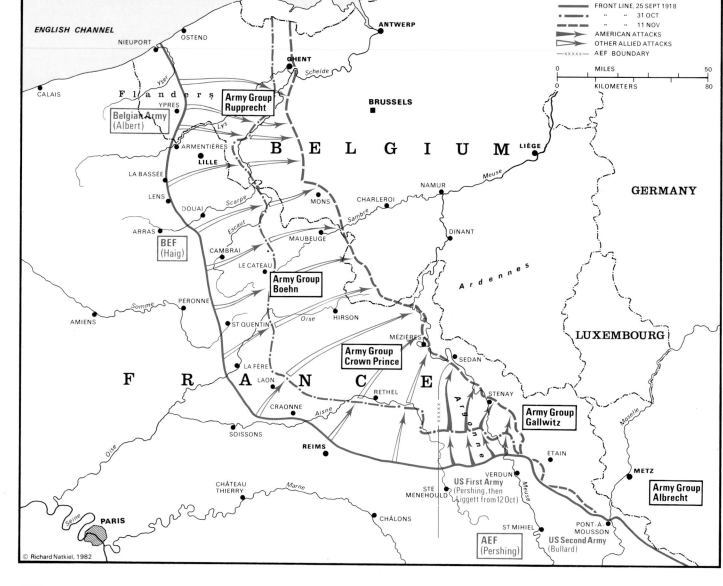

# The Allied Victory on the Western Front

Only a few days after the Battle of Amiens the Allies were ready to resume their offensive against the demoralized Germans. By the end of August the whole line north of the Marne was moving. The British gained ground along the Somme, while south of the Oise the French advanced to recapture ground lost in the recent German offensive. On 12 September General Pershing's US First Army attacked the St Mihiel salient just as the Germans were evacuating it, thereby winning a victory which, because it entailed few casualties, was an ideal introduction to real warfare for fresh troops. The Germans retreated to what in effect was their final defense, the Hindenburg Line. While the French busied themselves with collecting reserves to exploit a breakthrough, the British won positions from which the line could be assaulted.

The big breakthrough was planned for 26 September. On that day the French Fourth Army and the US First Army attacked between Reims and the River Meuse. Next day, the British Third and First Armies attacked farther north, near Lens. On the 28th the British Second Army and the French Sixth joined with the surviving units of the Belgian Army in an offensive between Armentières and the sea. Finally, around Epéhy, the French First Army and the British Fourth began an offensive. The Allies had 160 full strength divisions to pit against about 100 under-strength German divisions. It was the advance of the British Fourth Army which was decisive; helped by tanks, it broke through the Hindenburg Line in the first day of its attack.

Ludendorff, additionally unnerved by the decision of Germany's ally Bulgaria to seek an armistice, and knowing that this would open Austria to Allied attack from Greece, advised the Kaiser to seek an armistice. This took some weeks to arrange, and the last weeks of the war were weeks of retreat for the German Army. Before the Armistice was

signed, Ludendorff resigned in protest at its terms. He thereby protected his reputation on two fronts: the armistice he had suggested saved him from total defeat, while his resignation proclaimed that he was a man who would have preferred to fight on.

**Right: Austro-Hungarian troops in action on the Isonzo front.**

# Vittorio Veneto

The Italian stand on the Piave following their retreat from Caporetto had been bolstered by 11 British and French divisions sent from the Western Front. In their advance the German and Austrian forces had stretched their supply system and their consequently weakened attacks could not break through. These efforts came to an end in late December 1917. The new Italian commander, General Diaz, was more able than his predecessor Cadorna and under his direction the Italians spent the early months of 1918 re-forming and re-equipping their shattered forces. In this period also the German troops and six of the Anglo-French units were withdrawn to the Western Front.

With strong prompting from the Germans the Austrians renewed their attacks from 15–24 June 1918. The plan was for a two-pronged attack but neither General Boroević's group attacking over the Piave or Conrad's west of Monte Grappa was made sufficiently strong. Boroević gained some ground initially but air attacks and a rise in the river weakened the temporary bridges and the advance had to be abandoned. In the other sector the Austrians were quickly thrown back by British and French troops.

By 24 October the Italians themselves were ready to advance. Fourth Army made diversionary attacks in the Monte Grappa sector while crossings over the Piave were being won to the east. The most important initial gains were made by British and French troops which respectively formed part of the British and French led Tenth and Twelfth Armies. By 30 October the Austrian resistance was beginning to collapse and the Italian cavalry led a rapid pursuit. The battle is now known as the Battle of Vittorio Veneto. The armistice was agreed on 3 November.

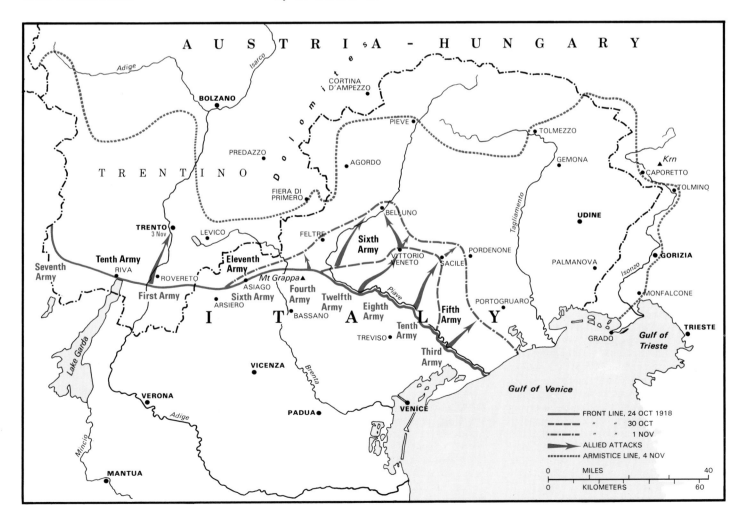

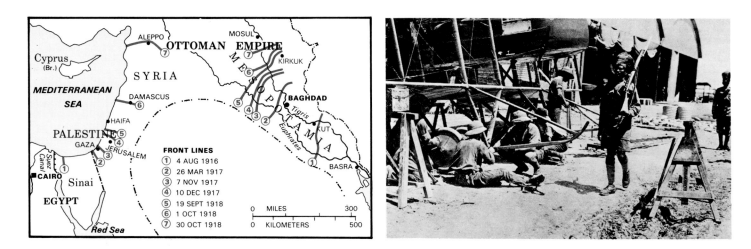

# The Mesopotamia Campaign

In November 1914 an expeditionary force of Britain's Indian Army landed at the head of the Persian Gulf with the intention of marching up the valley of the Tigris and Euphrates rivers. In doing so, it was expected to divert Turkish forces from other fronts and possibly, it was hoped, encourage the Arabs of the Turkish Empire to revolt. The Anglo-Indian force was very successful and pushed on faster than had originally been hoped. After Basra had been captured, the possession of Qurnah was thought necessary to secure it. Then to secure Qurnah, Amarah and Nasiriyah were taken, and it was realized that the whole situation would be improved if Kut were taken. Having got as far as Kut, it seemed a pity not to go on to capture Baghdad, from where the British could threaten the Turkish homeland in Anatolia, or advance into Turkish Syria and Palestine. To some, the fact that Baghdad was the terminus of the Berlin-Baghdad Railway, the legendary instrument of German influence in the Middle East, made it a specially attractive target.

General Townshend, the British commander, had made a well-planned attack on Kut, which he captured despite strong resistance by German-trained Turks. But by this time his supply routes were extended, and his men, although used to the Indian climate, were tired after a long campaign in arid conditions. Moreover, whereas the Turks could easily call up reinforcements,

Townshend had only 13,000 troops, of which two thirds were Indian. Nevertheless, a week after capturing Kut, Townshend was on his way, and by 12 November 1915 was within 24 miles of Baghdad, facing a Turkish defense line at Ctesiphon.

The Turks realized, just as well as the British, the strategic importance of Baghdad, and the defense they offered at Ctesiphon was strong, consisting of two lines of entrenchments on the eastern bank of the Tigris, with their right flank covered by a canal connecting the Tigris and Euphrates. Townshend's plan of attack was similar to that of his attack on Kut, but this time he succeeded only in capturing the outer Turkish line, and that only after heavy fighting. The arrival of reinforcements enabled the Turks to make counterattacks which, though costly, persuaded Townshend to withdraw. This withdrawal degenerated into a near-rout and ended only when the reduced British force was safe behind the walls of Kut. Here it was besieged from the beginning of December by strong Turkish forces under German command. The Turks were now able to transfer troops from the Gallipoli front, from which the Allied forces were withdrawing and mounted a fierce assault on 23 December which, however, failed. A Russian relief attempt through Persia was held back at Kermanshah, while a British relief force from the south almost reached Kut, but was impeded at the final stage by floodwater. On 29 April 1916 Townshend surrendered; his surviving 2,000 British and 6,000 Indian troops had been starved into submission.

The capture of Kut was only a temporary cause for Turkish rejoicing. While their own

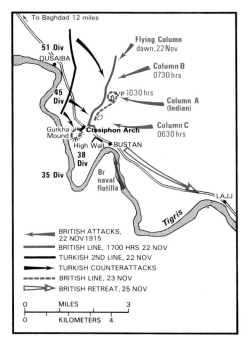

and the world's attention had been gripped by Mesopotamia, the Russians had advanced into Turkey from the Caucasus and, in a brilliant campaign in bitter temperatures, captured the city of Erzerum, reputed to be the strongest fortress in the Turkish Empire. Later, Russian cavalry from Persia would move forward to meet Anglo-Indian forces in Mesopotamia.

The British forces were strengthened during 1916 and by the end of the year had begun to advance once again. Kut was taken in February 1917 and the able and popular General Maude led his force on to capture Baghdad. Some further advances were made before a halt was called for the duration of the summer heat. There were important British victories at Ramadi and in the Tigris valley later in the year.

Following the Russian Revolution the main British concern for 1918 was to send a contingent, led by General Dunsterville, to north Persia to try and protect the oilfields there from a Turkish advance. This effort was only partially successful. The campaign in Mesopotamia was resumed in earnest in early October and the Turkish Sixth Army was quickly beaten. Mosul was occupied after the armistice.

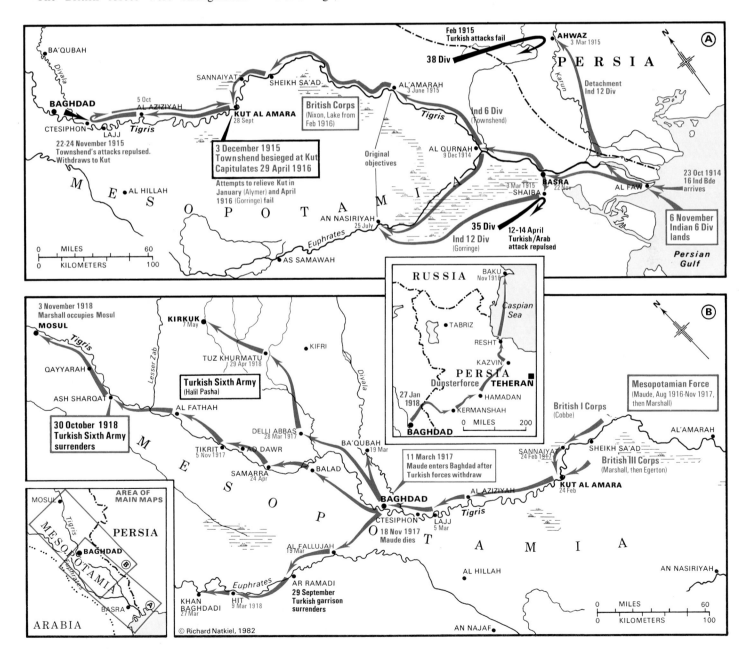

© Richard Natkiel, 1982

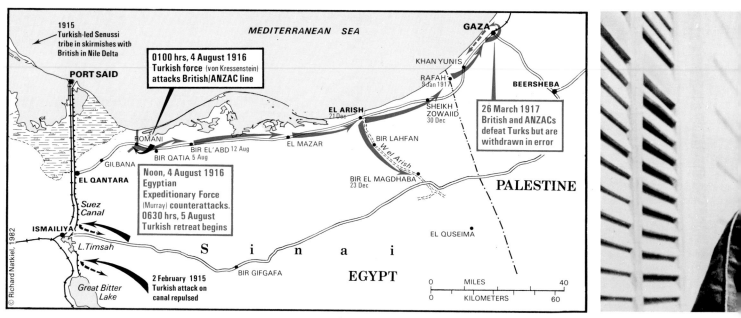

The map shows the Sinai and Palestine region with the following labels:

MEDITERRANEAN SEA

1915
Turkish-led Senussi tribe in skirmishes with British in Nile Delta

PORT SAID

0100 hrs, 4 August 1916
Turkish force (von Kressenstein) attacks British/ANZAC line

GAZA

KHAN YUNIS
RAFAH 9 Jan 1917
BEERSHEBA
SHEIKH ZOWAIID 30 Dec
EL ARISH 21 Dec

26 March 1917
British and ANZACs defeat Turks but are withdrawn in error

ROMANI
BIR EL'ABD 12 Aug
BIR QATIA 5 Aug
GILBANA
EL MAZAR
BIR LAHFAN
W el Arish

EL QANTARA

Noon, 4 August 1916
Egyptian Expeditionary Force (Murray) counterattacks.
0630 hrs, 5 August 1916
Turkish retreat begins

BIR EL MAGHDABA 23 Dec

PALESTINE

Suez Canal

ISMAILIYA

L. Timsah

S i n a i

EL QUSEIMA

2 February 1915
Turkish attack on canal repulsed

BIR GIFGAFA

EGYPT

Great Bitter Lake

© Richard Natkiel, 1982

MILES 0 — 40
KILOMETERS 0 — 60

# Crossing Sinai

Although Turkish attacks across the Sinai desert toward the Suez Canal had been unsuccessful in November 1914 and February 1915, the possibility of further attempts caused the British to keep in Egypt large forces which could have been better employed elsewhere. In late 1915 and early 1916 many of these troops were, however, withdrawn. At the same time the British forces were employed in putting down, successfully, a rebellion by Senussi tribesmen led by Turkish officers. Early in 1916 the British also began a slow advance into Sinai but with their involvement in Mesopotamia and the Caucasus the Turks could not mount a counterblow until the summer. When they did so their logistic arrangements were poor and, partly as a consequence, they were defeated in the Battle of Romani.

The careful British advance continued. A railroad was laboriously laid across the Sinai Desert eastward from Qantara to carry the essential supplies, including drinking water, which would be needed for a large-scale advance. On 21 December 1916 El Arish was captured and the Turkish troops who fled southward were surrounded and rounded up at Magdhaba. By March 1917 three infantry and two cavalry divisions were approaching Gaza which was defended by a strong Turkish force under German leadership. In the first Battle of Gaza on 26 March 1917 the British forces were on the verge of a victory when bad staff work and a breakdown in communications led to a premature withdrawal. By the time the supply situation allowed the attack to be renewed the Turks had been reinforced and the Second Battle of Gaza in April was a costly failure for the British forces.

# Palestine

After the British defeat in the Second Battle of Gaza General Allenby was appointed to command on this front, and was put under political pressure to capture Jerusalem 'in time for Christmas.' Making good use of his ample cavalry strength, he sent his artillery and infantry northward along the coastal plain, while his cavalry made sweeps inland to outflank the enemy. Von Falkenhayn, who had been replaced on the Western Front after he had failed to win dramatic victories, now commanded the Turkish forces, but although he was one of the most able generals of the war he was unable, with a force about one third in size of the British, to hold Allenby. In early November Allenby's men took Gaza; earlier frontal attacks had failed, but Allenby then outflanked it by capturing Beersheba. The advance continued rapidly, and as early as 14 November the railroad junction for the branchline to Jerusalem was captured and the Turkish defenders of that city thereby deprived of their supply route. Two days later Jaffa was captured. Allenby then contrived a pincer movement against Jerusalem and that city surrendered on 9 December; Allenby had succeeded where King Richard the Lionheart had failed. He was unable to advance further at this stage, partly because of supply difficulties, partly because many of his infantry units were withdrawn early in 1918 and sent to France to help meet the German spring offensives. Allenby retained his strong cavalry force and was sent some largely inexperienced Indian infantry.

Allenby's campaign was considerably aided by Arab irregular and guerrilla forces. A revolt in the Hejaz had begun early in 1916 and had become a powerful force under the inspiring leadership of a British officer T E Lawrence (Lawrence of Arabia) who was

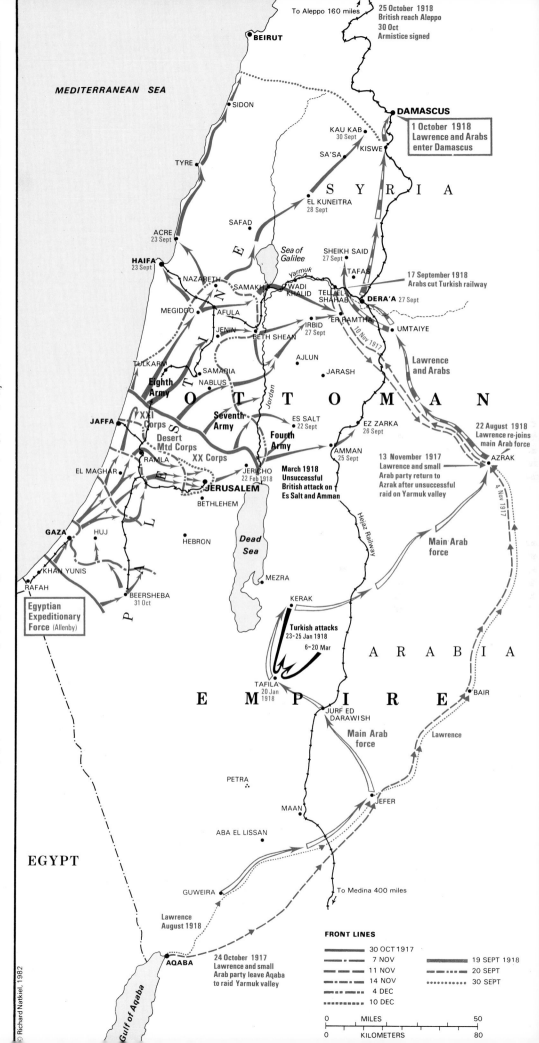

sent to join it in December 1916. Considerable Turkish forces were held down in the Hejaz at first while in the later stages of Allenby's campaign the Turkish flank was threatened and harassed.

In the summer of 1918 the British line in Palestine ran about 10 miles north of Jericho, Jerusalem and Jaffa, and by mid-September Allenby felt strong enough to launch an offensive which was destined to force Turkey out of the war. His infantry first drove the Turks back to the key railroad junction of Tulkarm, while his cavalry made a long fast ride through the night to reach Beth Shean and Nazareth. Here they turned south-east and cut off the Turks' retreat. This series of moves resulted in the virtual destruction of two Turkish armies, while the third fled across the Jordan and gradually decomposed; by this time the Turkish soldier was usually ready to surrender or desert. After this, there was nothing to stop Allenby. Damascus was captured on 1 October, Beirut fell to French units on 7 October, and meanwhile Turkey was reeling back in Mesopotamia and surrendering her entire army on the Tigris. Aleppo was taken on 25 October and on 30 October Turkey was forced to sign an armistice. In doing so she provided one more incentive for the German High Command to call for an end of the war.

**Top: Captain TE Lawrence, 'Lawrence of Arabia,' poses in Arab dress for photographers in 1918.**
**Left: part of the irregular Arab army which operated against Turkish rear areas during the Palestine campaign.**

MEDITERRANEAN SEA

To Aleppo 160 miles

25 October 1918 British reach Aleppo
30 Oct Armistice signed

BEIRUT
SIDON
DAMASCUS

1 October 1918 Lawrence and Arabs enter Damascus

KAU KAB 30 Sept
SA'SA
KISWE

TYRE
S Y R I A

EL KUNEITRA 28 Sept

ACRE 23 Sept
SAFAD
Sea of Galilee

SHEIKH SAID 27 Sept

HAIFA 23 Sept
NAZARETH
SAMAKH
Yarmuk
WADI KHALID
TAFAS

17 September 1918 Arabs cut Turkish railway

MEGIDDO
AFULA
JENIN
TELL EL SHAHAB
DERA'A 27 Sept
ER RAMTHA
UMTAIYE

BETH SHEAN
IRBID 27 Sept
AJLUN
JARASH

Lawrence and Arabs

TULKARM
SAMARIA
NABLUS
O T T O M A N

Eighth Army
Jordan

Seventh Army
ES SALT 22 Sept
EZ ZARKA 26 Sept

22 August 1918 Lawrence re-joins main Arab force

JAFFA
XXI Corps
Desert Mtd Corps
XX Corps
Fourth Army

AMMAN 25 Sept

13 November 1917 Lawrence and small Arab party return to Azrak after unsuccessful raid on Yarmuk valley

RAMLA
EL MAGHAR
JERICHO 22 Feb 1918
JERUSALEM
BETHLEHEM

March 1918 Unsuccessful British attack on Es Salt and Amman

AZRAK

GAZA
HUJ
HEBRON
Dead Sea

Hejaz Railway

Main Arab force

KHAN YUNIS
RAFAH
BEERSHEBA 31 Oct

MEZRA

KERAK

Egyptian Expeditionary Force (Allenby)

Turkish attacks 23-25 Jan 1918 6-20 Mar

A R A B I A

TAFILA 20 Jan 1918

BAIR

JURF ED DARAWISH

P A L E S T I N E

E M P I R E

Main Arab force
Lawrence

PETRA

EGYPT

MAAN
JEFER

ABA EL LISSAN

Lawrence August 1918

GUWEIRA
To Medina 400 miles

24 October 1917 Lawrence and small Arab party leave Aqaba to raid Yarmuk valley

AQABA
Gulf of Aqaba

FRONT LINES

30 OCT 1917
7 NOV
11 NOV
14 NOV
4 DEC
10 DEC

19 SEPT 1918
20 SEPT
30 SEPT

0        MILES        50
0      KILOMETERS      80

© Richard Natkiel, 1982

# Africa in 1914

What became known as the 'scramble for Africa' began in the mid-1880s and continued to 1914. There was a series of agreements in which colonizing powers divided up Africa among themselves. They agreed, for example, that King Leopold of Belgium could hold the Congo as his personal property (he later bequeathed it, as the Belgian Congo, to Belgium). The French, apart from their hold on the island of Madagascar, concentrated on the vast areas of northwest Africa. To this extensive territory they joined the region to the north of the Congo (French Equatorial Africa). British expansion, mainly through chartered trading companies, meant that by 1914 Britain had important colonies in East Africa (Kenya and Uganda, Somaliland) and West Africa (Nigeria, the Gold Coast, Gambia, and Sierra Leone). Cape Colony, Natal, the Orange Free State, and the Transvaal had united into the Union of South Africa under the British crown. Britain had also pushed northward into Bechuanaland, Rhodesia and Nyasaland, thereby interposing a wedge between German Southwest Africa and German East Africa.

The Germans, who had worked hard as latecomers to extend their colonies, possessed by 1914 the Kamerun, Togoland, Southwest Africa, and Tanganyika with Ruanda and Urundi. The Portuguese, asserting centuries-old rights of settlement, had the extensive territories of Angola and Mozambique, as well as Portuguese Guinea. The Italians, latecomers like the Germans, had managed to gain three barren territories, Libya, Eritrea and Italian Somaliland. There were a few small Spanish colonies, too, of which the most important was Spanish Morocco. By 1914 only Liberia and Abyssinia remained independent.

# The East African Campaign

The campaign in East Africa was one of the most remarkable of the war. Despite being completely cut off from outside help the German forces, led by General Paul von Lettow-Vorbeck, remained in being to the end of the war and succeeded in tying down enormously greater Allied forces. Lettow-Vorbeck's strength was never greater than 4000 German and 12,000 native troops.

The Allied campaign began with landings by Indian troops in November 1914 but these were quickly repulsed with heavy losses. The events of 1915 were mostly indecisive cross-border raids by both sides but the Allies did manage to gain control of the great lakes and also to sink the German cruiser *Königsberg*. Following the conclusion of the campaign in

© Richard Natkiel, 1982

**Bottom: a bridge on the Dar-es-Salaam to Mikese railroad blown up by German forces in September 1916.**
**Bottom right: a company of German askaris forms a firing line.**

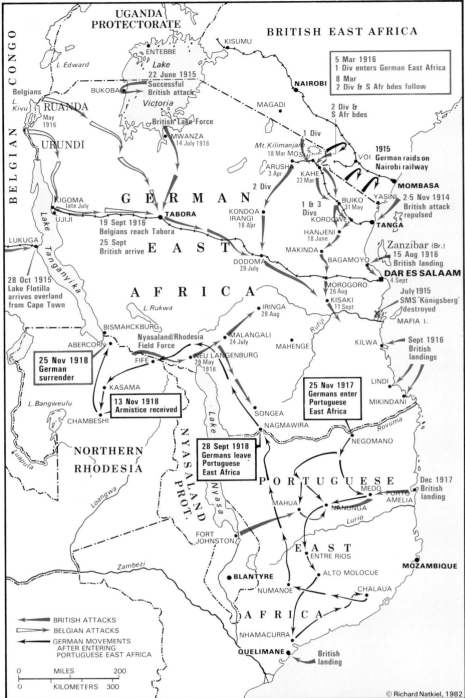

Southwest Africa in mid-1915 considerable South African forces were sent to East Africa. These units, under the command of General Smuts, led a major Allied offensive beginning in early 1916. Belgian forces from the Congo also began to advance. After much elaborate maneuvering but few major battles the German forces were gradually pushed southward. At the end of 1916 Smuts and most of the South African force left after suffering heavy losses to disease. They were replaced by British-trained East and West African troops.

When the fighting was resumed in July 1917 after the rainy season the Germans were forced even farther south and a large contingent was cut off at Mahenge and had to surrender. In November Lettow-Vorbeck led his remaining forces into Portugese East Africa. They were continually harried and occasionally small groups were captured but the Armistice in 1918 found the Germans in Rhodesia still ahead of their pursuers.

# Africa in 1919

Despite Lettow-Vorbeck's brilliant and prolonged resistance, by the end of the war German East Africa was firmly in Allied hands. The other German colonies had fallen far more quickly. Togoland was the first to go. Allied forces moved in from the east and west on 7 August 1914 and the Germans surrendered on the 26th. The Kamerun was also attacked first in August 1914 but a more resolute defense and difficulties of climate and disease prolonged the struggle to the end of 1915 when the remaining German forces entered Rio Muni and were interned by the Spanish authorities. Southwest Africa held out until 9 July 1915. After overcoming an anti-British Afrikaner revolt, South African units under General Botha soon took control of the railroad lines and forced the Germans to surrender.

The German possessions in Africa were formally stripped from her by the Treaty of Versailles in 1919. The Union of South Africa took over control of Southwest Africa by a League of Nations mandate. Most of German East Africa became British Tanganyika but two parts of it, Ruanda and Urundi, were attached to the Belgian Congo as some small compensation for the German occupation of Belgium during the war. Most of Kamerun went to France (as Cameroons) with a small portion being annexed to British Nigeria. Most of Togo also went to France with the rest joining the British Gold Coast. Thus the Treaty of Versailles, which was to champion the cause of national self determination, became an instrument for the expansion of the British and French Empires in Africa after World War I.

# Partition of the Pacific 1914–19

Britain's declaration of war against Germany in August 1914 did not automatically invoke the terms of the Anglo-Japanese alliance of 1902. Nevertheless the Japanese Empire was keen to make the most of the golden opportunity which Germany's preoccupation with European events provided. Much to the dismay of her British ally, Japan declared war against Germany in October 1914. She proceeded to seize every German territory in the Pacific she could lay her hands on. The first and most important of these was the greatest natural port in the whole of east Asia, Tsingtao, which included Kiaochow Bay and the coal-rich province of Shantung which had been effectively controlled by Germany and formed Tsingtao's hinterland. This conquest was not easy, but it was the only time in history that German and Japanese forces ever fought each other.

When the Japanese naval forces moved to occupy the Marshall, Marianas and Caroline Islands, Australia became nervous, as Kaiserwilhelmsland in northeastern New Guinea was directly adjacent to their own territory. Therefore Australian troops were ordered to Papua by their pugnacious Prime Minister Billy Hughes, and New Zealand forces moved to capture German Samoa.

At the Paris Peace Conference in 1919 the western allies sought to force Japan out of her newly won territories. After long discussion, German rights in China were given to Japan but the Japanese, under Allied pressure, withdrew from Shantung in 1926, after Japan had established her hegemony throughout North China. The Marshalls, Marianas and Carolines north of the Equator passed to Japan under a League of Nations mandate. The Australians took all German territory south of the Equator, including Kaiserwilhelmsland, New Britain, New Ireland and the Bismarck Archipelago, also under a League of Nations mandate. The phosphate-rich island of Nauru became a British colony. The New Zealanders established a mandate over western Samoa thereby sharing the island group with the United States. The partition of the German Empire in the Pacific established Japan as a major Pacific power.

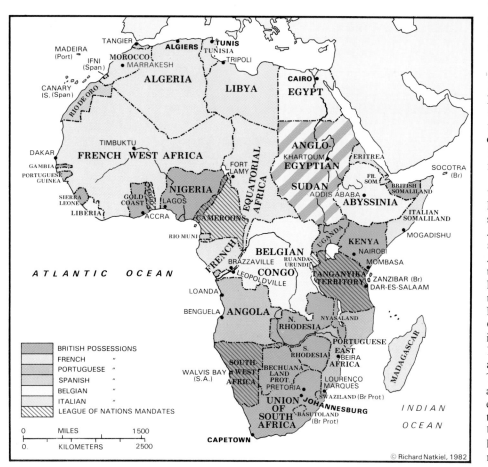

BRITISH POSSESSIONS
FRENCH "
PORTUGUESE "
SPANISH "
BELGIAN "
ITALIAN "
LEAGUE OF NATIONS MANDATES

0   MILES        1500
0.  KILOMETERS       2500

© Richard Natkiel, 1982

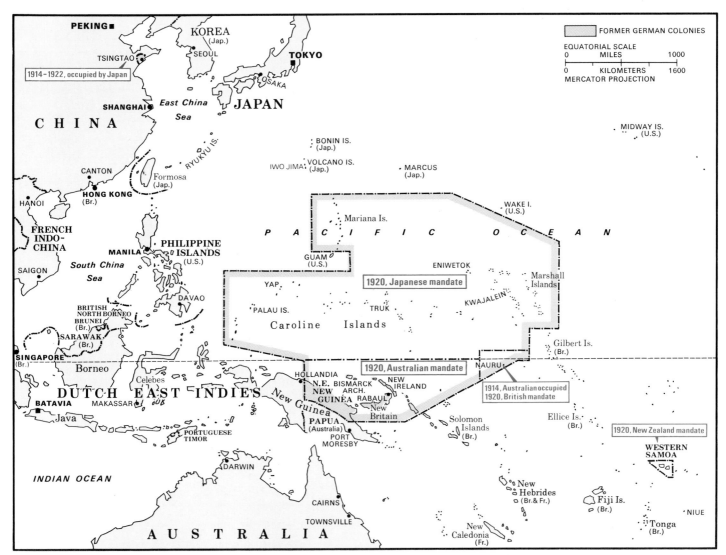

FORMER GERMAN COLONIES

EQUATORIAL SCALE
0        MILES        1000
0      KILOMETERS    1600
MERCATOR PROJECTION

PEKING■

KOREA
(Jap.)

SEOUL

TOKYO

TSINGTAO
1914–1922, occupied by Japan

OSAKA

East China Sea

JAPAN

SHANGHAI

CHINA

MIDWAY IS.
(U.S.)

RYUKYU IS.

BONIN IS.
(Jap.)

CANTON

Formosa
(Jap.)

IWO JIMA
VOLCANO IS.
(Jap.)

MARCUS
(Jap.)

HANOI

HONG KONG
(Br.)

P   A   C   I   F   I   C         O   C   E   A   N

WAKE I.
(U.S.)

Mariana Is.

FRENCH
INDO-
CHINA

MANILA

PHILIPPINE
ISLANDS
(U.S.)

GUAM
(U.S.)

ENIWETOK

Marshall
Islands

SAIGON

South China
Sea

YAP
1920, Japanese mandate

KWAJALEIN

DAVAO

PALAU IS.

TRUK

BRITISH
NORTH BORNEO

Caroline      Islands

BRUNEI
(Br.)

Gilbert Is.
(Br.)

SARAWAK
(Br.)

SINGAPORE
(Br.)

Borneo

1920, Australian mandate

NAURU

1914, Australian occupied
1920, British mandate

HOLLANDIA

Celebes

N.E. BISMARCK
ARCH.

NEW
IRELAND

Ellice Is.
(Br.)

DUTCH   EAST   INDIES

New Guinea

NEW
GUINEA

RABAUL

1920, New Zealand mandate

BATAVIA

MAKASSAR

New
Britain

Solomon
Islands
(Br.)

WESTERN
SAMOA

Java

PORTUGUESE
TIMOR

PAPUA
(Australia)

PORT
MORESBY

INDIAN OCEAN

DARWIN

New
Hebrides
(Br. & Fr.)

Fiji Is.
(Br.)

NIUE

CAIRNS

New
Caledonia
(Fr.)

Tonga
(Br.)

AUSTRALIA

TOWNSVILLE

Wir Protestieren gegen das Blutbad in der Chaussee-Str. Die Arbeiter „MERCUR" Flugzeugbau

# Between the Wars, 1919-38

**Soldiers and sailors lead a protest march in Berlin shortly after World War I.**

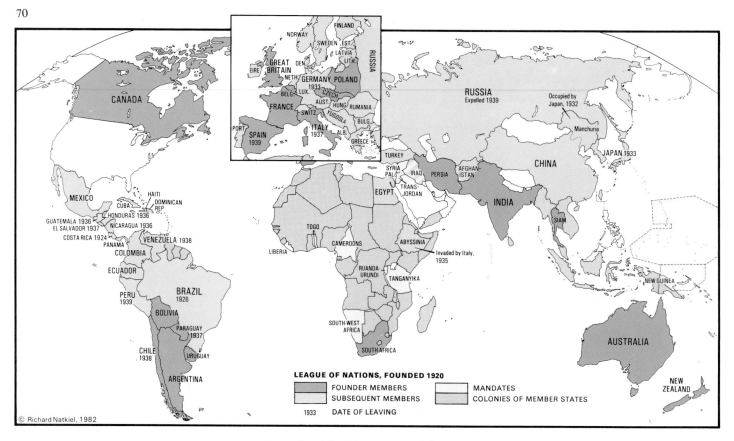

**LEAGUE OF NATIONS, FOUNDED 1920**

FOUNDER MEMBERS
SUBSEQUENT MEMBERS
MANDATES
COLONIES OF MEMBER STATES
1933    DATE OF LEAVING

© Richard Natkiel, 1982

# The League of Nations

An international organization which might prevent the outbreak of horrific wars like that being currently fought had been advocated during World War I by British and American figures, and notably by President Wilson of the USA, who was responsible for the inclusion in the Treaty of Versailles of the covenant of such an organization, the League of Nations. The terms of the covenant were a compromise, attempting to satisfy numerous claims and objections. For example, a clause, pressed by the Japanese, for outlawing racial discrimination, was finally rejected when Britain objected, at the bidding of Australia. A French protest, that the League could not function as arbitrator of international dis-

putes unless it had its own armed force, was unheeded.

However, the US Congress refused to ratify the Treaty of Versailles and this crippled the League from the start. It supervised some of the post-war frontier plebiscites and the establishment of the Free City of Danzig, and was ultimately responsible for the former colonies of Germany in Africa and the Pacific and of Turkey in Syria and Palestine, which it mandated to various powers. Many important states, including Germany and the Soviet Union, were members for only a few years. In its early days it did help to end the Turkish-Greek conflict of 1920–22. But without armed force its only weapon against offending states was to apply economic sanctions, which were dependent on the cooperation of all countries to be effective. It proved ineffective against Japanese aggression in Manchuria and China, and Italian aggression against Abyssinia.

**Right: the Palais des Nations in Geneva was the headquarters of the League of Nations, established by the Treaty of Versailles in 1919.**
**Below: these Bolshevik troops were captured at Yekaterinburg after a victory by White forces in September 1919. They are being guarded by British soldiers.**

# The Russian Civil War

The Bolshevik takeover of Petrograd (Leningrad) in November 1917 was followed by the withdrawal of Russia from World War I at the Treaty of Brest-Litovsk in the spring of 1918. This treaty guaranteed German domination of eastern Europe but it also guaranteed the enmity of Russia's former allies who, apart from being anti-Bolshevik in principle, felt they had been betrayed by the new regime as they were left to fight the German Empire alone without their strategically important but militarily inept eastern allies. The Germans set up states in Poland and the Ukraine which were amenable to her interests but when, in November 1918, the German government itself was overthrown and an armistice was signed with the allies, a power vacuum opened in eastern Europe and within the new Soviet Union. The Bolsheviks were effectively in control of little more than the corridor between Petrograd and Moscow. Finland and the Baltic states were created out of the western Russian provinces and an expanded Rumanian state rushed to claim Bessarabia. The newly formed state of Poland sought to expand in the east at Russian expense. For their part the Allies were hoping that the war between pro-Tsarist elements and the Bolsheviks would force Lenin's regime to collapse. The victorious western Allies helped the so-called White Armies by invading the northern ports of Murmansk and Archangel as well as the Black Sea ports.

Attacked from every direction, Leon Trotsky's newly formed Red Army struck back. Russian forces were at the gates of Warsaw before the French, led by General Maxime Weygand and Captain Charles de Gaulle, intervened. Although the French-backed Polish Army was able to capture large sections of White Russia, the Allied-supported Ukrainians were not so lucky. By the spring of 1920 the western allies and the White Russians whom they supported were thrown back and the armies dispersed. The Allies for their part were anxious to have their troops return home and the cohesiveness and power of the Red Army made it by far the most determined force in the field and it was ultimately victorious over all comers.

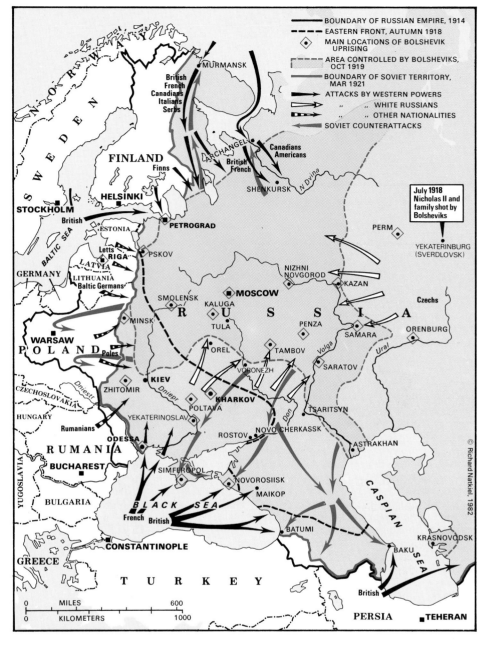

72

Below right: members of the Irish
Citizen Army pose on the roof of
Liberty Hall, Dublin, shortly after the
Easter Rising in 1916.
Below: Kemal Atatürk, the father of
modern Turkey, pictured in 1922.

# The Emergence of Turkey

Following Turkey's surrender to the Allies in 1918 there were internal political troubles in Turkey while the Allies were squabbling among themselves over the division of the Ottoman Empire, still nominally ruled by the Sultan. The Middle Eastern lands were eventually allocated to Britain and France under League of Nations mandates. As for the Turkish heartland on Asia Minor, Italy, France and Greece all nursed claims and in pursuit of these Italy made landings in the Adalia area. With support from Britain and France, Greek troops were sent to Smyrna where there was a considerable Greek population, to ensure Italian gains remained limited. These incursions, Greek control of most of eastern Thrace and international control of the Straits Zone were all recognized by the Treaty of Sèvres.

However, as early as May 1919 nationalist moves to resist this partitioning were begun under the leadership of Mustapha Kemal. He soon had a considerable following and was proclaimed head of a provisional government in April 1920. The Allied response was to occupy Constantinople and to urge the Greeks to begin an advance inland from Smyrna which they did in June 1920. Adrianople and most of Thrace were also overrun and in Anatolia there were inconclusive battles near Eskishehr (the First and Second Battles of the Inönu) and at Afiun in early 1921. In July a Greek victory at Afiun allowed the Greek forces to make a general advance toward Ankara but Kemal's forces won a bitter battle in the bend of the Sakaria River and the Greeks retired to their July positions. By this time the Turks were receiving some Soviet help while diplomatic efforts had persuaded the Italians to leave the Adalia area and the French were ready to move out of southwest Turkey (not shown on map). Kemal's popularity was unquestioned and the Greek forces were exhausted. A Turkish offensive in August 1922 quickly took Afiun and in a lightning advance the Greeks were bundled out of Smyrna. In October the Allies allowed Turkey to reoccupy the Straits area and Thrace, and these gains and Turkish independence were confirmed by the Treaty of Lausanne in July 1923.

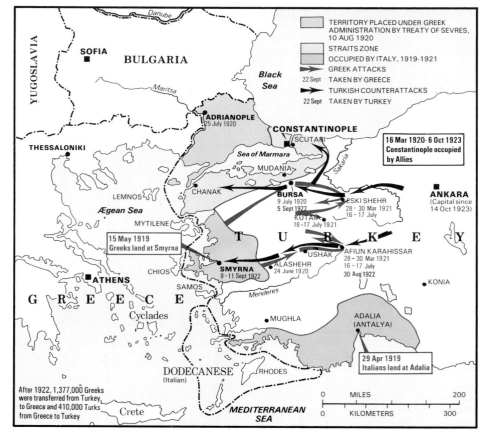

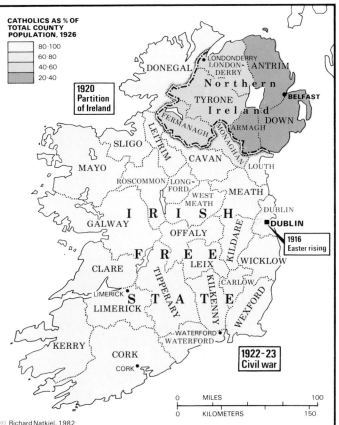

CATHOLICS AS % OF
TOTAL COUNTY
POPULATION, 1926

80-100
60-80
40-60
20-40

1920 Partition of Ireland

1916 Easter rising

1922-23 Civil war

© Richard Natkiel, 1982

# The Partition of Ireland

The outbreak of war in 1914 meant that a Home Rule Bill for Ireland, which had finally passed through the British parliament, was shelved, and the war years gave its opponents time to prepare. In Ulster, largely Protestant and industrial, opposition to being ruled from Catholic Dublin had been so strong that para-military formations to fight the Bill had appeared in 1914. In the south, the Sinn Fein organization, mainly Catholic, which was opposed to the link with the British monarchy, staged a rebellion in Dublin at Easter 1916. This was quelled, but the movement went on to electoral successes in 1918. The Sinn Fein majority refused to take seats in the British parliament but set up its own *Dail* (national assembly) in Dublin. Guerrilla warfare against the British Army, and between Sinn Feiners and Ulstermen, became savage after the war, and in 1921 the British offered dominion status for southern Ireland, with the six counties of Ulster remaining British. An Irish delegation signed a treaty in London setting up the Irish Free State as a dominion, but it was then disowned by De Valera, the Irish President, and his allies, who denounced the partition of Ireland into Ulster and the Irish Free State. However, the treaty was ratified and De Valera resigned, a 1922 election giving the Free State government a strong majority. But political opposition turned to violent opposition, and a civil war broke out which the government won. The boundary with Northern Ireland was then confirmed. Theoretically, it was determined by the predominant religion of each county, but initially it included areas with Catholic majorities. Although the economic effect of the new frontier was smaller than had been feared, it could not really achieve the separation of Catholics from Protestants, due to the religious intermixing of each locality. Partition, as a temporary measure, seemed justified in view of the strong demand for independence on the one hand and the antipathy between Protestants and Catholics on the other, but it was far from being the final solution for which many Ulstermen had hoped; a divided Ireland was a contradiction of geography and a source of resentment for Catholics in the north and south.

Right: smoke billows above Shanghai
during the Japanese occupation of the
city in 1937.
Below: Chinese soldiers such as these
faced the invading Japanese armies.

# The Rise of Chinese Communism – The Long March

For a number of years following the overthrow of the Manchu dynasty in 1911 there had been little real government in China. Instead local war lords had competed for control with the nationalist party, the Kuomintang, and later with the Chinese Communist Party (founded 1921). In the 1920s the Kuomintang, under the increasingly dominant leadership of Chiang Kai-shek, improved its position and in 1927 they moved powerfully against the communists with whom relations had previously been fairly good.

After some attempts to establish communist enclaves in the cities had proved unsuccessful, the communists instead began to concentrate on winning over the rural peasantry. This change in technique was developed by the new communist leader Mao Tse-tung and in 1931 the communists proclaimed the establishment of a Chinese Soviet Republic from their main stronghold in Kiangsi province. Although faced by an increasing Japanese threat following their takeover of Manchuria in October 1931, Chiang decided that his priority ought to be to defeat the communists. Accordingly from 1930–34 the Kuomintang conducted a series of so-called Bandit Suppression Campaigns against the communist revolutionary bases.

The communists found it increasingly difficult to hold out against these attacks and therefore in 1934 they decided to move their whole operation to a less vulnerable area.

In October 1934 the communist forces broke out of Kiangsi and began what is known as the Long March. The march lasted until November 1935 with some units covering as much as 6000 miles. There were very many casualties en route but a considerable force reached Yenan where Mao established a moderate socialist regime which was generally well-received by the inhabitants. The communists were also gaining support throughout China by their commitment to fighting the Japanese whereas Chiang seemed too concerned with fighting the communists. Chiang attempted to continue his bandit suppression operations but after a mutiny of some of his forces in Sian in late 1936 he was for a time personally in communist hands and was obliged to give undertakings to be more active against the Japanese. The Japanese attack in 1937 meant that these had to be fulfilled.

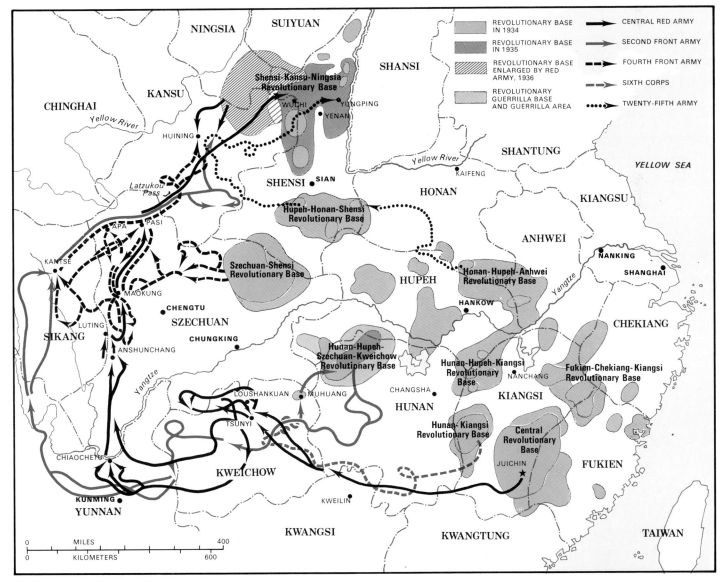

# The Italian Invasion of Ethiopia

Ethiopia (Abyssinia), was a Christian kingdom which had retained its independence for centuries. As late as 1896 it had decisively defeated an Italian invading army at Adowa. In 1930 Haile Selassie became Emperor, introduced modernizing reforms, but took care not to invite Italian experts for technical assistance. In Italy, Mussolini was in power and seeking foreign conquest as well as revenge for Adowa.

There were frontier incidents on Ethiopia's frontiers with neighboring Italian colonies of Eritrea and Somaliland. At an oasis, Walwal, claimed as their territory by both Italians and Ethiopians, there was a serious clash in December 1934. Both disputants agreed to accept League of Nations arbitration, but Mussolini continued to send reinforcements to his east African colonies. The arbitrators, after some months, decided that neither side had been to blame, but by that time Mussolini, with the tacit acquiescence of France, was preparing to invade as soon as the rainy season ended. On 3 October 1935 Italian troops invaded from Eritrea and captured Adowa, while

forces from Somaliland made somewhat slower progress. The League of Nations introduced economic sanctions against Italy but these were ineffective because key states, including Switzerland and Austria, did not comply with them. Although the Italian

advance was slowed by poor roads, modern weapons, including aircraft and poison gas, assured the defeat of the Ethiopians and on 5 May 1936 the capital, Addis Ababa, was captured. Haile Selassie fled, to return when the British drove out the Italians in 1941.

Bottom left: Nationalist troops close in on Madrid toward the end of the war.
Below: German-supplied Junkers Ju 52 trimotors ferried Nationalist troops into Spain from North Africa early in the Civil War.

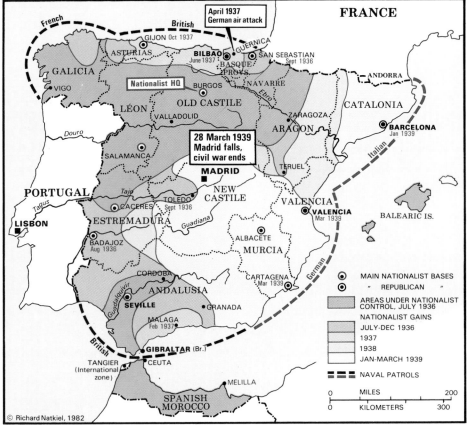

# The Spanish Civil War

In 1931, following a period of civil disturbance, the Spanish monarchy was replaced by a republic, and a left-wing government introduced reforms: separation of the state from the church, state education, and the break-up of large estates. Having moved faster than most people wished, it was defeated in a 1933 election by right-wing parties, which began to reverse the reforms but were in turn defeated by a 'popular front' of the left-wing in a 1936 election. Reform then continued, despite violent resistance by Spanish fascists, known as the Falange. There were political assassinations, followed by a revolt against the government started by army officers in Spanish Morocco. In October 1936 the insurgent General Franco, who had flown to the mainland in a chartered British plane from the Canary Islands, was declared 'Chief of the Spanish State.' The cities of Cadiz, Seville and Zaragoza declared for the insurgents, as did Burgos, where Franco made his headquarters. Soon fascist Italy and Nazi Germany were sending forces to help the insurgents (the Nationalists) while Russia

sent men and supplies to help the government (the Republicans). The latter were also reinforced, morally as much as militarily, by the International Brigade, made up of idealistic volunteers from various countries who saw this as the first great battle against European fascism.

By the end of 1936 the Nationalists held about half of Spain. They had benefited by their superior military strength and their supply routes through Portugal. The industrial areas as well as the Basque and Catalonian regions (which had been promised autonomy by the government) were strongly in support of the Republicans. In 1937 the Nationalists failed in an attempt to isolate Madrid by advancing toward Valencia from Teruel. The International Brigade, making an excursion from Madrid, defeated the Italians at Guadaljara and Teruel was recaptured. However the Nationalists captured the Republican stronghold of Bilbao. In 1938 increased German and Italian help, vainly obstructed by the British and French 'non-intervention' naval patrols, enabled the Nationalists to make gains at the same time as Soviet intrigues weakened the united front of the various Republican forces, and later resulted in the cutting off by Moscow of further aid. Madrid was besieged and Catalonia invaded by the Nationalists. In early 1939, with the loss of Barcelona, Valencia, and Madrid, the government's military resistance ended. About 750,000 lives had been lost in the war, many by execution.

As well as its importance for Spain, the

Civil War had significant influence on wider issues of international relations in several ways. It helped strengthen the relationship between Italy and Germany while weakening the possibility of anti-German agreements between France and the USSR because of the French refusal to help the Republicans. Both Britain and France appeared weak and unwilling to act decisively in support of their interests. Perhaps above all the war gave Hitler and Mussolini reason to believe that their aims could be achieved simply by ruthless military action. The fighting also gave the German and Italian armed forces useful experience. The German Luftwaffe in particular gave several rather misleading demonstrations of its power and effectiveness. Belief in the might of the Luftwaffe helped contribute to the appeasement policy followed by Britain and France up to 1939.

American landing ships are unloaded off
Leyte in 1944.

# Grand Strategy, 1939-45

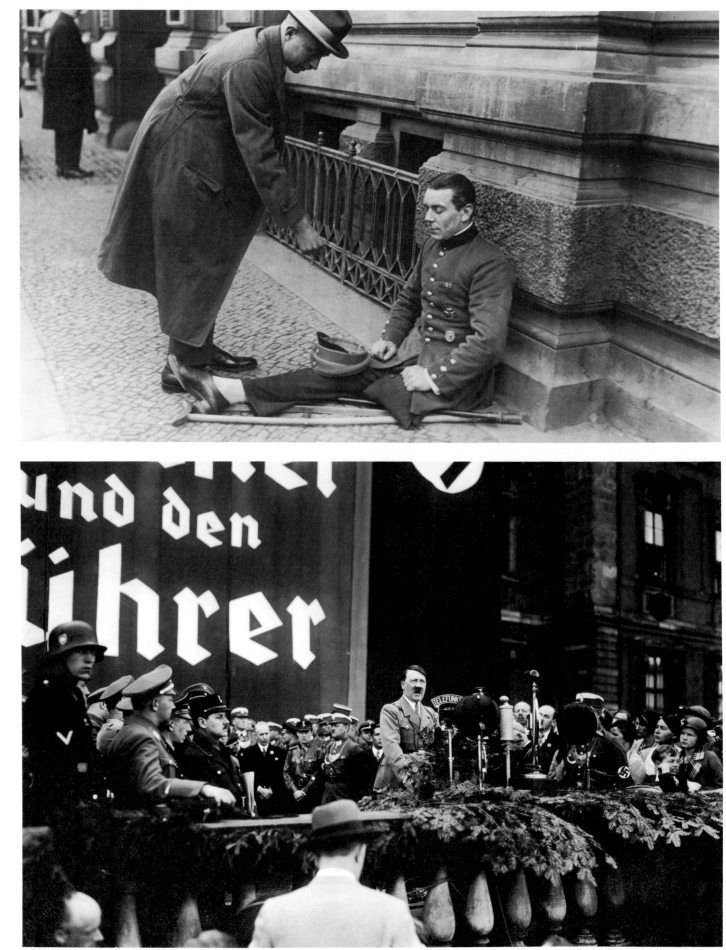

# The Treaty of Versailles

Germany, became an object of deep resentment in Germany. Germany also lost the city of Memel, which eventually went to Lithuania, and about 122 square miles which went to Czechoslovakia. In all, Germany lost 13 percent of her pre-war area. By another treaty, new states (Yugoslavia, Hungary, Poland, Czechoslovakia) had been established, largely at the expense of the old Austro-Hungarian Empire. But the Versailles Treaty expressly forbade a union of Germany with Austria, even though such a union was a possible solution to their problem of survival in the post-war world.

Unlike previous peace treaties, the Treaty of Versailles, signed by Germany in June 1919, was not negotiated, but imposed. It was also unfair and vengeful and therefore likely to lead to further conflict.

Under its provisions Germany lost all her colonies, mainly in Africa and the Pacific. Her army and navy were reduced to strengths characteristic of a third-rate power. The reparations clauses of the Treaty did not specify the payments in kind and in money which Germany was to pay to the victors, but left the door open for almost any demands which might be made. The moral basis for reparations were the so-called 'Honor' clauses of the Treaty, in which Germany admitted the entire blame for the outbreak of the war. This forced admission, which even in that emotional period must have been seen by most responsible statesmen as a lie, for long rankled with the German public and does much to explain the popularity of Hitler a dozen years later.

Territorially, Germany was required to return to France Alsace and Lorraine, taken by conquest in 1871. The mining area around Saarbrücken remained under German sovereignty but with commercial concessions for France. The west bank of the Rhine, which France unsuccessfully demanded in

perpetuity, was to be occupied by France for 15 years. Belgium acquired 400 square miles, including the towns of Eupen and Malmédy. It was proposed that Schleswig and Holstein, conquered in 1864, should be returned to Denmark. With a maturity lacking in other, greater, powers, Denmark refused this gift, contenting itself with the Danish-speaking parts, and that only after a plebiscite in 1920. In the east, Poland was newly independent, and seeking to expand at German expense and with French support. But it was stipulated that Upper Silesia should not go to Poland unless its population wished it to. A plebiscite was held in 1921, but satisfied nobody, and the problem of the German-Polish frontier was handed over to a League of Nations committee whose recommendation was adopted despite its absurdities (in places it passed not only through the middle of towns and villages, but also through factories). The German province of Posen became the Polish territory of Poznan. Elsewhere, in order that Poland might have access to the sea, Danzig (declared a free city) was connected to Poland proper by a wide strip of former Prussian territory henceforth known as the 'Polish Corridor.' This Polish strip, cutting off East Prussia from the rest of

**Facing page, top: returned veterans faced many problems in all countries after World War I. The Nazis were only one of many groups that tried to exploit these in Germany in the 1920s.**
**Facing page, bottom: Hitler addresses a meeting in May 1934. Much of the Nazi Party's appeal was developed in carefully organized public assemblies and demonstrations. Hitler's oratorical skills played a large part in this process.**

# The Rise of Nazi Germany

The financial penalties imposed on Germany by the Versailles Treaty and the wholesale boundary changes in central and eastern Europe laid many of the seeds of World War II but these were assiduously cultivated by Adolf Hitler and the German Nazi Party. By a combination of unscrupulous violent methods and careful political maneuvering Hitler exploited discontent with Germany's economic weakness and nationalist resentment with Versailles until, in March 1933, he took full control of the German government. The first concentration camp was established at Dachau during that month. By 1936 Hitler had consolidated his position at home and extended the persecution of Germany's Jewish population. In foreign and military affairs he had taken Germany out of the League of Nations, introduced compulsory military service and begun to create an air force while, despite these direct contraventions of the Versailles Treaty, he had negotiated a naval agreement with Britain. His success in all these clearly marked very important British and French weakness.

His first major move was the reoccupation of the Rhineland which was a complete success despite the tiny force which Germany could mobilize and Hitler's readiness to climb down if challenged. Emboldened, he next abrogated the Versailles Treaty and, in March 1938, annexed Austria. The next move, in the campaign supposedly to bring all German-speaking people under German rule, was against Czechoslovakia. In 1938, of the Czech population of 14 million, three million were German speaking, most of them living in the Sudeten area. Nazi-backed agitation by the Sudeten Germans had largely been controlled by the Czech authorities but British Prime Minister Chamberlain nonetheless flew to Munich to meet Hitler to try to find a solution to the crisis. Chamberlain seems to have believed that Hitler was a responsible and reasonable statesman who would keep his word and that, if his demands were met, there would be an end to the problem. According to this argument the issue at stake was purely a central European one and Britain should not, therefore, risk war on behalf of 'a far-off country of which we know little.' The French could not abandon their connections with Britain and, thus isolated, Czechoslovakia had to give in. Hitler completed his seizure of Czechoslovakia in March 1939 and immediately turned his acquisitive attentions to Poland. The British and French stepped up the pace of their rearmament programs but were still far from ready to fight.

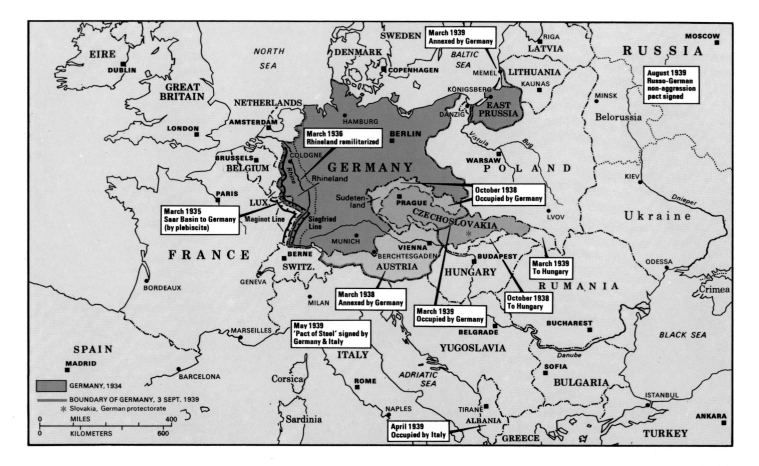

# German Gains 1939-40

After the outbreak of war Germany's military triumphs continued where Hitler's political successes had left off. Poland, Norway, Denmark and France were all quickly defeated. Although Britain temporarily staved off invasion her army had been shattered by the campaign in France and, despite Churchill's inspirational leadership, it was hard to see how a comeback could be made. Encouraged by German successes Mussolini had joined the war but by the end of 1940 the Italian armies in Greece and North Africa were struggling. The United States was increasing its supplies sent to Britain but the German U-Boats were taking an ever greater toll on the convoy routes despite the increasing strength of the escort forces.

Ceded Rumanian territories:
1. Bessarabia & N. Bukovina to Russia, June 1940
2. S. Dobruja to Bulgaria, August 1940
3. Transylvania to Hungary, September 1940

© Richard Natkiel. 1982

# The High Tide of German Expansion

Following his repulse in the Battle of Britain Hitler's thoughts turned to the Balkans and the USSR. By force or diplomacy the Balkans were brought under German influence by the early summer of 1941 while the Italian position in North Africa was propped up. Despite German confidence and enormous Soviet losses Operation Barbarossa was far from the expected easy victory. The Soviet Moscow counterattack demonstrated their resilience which was confirmed when the Germans were halted at Stalingrad despite their renewed victories in the summer of 1942. Although America had given Britain steadily increasing support only a foolish German declaration of war in the aftermath of Pearl Harbor confirmed that America would fight in Europe.

© Richard Natkiel, 1982

Below: a Panzer of the Afrika Korps
demonstrates German might in a street in
Libya, North Africa. The picture is taken
from a German propaganda magazine.

# Germany's Long Retreat

Although the counteroffensive at Kharkov for a time revived German hopes for victory in the east the defeat at Kursk ended this false optimism and the long retreat was resumed. Although the western allies were only able to invade France in June 1944 they had already knocked Italy out of the war and taken much of her territory. The threat to the Atlantic supply routes had been defeated in 1943 and after a long struggle throughout that year the British and American heavy bombers were beginning to achieve important results in their attacks on centers of population and industrial targets in Germany.

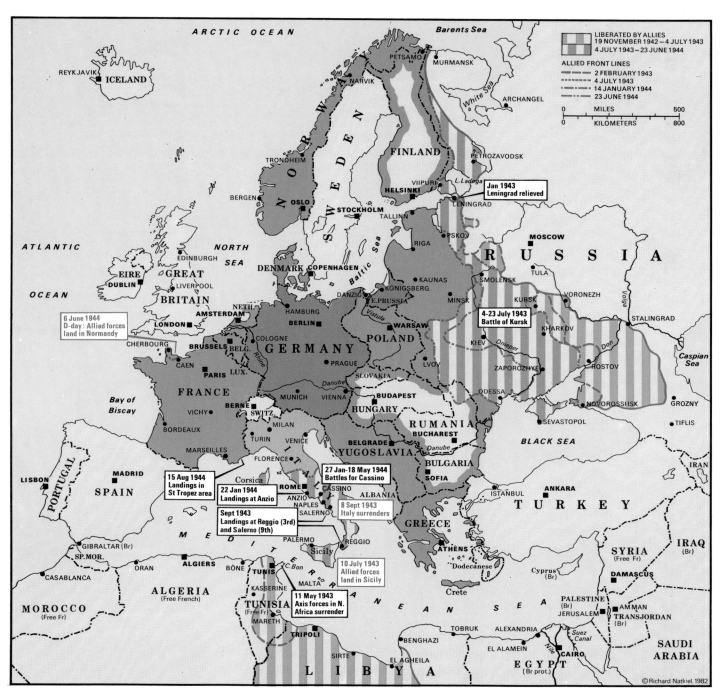

LIBERATED BY ALLIES
19 NOVEMBER 1942 – 4 JULY 1943
4 JULY 1943 – 23 JUNE 1944

ALLIED FRONT LINES
2 FEBRUARY 1943
4 JULY 1943
14 JANUARY 1944
23 JUNE 1944

Jan 1943
Leningrad relieved

6 June 1944
D-day: Allied forces land in Normandy

4–23 July 1943
Battle of Kursk

27 Jan–18 May 1944
Battles for Cassino

15 Aug 1944
Landings in St Tropez area

22 Jan 1944
Landings at Anzio

8 Sept 1943
Italy surrenders

Sept 1943
Landings at Reggio (3rd) and Salerno (9th)

10 July 1943
Allied forces land in Sicily

11 May 1943
Axis forces in N. Africa surrender

© Richard Natkiel, 1982

# The Fall of Hitler's Germany

By mid-1944 Germany's decline was completely irreversible. Her manpower losses had been immense; her industry was being pounded by Allied bombers; even her much-feared secret weapons were proving a disappointment. Although British resources were heavily strained by 1945 there was no doubt that the Allies were now far better organized and equipped. In the end despite the last German flurry in the Battle of the Bulge, there was no answer to the military and industrial might of the USA and USSR.

Long before the war ended it was becoming clear, however, that the Allies did not see eye-to-eye on the political future of the liberated European nations.

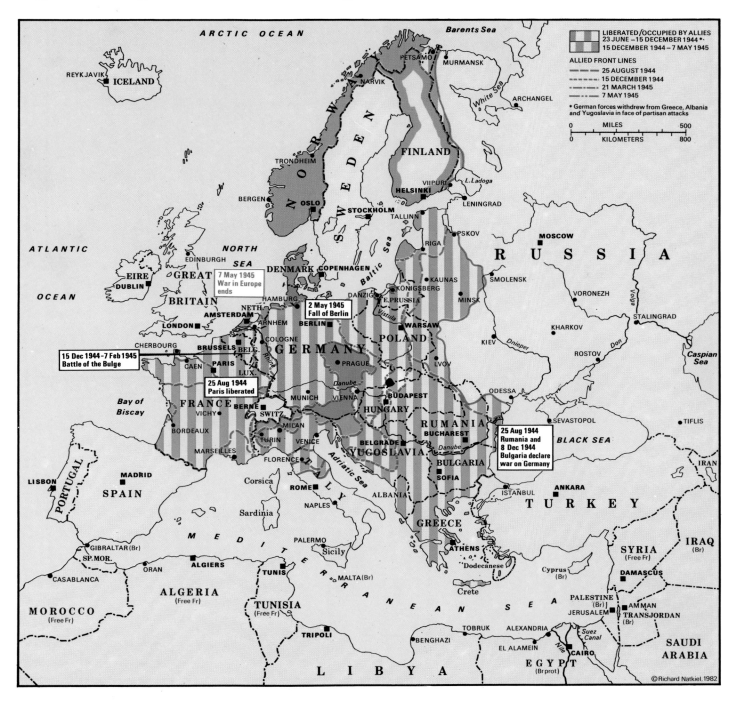

LIBERATED/OCCUPIED BY ALLIES
23 JUNE – 15 DECEMBER 1944 *
15 DECEMBER 1944 – 7 MAY 1945

ALLIED FRONT LINES
25 AUGUST 1944
15 DECEMBER 1944
21 MARCH 1945
7 MAY 1945
* German forces withdrew from Greece, Albania and Yugoslavia in face of partisan attacks

MILES 500
KILOMETERS 800

7 May 1945 War in Europe ends

2 May 1945 Fall of Berlin

15 Dec 1944–7 Feb 1945 Battle of the Bulge

25 Aug 1944 Paris liberated

25 Aug 1944 Rumania and 8 Dec 1944 Bulgaria declare war on Germany

© Richard Natkiel, 1982

# Japanese Expansion 1931-41

**1931**
**'The Mukden incident'**
**Japan overruns Manchuria**

**1933**
**Japan annexes Jehol**

**7 July 1937**
**Japan invades China**

**27 September 1940**
**Japan signs 'Tripartite' pact with Germany and Italy, and in April 1941, a non-aggression pact with Russia**

**August 1940**
**Japan establishes military bases in French Indo-China and in July 1941, occupies the country**

RUSSIA

ATTU

Sakhalin

Kurile Is

ETEROFU

Hitokappu B

ULAN BATOR

MONGOLIA

MANCHURIA
HARBIN
(MANCHUKUO)

Amur

VLADIVOSTOK

Hokkaido

Jehol

MUKDEN

SEA OF JAPAN

PEKING

C H I N A

KOREA
SEOUL

Honshu

Hwang Ho

TSINGTAO

TOKYO JAPAN

NANKING
HANKOW

NAGASAKI

Shikoku
Kyushu

DELHI

NEPAL

CHUNGKING

Yangtze

kiang

SHANGHAI

Kagoshima B

Ganges

CHANGSHA

Burma Road

Ryukyu Is

OKINAWA

BONIN IS

P A C

IMPHAL

KUNMING

CANTON

MARCUS

CALCUTTA

LASHIO

Formosa
(Taiwan)

IWO JIMA

MANDALAY

HANOI

O

I N D I A

BOMBAY

BURMA

HAIPHONG

HONG KONG

HAINAN

WAKE

RANGOON

THAI-
LAND

FRENCH
INDO-CHINA

Luzon

Mariana
Islands

SAIPAN

BAY OF BENGAL

BANGKOK

SAIGON

MANILA

PHILIPPINE
ISLANDS

GUAM

MADRAS

ANDAMAN
IS

LEYTE

ENIWETOK

KWAJALEIN

TRINCOMALEE

SOUTH CHINA
SEA

Mindanao

YAP

TRUK

Marshall
Is

COLOMBO

NICOBAR
IS

Str of Malacca

KOTA BHARU

DAVAO

MAJURO

Ceylon

MALAYA

N BORNEO

PALAU IS

C a r o l i n e   I s l a n d s

MAKIN

TARAWA

SARAWAK

Molucca Passage

Gilbert Is

Equator

SINGAPORE

HALMAHERA

Borneo

Makassar Str

ADMIRALTY
IS

NEW

NAURU

OCEAN

ADDU
ATOLL

Sumatra

Celebes

DUTCH   EAST   INDIES

New Guinea

BRITAIN

NEW IRELAND

RABAUL

BATAVIA

FLORES

BOUGAINVILLE

Solomon Is

Java

PAPUA

NEW
GEORGIA

GUADALCANAL

TIMOR

PORT
MORESBY

GUADALCANAL

SANTA CR
IS

COCOS IS

TIMOR SEA

DARWIN

CORAL SEA

ESPIRITU
SANTO

I N D I A N   O C E A N

CAIRNS

New
Hebrides

EFATE

Northern
Territory

New
Caledon

NOUMEA

Western
A U S T R A L I A
Australia

Queensland

ROCKHAMPTON

PERTH

South
Australia

BRISBANE

NORFOL

New
South Wales

SYDNEY

CANBERRA

ADELAIDE

Victoria

MELBOURNE

AUCKLA

JAPANESE EMPIRE, 1933

OCCUPIED BY JAPAN, 7 JULY 1937 – 7 DEC 1941

AREA UNDER JAPANESE CONTROL 7 DECEMBER 1941

MERCATOR'S PROJECTION

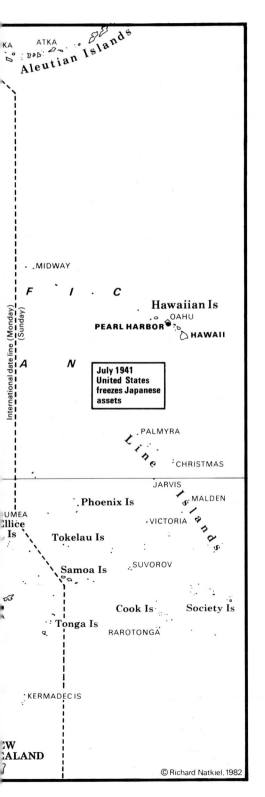

Japanese policy in the years before World War II cannot be described in the simple terms of single-minded leadership that can be applied to Hitler's Germany. Because of the nature of the Japanese constitution the military had a disproportionate influence over the usually more moderate civilian politicians. However, as well as disagreements between the army and navy affecting policy, both services were not able to control their members. So-called 'Patriotic Societies' and other interest groups were prepared to go to any lengths to achieve their ends. There was general resentment at the settlement of the Pacific at the end of World War I and with the Washington Naval Treaty agreed soon after. Many felt that Japan had been cheated on racist grounds. The rise of Chinese Nationalism in the 1920s was a further worry with its implied challenge to Japan's position as the leading Asian nation.

Several of these factors came together in 1931 when the Japanese Manchuria Army acted, independently of the government, to overrun the province following an incident which the army probably provoked deliberately. This confirmed Japanese isolation from the West. Japan left the League of Nations in 1933 and stepped up her previously unimpressive armament program. In the following years tension between Japan and China grew until serious fighting erupted in July 1937. Junior officers on both sides have been blamed for this outbreak. Whatever the cause Japan proceeded to occupy most of the major Chinese ports and much territory by early 1939. Pressure on French Indo-China was the next stage in an attempt to prevent supplies reaching the Chinese but in September 1940 this brought the first open US opposition, a minor export embargo.

Diplomatically the probable Japanese course was prepared by the Tripartite Pact and the Non-Aggression agreement with the USSR. This suggested that Japan was now likely to look south to the East Indies rather than to mainland Asia for future gains. The decision to occupy Indo-China confirmed this. The USA, UK and the Dutch retaliated by freezing Japanese assets and cancelling oil deals thus cutting off 75 percent of Japanese trade and 90 percent of her oil supplies. Japan's position was now simple: to avoid economic ruin she could make concessions or go to war before her oil stocks ran out. The militant General Tojo became prime minister in October and last minute diplomacy achieved nothing. On 2 December 1941 the Japanese aircraft carrier force, already on its way across the Pacific, was ordered to attack Pearl Harbor.

# Japan's Months of Triumph

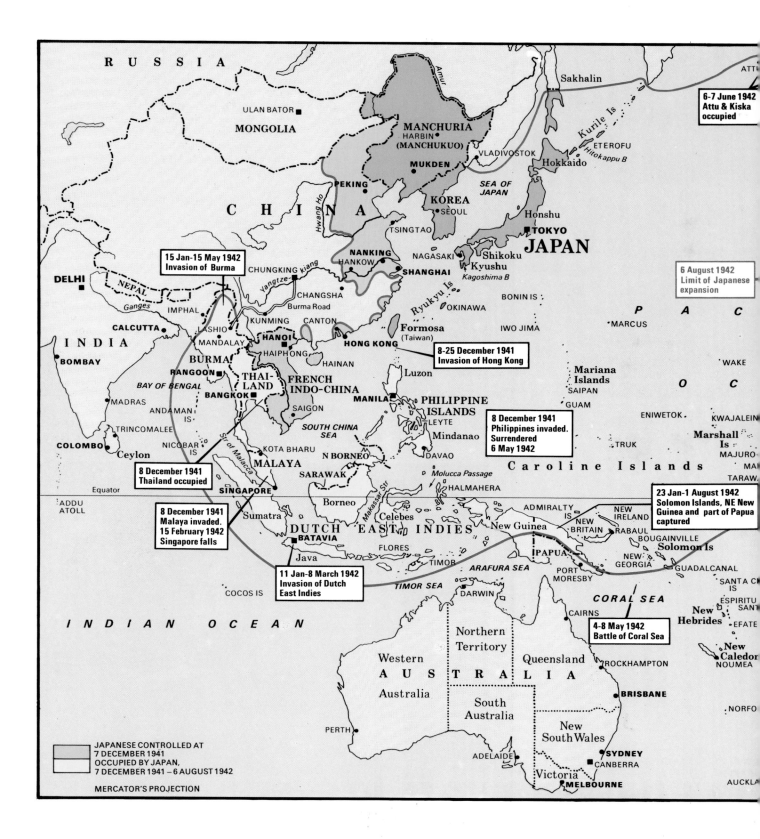

6-7 June 1942
Attu & Kiska
occupied

15 Jan-15 May 1942
Invasion of Burma

6 August 1942
Limit of Japanese
expansion

8-25 December 1941
Invasion of Hong Kong

8 December 1941
Philippines invaded.
Surrendered
6 May 1942

8 December 1941
Thailand occupied

23 Jan-1 August 1942
Solomon Islands, NE New
Guinea and part of Papua
captured

8 December 1941
Malaya invaded.
15 February 1942
Singapore falls

11 Jan-8 March 1942
Invasion of Dutch
East Indies

4-8 May 1942
Battle of Coral Sea

JAPANESE CONTROLLED AT
7 DECEMBER 1941
OCCUPIED BY JAPAN,
7 DECEMBER 1941 – 6 AUGUST 1942

MERCATOR'S PROJECTION

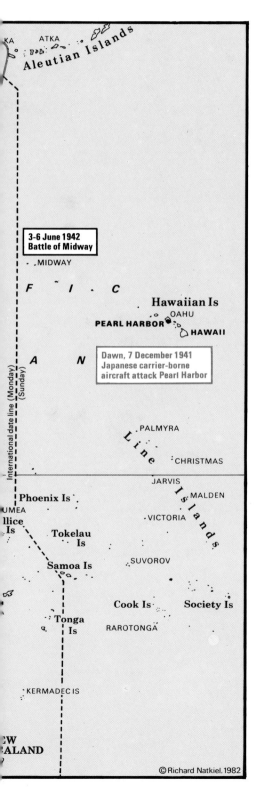

**3-6 June 1942
Battle of Midway**

Aleutian Islands

MIDWAY

F I C

Hawaiian Is
OAHU
PEARL HARBOR
HAWAII

**Dawn, 7 December 1941
Japanese carrier-borne
aircraft attack Pearl Harbor**

A N

International date line (Monday)
(Sunday)

PALMYRA
CHRISTMAS
JARVIS
Phoenix Is
MALDEN
UMEA
VICTORIA
llice Is
Tokelau Is
Line Islands
Samoa Is
SUVOROV

Cook Is
Society Is
Tonga Is
RAROTONGA

KERMADEC IS

EW
ALAND

© Richard Natkiel, 1982

The Japanese recognized that in a long war American strength would become dauntingly great. They therefore planned to seize the resource-producing areas that they lacked and perimeter bases to defend them. These would be taken in the first rapid campaigns and the decadent Europeans and Americans would, it was expected, make peace rather than mobilize their power against a much-strengthened Japan. The first stages of the fighting went almost according to plan but the Battle of the Coral Sea offered a slight check and the defeat at Midway was a serious setback.

**Below: although aircraft carriers played the most important role in the war at sea in the Pacific, battleships provided important softening-up bombardment prior to US landings.**

# The Allied Counteroffensive

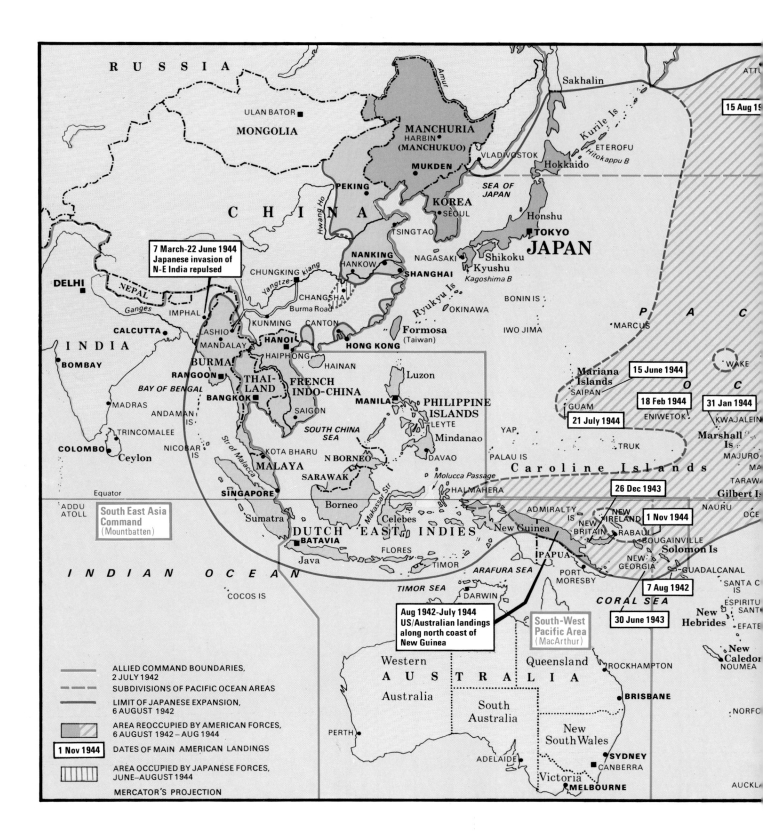

RUSSIA

Sakhalin

ATTU

15 Aug 19

ULAN BATOR
MONGOLIA

MANCHURIA
HARBIN
(MANCHUKUO)
MUKDEN

VLADIVOSTOK

Kurile Is

ETEROFU
Hitokappu B

Hokkaido

PEKING

KOREA

SÉOUL

SEA OF
JAPAN

Honshu

TOKYO
JAPAN

C H I N A

TSINGTAO

Hwang Ho

**7 March-22 June 1944**
**Japanese invasion of**
**N-E India repulsed**

NANKING
HANKOW
SHANGHAI

NAGASAKI

Shikoku
Kyushu
Kagoshima B

CHUNGKING kiang

DELHI

NEPAL

Yangtze-ho

CHANGSHA
Burma Road

Ryukyu Is

OKINAWA

BONIN IS

P    A    C    C

Ganges

IMPHAL

KUNMING

CANTON

Formosa
(Taiwan)

IWO JIMA

MARCUS

CALCUTTA

LASHIO
MANDALAY

HANOI
HAIPHONG

HONG KONG

Mariana
Islands

**15 June 1944**

WAKE

O    C

INDIA

BOMBAY

BURMA

RANGOON

THAI-
LAND

FRENCH
INDO-CHINA

HAINAN

Luzon

SAIPAN

**18 Feb 1944**

**31 Jan 1944**

BAY OF BENGAL

BANGKOK

MANILA

PHILIPPINE
ISLANDS

GUAM

**21 July 1944**

ENIWETOK

KWAJALEIN

MADRAS

ANDAMAN
IS

SAIGON

LEYTE

YAP

Marshall
Is

MAJURO

MA

TRINCOMALEE

SOUTH CHINA
SEA

Mindanao

PALAU IS

TRUK

TARAWA

COLOMBO

Ceylon

NICOBAR
IS

KOTA BHARU

N BORNEO

Davao

C a r o l i n e   I s l a n d s

Gilbert Is

Str of Malacca

MALAYA

SARAWAK

Molucca Passage

NAURU

OCE

Equator

SINGAPORE

Borneo

HALMAHERA

**26 Dec 1943**

ADMIRALTY
IS

NEW
IRELAND

**1 Nov 1944**

ADDU
ATOLL

**South East Asia**
**Command**
**(Mountbatten)**

Sumatra

Celebes

New Guinea

NEW
BRITAIN

RABAUL

BOUGAINVILLE

Solomon Is

DUTCH   EAST   INDIES

Makassar Str

BATAVIA

Java

FLORES

TIMOR

PAPUA

NEW
GEORGIA

GUADALCANAL

I N D I A N   O C E A N

ARAFURA SEA

PORT
MORESBY

**7 Aug 1942**

SANTA C
IS

COCOS IS

TIMOR SEA

DARWIN

CORAL SEA

ESPIRITU
SANT

New
Hebrides

EFATE

**Aug 1942-July 1944**
**US/Australian landings**
**along north coast of**
**New Guinea**

Western

Queensland

ROCKHAMPTON

**30 June 1943**

**South-West**
**Pacific Area**
**(MacArthur)**

New
Caledon
NOUMEA

A U S T R A L I A

Australia

South
Australia

BRISBANE

NORFC

PERTH

New
South Wales

ADELAIDE

SYDNEY
CANBERRA

Victoria

MELBOURNE

AUCKL

**Legend:**

— ALLIED COMMAND BOUNDARIES,
2 JULY 1942

--- SUBDIVISIONS OF PACIFIC OCEAN AREAS

— LIMIT OF JAPANESE EXPANSION,
6 AUGUST 1942

AREA REOCCUPIED BY AMERICAN FORCES,
6 AUGUST 1942 – AUG 1944

**1 Nov 1944** DATES OF MAIN AMERICAN LANDINGS

AREA OCCUPIED BY JAPANESE FORCES,
JUNE–AUGUST 1944

MERCATOR'S PROJECTION

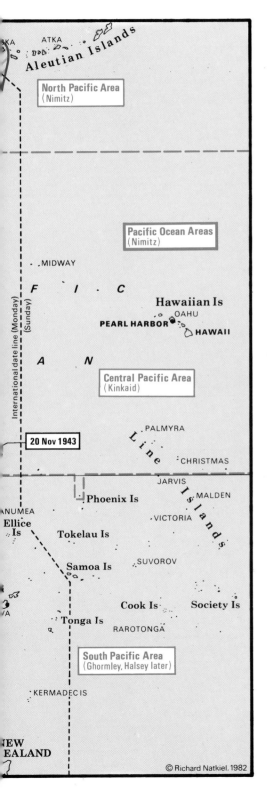

North Pacific Area
(Nimitz)

Pacific Ocean Areas
(Nimitz)

Central Pacific Area
(Kinkaid)

20 Nov 1943

Phoenix Is

South Pacific Area
(Ghormley, Halsey later)

© Richard Natkiel. 1982

America proved strong enough to mount two major lines of advance against the Japanese. The US Navy built up its carrier forces and its amphibious assault capability and backed them by the ability of the newly-created fleet train to keep the fighting ships in action at great distances from their bases. These units advanced by the islands of the central Pacific in a series of bloody battles of which the assault on Tarawa at the start of the campaign is perhaps the most notorious. The other wing of the Allied offensive was in the South-West Pacific where MacArthur's Australian and American forces advanced doggedly with enormous support from land-based air power.

**Below: the Mitsubishi Zero was the Japanese navy's main fighter aircraft throughout the Pacific War. This one was downed during the Solomons campaign.**

# The Japanese Defeat

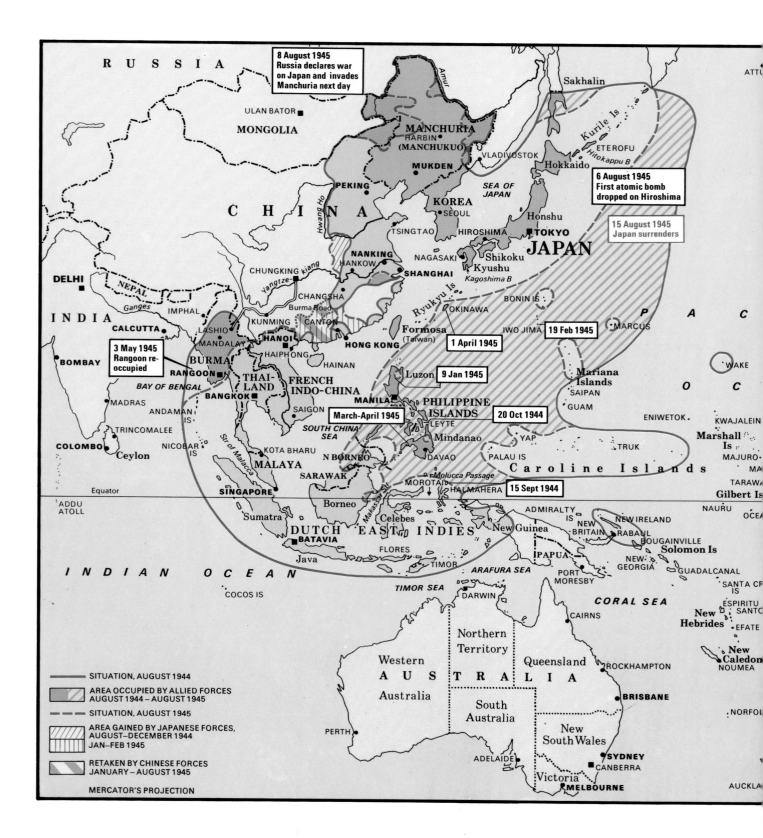

8 August 1945
Russia declares war on Japan and invades Manchuria next day

6 August 1945
First atomic bomb dropped on Hiroshima

15 August 1945
Japan surrenders

3 May 1945
Rangoon re-occupied

1 April 1945

19 Feb 1945

9 Jan 1945

20 Oct 1944

March–April 1945

15 Sept 1944

RUSSIA

MONGOLIA
ULAN BATOR

MANCHURIA
(MANCHUKUO)
HARBIN
MUKDEN
VLADIVOSTOK

Sakhalin

ATTU

Kurile Is
ETEROFU
Hitokappu B

Hokkaido

C H I N A
PEKING
Hwang Ho
KOREA
SEOUL
TSINGTAO

SEA OF JAPAN

HIROSHIMA

Honshu

TOKYO
JAPAN
Shikoku
NAGASAKI
Kyushu
Kagoshima B

NANKING
HANKOW
SHANGHAI
CHUNGKING
Yangtze-kiang
CHANGSHA
Burma Road

DELHI
NEPAL
Ganges
IMPHAL
INDIA
CALCUTTA
BOMBAY

LASHIO
MANDALAY
KUNMING
CANTON
HANOI
HAIPHONG
HAINAN
BURMA
RANGOON
THAI-LAND
BANGKOK
FRENCH INDO-CHINA
SAIGON

Ryukyu Is
Formosa (Taiwan)
HONG KONG

BONIN IS

OKINAWA
IWO JIMA
MARCUS

P A C

MARIANA Islands
SAIPAN
GUAM

WAKE

O C

ENIWETOK
KWAJALEIN
Marshall Is
MAJURO
MA

BAY OF BENGAL
MADRAS
ANDAMAN IS
TRINCOMALEE
COLOMBO
Ceylon
NICOBAR IS

Str of Malacca
KOTA BHARU
MALAYA
SARAWAK
N BORNEO

SOUTH CHINA SEA
Luzon
MANILA
PHILIPPINE ISLANDS
LEYTE
Mindanao
DAVAO

YAP
PALAU IS
TRUK
Caroline Islands

TARAWA
Gilbert Is

Equator
ADDU ATOLL
SINGAPORE
Sumatra
Java
BATAVIA
DUTCH EAST INDIES
Borneo
Makassar Str
Celebes
FLORES
TIMOR
Molucca Passage
MOROTAI
HALMAHERA

ADMIRALTY IS
New Guinea
NEW BRITAIN
NEW IRELAND
RABAUL
BOUGAINVILLE
Solomon Is
NEW GEORGIA
GUADALCANAL
PAPUA
PORT MORESBY

NAURU
OCEA

INDIAN OCEAN
COCOS IS

TIMOR SEA
DARWIN

ARAFURA SEA

CORAL SEA

CAIRNS

ESPIRITU SANTO
New Hebrides
EFATE

SANTA CR IS

New Caledon
NOUMEA

ROCKHAMPTON

Western Australia
Northern Territory
Queensland
A U S T R A L I A
South Australia
New South Wales
PERTH
ADELAIDE
Victoria
MELBOURNE
BRISBANE
SYDNEY
CANBERRA

NORFOL
AUCKLA

SITUATION, AUGUST 1944

AREA OCCUPIED BY ALLIED FORCES AUGUST 1944 – AUGUST 1945

SITUATION, AUGUST 1945

AREA GAINED BY JAPANESE FORCES, AUGUST–DECEMBER 1944
JAN–FEB 1945

RETAKEN BY CHINESE FORCES JANUARY – AUGUST 1945

MERCATOR'S PROJECTION

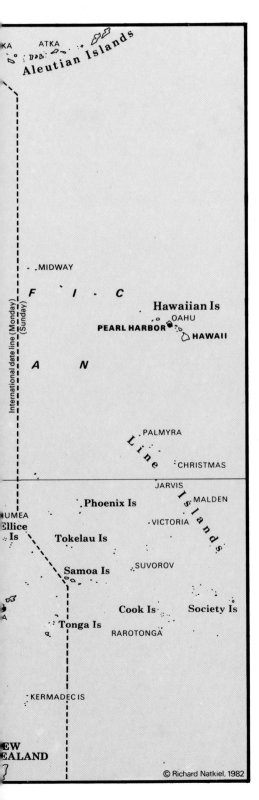

The final year of the war saw the Japanese defeated on all fronts, being thrown out of Burma, Iwo Jima and Okinawa and confined to unimportant pockets in the Philippines. At the same time US bomber forces were built up in the Marianas and, after a change in tactics in March 1945, they devastated city after city on the Japanese Home Islands. The first atomic bomb was dropped on 6 August. Faced by this new threat and the Soviet invasion of Manchuria, Japan capitulated.

**Below: MacArthur led the land forces which retook the Philippines in an 'island-hopping' campaign.**

A German antitank gun in action on the
Russian Front early in the war.

# The World at War, 1939-45

# The Invasion and Partition of Poland

No sooner had Hitler finished dismembering Czechoslovakia and seizing the Memel district from Lithuania in March 1939 than it became obvious that Poland would be considered next. Britain and France quickly issued a joint guarantee to Poland and hoped that with this lever they could persuade the Poles to make concessions like the Czechs at Munich, while still convincing Hitler of the need to be reasonable. However, throughout the spring and summer Hitler's aggressive attitude became more obvious especially after April when he revoked the 1934 German-Polish Non-Aggression Pact and the 1935 Anglo-German Naval Agreement. During this period both the western Allies and the Germans were courting Soviet assistance. The British and French efforts were poorly managed and, in any case, it soon became clear that Stalin wanted virtually a free hand in Eastern Europe in return for his help. The talks came to nothing. Instead, in August, the German diplomacy bore fruit and Foreign Minister Ribbentrop concluded first an economic agreement and then a Non-Aggression Pact with the USSR.

Despite some last minute uncertainty on Hitler's part, the German attack on Poland was free to begin on 1 September 1939. France and Britain each responded with an ultimatum to Germany demanding a withdrawal and when no satisfactory reply was received both countries declared war on Germany on 3 September 1939. Australia and New Zealand immediately followed suit and after some debate South Africa joined the war on 6 September. The Germans claimed that Polish provocation had caused the war and, to prove this, evidence of a Polish attack on a German radio station near the border at Gliewitz was shown to foreign pressmen. In fact the 'attack' was staged by the SS and the bodies in Polish uniforms left at the scene were those of concentration camp inmates.

The Germans deployed 53 divisions for the campaign against Poland leaving, by their own estimate, 10 divisions fit for action on the Western Front. Their six tank and their few motorized divisions were in the attack and together were used to form the

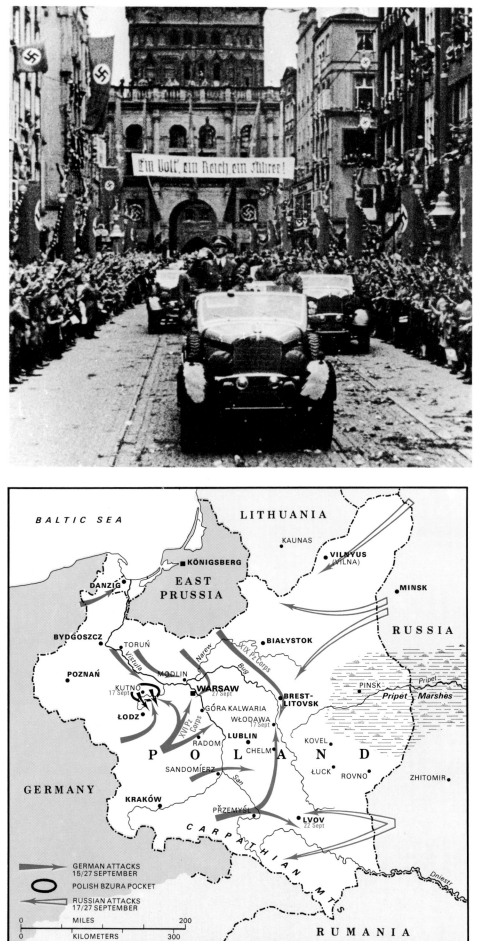

various panzer corps. The German Army Commander in Chief, Field Marshal Brauchitsch controlled the campaign, largely without interference from Hitler. In their preplanning and their retrospective appreciations the German Army described the campaign in terms of traditional infantry and artillery battles, allocating the tanks subordinate supporting roles. Only a few enthusiasts supported theories emphasizing the part played by the armored forces. To support their armies the Germans had an enormous superiority in the air with about 1600 modern planes facing the 500 largely obsolescent machines possessed by the Poles. The Polish mobilization was not begun until 30 August so the German attack found the Poles with 23 infantry divisions deployed and another seven assembling. All units were short of artillery, there was one weak armored division and a mass of ineffective cavalry. The Polish forces had been foolishly placed by Marshal Rydz-Smigly, their Commander in Chief, in forward positions near the frontier and, although they fought bravely, the campaign was decided within a few days. There was a Polish counterattack along the Bzura River from 9–15 September but this only caused the Germans brief worries. Warsaw fell after a vicious air bombardment on 27 September and by 3 October the last significant resistance had been wiped out.

On 17 September Soviet forces invaded Poland from the east and on 19 September a German-Soviet Treaty of Friendship was announced. This confirmed the arrangements for the partition of Poland that had been secretly agreed in August. This partition had now been achieved.

# The Russo-Finnish War

The Russo-Finnish War, or Winter War as it is sometimes known, is usually remembered for the astonishing resistance of the small and poorly armed Finnish forces against the overwhelming Soviet might. The Finnish strength never exceeded 200,000 and yet they inflicted at least 208,000 casualties (official Soviet figures) on the Soviet forces which eventually employed 1,200,000 men.

The conflict developed from Soviet demands first expressed early in October 1939 for territorial concessions similar to those eventually exacted and shown on the map, although at this stage compensatory changes in the Suomussalmi area were offered by the Soviets. On the Soviet side these demands probably arose from genuine worries about Baltic security similar to those inspiring the contemporaneous moves against the Baltic States. The Finns were naturally reluctant to grant such concessions believing that, if they acceded more demands would follow, and that, in any case, Soviet willingness to negotiate implied that their commitment might be weak.

Negotiations in fact broke down in November and the Soviet attack began on the 30th, employing 26 divisions and a massive prepondrance of tanks and artillery against 9 Finnish divisions with few guns, little ammunition and almost no tanks. Despite these advantages, for the first month almost every Soviet attack was resoundingly defeated by the well-trained and confident

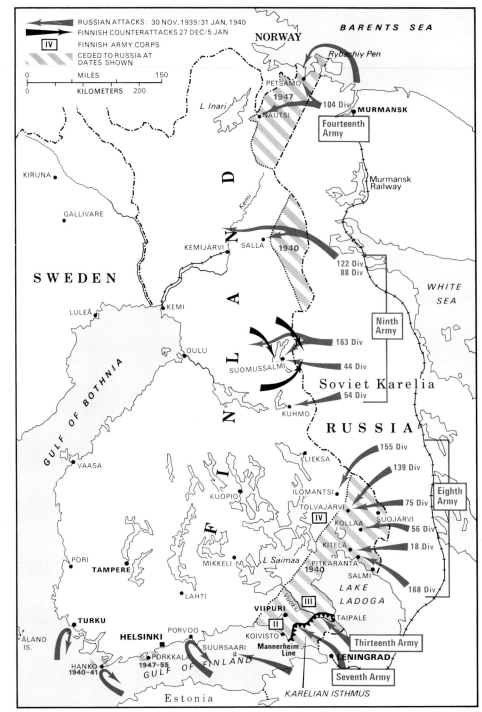

**Bottom left: Finnish ski troops consistently outmaneuvered the less mobile Soviet forces during the Winter War.
Bottom: civilians in snow-colored capes take cover during a Soviet air raid.
Right: the Soviet army did not perform well against the Finns in 1939–40 despite its propaganda image.**

Finnish forces. The Finns were more mobile in the difficult winter conditions and were able to isolate the clumsy Soviet attack columns and defeat them in detail. By January, however, the Soviets were learning to employ their firepower more effectively in defense and this stiffening was developed by Marshal Timoshenko who was appointed to lead the Soviet forces early in the month. Soviet pressure was stepped up during February and by early March the Finns had been beaten in a series of full-scale battles. An Armistice was agreed on the 11th and became effective on the 13th.

The Russo-Finnish War was important in wider international affairs for several reasons. It began by providing the final humiliation for the League of Nations when the Soviet Union remained unworried by its expulsion after ignoring a League attempt to mediate. Secondly the war illustrated the fumbling weakness of the British and French governments who were unable to decide whether help should be sent to Finland and what form it should take. (An important inducement was the possibility of interrupting supplies to Germany of iron ore from the Kiruna and Gällivare areas.) Although it is now clear that it would have been foolish in the long term to have aroused Soviet hostility by help to Finland, in France Premier Daladier's government fell because of this failure. The more vigorous Reynaud took over. Finally the war was important because of the impression it gave of Soviet inefficiency. This seems to have contributed to Hitler's decision to attack the USSR while it certainly encouraged many much-needed reforms to be carried out within the Red Army.

# Russian Annexations 1939–40

The Molotov-Ribbentrop Pact of August 1939 paved the way for Soviet expansion westward. Once Germany had attacked Poland on 1 September 1939, the way was laid open for the Soviet Union to annex Poland's White Russian provinces. On 17 September 1939 Russian Troops entered Poland and encountered almost no oposition. Included in the annexations were the White Russian territories up to and including Bialystok, Brest-Litovsk and Lvov, which had been part of the Russian Empire before 1920, as well as the territory around Wilno, which was largely Jewish and Lithuanian in its ethnic balance.

The Polish annexations were followed swiftly by the Russo-Finnish War, and although the world was amazed by the difficulty the Soviets had in defeating their small neighbor, the war, which began on 30 November 1939, ended in the late winter of 1940 with Soviet territorial gains including eastern Karelia. The annexation of Vyborg gave the Soviet Union total control of Lake Ladoga, a fact which was crucial in the defense of Leningrad during the war against Germany.

Prior to their Finnish annexations, the Soviet Union moved in to control the three Baltic states which before World War I had formed a part of their territory. By the summer of 1940 these nations of Estonia, Latvia and Lithuania were annexed to the Soviet Union, and were later to become separate socialist republics within the USSR. A similar fate was Rumania's, which was one of the successor states of the Austro-Hungarian Empire, and whose territory was composed largely of non-Rumanian speaking people. The territories of northern Bukovina and Bessarabia, the latter being a political football throughout the 19th century, belonging to Rumania and to Russia alternately, were reannexed by the Soviet Union in June 1940. With these annexations the Soviet Union improved its defenses against Germany.

Right: the Norwegian Campaign saw the
first extensive naval engagements of
World War II.
Bottom: German soldiers advance through
a burning village during their occupation
of Norway.

# Norway

The German invasion of Norway and Denmark brought the Phony War to an end. British and French ideas throughout this period had been to avoid costly battles on the Western Front in the style of World War I and instead to rely on the British naval blockade and a strategy of encirclement rather than direct attack. The abortive plans to assist Finland and the related interest in Norway were based on such ideas. The German aims in Scandinavia were to frustrate the Allied plans and, more specifically, to protect imports of iron ore from Sweden. Much of the iron ore traffic passed from Narvik in north Norway by coastal ship to Germany. Hitler became convinced that the Allies were ready to intervene after the *Altmark* incident of February 1940, in which a German ship carrying British prisoners was boarded in Norwegian territorial waters by the British. The Germans had some encouragement from the very small Norwegian Nazi Party led by Vidkung Quisling.

The Germans and the Allies both rapidly improvised plans in the early months of 1940. The Germans moved first by a matter of hours and held the initiative for the rest of the campaign. The German plan was very bold, if not rash, and the naval forces sent to escort the Narvik landing lost very heavily. However, the Germans did succeed in seizing a number of vital airfields at the outset, enabling them to reinforce their assault units rapidly and continue to dominate the coastal waters even when the full strength of the British Royal Navy could be deployed. The Norwegian defense forces were very weak and in many cases arms depots were captured so quickly by the Germans that belatedly mobilizing Norwegian reservists were left without arms. As in other early campaigns of the war the Allied organization was woefully inadequate. The troops were not properly armed, prepared or supplied and German professionalism and air power completed the story. There was a brief Allied revival at Narvik in May but in the light of events in France this foothold was evacuated in June.

Both Denmark and Norway remained under German occupation for the remainder of the war. The Germans gained useful Atlantic bases for striking against the Arctic convoys to the USSR but in the longer term disproportionate German forces were tied up in Norway. In the short term German naval losses helped complicate German planning for an invasion of Britain after the fall of France.

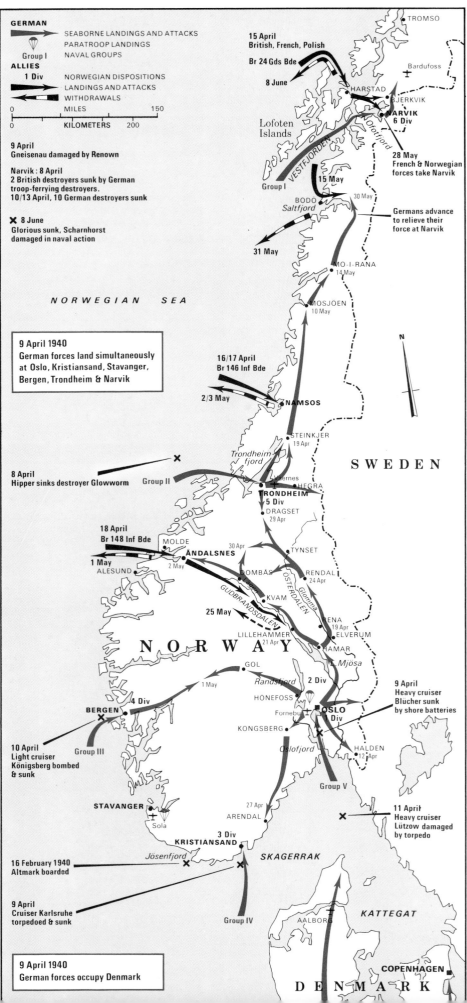

GERMAN
━━▶ SEABORNE LANDINGS AND ATTACKS
⛓ PARATROOP LANDINGS
Group I NAVAL GROUPS
ALLIES
1 Div NORWEGIAN DISPOSITIONS
━━▶ LANDINGS AND ATTACKS
◀━━ WITHDRAWALS

0 MILES 150
0 KILOMETERS 200

9 April
Gneisenau damaged by Renown

Narvik : 8 April
2 British destroyers sunk by German
troop-ferrying destroyers.
10/13 April, 10 German destroyers sunk

✗ 8 June
Glorious sunk, Scharnhorst
damaged in naval action

9 April 1940
German forces land simultaneously
at Oslo, Kristiansand, Stavanger,
Bergen, Trondheim & Narvik

8 April
Hipper sinks destroyer Glowworm   Group II

18 April
Br 148 Inf Bde

1 May
ALESUND

10 April
Light cruiser
Königsberg bombed
& sunk   Group III

16 February 1940
Altmark boarded

9 April
Cruiser Karlsruhe
torpedoed & sunk

9 April 1940
German forces occupy Denmark

TROMSO
15 April
British, French, Polish
Br 24 Gds Bde
8 June
Bardufoss
HARSTAD
BJERKVIK
NARVIK
6 Div
28 May
French & Norwegian
forces take Narvik
Lofoten
Islands
Ofotfjord
VESTFJORDEN
Group I   15 May
30 May   Germans advance
to relieve their
force at Narvik
BODO
Saltfjord
31 May
MO-I-RANA
14 May
NORWEGIAN SEA
MOSJOEN
10 May
N
16/17 April
Br 146 Inf Bde
2/3 May   NAMSOS
STEINKJER
19 Apr   SWEDEN
Trondheim
fjord   Vaernes   HEGRA
Group II   TRONDHEIM
5 Div
DRAGSET
29 Apr
MOLDE   30 Apr
ANDALSNES   TYNSET
2 May   DOMBÅS   RENDAL
24 Apr
GUDBRANDSDALEN   KVAM   OSTERDALEN
25 May   Glomma
LILLEHAMMER   RENA   19 Apr
21 Apr   HAMAR   ELVERUM
L. Mjösa
GOL   2 Div
Randsfjord   9 April
HONEFOSS   Heavy cruiser
1 May   Blücher sunk
by shore batteries
BERGEN   4 Div   Fornebu   OSLO
Div
KONGSBERG
Oslofjord   HALDEN
12 Apr
Group V
27 Apr   11 April
STAVANGER   ARENDAL   Heavy cruiser
Sola   Lützow damaged
by torpedo
3 Div
KRISTIANSAND
Jösenfjord   SKAGERRAK
KATTEGAT
Group IV   AALBORG
COPENHAGEN
DENMARK

104

Bottom: French troops lay down their
arms after the surrender of Lille to the
Germans in May 1940.

# The Fall of France, 1940

The period from the end of the Polish campaign until the invasion of Norway and Denmark was known as the 'Phony War' because of the apparent inactivity along the Western Front. In fact many preparations were made.

Hitler initially wanted to attack in November 1939 but after several postponements a decision was made in January 1940 to wait until May. One reason for this hesitancy was difficulty in finding a satisfactory plan. Limited advances into Belgium and Holland were considered, as were variations on the 1914 Schlieffen Plan. None of these seemed adequate because, although they avoided the difficulties of a frontal attack on the French Maginot Line fortifications, they seemed too predictable and easy to counter. The plan finally adopted under the code name Sickle-stroke was largely developed by General von Manstein. He proposed that attacks into Belgium and Holland should be made (by Army Group B) to draw British and French forces forward from their prepared positions on the Franco-Belgian border. At the same time the main German advance (Army Group A), led by powerful tank forces, would move as quickly and secretly as possible through Luxembourg and the wooded and hilly Ardennes area to the Meuse River, cross it and drive to the Channel, cutting off the Belgians and Dutch and all the Allied forces which had advanced to help them.

The British and French took no account of any such possibility in their plans largely because they believed that the terrain in the Ardennes was not suitable for a large-scale advance. Instead they expected a variation on the Schlieffen Plan. The Maginot Line was garrisoned and the remaining forces deployed along the Franco-Belgian border ready for an advance to the line of the River Dyle if the Belgians should ask for help. The best French units and the British were earmarked for this advance. The weakest part of the Allied line was the sector opposite the Ardennes.

Clearly the Allied plan depended a great deal on co-operation from the Belgians and Dutch but this was never really established before 10 May because the Belgians and Dutch feared to compromise their neutrality and provoke the Germans into attacking. As well as this problem there were other basic weaknesses in the Allied position. General Gamelin, the Commander in Chief, was 68 years old and far from vigorous. His headquarters were badly sited with poor communications and the chain of command,

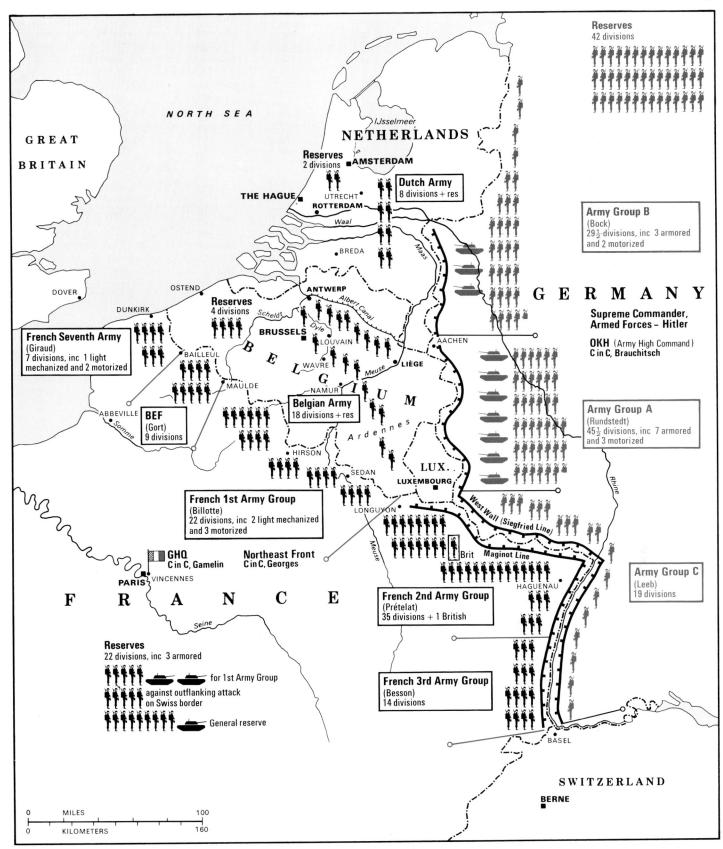

**Reserves**
42 divisions

NORTH SEA

GREAT
BRITAIN

*IJsselmeer*

NETHERLANDS

**Reserves**
2 divisions ■ AMSTERDAM

THE HAGUE ■ UTRECHT

ROTTERDAM

**Dutch Army**
8 divisions + res

*Waal*

BREDA

*Maas*

**Army Group B**
(Bock)
29½ divisions, inc 3 armored
and 2 motorized

DOVER

OSTEND

ANTWERP

*Albert Canal*

*Scheldt*

**Reserves**
4 divisions

*Dyle*

BRUSSELS

LOUVAIN

GERMANY

AACHEN

**Supreme Commander,
Armed Forces – Hitler**

DUNKIRK

**French Seventh Army**
(Giraud)
7 divisions, inc 1 light
mechanized and 2 motorized

BAILLEUL

B E L G I U M

WAVRE

*Meuse*

LIÈGE

**OKH** (Army High Command)
C in C, Brauchitsch

MAULDE

NAMUR

ABBEVILLE

*Somme*

**BEF**
(Gort)
9 divisions

**Belgian Army**
18 divisions + res

*Ardennes*

**Army Group A**
(Rundstedt)
45½ divisions, inc 7 armored
and 3 motorized

HIRSON

SEDAN

LUX.

LUXEMBOURG ■

**French 1st Army Group**
(Billotte)
22 divisions, inc 2 light mechanized
and 3 motorized

LONGUYON

*Meuse*

*Rhine*

GHQ
C in C, Gamelin

**Northeast Front**
C in C, Georges

**West Wall** (Siegfried Line)

Brit

*Maginot Line*

PARIS ■ VINCENNES

F R A N C E

**French 2nd Army Group**
(Prételat)
35 divisions + 1 British

HAGUENAU

**Army Group C**
(Leeb)
19 divisions

*Seine*

**Reserves**
22 divisions, inc 3 armored

for 1st Army Group

against outflanking attack
on Swiss border

General reserve

**French 3rd Army Group**
(Besson)
14 divisions

BASEL

SWITZERLAND

BERNE ■

| 0 | MILES | 100 |
| 0 | KILOMETERS | 160 |

through Georges to the Army Group commanders, was unnecessarily complicated. Relations between the British and French were not at all perfect and General Gort's responsibilities to his own government as well as the French command were a potential source of difficulty. The German command arrangements were sensible and workmanlike.

The ground forces of the two sides were fairly evenly matched in numbers. Counting all nationalities the Allies had 149 divisions against 136 German with 3000 tanks against 2700. However there was no comparison in standards of training, leadership, especially at junior levels, or in tactical doctrine and organization. The German armor in particular was far better placed with almost all of their fighting vehicles being formed in panzer divisions and these divisions in turn being grouped together. Most of the strong

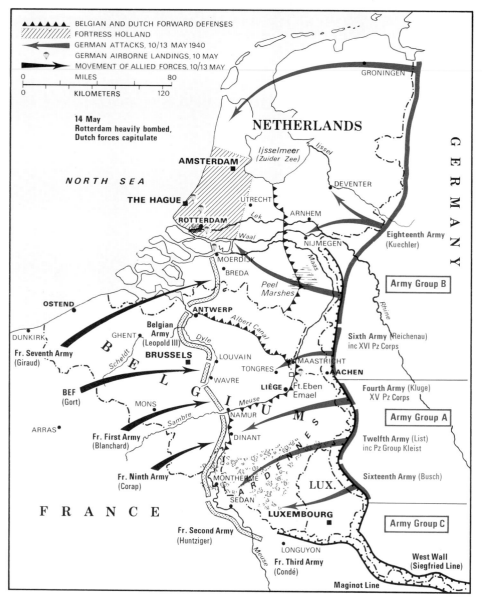

**KEY:**
- ▲▲▲ BELGIAN AND DUTCH FORWARD DEFENSES
- ///// FORTRESS HOLLAND
- → GERMAN ATTACKS, 10/13 MAY 1940
- ⬇ GERMAN AIRBORNE LANDINGS, 10 MAY
- ➡ MOVEMENT OF ALLIED FORCES, 10/13 MAY

0 MILES 80
0 KILOMETERS 120

14 May
Rotterdam heavily bombed,
Dutch forces capitulate

NETHERLANDS

GERMANY

Ijsselmeer
(Zuider Zee)

Ijssel

NORTH SEA

AMSTERDAM
THE HAGUE
ROTTERDAM

UTRECHT

DEVENTER

ARNHEM

Lek

Waal

NIJMEGEN

Maas

Eighteenth Army
(Kuechler)

MOERDIJK
BREDA

Peel
Marshes

OSTEND

Rhine

Army Group B

ANTWERP

Albert Canal

Sixth Army (Reichenau)
inc XVI Pz Corps

DUNKIRK

GHENT

Belgian
Army
(Leopold III)

Scheldt

Dyle

LOUVAIN

MAASTRICHT
TONGRES
AACHEN

Fr. Seventh Army
(Giraud)

BRUSSELS

WAVRE

LIÈGE
Ft.Eben
Emael

Fourth Army (Kluge)
XV Pz Corps

BEF
(Gort)

MONS

Meuse

NAMUR

Army Group A

ARRAS

Fr. First Army
(Blanchard)

Sambre

DINANT

Twelfth Army (List)
inc Pz Group Kleist

Fr. Ninth Army
(Corap)

MONTHERME

ARDENNES

LUX.

Sixteenth Army (Busch)

SEDAN

LUXEMBOURG

FRANCE

Fr. Second Army
(Huntziger)

Army Group C

LONGUYON

Meuse

West Wall
(Siegfried Line)

Fr. Third Army
(Condé)

Maginot Line

**Bottom: a French truck-mounted antitank gun takes up a camouflaged position. Right: the wreckage left by the retreating British Expeditionary Force at Dunkirk. The British had to leave behind almost all their heavy equipment during the evacuation.**

French tank force was wastefully dispersed in small infantry support units and on the day the battle began there was no British armored division in position in France. (One such unit was sent, not fully prepared, immediately fighting began.) Perhaps the most telling German advantage, however, was in the air where the Luftwaffe had over 3000 modern aircraft with well trained pilots and crews to face a mixed bag of less than 2000 Allied machines. (The Allied forces could expect some help and reinforcement from UK-based RAF units.)

The combination of tanks and air power was central to the German success. The aircraft, and particularly the dive-bombing Stukas, acted almost as artillery support to the army both when it was necessary for the tanks to break through solid defenses and also when, in the advance to exploit success, armored columns ran into pockets of resistance after having left their own artillery behind. Few even in the German Army understood the potential of such a system but their leadership was so dynamic that the *Blitzkrieg* or lightning war which they advocated became a byword for military skill and success.

The German attack began on 10 May and for the first few days attention was held, as the Germans had hoped, by events in the

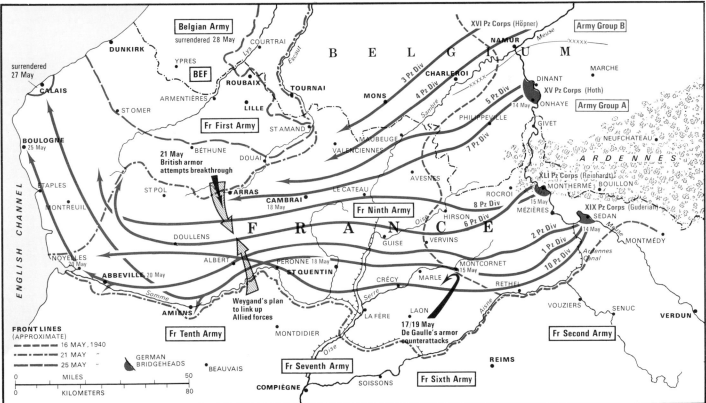

XVI Pz Corps (Höpner)

Army Group B

COURTRAI

B E L G I U M

NAMUR

Meuse

xxxxx

DUNKIRK

YPRES

Lys

MONS

CHARLEROI

3 Pz Div

DINANT

MARCHE

surrendered
27 May

BEF

ROUBAIX

TOURNAI

4 Pz Div

Sambre

xxxxx

XV Pz Corps (Hoth)

CALAIS

ARMENTIÈRES

LILLE

5 Pz Div

14 May

ONHAYE

Army Group A

ST OMER

Fr First Army

ST AMAND

MAUBEUGE

PHILIPPEVILLE

GIVET

BOULOGNE
25 May

BÉTHUNE

DOUAI

VALENCIENNES

7 Pz Div

NEUFCHATEAU

21 May
British armor
attempts breakthrough

ARRAS

7 Pz Div

A R D E N N E S

ÉTAPLES

ST POL

CAMBRAI
18 May

LE CATEAU

AVESNES

ROCROI

XLI Pz Corps (Reinhardt)

MONTHERME

BOUILLON

MONTREUIL

8 Pz Div

Oise

Fr Ninth Army

HIRSON

6 Pz Div

MÉZIÈRES

15 May

XIX Pz Corps (Guderian)

ENGLISH CHANNEL

F R A N C E

GUISE

VERVINS

SEDAN

14 May

Meuse

DOULLENS

2 Pz Div

MONTMÉDY

NOYELLES
20 May

ALBERT

PÉRONNE 18 May

ST QUENTIN

CRÉCY

MARLE

MONTCORNET
15 May

1 Pz Div

10 Pz Div

Ardennes
Canal

ABBEVILLE 20 May

Somme

Serre

LA FÈRE

LAON

RETHEL

Aisne

VOUZIERS

SENUC

VERDUN

Weygand's plan
to link up
Allied forces

AMIENS

Oise

17/19 May
De Gaulle's armor
counterattacks

Fr Tenth Army

MONTDIDIER

MONTDIDIER

Fr Second Army

FRONT LINES
(APPROXIMATE)
———— 16 MAY, 1940
–·–·– 21 MAY
– – – 25 MAY

GERMAN
BRIDGEHEADS

BEAUVAIS

Fr Seventh Army

REIMS

0        MILES        50

0      KILOMETERS      80

COMPIÈGNE

SOISSONS

Fr Sixth Army

108

Bottom right: lines of British and French troops wait to be evacuated from the Dunkirk beaches in May/June 1940. Still greater numbers were lifted from the harbor at Dunkirk itself.

Low Countries. The Germans began with a number of daring paratroop and ground force attacks on important border defenses in both Belgium and Holland. These made important gains particularly the capture of Fort Eben Emael. The Dutch forces were left totally disorganized by a combination of paratroop drops and air attacks. Their defenses were never properly put into operation and after a particularly vicious air raid on Rotterdam on 14 May the Dutch surrendered. The French Seventh Army attempted to intervene but was thrown back.

Queen Wilhelmina and her government were evacuated to England from where they hoped to continue the fight.

In Belgium the German attacks were soon making good progress both in the north and in the tank advance to the Meuse. The British and French had advanced as planned to the Dyle but found that their positions there were weak and called in reinforcements from the reserve. Despite thus playing into the German hands, by 15 May it was necessary to order the evacuation of the Dyle Line in the face of the German attack. This was

even before the German tank advance became an obvious threat.

The German tank forces had quickly penetrated through the Ardennes and on 14 May they secured vital bridgeheads over the Meuse in what were probably the most decisive actions of the whole campaign. The local French forces failed to counterattack. The German armor then began rushing forward to the sea, hindered more by the caution of the higher German commanders than by the British or the French. General Weygand replaced Gamelin as French Commander in Chief and tried to organize a counteroffensive but the only significant response was a limited British attack near Arras.

After this effort there was little the Allied forces could do but retreat to the sea. They were helped in this by a strange order from Hitler and Rundstedt which largely halted the German armored advance from 23–26 May. Most of the Allied force was able to fall back to the Dunkirk perimeter and 338,000 men, including 120,000 French, were evacuated in the nine-day operation (26 May–4 June) at heavy cost in transport ships and covering aircraft.

While the Germans were concentrating on Dunkirk Weygand was trying to organize the remaining French forces for defense of the line of the Somme. The Germans began to attack south on 5 June and the line was soon broken despite brave resistance from many French units. The German advance continued apace and on 16 June Premier Reynaud and his government resigned. The new head of government was Marshal Pétain and on the 17th he announced that France was seeking an armistice. The armistice was signed on 22 June.

France was divided into an occupied and an unoccupied zone. The unoccupied zone was ruled by the Pétain government from Vichy and, although its independence was nominally preserved, on many issues there was complete co-operation with Germany. A comparatively junior army officer and politician, General de Gaulle, escaped to Britain with a small following and proclaimed himself leader of Free France, announcing that France had lost a battle but had not lost the war.

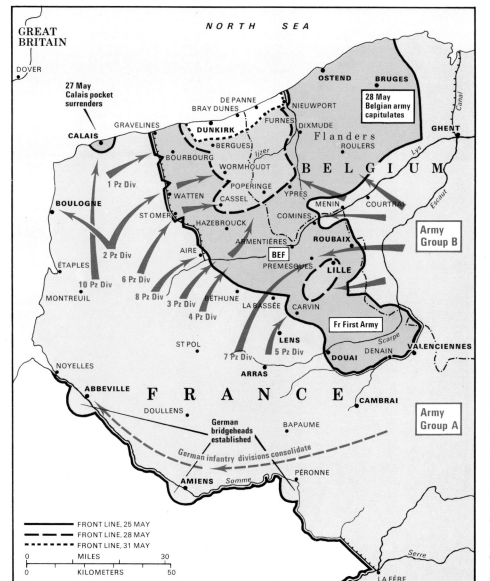

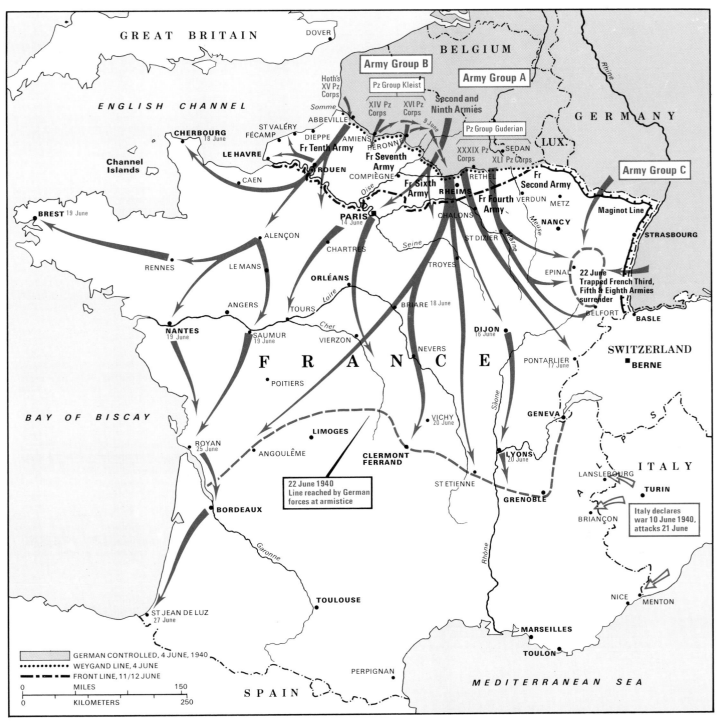

GREAT BRITAIN

DOVER

BELGIUM

**Army Group B**

Hoth's XV Pz Corps

Pz Group Kleist

XIV Pz Corps  XVI Pz Corps

**Army Group A**

GERMANY

ENGLISH CHANNEL

Somme

Second and Ninth Armies

Rhine

LUX.

Pz Group Guderian

ABBEVILLE

9 June

**Army Group C**

CHERBOURG 18 June

ST VALÉRY FÉCAMP

DIEPPE

AMIENS PÉRONNE

XXXIX Pz Corps

SEDAN

LE HAVRE

**Fr Tenth Army**

**Fr Seventh Army**

XLI Pz Corps

Channel Islands

CAEN

ROUEN

COMPIÈGNE

RETHEL

**Fr Second Army**

VERDUN METZ

Maginot Line

Oise

**Fr Sixth Army**

RHEIMS

**Fr Fourth Army**

STRASBOURG

BREST 19 June

PARIS 14 June

CHÂLONS

ST DIZIER

Meuse

NANCY

ALENÇON

CHARTRES

Seine

Marne

EPINAL

**22 June Trapped French Third, Fifth & Eighth Armies surrender**

RENNES

LE MANS

TROYES

BELFORT

ANGERS

ORLÉANS

Loire

TOURS

BRIARE 18 June

DIJON 16 June

BASLE

NANTES 19 June

SAUMUR 19 June

VIERZON

Cher

NEVERS

PONTARLIER 17 June

SWITZERLAND

BERNE

POITIERS

F R A N C E

Saône

BAY OF BISCAY

ROYAN 25 June

LIMOGES

VICHY 20 June

GENEVA

ITALY

ANGOULÊME

CLERMONT FERRAND

LYONS 20 June

LANSLEBOURG

TURIN

**22 June 1940 Line reached by German forces at armistice**

ST ETIENNE

GRENOBLE

BRIANÇON

**Italy declares war 10 June 1940, attacks 21 June**

BORDEAUX

Garonne

Rhône

ST JEAN DE LUZ 27 June

TOULOUSE

NICE  MENTON

MARSEILLES

TOULON

PERPIGNAN

SPAIN

MEDITERRANEAN SEA

GERMAN CONTROLLED, 4 JUNE, 1940
WEYGAND LINE, 4 JUNE
FRONT LINE, 11/12 JUNE

0      MILES      150
0      KILOMETERS      250

# Battle of Britain

On 16 July 1940 Hitler issued his Directive 16 to the German Armed Forces. It began, 'I have decided to begin to prepare for, and, if necessary, to carry out, an invasion of England.' It went on to explain that the Luftwaffe must defeat the RAF so that the Royal Navy would be unprotected if it tried to interfere with an invasion force crossing the Channel.

If the British were to survive this threat the RAF had to gain time for the army to reequip after the losses of Dunkirk and if possible to hold the Germans off until bad weather in the fall made an invasion impossible.

The RAF was none too strong for its task but was well organized and led. Air Chief Marshal Dowding, who led Fighter Command, and his principal lieutenant, Air Vice-Marshal Park, were both particularly able and perceptive officers. The British

fighter direction system was well thought out with radar and other information being coordinated and instructions issued from operations rooms in each RAF sector. Although they understood its technical capabilities the Germans failed to appreciate the importance of radar within the British system and did little to attack the radar stations. In a sense this was part of the 'home advantage' which the British had throughout the battle. In order to plan, the Germans needed, and did not get, accurate information on damage done and losses inflicted while the RAF had a more clear-cut task and could husband its resources accordingly. The RAF's principal shortage was of trained fighter pilots and it was, therefore, of considerable importance that defending pilots who were shot down unwounded could immediately return to service. The Germans, of course, had no such second chance and their principal fighter aircraft, the short-range Messerschmitt Bf 109, could only fight over southern England for a very limited time.

All these British advantages would not have cancelled out the greater German strength and the experience of their pilots unless the German High Command had not been found wanting. Reichsmarshal Göring, the Commander in Chief of the Luftwaffe, controlled the German attack and made many wrong decisions. There was no real understanding of the urgency of the invasion timetable – the all-out Luftwaffe attacks only began on 13 August, more than two months after Dunkirk. There was, too, no clear understanding of the exact aim. For a few days in late August and early September the Germans came close to winning the battle, with attacks on No 11 Group airfields, but on 7 September the main German target became London and the RAF was allowed to recover. Although it was not obvious at the time, the last major German effort was on 15 September. There were many later daytime attacks, and the night 'Blitz' on Britain's cities continued well into 1941, but Hitler postponed the invasion on 17 September.

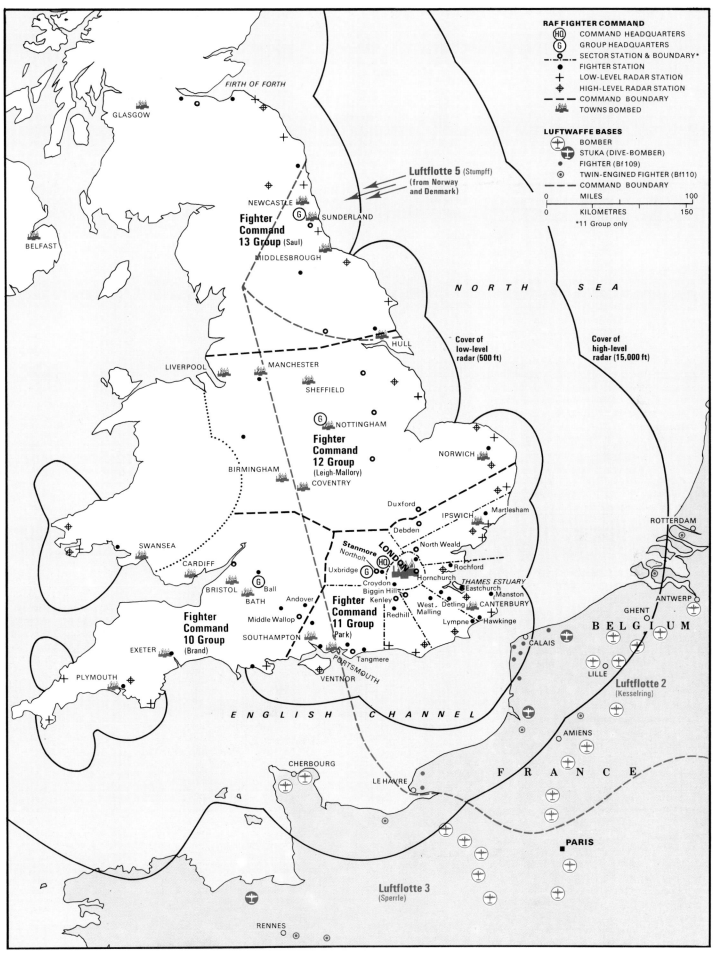

Below: Italian troops, laden with bundles of barbed wire, move through a mountain pass during the disastrous war with Greece in the winter of 1940–41. The Italians were no match for the Greeks in this mountain campaign.

# Greece

Although Hitler's plans for 1941 were dominated by the idea of attacking the USSR he also intended to secure German domination of southeastern Europe and the natural resources of that area. The allegiance of Hungary, Rumania and Bulgaria was secured during the winter of 1940–41 but Greece and Yugoslavia presented different problems. Italy had occupied Albania in 1939 and late in October 1940 had begun a war with Greece. Despite Mussolini's blustering confidence the Italians fared badly and by mid-March 1941 had suffered many defeats and had lost control of a large part of Albania. By that time also the Greeks were receiving help from Britain. The combination of defeat for his Italian ally and the prospect of British forces within striking distance of the oil fields of Rumania was clearly unacceptable to Hitler and he confirmed the plan to attack Greece which had been in preparation since late 1940.

To defend Greece the Allies had, in addition to the forces facing the Italians, seven weak Greek divisions, the New Zealand Division, part of the 6th Australian Division and a British armored brigade. The Germans employed three full army corps including a strong armored element. They had overwhelming air support. The British leaders hoped to base their defense on the naturally strong Aliakmon Line and have forces in hand to cover the Monastir Gap but despite this sensible advice the Greek Commander in Chief, General Papagos, insisted that he could not abandon Greek Macedonia and deployed much of his available strength on the weaker Metaxas Line covering that region. The Germans planned to destroy this force in direct attacks and push other units through the Monastir Gap to outflank the defense lines.

The attack began on 6 April and the map shows the speed with which the German plan was completed. By 10 April the Aliakmon Line was being evacuated and General Wavell's decision of 16 April to stop reinforcements being sent from Egypt effectively meant that the fight in Greece was being abandoned.

In a postscript to the Greek campaign German airborne troops landed on Crete on 20 May and despite a fierce struggle had captured the island by the end of the month.

Below: Italian troops, laden with bundles of barbed wire, move through a mountain pass during the disastrous war with Greece in the winter of 1940–41. The Italians were no match for the Greeks in this mountain campaign.

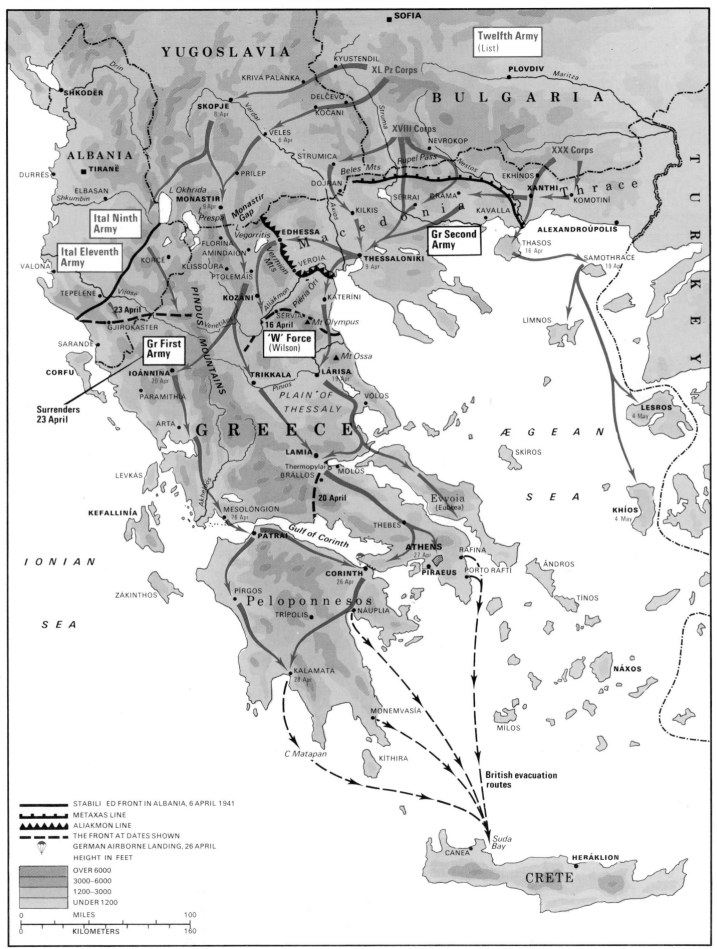

YUGOSLAVIA

SOFIA

KYUSTENDIL

KRIVA PALANKA

Twelfth Army
(List)

PLOVDIV

*Maritza*

BULGARIA

XL Pz Corps

SKOPJE
8 Apr

*Drin*

SHKODËR

DELČEVO

KOČANI

*Vardar*

VELES
6 Apr

PRILEP

STRUMICA

*Struma*

NEVROKOP

XVIII Corps

XXX Corps

*Thrace*

EKHÍNOS

KOMOTINÍ

XANTHI

ALBANIA

TIRANË

DURRËS

ELBASAN

*Shkumbin*

L. Okhrida

MONASTIR
9 Apr

L. Prespa

L. Vegoritis

Monastir
Gap

*Beles Mts*

DOJRAN

Rupel Pass

*Nestos*

SERRAI

DRAMA

KAVALLA

ALEXANDROÚPOLIS

*Macedonia*

AXIOS

KILKIS

THESSALONIKI
9 Apr

Gr Second
Army

THASOS
16 Apr

SAMOTHRACE
19 Apr

TURKEY

Ital Ninth
Army

EDHESSA

FLORINA

AMINDAION

VEROIA

Ital Eleventh
Army

VALONA

KORČE

KLISSOURA

PTOLEMAÏS

*Vermion Mts*

KATERÍNI

LÍMNOS

TEPELENË

*Vijosë*

GJIROKASTER

23 April

*PINDUS MOUNTAINS*

KOZANI

*Aliakmon*

SERVIA
16 April

*Piéria Óri*

▲ Mt Olympus

LESBOS
4 May

SARANDË

CORFU

Gr First
Army

IOÁNNINA
20 Apr

PARAMITHIA

ÁRTA

*Venetikos*

'W' Force
(Wilson)

TRIKKALA

*Pinios*

LÁRISA
19 Apr

▲ Mt Ossa

VÓLOS

ÆGEAN

Surrenders
23 April

GREECE

PLAIN OF
THESSALY

SKÍROS

KHÍOS
4 May

LEVKÁS

LAMIA

*Akheloos*

KEFALLINÍA

MESOLÓNGION
26 Apr

Thermopylai
BRÁLLOS

MOLOS

20 April

*Evvoia*
*(Euboea)*

SEA

IONIAN

Gulf of Corinth

PÁTRAI

THEBES

ATHENS
27 Apr

PIRAEUS

RAFINA

PORTO RAFTI

ÁNDROS

TÍNOS

SEA

ZÁKINTHOS

PÍRGOS

*Peloponnesos*

TRÍPOLIS

CORINTH
26 Apr

NÁUPLIA

NÁXOS

KALAMATA
28 Apr

MONEMVASÍA

MÍLOS

C Matapan

KÍTHIRA

British evacuation
routes

*Suda Bay*

CANEA

HERÁKLION

CRETE

STABILISED FRONT IN ALBANIA, 6 APRIL 1941

METAXAS LINE

ALIAKMON LINE

THE FRONT AT DATES SHOWN

GERMAN AIRBORNE LANDING, 26 APRIL

HEIGHT IN FEET

OVER 6000

3000–6000

1200–3000

UNDER 1200

0                MILES                100

0                KILOMETERS                160

# Yugoslavia

As the other Balkan countries fell under German influence one by one during the winter of 1940–41 pressure on Yugoslavia to follow suit increased. On 25 March, with the agreement of Prince Paul the Regent, the government gave in and signed the Tripartite Pact but this decision was overturned on the 27th by a largely Serbian-backed coup deposing Prince Paul and his government in favor of King Peter. Hitler responded by immediately ordering his forces to prepare to invade Yugoslavia and also to carry out the attack on Greece which was already planned.

The attack began on 6 April with heavy air raids on Belgrade and against the Yugoslav Air Force which was soon out of the fight. On the same day units of List's Twelfth Army moved into Yugoslavia toward Strumica and Monastir but these were really part of the force attacking Greece. The land attack on Yugoslavia proper began on 8 April when Kleist's First Panzer Group crossed the Bulgarian border. Weich's Second Army joined in on the 9th and on the 11th the remaining Italian, Hungarian and German units began their efforts. There was little resistance to any of the attacks and the country was quickly overrun. King Peter and his government fled and on the 17th an armistice was agreed. The defense was vitiated by a senseless cordon deployment and by internal dissension, particularly Croatian disaffection. The Germans lost less than 200 dead in the whole campaign.

It has often been suggested that, although at the time the Greek and Yugoslavian campaign seemed disasters for the Allied cause they were indirectly beneficial by crucially delaying the attack on the USSR. Modern historical research suggests that this is not so. Any delay was caused rather more by weather and supply problems and, although it certainly took time to redeploy forces from the Balkans to face the USSR, it is not clear that the units involved were essential in the initial stages of the attack. If it had been necessary to move them to their Barbarossa positions quicker this could have been done also.

Below left: a 15cm howitzer, mounted on a Panzer I chassis, operating in Yugoslavia in the spring of 1941.
Bottom left: a formation of Junkers Ju 87 Stukas flies over the Bosnian mountains during an operation against Yugoslavian guerrilla forces.
Bottom: a German half-track fords a river in Yugoslavia during an attack on Partisan forces.

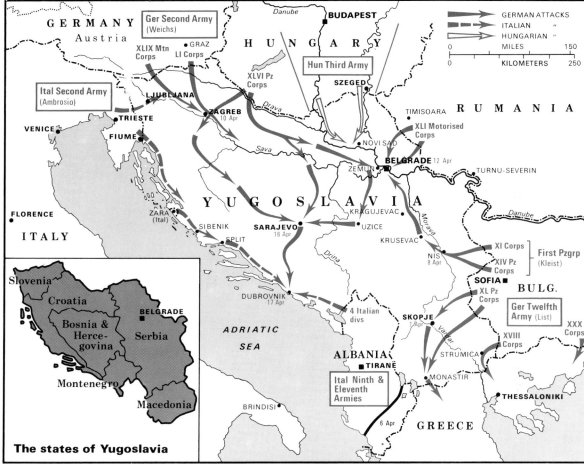

**The states of Yugoslavia**

# War in the Desert, 1940–41

In its repeated changes of fortune the North African campaign was unlike any other of the war. Between the Axis base at Tripoli and the British base in the Nile Delta there was a 1500-mile expanse of waterless and largely roadless desert. Both sides' attempts to build up the supplies and reinforcements necessary for any sustained advance in such terrain were continually hampered by the demands of other theaters and other problems. Thus in 1940–41 the British Middle East Command fought successful campaigns in East Africa and Syria and unsuccessfully in Greece and Crete. At the end of 1941, even as the British were advancing once again, units had to be withdrawn to be sent east to face the Japanese. It was by no means a one-sided process. The Germans soon assumed the dominant role in the Axis partnership, and constraints on their commander, General Rommel, were soon apparent. The German High Command saw North Africa as a distinctly minor theater and allocated forces and supplies accordingly. The proportion of these supplies reaching Rommel was also highly variable. When the German Mediterranean air forces were strong as at the beginning of 1941 or at the same time in 1942, Rommel tended to do well, whereas when the British naval and air forces were strong, particularly those based in Malta, Rommel did badly. Many of Rommel's supply and other problems would have been much less acute with wholehearted

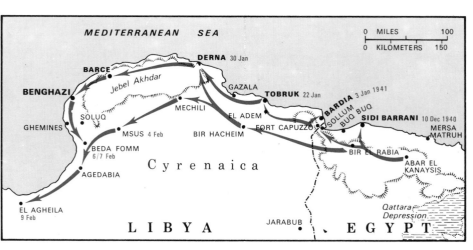

and efficient cooperation from his Italian allies. These general difficulties affected each side almost independently of the prevailing tactical situation but because of the poor land communications and the lack of suitable ports the military dictum, that an army becomes weaker as it advances away from its base and stronger as it retires, was a formula with special relevance to the North African battle. Only if this whole list of constraints and imperatives is taken into account can the unique rhythms of the fighting in North Africa be understood.

Italy declared war on Britain on 10 June 1940 and in September the numerically strong Italian Tenth Army made a short tentative advance into Egypt. By December the much smaller British and Imperial force was ready to attack under the able leadership of Generals Wavell and O'Connor. The Italians were successively hustled out of defensive positions at Sidi Barrani, Bardia

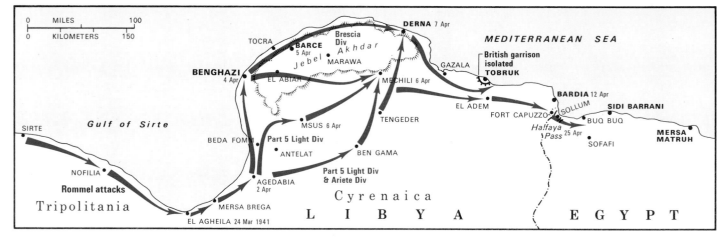

**Left: a Panzer III of the Afrika Korps
goes into action in the Western Desert.
Below left: a Messerschmitt Bf 109E
fighter operating from a desert airfield.
Below far left: German troops examine a
knocked-out British Matilda tank.**

and Tobruk and thrown into abject retreat along the coast road. The Italian defeat was completed when a force sent across the Cyrenaica Plateau cut their retreat at Beda Fomm. In those two months the British forces never had more than two divisions in the fight. Ten Italian divisions were destroyed and 130,000 prisoners taken for the loss of 550 dead and 1400 wounded. Already, however, the British position was deteriorating. Troops had been withdrawn to East Africa and more were about to go to Greece. Even those forces remaining could not all be supplied at the front and so it was not solidly held, the more so because many of the tanks were worn out.

General Rommel arrived in Africa on 12 February 1941 with a small German force and instructions to block any further British advance. He quickly discerned the British weakness and by early April had begun an all-out attack which quickly overwhelmed the depleted British force. However, although the main front line was pushed back into Egypt, Rommel was unsuccessful in desperate attempts to capture Tobruk before his own acute supply problems forced a pause.

During the next phase of the campaign both sides tried to build up their forces and supply stocks for an offensive. A premature British attack in June, Operation Battleaxe, was soundly defeated but Tobruk remained a thorn in the German side. The British were again ready to attack in November 1941 under a new Commander in Chief, General Auchinleck and Operation Crusader accordingly began on the 18th. The British had far greater resources initially but the individual German units were better led and far more professional in their approach. The result, when combined with errors in generalship on both sides, was a prolonged and highly confused battle in the area between Tobruk and the Egyptian frontier. After very heavy losses on both sides Rommel was forced to retreat and because of the lack of suitable defensive positions and the danger of being outflanked he had to go back as far as El Agheila. Once more, however, there were signs of a change: Malta was coming under heavier attack and the British naval forces had recently suffered serious losses; Rommel was receiving reinforcements even as he retreated and British and Australian troops were being withdrawn to reinforce the Far East against the threat from Japan.

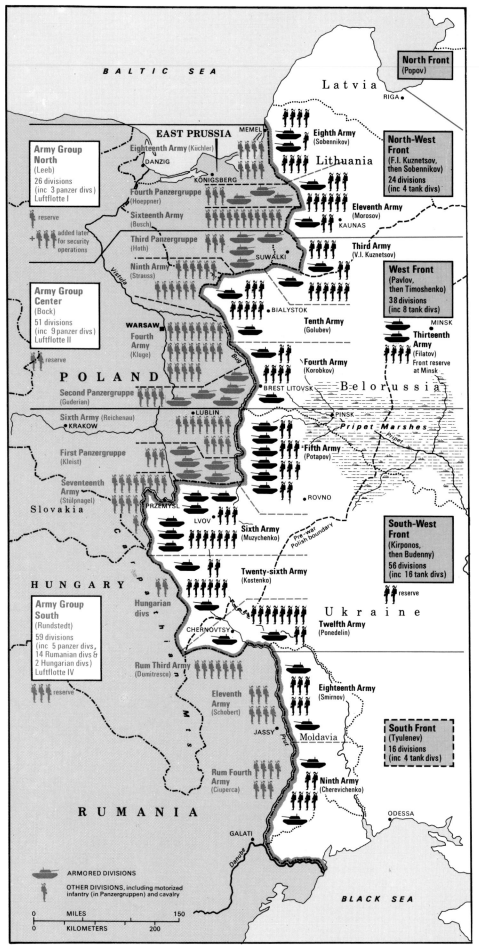

**BALTIC SEA**

Latvia

RIGA •

**North Front**
(Popov)

**EAST PRUSSIA**    MEMEL

**Eighteenth Army** (Küchler)

DANZIG

**Army Group North**
(Leeb)
26 divisions
(inc 3 panzer divs)
Luftflotte I

reserve

added later for security operations

KÖNIGSBERG

**Fourth Panzergruppe**
(Hoeppner)

**Sixteenth Army**
(Busch)

Lithuania

**Eighth Army**
(Sobennikov)

**North-West Front**
(F.I. Kuznetsov,
then Sobennikov)
24 divisions
(inc 4 tank divs)

**Eleventh Army**
(Morosov)
KAUNAS

**Third Panzergruppe**
(Hoth)

SUWALKI

**Third Army**
(V.I. Kuznetsov)

Vistula

**Ninth Army** (Strauss)

**Army Group Center**
(Bock)
51 divisions
(inc 9 panzer divs)
Luftflotte II

reserve

WARSAW

**Fourth Army**
(Kluge)

**West Front**
(Pavlov,
then Timoshenko)
38 divisions
(inc 8 tank divs)

BIALYSTOK

**Tenth Army**
(Golubev)

MINSK

**Thirteenth Army**
(Filatov)
Front reserve
at Minsk

**P O L A N D**

Bug

**Second Panzergruppe**
(Guderian)

**Fourth Army**
(Korobkov)

BREST LITOVSK

**Belorussia**

PINSK

*Pripet Marshes*

**Sixth Army** (Reichenau)
• KRAKOW

LUBLIN

Pripet

**First Panzergruppe**
(Kleist)

**Fifth Army**
(Potapov)

**Seventeenth Army**
(Stülpnagel)

Slovakia

PRZEMYSL

• ROVNO

LVOV

Pre-war Polish boundary

**Sixth Army**
(Muzychenko)

**South-West Front**
(Kirponos,
then Budenny)
56 divisions
(inc 16 tank divs)

reserve

**Twenty-sixth Army**
(Kostenko)

**H U N G A R Y**

Hungarian
divs

**U k r a i n e**

CHERNOVTSY

**Twelfth Army**
(Ponedelin)

**Army Group South**
(Rundstedt)
59 divisions
(inc 5 panzer divs,
14 Rumanian divs &
2 Hungarian divs)
Luftflotte IV

reserve

**Rum Third Army**
(Dumitrescu)

Mts

**Eleventh Army**
(Schobert)

JASSY

Prut

Moldavia

**Eighteenth Army**
(Smirnov)

**South Front**
(Tyulenev)
16 divisions
(inc 4 tank divs)

**R U M A N I A**

**Rum Fourth Army**
(Ciuperca)

**Ninth Army**
(Cherevichenko)

ODESSA •

GALATI •

Danube

ARMORED DIVISIONS

OTHER DIVISIONS, including motorized
infantry (in Panzergruppen) and cavalry

MILES    0 ——— 150
KILOMETERS    0 ——— 200

**BLACK SEA**

# Operation Barbarossa

In February 1941 a sympathetic German printer showed to Soviet diplomats in Berlin a new Russian phrasebook he had been ordered to print in large quantities, and which included phrases like 'Hands up or I'll shoot!' and 'Are you a communist?' This was just one of several signs that Hitler was preparing to turn against the USSR. He had in fact issued a general directive plan in December 1940 which, drawing on the experience and self-confidence gained in the French campaign, proposed that the initial aim should be nothing less than the complete destruction of the Red Army. This would be facilitated by the circumstance that the Russians, whose prevailing military doctrine was the doctrine of the offensive, had placed almost their entire active army close to the frontiers. Deep penetrations by German armor would be able to cut off the retreat of these Soviet formations. Having accomplished this, the German forces were to press eastward and establish a line running roughly from Archangel to Astrakhan.

22 June 1941 was the date finally fixed for this Operation Barbarossa. In the preceding weeks the Soviet government, despite ominous indications of German preparations, had issued orders that no Soviet preparations should be made, as the Germans might regard these as a provocation to attack. When war came, therefore, Stalin and his colleagues were in the unusual situation of being both unsurprised and unprepared and, long after the British and French had shown the perils of appeasement, stood revealed as the greatest appeasers of all. The Soviet formations were taken, catastrophically, by surprise.

After heavy German air attacks, directed mainly at airfields close to the frontier, and which had the effect of shattering the Red Air Force, German troops advanced across the frontier at dawn on 22 June. Army Group Center made a pincer movement from East Prussia and Poland toward Minsk, cutting off parts of two Soviet armies whose men, after a little confused resistance, surrendered en masse. Meanwhile Army Group South entered the Ukraine and, aided by Rumanian troops, also forced large Soviet concentrations to surrender.

In September Budenny, a cavalryman and crony of Stalin since the Russian Civil

SWEDEN

FINLAND

TURKU

HELSINKI

HANKO
(USSR)
3 Dec 1941
Evacuated by Russia

Gulf of Finland

LAKE LADOGA

Lake Oneg

Svir

VIIPURI

Twenty-third
Army

Forty-second &
Fifty-second Armies

VOLKHOV
Eighth Army
TIKHVIN

LENINGRAD

Fifty-fourth Army
Fourth Army

Fifty-ninth Army
Second Shock Army

NOVGOROD

Eleventh Army

TALLINN

NARVA

Estonia

TARTU

L Peipus

PSKOV

STARAYA
RUSSA

L Ilmen

Lovat

Volkhov

Luga

Luga

BALTIC
SEA

VENTSPILS

RIGA

OSTROV

REZEKNE

Dvina

IDRITSA

VELIKIYE
LUKI

KHOLM

Thirty-
fourth Army

Third Shock Army

OSTASHKOV
Twenty-seventh Army
Twenty-second Army

Twenty-ninth
Army

BELYY

RZHEV

KALININ

Volga

**North-West Front**
(Voroshilov)

MOSCOW

Latvia

SIAULIAI

Eighth
Army

**Army Group
North** (Leeb)

MEMEL

Eighteenth
Army

EAST
PRUSSIA

Fourth Pzgrp
Sixteenth Army

Ninth Army
Third Pzgrp

Lithuania

Neman

KAUNAS

VILNYUS

Eleventh
Army

POLOTSK

VITEBSK

VELIZH

YARTSEVO

SMOLENSK

VYAZMA

Dniepr

ORSHA

Thirtieth Army
Nineteenth Army
Sixteenth Army

Thirty-second Army

Twentieth Army

KALUGA

TULA

NOVI BOROSOV

Moscow
Highway

Berezina

MOGILEV

ROSLAVL

Twenty-fourth Army

Twenty-eighth
Army

Forty-third Army

Fiftieth Army

BRYANSK

OREL

**West Front**
(Timoshenko)

MINSK

GORODISHCHE

GRODNO

NOVO
BYKHOV

KRICHE

Sozh

Third
Army

BIALYSTOK

Tenth
Army

Fourth
Army

BOBRUYSK

GOMEL

STARODUB

Second
Pzgrp

NOVGOROD
SEVERSKI

Third Army

Thirteenth
Army

KURSK

WARSAW

Vistula

Fourth Army
Second Pzgrp

BREST-LITOVSK

PINSK

Pripet

**Army Group
Center** (Bock)

Belorussia

Pripet Marshes

Twenty-
first Army

RECHITSA

MOZYR

CHERNIGOV

Desna

KONOTOP

**South-West
Front** (Budenny)

Bug

POLAND

KOVEL

KOROSTEN

Fifth Army

Fortieth
Army

Sixth Army
First Pzgrp

Fifth Army

ROVNO

ZHITOMIR

KIEV

Thirty-
seventh
Army

BAKHMACH

Second
Army

LOKHVITSA

Twenty-first
Army

KHARKOV

Donets

Seventeenth
Army

LWOW

Sixth Army

TERNOPOL

BERDICHEV

KAZATIN

First Pzgrp

CHERKASSY

POLTAVA

Psel

Thirty-
eighth Army

Slovakia

Dniestr

Twenty-sixth
Army

KAMENETS-PODOLSKY

Ukraine

VINNITSA

UMAN

PERVOMAYSK

KREMENCHUG

Sixth
Army

DNEPROPETROVSK

Twelfth
Army

ZAPOROZHYE

**Army Group
South** (Rundstedt)

Carpathian Mts

Twelfth Army

CHERNOVTSY

HUNGARY

Rum Third
Army

Eighteenth
Army

Eleventh
Army

Prut

Moldavia

Rum Fourth
Army

KISHINEV

Ninth
Army

Yuzhni Bug

Seventeenth
Army

KRIVOY ROG

Eleventh
Army

NIKOLAYEV

Dniepr

Eighteenth
Army

MELITOPOL

Ninth
Army

ODESSA
16 Oct

PEREKOP

Sea of
Azov

Fifty-first
Army

Crimea

RUMANIA

BUCHAREST

SEVASTOPOL

Danube

CONSTANTA

BLACK SEA

▼▼▼ ▼▼▼▼   STALIN LINE
――――   FRONT LINE, 21 JUNE 1941
– – – –   "     "   9 JULY
· · · · ·   "     "   1 SEPTEMBER
· – · – ·   "     "   30 SEPTEMBER
⬅   RUSSIAN COUNTERATTACKS
▨   TRAPPED RUSSIAN POCKETS

0        MILES        200
0      KILOMETERS     300

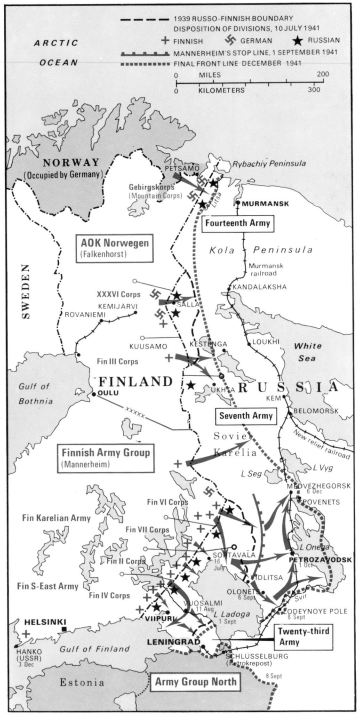

War, allowed his South-West Front (that is – army group) to engage in catastrophic battles rather than retreat in good time. At Kiev alone half a million Red soldiers were taken prisoner, and by mid-November Rostov had been taken by the invaders, as well as the Perekop Isthmus commanding the Crimea. In the center there had been a big tank battle near Smolensk, and a second battle at Bryansk had allowed the Germans to take Orel, Tula and Vyazma. In the north the Baltic states had been occupied and some formations had penetrated east of Leningrad. The much-publicized 'Stalin Line,' had been shown to be virtually non-existent.

# The Finnish Front, 1941

After their defeat by Russia in 1940 the Finns were, understandably enough, ready to join Germany in the Barbarossa attack in 1941 with the aim of recovering their lost territory. The Finnish front was strategically important because attacks there would probably help the German Army Group North to reach Leningrad.

With German help the Finnish forces were better prepared than in 1940. The Finnish mobilization system had been overhauled to increase the proportion of the country's manpower called up for military service and training had been improved.

The joint German and Finnish attack began on 19 June 1941. The earliest successes were in the area immediately north of Lake Ladoga and in August there were also important gains on the Karelian Isthmus. These almost reached Leningrad before being halted on Mannerheim's orders. In September, October and November there were further Finnish advances toward Lake Onega and farther north but by December the Finns had gone over completely to the defensive.

Opposite left: German troops take a rest
in recently captured Soviet trenches during
the early months of Barbarossa.
Below: Cossack cavalry charge across a
snowfield. Their main usefulness was in
harassing enemy rear areas.
Bottom: a German motor convoy drives
through a snowstorm during the first
winter of the Russian campaign.

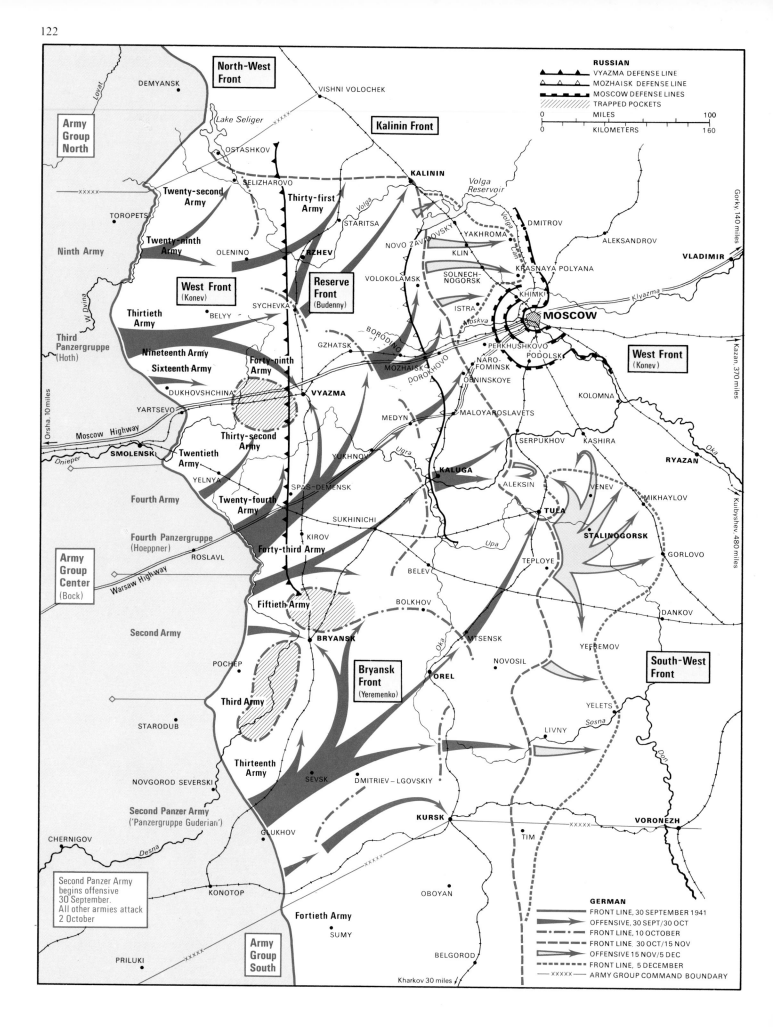

**North-West Front**

DEMYANSK

*Lovat*

**Army Group North**

**Ninth Army**

*Lake Seliger*

OSTASHKOV

SELIZHAROVO

TOROPETS

**Twenty-second Army**

**Twenty-ninth Army**

OLENINO

**Thirty-first Army**

RZHEV

*Volga*

STARITSA

VISHNI VOLOCHEK

**Kalinin Front**

KALININ

*Volga Reservoir*

NOVO ZAVIDOVSKY

YAKHROMA

KLIN

DMITROV

ALEKSANDROV

**VLADIMIR**

*Gorky, 140 miles*

*Kazan, 370 miles*

**RUSSIAN**
VYAZMA DEFENSE LINE
MOZHAISK DEFENSE LINE
MOSCOW DEFENSE LINES
TRAPPED POCKETS

0    MILES    100
0    KILOMETERS    160

**West Front**
(Konev)

SYCHEVKA

**Reserve Front**
(Budenny)

VOLOKOLAMSK

KRASNAYA POLYANA

SOLNECH-NOGORSK

HIMKI

ISTRA

*Moskva*

*Volga Can*

**Third Panzergruppe** (Hoth)

**Thirtieth Army**

BELYY

BORODINO

GZHATSK

MOZHAISK

DOROKHOVO

PERKHUSHKOVO

**MOSCOW**

PODOLSK

*Klyazma*

**West Front**
(Konev)

*Orsha, 10 miles*

**Nineteenth Army**

**Sixteenth Army**

**Forty-ninth Army**

DUKHOVSHCHINA

*W. Dvina*

YARTSEVO

VYAZMA

MEDYN

NARO-FOMINSK

OBNINSKOYE

MALOYAROSLAVETS

KOLOMNA

SERPUKHOV

KASHIRA

*Oka*

**RYAZAN**

*Kuibyshev, 480 miles*

Moscow Highway

**SMOLENSK**

**Twentieth Army**

**Thirty-second Army**

YELNYA

YUKHNOV

*Ugra*

KALUGA

ALEKSIN

VENEV

MIKHAYLOV

**Fourth Army**

YELNYA

SPAS-DEMENSK

**Twenty-fourth Army**

KIROV

**TULA**

**STALINOGORSK**

GORLOVO

**Fourth Panzergruppe** (Hoeppner)

ROSLAVL

*Upa*

TEPLOYE

**Forty-third Army**

SUKHINICHI

BELEV

DANKOV

**Army Group Center**
(Bock)

Warsaw Highway

*Dnieper*

**Fiftieth Army**

BOLKHOV

MTSENSK

YEFREMOV

**South-West Front**

**Second Army**

**Third Army**

POCHEP

**BRYANSK**

**Bryansk Front**
(Yeremenko)

*Oka*

**OREL**

NOVOSIL

YELETS

LIVNY

*Sosna*

STARODUB

**Thirteenth Army**

NOVGOROD SEVERSKI

SEVSK

DMITRIEV – LGOVSKIY

*Don*

**Second Panzer Army**
('Panzergruppe Guderian')

GLUKHOV

CHERNIGOV

*Desna*

Second Panzer Army begins offensive 30 September. All other armies attack 2 October

KONOTOP

**KURSK**

TIM

**VORONEZH**

**Fortieth Army**

SUMY

OBOYAN

BELGOROD

**Army Group South**

*Kharkov 30 miles*

PRILUKI

**GERMAN**
FRONT LINE, 30 SEPTEMBER 1941
OFFENSIVE, 30 SEPT/30 OCT
FRONT LINE, 10 OCTOBER
FRONT LINE, 30 OCT/15 NOV
OFFENSIVE 15 NOV/5 DEC
FRONT LINE, 5 DECEMBER
XXXXX — ARMY GROUP COMMAND BOUNDARY

Bottom: a German soldier struggles to extricate his motorcycle combination from the ubiquitous Russian mud. Particularly during the spring thaw, soft ground could virtually prevent movement by any type of vehicle.

# The German Attack on Moscow

Although the Russians had failed to hold Smolensk, the sturdy defense of that city had delayed the German advance on Moscow. Meanwhile, ahead of the German advance, the Russians were evacuating as much as possible of their factory equipment and key workers, intent on relocating them far to the east. The evacuation of railroad equipment meant that the Soviets had more locomotives and freightcars per mile of track, so Hitler's expectation of a transport breakdown was disappointed. The order for the capture of Moscow was issued on 2 October, and specified the encirclement of the city by 51 divisions, including 13 armored divisions. As the Germans closed in on the capital the fighting grew fiercer and,

for both sides, more desperate. The German and Russian high commands both knew that the delay at Smolensk meant that there would be little time to capture the Soviet capital before the onset of winter. In fact, the Germans never succeeded in totally encircling the city, whose lines of communication to the east remained open. This enabled the ministries to be evacuated and, in due course, permitted the arrival by train of fresh divisions from Siberia.

The Germans had virtual command of the air, although this advantage was not properly exploited so far as the ground fighting was concerned. Nevertheless, bombing was intense enough to cause the anniversary of the Russian revolution to be celebrated in an underground station of the Moscow Metro. Russian workers were given a week's training and sent to the front, while Moscow's women dug trenches and helped with supplies. By the end of November German units had reached the western suburbs but

two attempts to take the entire city by assault had failed. The encirclement was still incomplete and, moreoever, just as had happened to Napoleon's army in 1812, there had been an early onset of winter. In 1941, the temperature dropped to 40 degrees below zero as early as the first week of November. The Germans were not provided with winter clothing, nor was their equipment properly prepared. Engines of lorries and tanks froze up, with their cylinders sometimes cracking. Meanwhile the Siberian units had begun to arrive. On 8 December Hitler called off the attack for the duration of the winter. In effect this meant that, despite the shattering of the Red Army, Operation Barbarossa had failed. Neither Moscow nor Leningrad had been captured. Through Archangel, Murmansk, Persia and Vladivostok the USSR was beginning to receive shipments of war material from the west, while her own armaments industry was being re-established far behind the front.

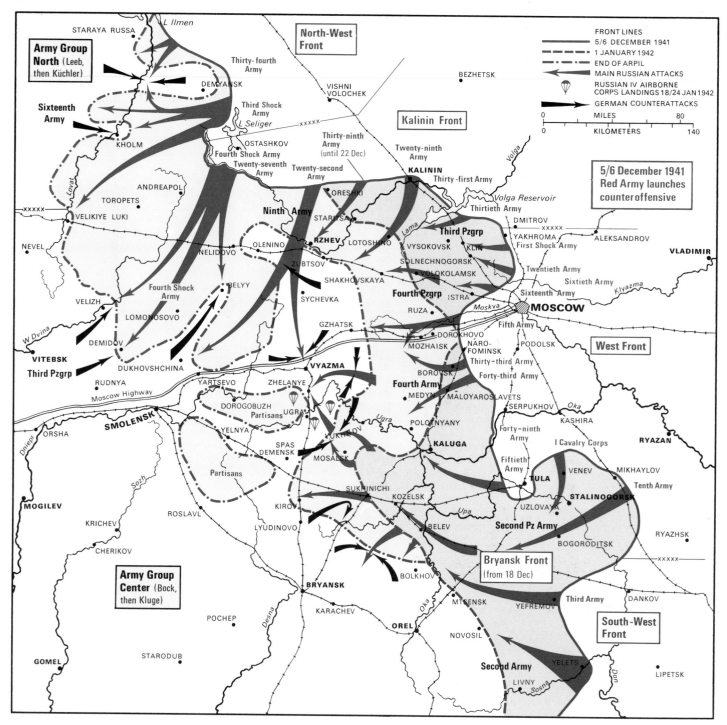

FRONT LINES
5/6 DECEMBER 1941
1 JANUARY 1942
END OF ARPIL
MAIN RUSSIAN ATTACKS
RUSSIAN IV AIRBORNE CORPS LANDINGS 18/24 JAN 1942
GERMAN COUNTERATTACKS

MILES 0 — 80
KILOMETERS 0 — 140

**5/6 December 1941 Red Army launches counter offensive**

# The Russian Counterattack, Moscow

On 8 December 1941 Hitler had announced a temporary suspension of operations outside Moscow, but the Soviet High Command soon showed that this was wishful thinking. It was, in fact, on the point of launching a counter-offensive for which it had been accumulating reserves over the previous weeks. Again, the situation of 1812 repeated itself, for the Soviet advance took

the form of a mass infiltration which avoided the strongest German points. Passing over fields rather than following the roads, making great use of Cossacks, ski troops and guerilla forces, the Soviets forced the Germans to withdraw from one position after another by threatening them with attacks from the flank or rear. The Germans were handicapped by the effect of low temperatures on their internal-combustion engines, which effectively put the Luftwaffe out of action, and by their difficult supply position, which relied on thinly spread railroad links, hampered by a change of gauge, and the very poor Russian roads.

The Germans were pushed back most in the center. Kalinin and Tula were retaken,

and the immediate threat to Moscow removed. The offensive continued to late February, by which time both sides were in need of rest and consolidation. This winter offensive had brought the Russians back as far as Velikiye Luki and Mozhaisk. At the same time, in the north the Germans had given ground around Leningrad, losing Tikhvin and control of Lake Ladoga, across which the Russians built a temporary ice road to the city. In the south the Kerch Isthmus was retaken and the Crimea re-entered, with Feodosia being reoccupied. In these Crimean operations the Red Navy played some role; it had been seriously crippled in the early days of the war and, neither very big nor very effective, its work

# The War at Sea

As well as the full-scale carrier battles of the Pacific War and the U-Boat struggle in the Atlantic (which are treated elsewhere) there were many other important and exciting facets of the worldwide naval war.

German U-Boats and surface raiders in fact served in every ocean of the world. The surface raiders, fast, long-range and heavily armed merchant ships, were most active in 1940–41 and during that time they sank more than 600,000 tons of Allied shipping. Major German warships also made a number of commerce-destroying sorties but these were less effective, largely because of restrictive orders from Hitler.

As well as the main transatlantic convoys the Allies had to protect the supplies being sent to northern Russia. If the inhospitable Arctic weather was not enough, these convoys passed close to German air and submarine bases and often came under constant attack. One convoy, PQ.17, was a notable disaster. Equally hard-fought were the battles to send supplies to Malta.

As well as their successively greater losses in the major battles the Japanese Navy found itself at an increasing disadvantage in small scale actions and in the Pacific-wide underwater war. Particularly in the later stages of the New Guinea and Solomons campaigns, the American PT-Boats and other small warships inflicted many losses on the Japanese supply units. There was an even greater imbalance in the effectiveness of the two submarine forces. Both sides succeeded in sinking some major warships but the Japanese had a very poor grasp of the importance of attacking supply and merchant ships. By contrast the Americans achieved a steadily growing degree of success in this field after early equipment problems had been overcome. The Japanese were very slow to institute a convoy system and their escorts' submarine detection equipment and antisubmarine armament were poor. At the outbreak of the war the Japanese merchant fleet had a carrying capacity of about six million tons. At the end of the war, despite the addition of new construction and captures, this had been reduced to just over one million tons. Expressed in other terms, Japan had gone to war largely to win access to the raw material resources of southeast Asia and the East Indies, and although much of this territory was still held by the Japanese in 1945 the resources were useless without the means of transporting them. Even round the Japanese Home Islands sea traffic was reduced to very small coastal vessels by 1945. The US submarine force played a vital part in the final Allied victory.

in the war would be largely confined to cooperation with the Red Army.

Meanwhile, the Germans, still ill-prepared for winter, settled down in their 'hedgehogs,' strongly fortified defensive positions, and awaited the arrival of fresh troops which Hitler had reluctantly decided to dispatch eastward.

When the Soviet offensive began Hitler immediately ordered that there should be no retreat by the German forces. Although the Germans were in fact pushed back in many areas it is now generally agreed by historians that Hitler's policy was correct in this case. After the initial Soviet strength had been expended it was found that the individual German positions could hold out, often with the help of supplies brought in by air, whereas a full scale retreat might well have been completely disastrous. The comparative success of the no retreat policy confirmed Hitler's belief in his own military judgment and his disdain for the advice of his generals.

ARCTIC OCEAN

Scharnhorst sunk,
26 Dec 1943

from
1941

MURMANSK

Arctic Circle

ARCHANGEL

REYKJAVIK

TRONDHEIM?

Supplies to Russ

LIVERPOOL

MOSCOW

KIEL

Battle of the Atlantic
(Peak 1941-43)

WILHELMSHAVEN

QUEBEC

ST. JOHNS

MONTREAL

LORIENT

HALIFAX

Bismarck sunk,
27 May 1941

NEW YORK

Mediterranean
partially closed
1940-43

1942

AZORES

GIBRALTAR

MALTA

Supplies
to Russia

HAIFA

ALEXANDRIA

1943-44

BA
SH

ATLANTIC OCEAN

SUEZ

1942

German Mid-Atlantic
refuelling zone

CAPE VERDE
IS

DAKAR

1942

Airborne supplies
to Middle East

PANAMA

PORT OF SPAIN

1942

TAKORADI

LAGOS

1943-

Equator

NATAL

1942

ASCENSION I

1939-40

1939-44

RIO DE JANEIRO

LOURENÇO
MARQUES

1939-44

CAPETOWN

MONTEVIDEO

Battle of the River Plate,
13 Dec 1939

1939-44

Graf Spee sunk,
13 Dec 1939

ANTARCTIC OCEAN

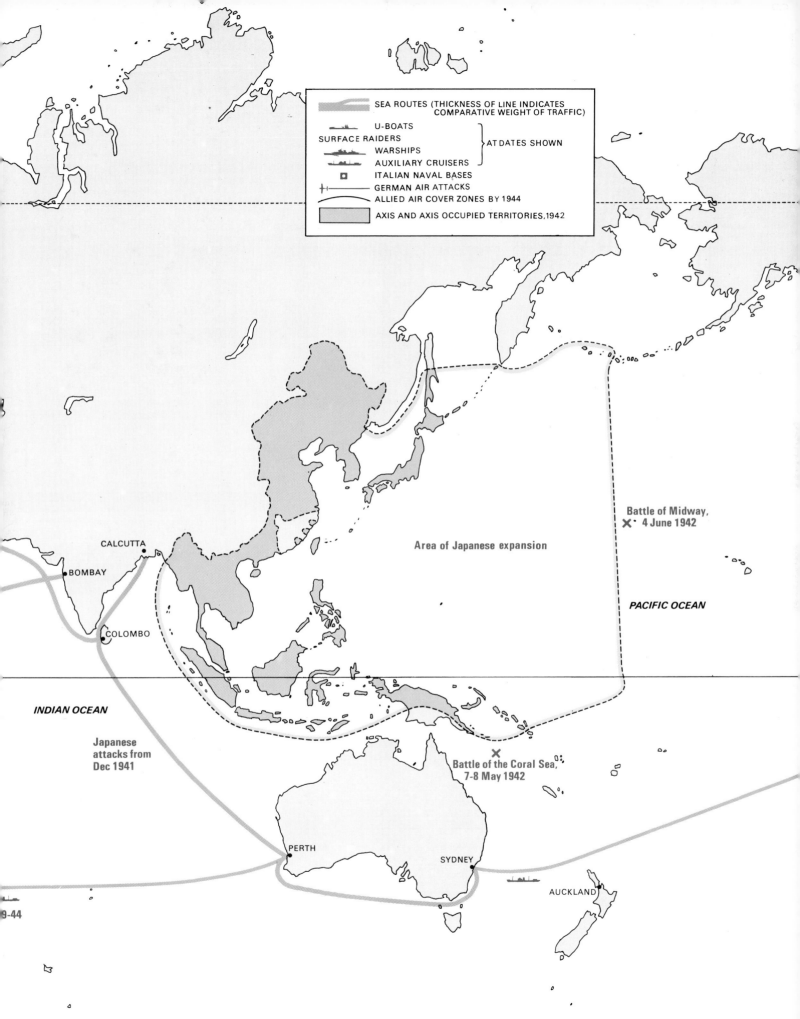

SEA ROUTES (THICKNESS OF LINE INDICATES COMPARATIVE WEIGHT OF TRAFFIC)

U-BOATS

SURFACE RAIDERS

WARSHIPS

AUXILIARY CRUISERS

ITALIAN NAVAL BASES

GERMAN AIR ATTACKS

ALLIED AIR COVER ZONES BY 1944

AXIS AND AXIS OCCUPIED TERRITORIES, 1942

AT DATES SHOWN

CALCUTTA

BOMBAY

COLOMBO

Area of Japanese expansion

Battle of Midway,
4 June 1942

PACIFIC OCEAN

INDIAN OCEAN

Japanese
attacks from
Dec 1941

Battle of the Coral Sea,
7-8 May 1942

PERTH

SYDNEY

AUCKLAND

9-44

MERCATOR PROJECTION

128

# The Battle of the Atlantic

Although the German submarine campaign of 1917 had nearly defeated Britain, Hitler's navy was not particularly well prepared to try to improve on this. Submarine building had not been given the highest priority and in the early months of the war Hitler imposed various restrictions on U-Boat operations to try to avoid offending neutral opinion. Drawing on the lessons of 1917 the British immediately introduced a convoy system but escorts could only be provided for part of some voyages and many ships sailed independently. Initially almost all U-Boat successes were from among these 'independents.' Nonetheless, in the first months of war U-Boat successes, although a serious problem, were certainly not out of control.

The events of June 1940 brought about a complete change. British naval responsibilities increased with the Italian entry into the war and the loss of the support of the French fleet, while the German strategic position was transformed by acquisition of bases in western France and Norway for the U-Boats and their supporting long-range reconnaissance aircraft. At this time also the U-Boats had many technical advantages. Their intelligence was good with the German Navy's B Dienst signals service having far more success with the British codes than the British were having with the German Enigma cipher machine. Although the British had Asdic equipment for detecting submerged submarines, radar was still comparatively primitive and escorts did not have sets capable of detecting U-Boats on the surface. A submarine on the surface could only be detected visually and at night a submarine was small and inconspicuous indeed. British patrol aircraft were few in number and, as well as lacking detection equipment, at this stage they were only armed with ineffective antisubmarine bombs. The Battle of the Atlantic became a struggle in all these fields; intelligence, technology, tactics, air support and others, as well as being in the obvious sense an industrial competition with graphs of merchant ship sinkings and cargoes delivered being compared with figures for new construction on both sides and for U-Boats lost. In each of these fields

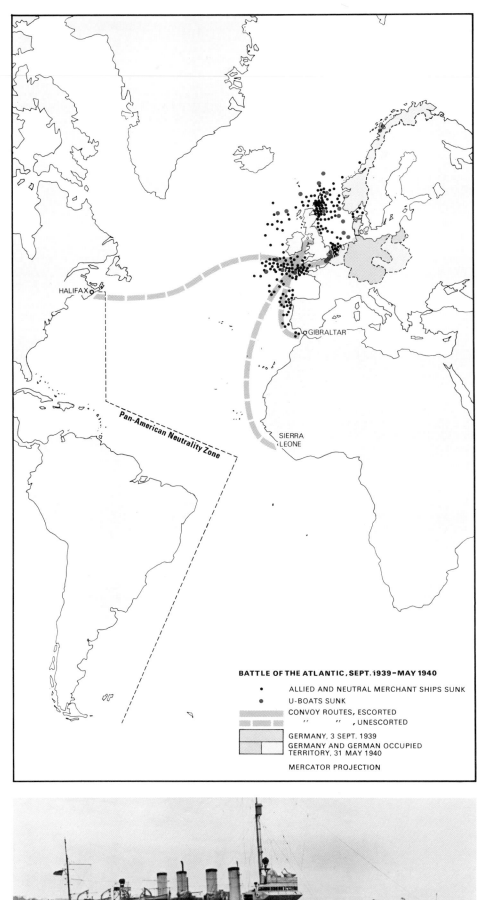

Bottom left: the American destroyer
*Reuben James* was the first US Navy ship
to be lost in World War II. She was sunk
by a U-Boat in October 1941 before the
USA joined the war.
Below: Admiral Dönitz directed the
German U-Boat offensive against Allied
merchant shipping.
Bottom: a tanker blazes after being
torpedoed by a U-Boat.

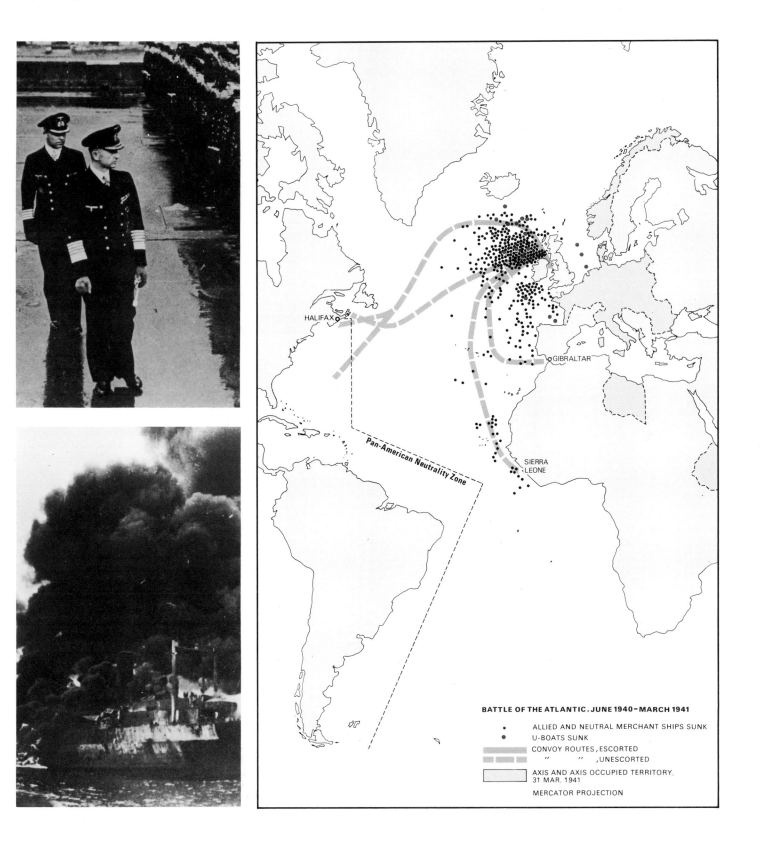

BATTLE OF THE ATLANTIC, JUNE 1940 – MARCH 1941

· ALLIED AND NEUTRAL MERCHANT SHIPS SUNK
● U-BOATS SUNK

CONVOY ROUTES, ESCORTED
" " , UNESCORTED

AXIS AND AXIS OCCUPIED TERRITORY,
31 MAR. 1941

MERCATOR PROJECTION

HALIFAX

GIBRALTAR

Pan-American Neutrality Zone

SIERRA
LEONE

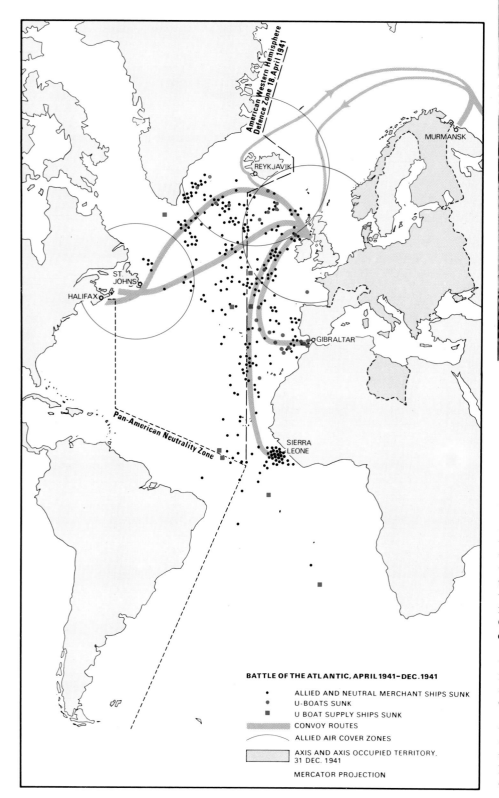

American Western Hemisphere
Defence Zone 18 April 1941

MURMANSK

REYKJAVIK

ST. JOHNS

HALIFAX

GIBRALTAR

Pan-American Neutrality Zone

SIERRA
LEONE

**BATTLE OF THE ATLANTIC, APRIL 1941–DEC. 1941**

· ALLIED AND NEUTRAL MERCHANT SHIPS SUNK

• U-BOATS SUNK

■ U BOAT SUPPLY SHIPS SUNK

CONVOY ROUTES

ALLIED AIR COVER ZONES

AXIS AND AXIS OCCUPIED TERRITORY,
31 DEC. 1941

MERCATOR PROJECTION

there were gradual developments and sudden breakthroughs.

For the second half of 1940 the U-Boats were on top and the period was known to the German submariners as the 'happy time.' A number of 'ace' commanders each achieved many successes. 'Wolf pack' tactics were developed in which a group of U-Boats made co-ordinated attacks on a convoy in order to swamp the escorts. However, by March 1941 the happy time was definitely over. The German U-Boat strength was virtually at its lowest point, the escort forces were becoming stronger, radar equipment was more widely available and in March three of the highest-scoring U-Boat aces were lost. Also in that month Churchill formed a high-level Battle of the Atlantic Committee (the first use of this title for the campaign) to oversee British efforts in all aspects of the struggle. The careful organization of military, industrial and scientific resources that this encouraged outmatched anything the Germans created and in time contributed greatly to Allied success.

The period from April to December 1941 was one of balance. The strength of the German operational U-Boat fleet was trebled but November 1941 showed the lowest shipping losses of the war to that date. There were various reasons for the

**Left: a US Navy submarine-chaser fires a depth charge at a suspected U-Boat contact off the United States Atlantic coast in 1942.**

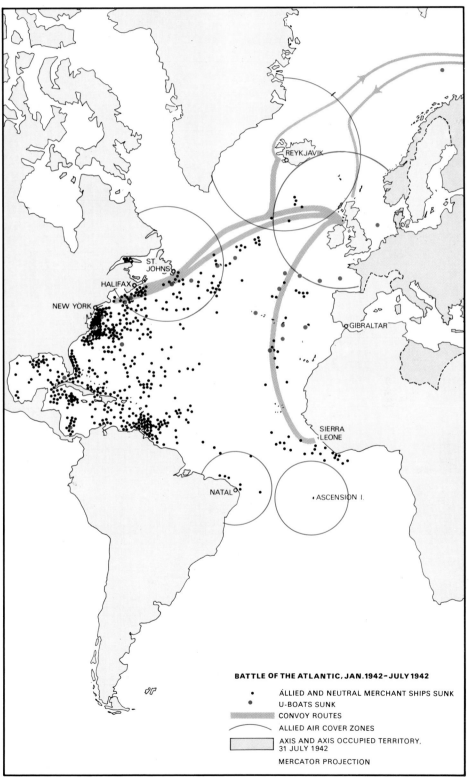

**BATTLE OF THE ATLANTIC, JAN. 1942 – JULY 1942**

- • ALLIED AND NEUTRAL MERCHANT SHIPS SUNK
- ● U-BOATS SUNK
- CONVOY ROUTES
- ALLIED AIR COVER ZONES
- AXIS AND AXIS OCCUPIED TERRITORY, 31 JULY 1942

MERCATOR PROJECTION

better Allied performance. The United States was moving into a more belligerent position both as an industrial supplier and as a military partner providing escorts for convoys in some areas. Following a breakthrough in May 1941 British intelligence was able to read many German signals until changes in February 1942. Convoys were therefore diverted away from U-Boat packs and U-Boats and their supply ships were intercepted and sunk.

The situation was transformed once more with the US entry into the war. U-Boats quickly began operations off the US East Coast and to their delight found virtually peacetime conditions prevailing. Ships sailed unescorted, showed lights at night and even on occasion sent radio signals giving their positions in plain language. The US Navy was naturally distracted by the sudden demands of the Pacific war but the anti-submarine patrols mounted were easily avoided by the U-Boats and were no substitute for even the least effective convoy system. Gradually, however, a convoy system was introduced and in July 1942 was extended south from Florida to cover most of the Caribbean. By the end of July the U-Boats were beginning to resume the struggle for the main North Atlantic convoy routes and their second happy time was over.

**Right: Pearl Harbor under attack by warplanes of the Imperial Japanese Navy on 7 December 1941.**

# Pearl Harbor

At 0755 local time on 7 December 1941 Japanese carrier aircraft attacked the main base of the US Pacific Fleet at Pearl Harbor. They gained complete strategic and tactical surprise. They sank or crippled five of the eight battleships in the port and destroyed 188 aircraft for the loss of 29 of the attacking planes.

The Japanese attack was planned by Admiral Yamamoto and the six aircraft carriers and two battleships of the strike force were led by Admiral Nagumo. The pilots were well trained and their equipment, some of it specially developed, was good. The fine Zero fighter in particular presented the Allies with many unforeseen problems in the months to come. There were, however, two omissions in the Japanese achievement. The US Pacific Fleet aircraft carriers were absent and escaped damage and the massive oil-storage facilities of the base were not struck as Nagumo's staff recommended. These factors combined to provide a solid foundation on which the industrial power of the United States could prepare a comeback. As the far-sighted Admiral Yamamoto had warned the other Japanese leaders,

Japan could expect a few months of success but would then be swamped.

Nonetheless the American authorities had little reason for complacency. US codebreaking services had intercepted a mass of low-level Japanese radio traffic which suggested that an attack, perhaps on Pearl Harbor, was imminent. More importantly, the highest-level Japanese diplomatic cipher had been broken and the final message to the Japanese ambassador in Washington was intercepted. Partly because it was a Sunday, this intercept was passed slowly and there was a delay in sending a warning.

The warning did not reach Pearl Harbor until around midday.

Peacetime customs and inexperience had important detailed effects also. Aircraft on Oahu airfields were parked vulnerably close together; boxes for antiaircraft ammunition were kept locked; large portions of ships' crews were ashore for the day; a submarine sighting by a patrol ship was ignored and a radar warning was disregarded.

The 'day of infamy' (President Roosevelt's description) convinced the American people of the need for war and in the end Yamamoto's prediction was proved correct.

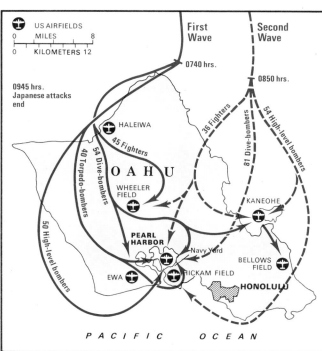

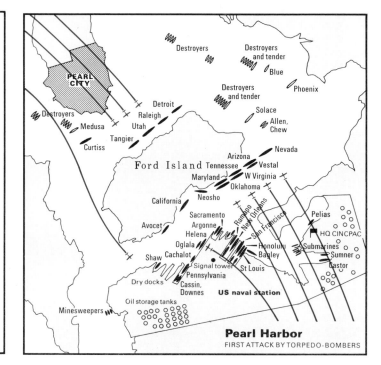

**Pearl Harbor**
FIRST ATTACK BY TORPEDO-BOMBERS

# The Conquest of Malaya

The British withdrawal in Malaya and the fall of Singapore on 15 February 1942 were described by Churchill as the worst disaster in British military history. The British, Australian and Indian forces lost 138,000 men. Many of the prisoners later died of maltreatment or were murdered in the Japanese prison camps. The Japanese lost less than 10,000 casualties. By their own most optimistic assessments the campaign was expected to last 100 days. It took only 70.

The Japanese forces deployed for the attack were three divisions from General Yamashita's Twenty-fifth Army. They were supported by about 200 tanks and 500 aircraft. The Allied infantry force was at least as strong but had virtually no tanks and few antitank weapons. General Percival was in command. The RAF had about 150 aircraft in Malaya, most of them old and inferior types. As well as their crucial advantages in tanks and aircraft the Japanese forces were much better trained and led. By contrast the British military and civilian administration of Malaya was riddled with lethargy and inefficiency. Disruptive peacetime practices of all sorts were maintained up to the start of hostilities and beyond. There was a prevailing attitude of racial contempt for the Japanese who were held to be technologically backward and individually unsuited for military service. Such obtuse racist attitudes were even applied in part to Indian and Malayan soldiers and officers in British service with obvious effects on their morale and fighting efficiency. In a more purely military reckoning the British forces were organized and prepared logistically for a European style of campaign which, in Malayan conditions, made them totally dependent on the few main roads for supplies and tactical movement. The Japanese preferred to travel light, often by bicycle with a ration bag slung over the handlebars, making use of minor roads and tracks and, on the west coast, minor amphibious operations. Little movement was attempted by either side in the true jungle but the Japanese were nonetheless much more flexible and mobile despite, and in part because of, the more lavish scale on which the Allied forces were provided with motor transport. The Jap-

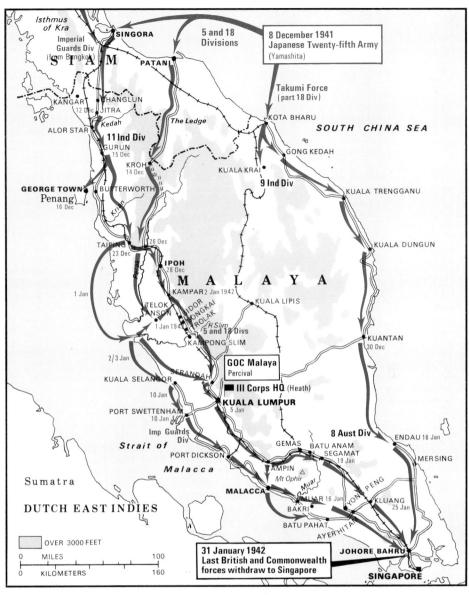

anese tactics were normally based on a combination of two simple techniques. Whenever possible minor roads or paths were used to outflank British forces who were consistently unable to tell whether they were being surrounded by a major force or being bluffed into retreat by a patrol. Alternatively when the Allied units held a strong position the Japanese tanks would break into the position along the main roads and force a retreat. In these ways the Allies were hustled from one defense line to another becoming more disorganized and dispirited as they went.

By the end of January only Singapore remained in British hands. The fleet which the great Singapore naval base had been built to nurture was already gone. The new battleship *Prince of Wales* and the older *Repulse* had been sent to Singapore specifically to deter the Japanese from attacking. They arrived only a few days before the outbreak of war, sailed to attack the Japanese landings on 8 December and were sunk with ease by Japanese aircraft on the 10th, leaving the Allies without a battleship in the Pacific.

The Singapore base did not long survive them. Japanese landings on Singapore Island began on the night of 8/9 February and the British forces surrendered on the 15th. The blow to British and European prestige was felt throughout southeast Asia.

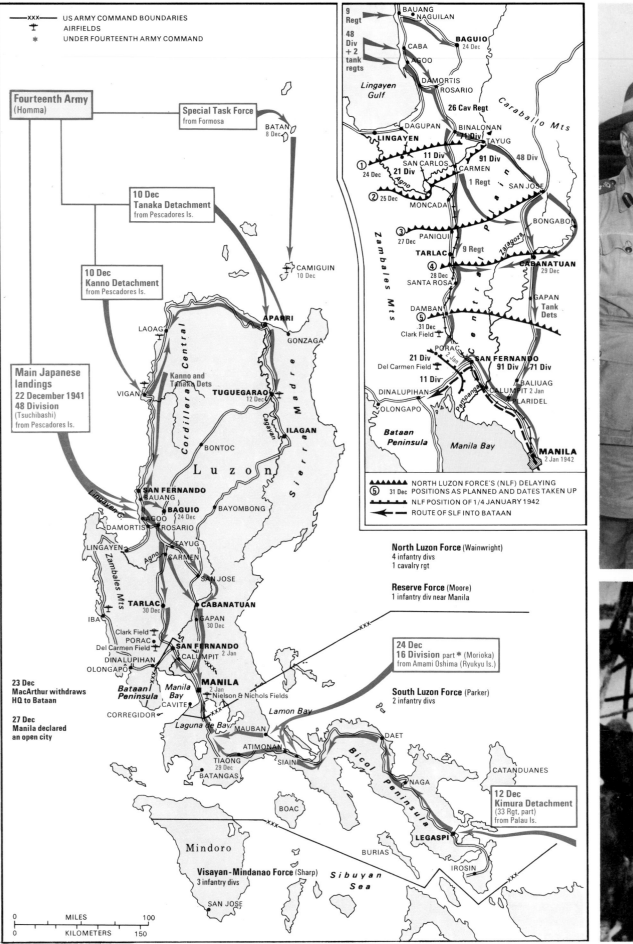

US ARMY COMMAND BOUNDARIES
✈ AIRFIELDS
∗ UNDER FOURTEENTH ARMY COMMAND

Fourteenth Army (Homma)

Special Task Force from Formosa
BATAN 8 Dec

10 Dec Tanaka Detachment from Pescadores Is.

10 Dec Kanno Detachment from Pescadores Is.

CAMIGUIN 10 Dec

Main Japanese landings 22 December 1941 48 Division (Tsuchibashi) from Pescadores Is.

APARRI
LAOAG
GONZAGA
Kanno and Tanaka Dets
VIGAN
TUGUEGARAO 12 Dec
ILAGAN
Cordillera Central
BONTOC
Luzon
Sierra Madre
Cagayan
SAN FERNANDO
BAUANG
BAGUIO 24 Dec
AGOO
ROSARIO
DAMORTIS
BAYOMBONG
Lingayen G.
Zambales Mts
LINGAYEN
TAYUG
Agno
CARMEN
SAN JOSE
IBA
TARLAC 30 Dec
CABANATUAN
GAPAN 30 Dec
Clark Field
PORAC
Del Carmen Field
SAN FERNANDO 2 Jan
DINALUPIHAN
CALUMPIT
OLONGAPO
Bataan Peninsula
Manila Bay
MANILA 2 Jan
Nielson & Nichols Fields
CAVITE
CORREGIDOR
Laguna de Bay
MAUBAN
Lamon Bay
TIAONG 29 Dec
ATIMONAN
SIAIN
BATANGAS
DAET
Bicol Peninsula
CATANDUANES
BOAC
NAGA
Mindoro
BURIAS
IROSIN
LEGASPI
Visayan-Mindanao Force (Sharp) 3 infantry divs
SAN JOSE
Sibuyan Sea

23 Dec MacArthur withdraws HQ to Bataan

27 Dec Manila declared an open city

MILES 0 100
KILOMETERS 0 150

North Luzon Force (Wainwright) 4 infantry divs 1 cavalry rgt

Reserve Force (Moore) 1 infantry div near Manila

24 Dec 16 Division part ∗ (Morioka) from Amami Oshima (Ryukyu Is.)

South Luzon Force (Parker) 2 infantry divs

12 Dec Kimura Detachment (33 Rgt, part) from Palau Is.

9 Regt
BAUANG
NAGUILAN
48 Div + 2 tank regts
CABA
BAGUIO 24 Dec
AGOO
DAMORTIS
ROSARIO
Lingayen Gulf
26 Cav Regt
Caraballo Mts
DAGUPAN
BINALONAN
71 Div
TAYUG
LINGAYEN
11 Div
91 Div
48 Div
① 24 Dec
SAN CARLOS
21 Div
CARMEN
1 Regt
SAN JOSE
② 25 Dec
Agno
MONCADA
BONGABON
③ 27 Dec
PANIQUI
Zaragoza
9 Regt
TARLAC
CABANATUAN 29 Dec
④ 28 Dec
SANTA ROSA
GAPAN Tank Dets
DAMBAN
⑤ 31 Dec
Clark Field
PORAC
Del Carmen Field 2 Jan
21 Div
SAN FERNANDO
91 Div
71 Div
11 Div
DINALUPIHAN
BALIUAG
Pampanga
CALUMPIT 2 Jan
PLARIDEL
OLONGAPO
Bataan Peninsula
Manila Bay
MANILA 2 Jan 1942

▲▲▲ NORTH LUZON FORCE'S (NLF) DELAYING
⑤ 31 Dec POSITIONS AS PLANNED AND DATES TAKEN UP
NLF POSITION OF 1/4 JANUARY 1942
ROUTE OF SLF INTO BATAAN

Left: General Douglas MacArthur commanded in the Philippines until President Roosevelt ordered him to leave. He is seen with General Blamey who led Australian troops in New Guinea under MacArthur's command later in the war. Bottom: Japanese Marines advance through Caba on Lingayen Gulf in December 1941.

# The Fall of the Philippines

As was the case elsewhere in Asia and the Pacific the Allied forces in the Philippines were ill-armed and badly prepared for war. Although the US and Filipino forces had been joined under General MacArthur's command since late July 1941 their training and equipment remained inadequate. MacArthur had about 31,000 regular troops, 19,000 of them American, and something over 100,000 Filipino conscripts to defend the Philippine archipelago. Although the largest force was on Luzon many units were unavoidably dispersed to the other islands of the group. The units on Luzon were divided into the North and South Luzon Forces. The prewar US plan for defending the Philippines was for strong ground and air forces there to hold out until the US Pacific Fleet could bring help. Clearly this would not be forthcoming after the Pearl Harbor attack. Much therefore depended on MacArthur's air strength but at the outbreak of war his air commander General Brereton only had 150 aircraft. By a combination of mismanagement and ill-luck more than half of these were knocked out in Japanese raids on the first day of war. (7 December, Pearl Harbor = 8 December Philippines because of the International Date Line.)

After some early landings to seize airfields for tactical support the main Japanese operation began on 22 December and by 24 December it was clear to MacArthur that he would have to order all his forces to retreat to the Bataan Peninsula. This retreat was successfully accomplished in the subsequent week. The Japanese believed that the campaign was then virtually over and withdrew their best infantry unit, the 48th Division, and a large part of their air support to be used in operations in the East Indies. Attacks by the less experienced Japanese units that remained had some success but by the end of January both they and the defenders were worn out and a long pause ensued. By April, however, the Japanese had built up their forces once more and their renewed attacks compelled an American surrender on the 9th. The final US positions on Corregidor were overrun on 5–6 May. General MacArthur had been evacuated from Bataan in March on orders from President Roosevelt, promising 'I shall return.'

# The Dutch East Indies

Owing to their important oil and other resources, the islands of the East Indies were a natural target for the Japanese offensive and once again Japanese air and naval superiority came into its own as the widely spaced garrisons were overwhelmed in turn. The elaborate Japanese plan called for three main lines of attack with comparatively limited ground and air forces being employed in each. The Eastern Force, for example, seized airfields at the northern tip of the Celebes and then used these air bases to cover attacks by the same units on Kendari and Amboina which in turn became bases for the next moves. This leap-frogging technique was repeated in each sector and made efficient and economical use of the forces available and every phase of the operation had powerful air support.

The outnumbered Allied ground and air forces generally fought well but any real check to the Japanese had to come from naval units. Two small actions – off Balikpapan on 24 January and in the Lombok Strait on 19/20 February – failed to achieve any conclusive success. In the larger scale Battle of the Java Sea on 27 February the Allied cruiser and destroyer squadron was decisively beaten and, having been dispersed, was almost wiped out in the next two days. Japanese naval and air supremacy was confirmed on 19 February when carrier aircraft led a devastating raid on Darwin in northern Australia. The Allied forces on Java were the last to succumb on 8 March. A formal surrender was agreed on 12 March 1942.

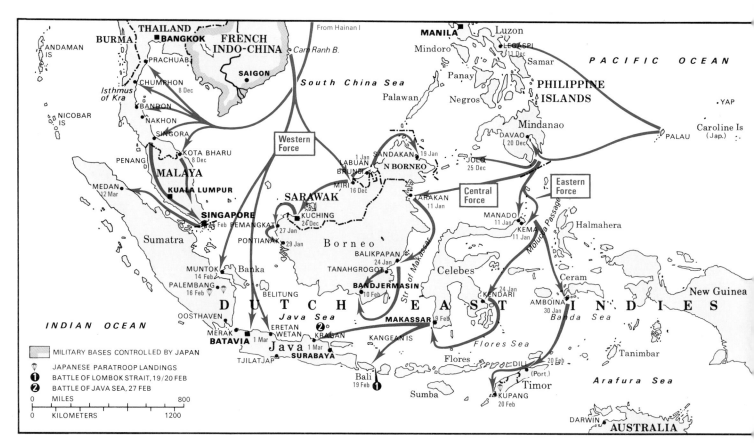

# The Japanese Invasion of Burma

With the invasion of Malaya going well the Japanese were ready to extend their offensive into Burma as they had planned. The attack began in mid-January when small units forced the British to abandon their airfields at Victoria Point and Mergui and was extended a few days later when the main body of Fifteenth Army, 33rd and 35th Divisions, moved on Moulmein. The defending forces were also about two divisions strong at this stage but the units had had little collective training and their equipment was poor.

The British plan was simply to defend as stubbornly as possible to prevent the Japanese from reaching Rangoon, the port through which all supplies and reinforcements had to flow. The Allied air forces initially had only one RAF squadron and one squadron of Chennault's American Volunteer Group (The Flying Tigers) to face over 200 Japanese aircraft, but they nonetheless had many successes both in defense of Rangoon and over the front line. On the ground too the battle was fairly well managed for the first three weeks of February, with the Allied forces gradually retreating to the Sittang River. Unfortunately on 23 February the one available bridge over the river was demolished prematurely when most of the 17th Indian Division was still on the wrong side.

After this disaster the pace of the Japanese advance increased and despite the appointment of General Alexander to take command of the British force and the arrival of the veteran British 7th Armoured Brigade, Rangoon quickly fell. The Japanese were now able to draw ground and air reinforcements from Malaya and advance in strength up the great river valleys. Chinese armies (each equivalent in strength to a European division) had by this time arrived to join the Allied forces but the best efforts of their American commander, General Stilwell, could not always make them fight effectively. Both they and the British were soon forced into rapid and continuous retreat. The remnants of the Allied force reached India in mid-May just as the monsoon was beginning to break. They had lost virtually all their heavy equipment.

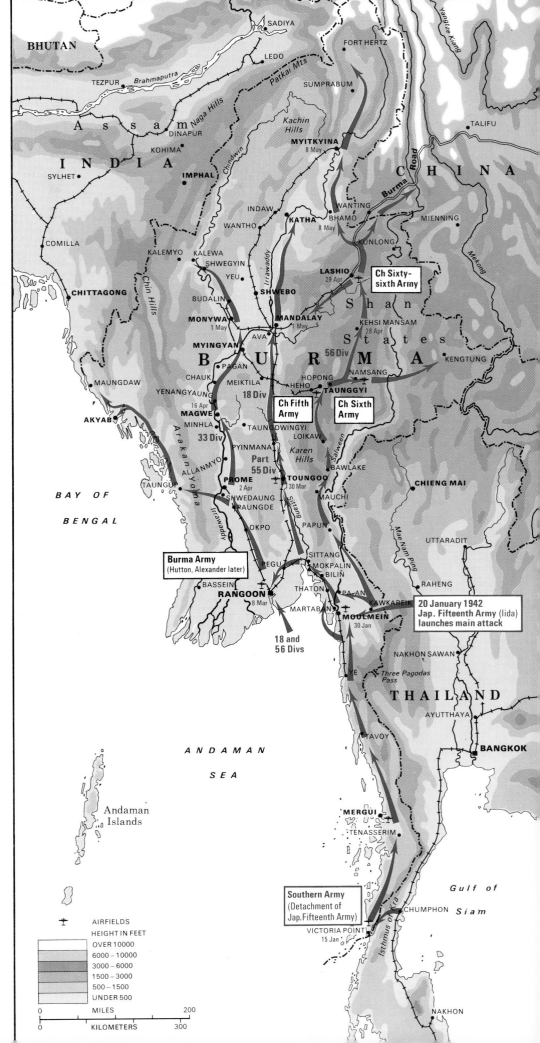

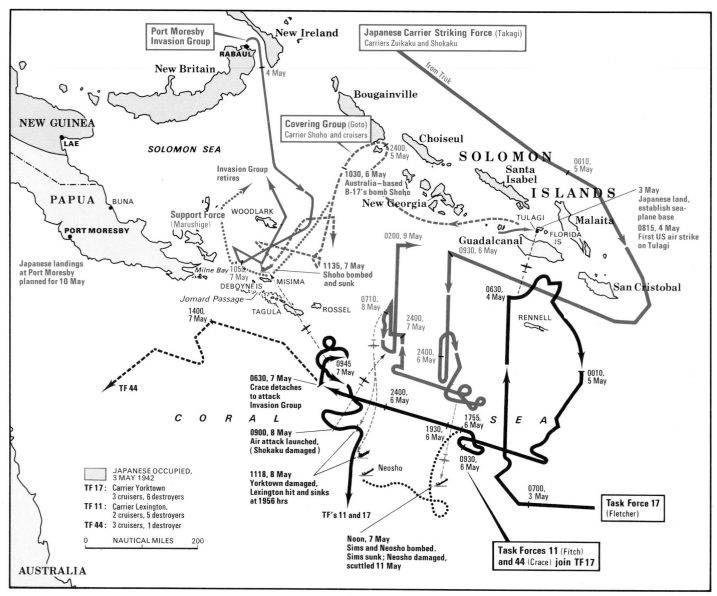

Port Moresby Invasion Group
RABAUL
New Ireland
Japanese Carrier Striking Force (Takagi)
Carriers Zuikaku and Shokaku
4 May
from Truk

New Britain
Bougainville

NEW GUINEA
LAE
SOLOMON SEA

Covering Group (Goto)
Carrier Shoho and cruisers

Choiseul
SOLOMON
Santa Isabel
0010, 5 May

2400, 5 May
Invasion Group retires

1030, 6 May
Australia–based
B-17's bomb Shoho

New Georgia
ISLANDS

3 May
Japanese land,
establish sea-
plane base
0815, 4 May
First US air strike
on Tulagi

PAPUA
BUNA

Support Force
(Marushige)
WOODLARK

TULAGI
Malaita

PORT MORESBY

Japanese landings
at Port Moresby
planned for 10 May

Milne Bay
DEBOYNE IS
1050, 7 May

1135, 7 May
Shoho bombed
and sunk

Guadalcanal
0930, 6 May
FLORIDA IS

San Cristobal

Jomard Passage
1400, 7 May
TAGULA
MISIMA
ROSSEL

0710, 8 May
0200, 9 May

0630, 4 May

RENNELL

0010, 5 May

TF 44

0945, 7 May

2400, 7 May

2400, 6 May

C O R A L

0630, 7 May
Crace detaches
to attack
Invasion Group

2400, 6 May

1755, 6 May
S E A

0900, 8 May
Air attack launched,
( Shokaku damaged )

1930, 6 May

0930, 6 May

0700, 3 May

1118, 8 May
Yorktown damaged,
Lexington hit and sinks
at 1956 hrs

Neosho

Task Force 17
(Fletcher)

JAPANESE OCCUPIED,
3 MAY 1942
TF 17 : Carrier Yorktown
3 cruisers, 6 destroyers
TF 11 : Carrier Lexington,
2 cruisers, 5 destroyers
TF 44 : 3 cruisers, 1 destroyer

0    NAUTICAL MILES    200

TF's 11 and 17

Noon, 7 May
Sims and Neosho bombed.
Sims sunk ; Neosho damaged,
scuttled 11 May

Task Forces 11 (Fitch)
and 44 (Crace) join TF 17

AUSTRALIA

# The Battle of the Coral Sea

Because of the ease with which they had achieved their many successes in the first months of 1942, the Japanese High Command began to consider extending the defensive perimeter which was being set up. This intention was confirmed by the Doolittle Raid on 18 April when bombers launched from an aircraft carrier attacked Tokyo to the shock and dismay of the Japanese leaders. Part of the plan for extending the perimeter was a decision to move into southern Papua by an amphibious attack on Port Moresby. This led to the Battle of the Coral Sea.

The Battle of the Coral Sea holds an important place in naval history as the first naval battle in which the opposing fleets were never in visual contact, leaving the action to be fought entirely by aircraft. Forewarned by codebreaking information the

Americans were able to have two carriers in position to face the Japanese as well as a force of cruisers and destroyers. In addition to the two carriers sent to cover the whole operation the Japanese had a third small carrier in closer support of the invasion group.

The first flurry of action was on 3–4 May when a Japanese seaplane base was established on Tulagi and then attacked the next day by aircraft from the USS Yorktown. The Americans then moved south to concentrate their forces and refuel just as the main Japanese operations were getting under way. The action was not renewed until 7 May when Japanese carrier aircraft successfully attacked an American tanker and a destroyer while heavy attacks by land-based aircraft failed to damage any ships of TF.44 which had been unwisely sent to cut off the Japanese Invasion Group. However, American carrier aircraft scored an important success by sinking the Sholo. By now the main carrier groups each knew the other's position and a full-scale battle was fought on the 8th. The Japanese lost more aircraft but did

more damage to the American ships especially after errors in damage control contributed to the loss of the Lexington. However, with their air strength dissipated the Japanese carriers had to withdraw and the invasion of Port Moresby was cancelled. Thus although the battle was perhaps a draw tactically it was a clear strategic victory for the Americans.

**Below left: Yamamoto, Japan's greatest naval strategist and architect of the Pearl Harbor attack.**
**Right: the Japanese heavy cruiser *Mikuma* abandoned and sinking on 6 June 1942 during the Battle of Midway.**

# The Battle of Midway

The Japanese High Command decision to extend their defensive perimeter had led firstly to the Battle of the Coral Sea but it was also the motive for the Japanese attack on Midway and the decisive battle which developed there. The Coral Sea battle had important effects on the Midway operation. The two Japanese carriers from the earlier battle were not repaired quickly enough to go to Midway nor were the survivors of their air groups used to bolster the Japanese strength on the other carriers. The Japanese also believed that the *Yorktown* was too seriously damaged to be made ready in time for Midway. In fact she returned to Pearl Harbor with damage that would certainly have taken months to repair in peacetime but she was patched up in 48 hours.

The false assessment of *Yorktown*'s status was only one of a number of intelligence and planning factors that contributed to the Japanese defeat. Admiral Yamamoto believed that, as well as the *Yorktown* being out of action, the other American carriers available, the *Enterprise* and *Hornet*, were likely to be in the South Pacific. Even if this was not the case diversionary attacks on the Aleutians were planned so that the Americans would be distracted from the landings on Midway. Once the capture of the island was complete, the Japanese, warned by their submarine patrols, would destroy the American forces in an all-out battle. Unfortunately for the Japanese the Americans were able to repeat their previous codebreaking successes and thus forewarned they were able to move their carriers into position before the Japanese patrols were established and equally able to disregard the Aleutians attacks so that these became in effect a wasteful dispersal of the Japanese resources (two powerful light carriers and many other ships were employed in the Aleutian operations). The various Midway forces were also widely dispersed leaving further small aircraft and seaplane carriers effectively out of the battle when their scout planes might well have been of decisive help and leaving Nagumo's carriers with only a few ships in company to provide supporting AA fire.

The Japanese were sighted approaching on 3 June and the action began in earnest on 4 June. The Japanese started by virtually wiping out the defending aircraft based on Midway at little cost to themselves. However it was not until the Japanese were ready to recover their aircraft from the first strike that their scouts found the American carriers. The American carrier aircraft were already on their way and made a series of attacks before the Japanese had reorganized to defend properly. Three of the four Japanese carriers were crippled and later sank. The fourth Japanese carrier, the *Hiryu*, fought back causing the *Yorktown* to be abandoned but the *Hiryu* herself was put out of action later in the day. The Japanese leaders made half-hearted attempts on 5 June to close in and fight a gun action with their vastly superior surface forces but the Americans refused to be drawn and the whole operation was abandoned.

Midway was one of the most decisive battles of the war for not only had the Japanese lost four of their best aircraft carriers but with them had gone the cream of their carrier pilots and crews. While they still had a useful supply of aircraft and aircraft carriers the veteran flyers could not be replaced. The next major naval battles in the Pacific, although close fought, would follow the American advance against Guadalcanal. The Japanese had irrevocably lost the initiative.

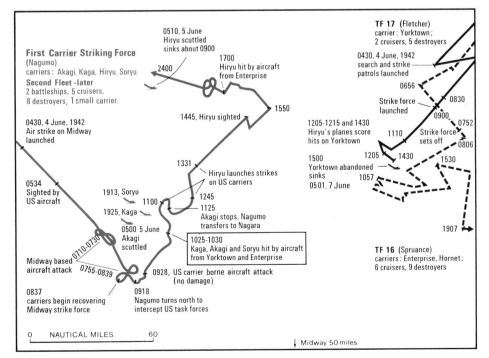

**Right:** Rommel in a *Befehlswagen*
(command vehicle) in North Africa in 1942.
Rommel always tried to keep in close touch
with events in the front line.

# Rommel's Advance into Egypt

Even as he retreated following the prolonged
Crusader battles for Tobruk Rommel was
looking for an opportunity to riposte. His
supply and reinforcement position was improving as Malta came under ever heavier
attack and the British communications
were naturally being extended by their
advance as well as their forces being weakened by withdrawals of troops for the Far
East leaving inexperienced units, notably
1st Armoured Division, at the front.

Rommel's German Units (DAK,
*Deutsches Afrika Korps*) began probing
attacks on 21 January 1942 and in less than
three weeks had hustled the British forces
back to a line from Gazala to Bir Hacheim,
inflicting many casualties. Eighth Army
morale was severely damaged in the process,
with the lack of trust between infantry and
tank units that had become evident during
the Crusader battles being further confirmed.

This lack of trust and cooperation became
even more obvious when Rommel resumed
his offensive on 26 May. Faulty intelligence
information and Rommel's bold plan placed
the German forces in a very weak position
initially but General Ritchie failed to order
counterattacks sufficiently promptly to take
advantage. When the counterattacks were
made they were poorly organized and the
numerically-superior British armor was
squandered. Rommel's forces then burst
forward and stormed into Tobruk on 20
June capturing men and supplies.

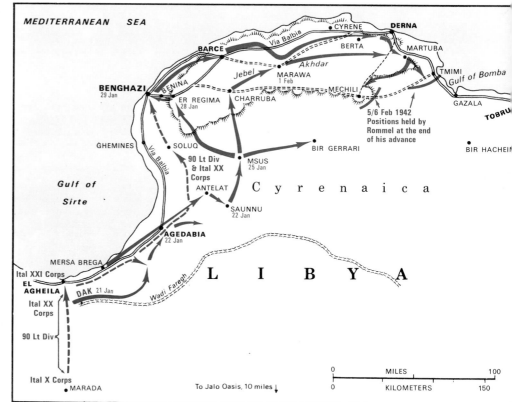

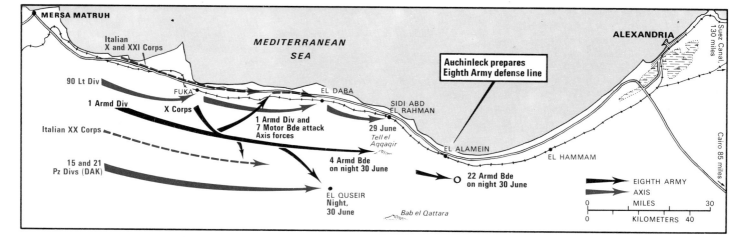

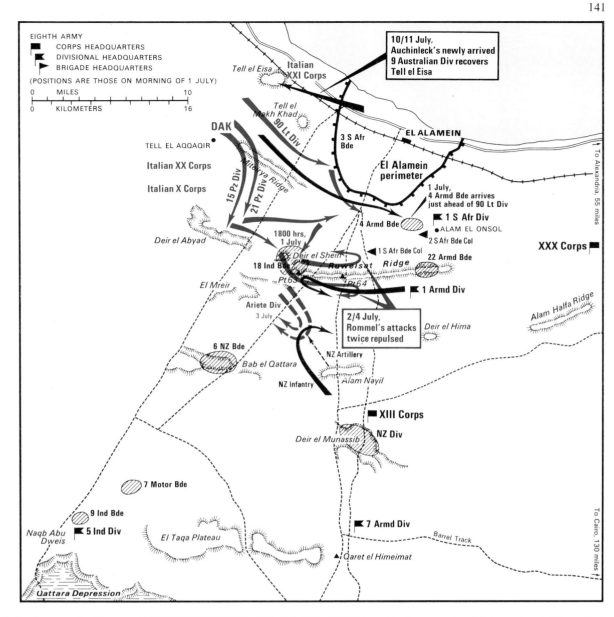

# The First Battle of Alamein

At this point the Axis plan was for Rommel to pause while the German and Italian naval and air forces concentrated for an invasion of Malta but, as the hero of the hour, the newly promoted Field Marshal Rommel successfully argued for this plan to be abandoned in favor of an advance to Egypt using the newly captured supplies.

Nonetheless there is no doubt that the British were in considerable disarray and their next attempt to halt Rommel, at Mersa Matruh on 26–27 June, was soon overcome leaving yet more booty to fall into German hands. General Auchinleck, the British Commander in Chief, Middle East, had now taken over tactical command of Eighth Army having sacked General Ritchie, and his firmer control soon became evident. However the retreat had to continue to the next defensible position which was being prepared by Auchinleck's few reserve units in a line south from a small rail station called El Alamein. The move from Mersa Matruh to Alamein was one of the most curious of the war, with advancing Axis columns mixed with retreating British.

After the headlong retreat from Mersa Matruh the next defensible position for the Eighth Army was at El Alamein where the gap between the more or less impassable Qattara Depression and the sea was fairly narrow. Although Auchinleck had only a few imperfectly organized reserve units with which to prepare the position in addition to those retreating to it, Rommel's situation was hardly better. He was relying almost entirely on the booty from Tobruk and Mersa Matruh to provide his fuel and other supplies. The recent battles had also reduced his strength severely until he had less than 2000 German infantry and perhaps 65 German tanks. Nonetheless Rommel was confident that if he could maintain his momentum he could bounce the British out of their position and strike for the Nile.

However the initial German and Italian attacks were fought to a standstill on 2–4 July, a feature of the battle being the improved coordination of Eighth Army's artillery units. Auchinleck was now ready to make some limited counterattacks and chose the Italian *Sabratha* Division at Tell El Eisa as his first victim on 10–11 July. This and other minor operations over the next few days compelled Rommel to spend precious fuel moving his German units to help the Italian formations which were the deliberately-chosen British targets. There were larger Allied efforts in the Ruweisat Ridge area on 14 and 21–22 July and, although the British armor lost heavily because of poor cooperation with its supporting infantry and poor tactics, Rommel's forces too were worn out.

Although General Auchinleck's refusal to continue these attacks completed Churchill's disillusion with his leadership and lost him his command, many commentators now regard this series of actions, together known as the First Battle of El Alamein, as marking the real turning point in North Africa rather than the famous Second Battle.

# The German Advance to Stalingrad

In early April Hitler issued his instructions for the 1942 offensive. This time the central sector was to remain fairly quiet, while in the north the capture of Leningrad was envisioned. However, the main effort was to be in the south. Here the Red Army was to be engaged and beaten on the River Don, which would permit an advance to the prized Caucasian oilfields and the capture or neutralization of Stalingrad which, apart from being 'Stalin's City,' was an important rail and river center, and also the site of tank and armament factories. In preparation for this campaign General Manstein expelled the Red Army from the Kerch Peninsula and captured the Crimea, including the naval base of Sevastopol.

The main offensive by Army Group South was delayed for four weeks by a big Soviet attack at Kharkov, so it did not begin until the end of June. But it made good progress and reached the Don in mid-July. Here it was held by a Soviet counteroffensive at Voronezh, but in the south Rostov was again captured by the Germans. At this point

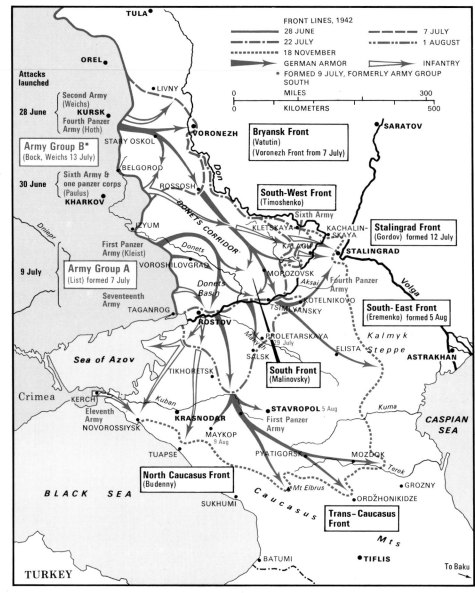

Below left: a Soviet gun crew firing in
Stalingrad's factory district during the
bitter fighting in 1942.
Below: Soviet Illyushin IL-2s were very
successful ground-attack aircraft, but
suffered heavy losses.

Hitler appears to have changed the emphasis of his attack; Stalingrad was to be the main target, although the Caucasian oilfields were to remain a priority. His staff officers realized that, with the Red Army still not decisively beaten, this division of effort was strategically risky, but they were overruled and some were dismissed by Hitler.

In the Caucasus the German Army Group A did make a rapid advance, capturing Novorossiysk. Paradoxically, shortly after occupying the outlying Maykop oilfield, the German advance ran out of fuel. The main

Caucasian oilfields remained out of reach; the allocation of 300,000 troops to the capture of Stalingrad meant that the Caucasus thrust had not achieved its main object.

The German attack on Stalingrad was a simple frontal assault. To have encircled the city would have entailed crossing the Volga, which the Germans felt unable to undertake with the resources available. The Russians deliberately kept as few men as possible in the city itself, relying on high morale and determination to ensure that the Germans would need to fight bitterly for every street

and building. This in fact is what happened. Soviet soldiers, joined by armed civilians, withdrew only inch by inch as shells and bombs destroyed the city about their ears. More and more German units were drawn into the brutal struggle while the Soviet commanders were able to husband their forces and prepare for a counteroffensive.

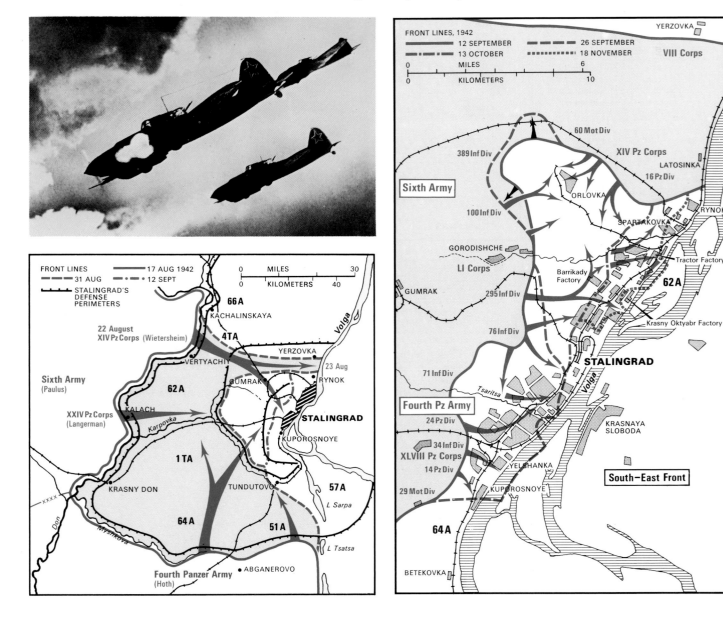

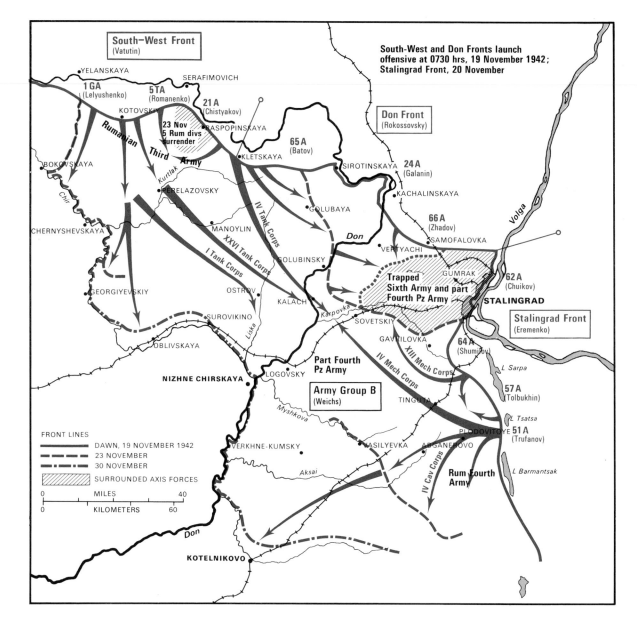

Map labels:

South-West Front (Vatutin)

South-West and Don Fronts launch offensive at 0730 hrs, 19 November 1942; Stalingrad Front, 20 November

YELANSKAYA
1 GA (Lelyushenko)
5 TA (Romanenko)
SERAFIMOVICH
21 A (Chistyakov)
KOTOVSKIY
RASPOPINSKAYA
23 Nov 5 Rum divs surrender
Rumanian Third Army
Kurtlak
Chir
BOKOVSKAYA
PERELAZOVSKY
CHERNYSHEVSKAYA
MANOYLIN
XXVI Tank Corps
IV Tank Corps
I Tank Corps
GEORGIYEVSKIY
OSTROV
SUROVIKINO
Liska
OBLIVSKAYA
KLETSKAYA
65 A (Batov)
GOLUBAYA
GOLUBINSKY
KALACH
Karpovka
SOVETSKIY
Don
SIROTINSKAYA
24 A (Galanin)
KACHALINSKAYA
Don Front (Rokossovsky)
66 A (Zhadov)
SAMOFALOVKA
VERTYACHI
Trapped Sixth Army and part Fourth Pz Army
GUMRAK
62 A (Chuikov)
STALINGRAD
Volga
Stalingrad Front (Eremenko)
64 A (Shumilov)
L Sarpa
Part Fourth Pz Army
GAVRILOVKA
XIII Mech Corps
IV Mech Corps
57 A (Tolbukhin)
NIZHNE CHIRSKAYA
LOGOVSKY
Army Group B (Weichs)
TINGUTA
L Tsatsa
Myshkova
VERKHNE-KUMSKY
VASILYEVKA
ABGANEROVO
PLODOVITOYE
51 A (Trufanov)
Rum Fourth Army
L Barmantsak
Aksai
IV Cav Corps
Don
KOTELNIKOVO

FRONT LINES
——— DAWN, 19 NOVEMBER 1942
—·—·— 23 NOVEMBER
—··—··— 30 NOVEMBER
▨ SURROUNDED AXIS FORCES
0 MILES 40
0 KILOMETERS 60

# The Stalingrad Counteroffensive

While Soviet resistance inside Stalingrad prevented the Germans capturing that city in its entirety, the Soviet High Command was assembling forces north of the Don for a counteroffensive. The general situation was that the German general, Paulus, had about 300,000 men concentrated to the west of Stalingrad. His northwest flank was protected by Italian and Rumanian troops while on his southern flank he had more Rumanian units.

The Soviet offensive began on 19 November 1942. It consisted of some diversionary action on the central, Moscow, front with the aim of attracting German reinforcements which otherwise might be sent to Stalingrad, and the main thrust, which was to relieve Stalingrad. General Zhukov, disposing of the whole Soviet operational reserve, had three army groups ['fronts'] which were to attack from the north, south, and northwest, initially concentrating their blows on the Italians and Rumanians, whose morale was lower than the Germans'. In fact the Italian and Rumanian positions in the northwest soon crumbled, enabling the Soviet troops to penetrate into the German rear and then link up with the Stalingrad Front advancing westward from its concentration area in the south. Paulus was now surrounded but Hitler, assured by Göring that an airlift could keep the encircled troops supplied, insisted that the siege of Stalingrad should continue. In mid-December General Manstein led an attack which broke through the Russian lines, by then far to the west, in an attempt to relieve Paulus, but the Soviet high command, diverting troops from the battle with Paulus, blocked this move. With Hitler's agreement Paulus made no attempt to break out and join Manstein. The Red Army could then turn back to the steady destruction of Paulus's Sixth Army. On 2 February 1943 the German forces at Stalingrad surrendered, after being reduced to little more than a headquarters and isolated detachments. Although the Germans had been defeated earlier by the British at El Alamein, this was the first really major defeat suffered by the German Army and had an enormous psychological effect. Hitler had shown incompetent generalship; his refusal to allow Paulus to withdraw from Stalingrad while there was still time was directly responsible for this catastrophic defeat. Many thousands of the German troops taken prisoner died in Russian camps. Many were held for several years after the end of the war.

# The Battle of Alam Halfa

Despite the defensive success of the First Battle of El Alamein, Churchill arrived in the Middle East early in August 1942 determined to make changes. After some deliberation General Alexander was chosen to replace Auchinleck as Commander in Chief and Montgomery arrived to take over at Eighth Army. It was clear that Rommel was going to attack again soon in an effort to reach the Nile before the British forces were fully rebuilt after the disasters of the summer. While historians generally compliment Montgomery on his conduct of the Battle of Alam Halfa which resulted, most believe that it was fought along lines already laid down by Auchinleck. However, some authorities suggest that Montgomery's determined and vigorous leadership was needed to transform a previously half-hearted plan.

Broadly speaking the defense plan was to hold the northern half of the line very strongly while guarding against a 'right hook' outflanking maneuver by fortifying the Alam Halfa Ridge and deploying strong armored forces in the southern area. Such an outflanking move was exactly Rommel's aim but a combination of unexpectedly strong British forward defenses, harrassing air attacks and fuel shortages forced him to turn north earlier than planned. Although some British tank units suffered heavily, the German attacks on Alam Halfa Ridge foundered on an improved British antitank defense system. On 2 September Rommel ordered a retreat. By 6 September the Axis forces were back where they started and settling down to meet a British attack.

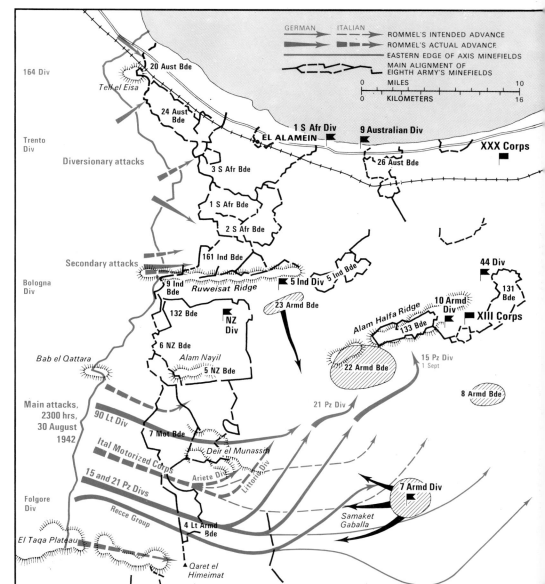

# Advance in the Caucasus

Even before Paulus surrendered at Stalingrad the Soviet High Command was able to divert part of its southern, Stalingrad Front to the southwest toward Rostov, the aim being to cut off the German Army Group A in the Caucasus. The Soviet advance was so rapid that Rostov was indeed threatened by the beginning of January. At the same time, the Russian Trans-Caucasus Front, which hitherto had been merely holding back the Germans on the line of the Terek River, launched a counteroffensive. Threatened from both north and south, Kleist, the commander of Army Group A, decided that an immediate withdrawal was the only guarantee of survival. But he was too late to escape through Rostov. Only one of his armies, the motorized First Panzer Army, achieved this. The remainder of Kleist's troops took refuge in the Taman Peninsula.

Here they were beset by both Soviet fronts and driven into a small defended area around Novorossiysk. Rostov fell in mid-February.

By this time, although the Russian tactics of mass assault continued to cause them casualties several times higher than those suffered by the Germans, and although the losses of the first months of the war had not been replaced, the Red Army had become a formidable fighting force. One reason for this was the psychological effect of the Stalingrad battle which removed the last trace of defeatism from the Russian ranks. Another was that the ineffective Party generals like Voroshilov and Budyenny had been removed to positions where they could do less harm to the military effort.

**Right: Manstein headed the German Army Group Don during the Kharkov battles. He had devised the plan for the attack on France in 1940 and is regarded as one of the most able generals of the war.**

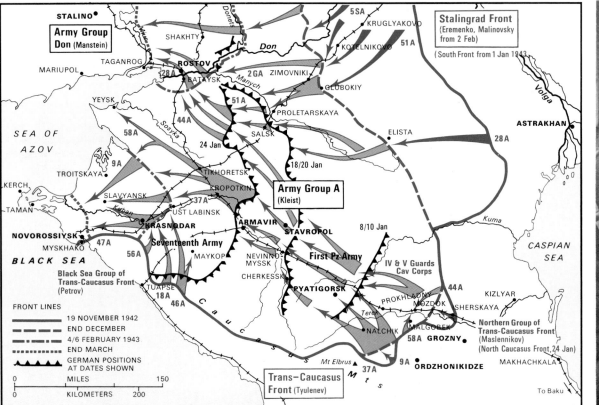

**Bottom: Russian soldiers in the northern Caucasus during the battle for Yuzel settlement. The soldier on the left is armed with an obsolescent antitank rifle.**

# The Advance to Kharkhov and the German Counterattack

Before the defeats of World War I the Russian Army had been popularly known as the 'Russian Steamroller.' By 1943 it was evident to the Germans that this description was still applicable. The USSR had lost millions of men and enormous expanses of its most productive territory, yet more and more well-equipped divisions were entering service. Even while they were squeezing the last remnants of Paulus's army in Stalingrad, the Russians were undertaking offensives not only in the Caucasus, but also in the Ukraine, with Kharkov as its main objective.

The Soviet High Command devoted four fronts to this attack, including the new

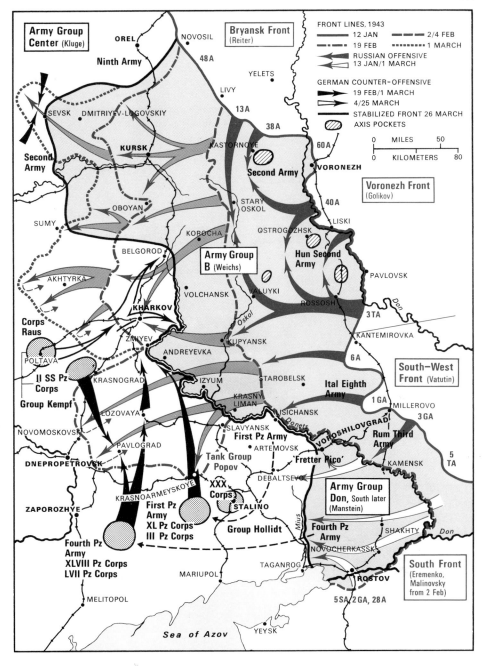

South Front comprising divisions released from Stalingrad. The northern prong of the attack made dramatic advances, surrounding much of the German Second Army and putting the rest to flight. In the center, Kharkov was captured early in February, while in the south the Russian advance went equally well at first, although in its onward rush it created vulnerable salients Manstein, commanding Army Group Don, exploited the opportunity to attack the strong but over-extended Southwest Front. He assembled a reconstituted army of 24 divisions, of which 12 were armored, around Dnepropetrovsk and moved north to engage the Russians south of Kharkov, pushing them back over the River Donets and, on 2 March, recapturing Kharkov. After this effort the exhaustion of both sides, and the onset of the thaw, brought the winter campaign of 1942–43 to a halt. Despite

Manstein's technically brilliant attacks the manpower losses of the winter campaign had been disastrous for the Germans.

Right: British Crusader Mark III cruiser tanks in North Africa.
Below: Allied tanks await orders to move forward during the Battle of El Alamein. The wartime censor has removed the unit markings on the tank.
Below far right: One member of a German tank crew surrenders as British infantry rush his tank.

# El Alamein

Following their defeat in the Battle of Alam Halfa and bearing in mind their continuing fuel supply problems which that battle highlighted, the German leaders prepared to conduct the next battle in the North African theater from strong defense lines rather than rely on the mobility which had been the Afrika Korps' trade mark in the past. Although the forward defenses were mainly manned by Italian troops, German units were intermingled with them to provide extra strength and reliability. The fuel shortage meant that the armored reserve had to be split up to ensure that at least part of it would have enough fuel to reach any threatened sector. For the month before the battle Rommel was in Germany on sick leave and General Stumme commanded in his place. Rommel returned to Africa on 25 October after the battle was under way.

Throughout his earlier career General Montgomery had shown himself to be deeply concerned with improving the morale and training of the troops, and planning the battle meticulously before beginning to fight. This concern was nowhere more evident than in the preparation for Alamein. Many of the faults which had affected Eighth Army in the past were ironed out and confidence was high. The plan, as shown below, was for infantry units of XXX Corps to win corridors through the Axis minefields through which the armor of X Corps would pass unhindered, ready to meet and destroy the German tanks in open ground.

Despite the careful preparations on which Montgomery insisted, the actual events were only broadly similar to this plan. The powerful preparatory artillery barrage helped the infantry attacks to make a good start

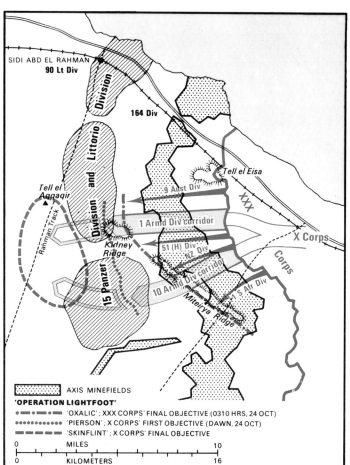

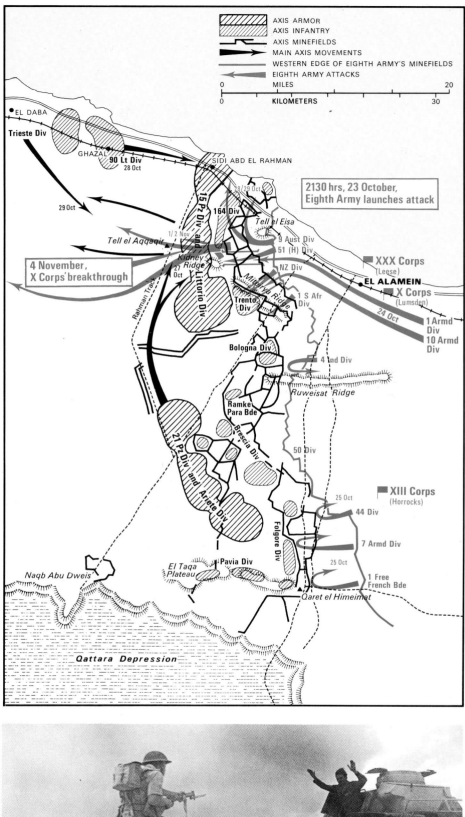

but it proved impossible to move the tanks forward in the way envisioned. The German defense was not helped by General Stumme's death from a heart attack on the afternoon of the 24th as heavy fighting continued. The German 21st Panzer Division was kept out of the main battle for the first days by diversionary efforts by XIII Corps. Although attempts to push the main British armored force forward continued, by the 26th it was clear that it had becomed bogged down and Montgomery largely halted his forces for regrouping. The chief events of the following five days were unsucessful German counterattacks throughout the main sector and a powerful northward advance by 9th Australian Division which drew in the German reserves. Montgomery's revised breakthrough plan, Operation Supercharge, was put into action on the night of 1/2 November. Although Rommel's forces fought well, by the end of the 2nd he was left with only 35 tanks. He signalled to Hitler that he must retreat. Hitler immediately forbade this but by 4 November further German and Italian losses made the retreat inevitable. Although the Battle of El Alamein was undoubtedly a decisive success for the Allies, Montgomery was unable to follow up his victory quickly enough and the remainder of Rommel's forces was able to make good its retreat.

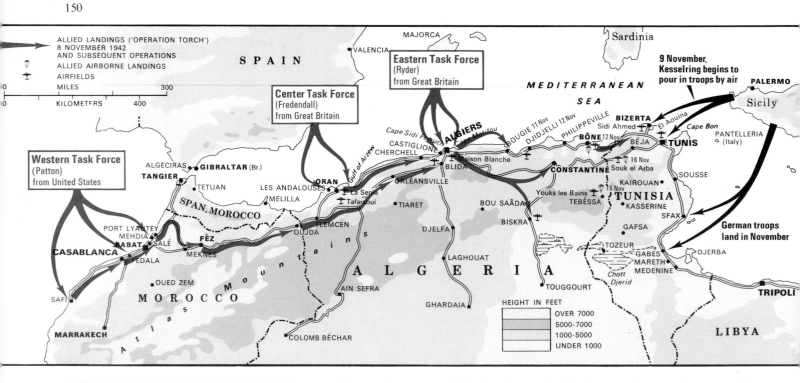

# Operation Torch

On 8 November 1942 as Rommel's forces were retreating from Egypt, American and British troops began a series of landings in French North Africa. The codename for the landings was Operation Torch. Although the operation gave US ground forces their first large-scale opportunity to fight in the European war, the plan had been strongly opposed by the US Chiefs of Staff who saw it as a diversion from their preferred strategy of preparing exclusively for a direct invasion of western Europe. This

opposition had been overruled by President Roosevelt because he believed that if the US delayed becoming involved in Europe then pressure would grow in US political circles for the abandonment of the policy of putting the defeat of Germany first.

In preparation for the landings there had been secret talks with various local French leaders (the USA had maintained diplomatic links with Vichy France) in an effort to ensure that the landings would not be resisted by the strong Vichy forces in North Africa. The Americans had taken the lead in this as much Anglo-French hostility remained as a legacy of events of 1940. For this reason also the American presence in the

initial phases of the operation was deliberately increased and publicly exaggerated when in fact the British contribution, particularly in warships and transport shipping, was rather larger. Nonetheless Torch was certainly the first truly combined Allied operation of the war. Whatever his other shortcomings as a general, the Commander in Chief, General Eisenhower, from the outset demonstrated the ability to create a genuinely integrated and efficient staff.

The map shows the three main landing areas and the early advances. Although there was sporadic resistance from the Vichy forces in most areas the landings generally went well with less than 2000

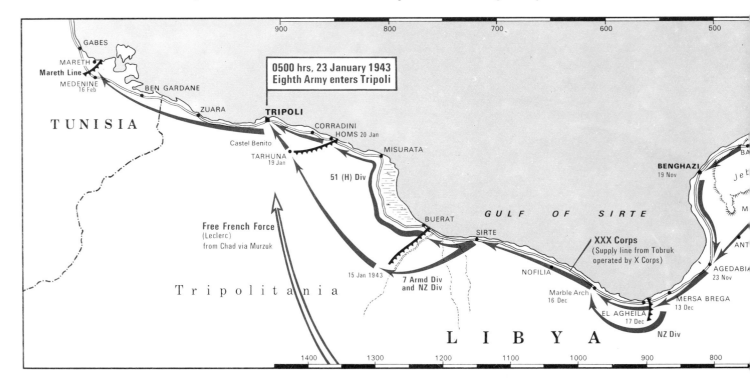

Below: smashed and burned-out German equipment on the battlefield after Rommel's retreat in North Africa. In the background, a disabled 88mm gun and its tractor.

casualties all told. Admiral Darlan, one of the principal leaders of the Vichy government happened to be in Algiers on private business and was captured and persuaded to use his considerable influence in the Allied cause.

Despite the comparative success of the initial landings there were obviously logistic difficulties involved in pushing any large force quickly forward the 400 miles to Tunis. In retrospect it would probably have been better, as some of the planners of the operation had urged, for the initial landings to have been extended as far east as Bône. In the event the Germans reacted with very great speed and on instructions from Hitler and the Commander in Chief, Mediterranean, Field Marshal Kesselring, they poured in troops and aircraft. The Vichy forces in Tunisia made little attempt to resist this move and in a series of battles in late November and December the Germans were able to halt the Allied advance.

# El Alamein to Tripoli

Montgomery is often criticized for the slow pace of Eighth Army's pursuit of Rommel's broken forces at the end of the Battle of El Alamein. A number of factors contributed to this slowness. Heavy rain made some areas impassible and there were massive traffic holdups in the corridors through the Alamein minefield belts. Both the pursuing units and their supplies were delayed as a result. Nonetheless Agedabia was reached before there had to be a major halt to allow the supplies to catch up. The advance was resumed on 12 December and the El Aghelia position was quickly outflanked. The German rear guard skilfully delayed the advance to Sirte and Buerat but once these positions were turned Eighth Army quickly pushed forward to Tripoli.

The Germans had done what they could to wreck the port installations at Tripoli and although it was partly in use by the end of January Eighth Army's supply difficulties remained acute. Small British units entered Tunisia on 4 February and had pushed forward to Medenine by the end of the month. Montgomery was still worried,

rightly, about his supplies and only advanced as far as this in an attempt to distract the Germans from their Kasserine attack. As a result his forward units were only just reinforced in time to beat off a German attack on 6 March. The advance was resumed two weeks later by which time Tripoli was in fairly full use.

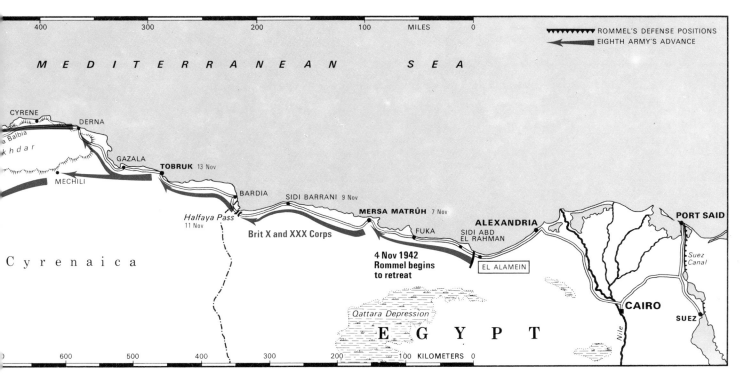

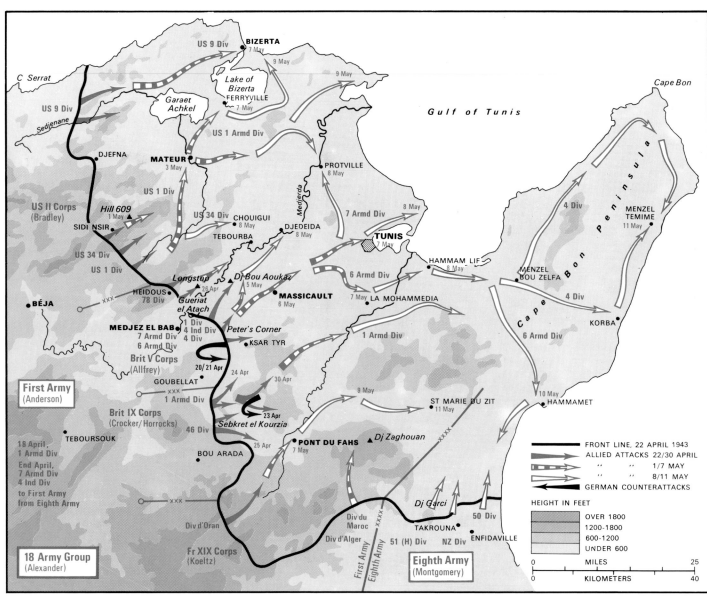

# Tunisia

Although the German and Italian forces had fought a brave series of delaying actions during their retreat into Tunisia, particularly on the Mareth Line and at Wadi Akarit, by April 1943 Eighth Army had pushed well forward. Similarly, although the Allied units from the Torch landings had suffered heavily in mid-February when the Germans attacked at Kasserine, this setback had been overcome and the Axis forces driven back. By 14 April the Germans and Italians had taken up the positions shown on the map defending the last line of hills before the plain around Tunis and Bizerta.

Allied attacks on this line began on 22 April especially in the sectors between Hill 609 and Peter's Corner. Although some progress was made by American forces at Hill 609 and in the nearby Mousetrap Valley and by the British at Longstop Hill and toward Djebel Bou Aoukaz, no decisive gains were made at first. General Alexander

decided to switch experienced British units from Eighth Army to V Corps and with their help renewed British and US attacks from 5 May soon broke through. The German and Italian resistance collapsed and by 12 May Marshal Messe and General von Arnim had surrendered along with 250,000 troops.

Rommel had left Africa on 9 March and had urged that the German and Italian forces be evacuated. Hitler refused to countenance this and there can be little doubt that, despite the delaying actions they fought, the forces lost in Africa would have served the Axis better in defending Sicily and Italy against the seaborne assaults that would be the British and Americans' next move. The early stages of the battle for Tunisia also contributed to another German disaster by occupying large numbers of transport aircraft at a time when Göring was failing to fulfill his promise to supply Stalingrad by air.

**Right: Italian troops on a desert reconnaissance mission.**

# The Battle of Kursk

For the summer of 1943 the German High Command planned no big offensive in Russia. It needed time to re-equip and, moreover, expected that its resources would be needed in other theaters. Nevertheless, to regain a psychological advantage, and to throw the expected Soviet offensive off balance, it was decided to stage a large but essentially limited attack toward Kursk. Here the Russians had ended the 1942–43 winter campaign holding a large salient which seemed very vulnerable to the kind of pincer movement which had won so many German successes in 1941.

Through various espionage channels, the Soviets were well informed of the German intentions, although they were probably not prepared for the repeated postponement of the operation; some German commanders were having second thoughts and were not in a hurry to get into position. All this enabled the Soviets to construct three lines of defense around the salient, each line consisting of elaborate trenches and antitank positions with appropriate artillery cover. The Germans began their advance on 5 July, in the belief that they were making a surprise

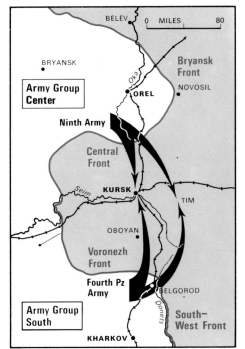

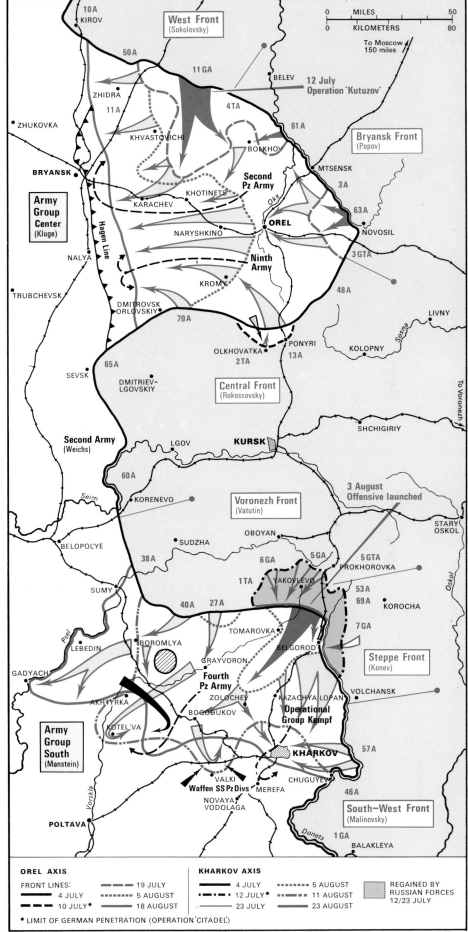

154

Below: a disabled Elefant tank destroyer pictured on the battlefield at Kursk. Following their unpromising debut at Kursk most of the surviving Elefants were redeployed to Italy.

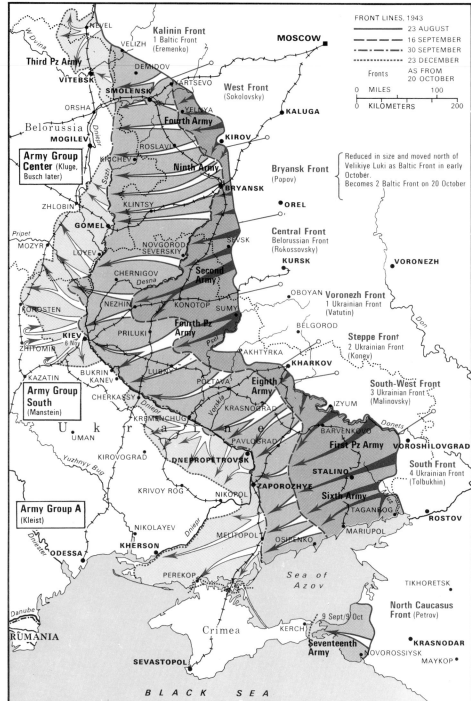

attack, but immediately encountered resistance far stiffer than they had expected. Moreover, the Soviets were technically better-off than they had been earlier in the war. Their T.34 tank was robust and reliable and available in large numbers, whereas the new types of German tank were not quite out of their teething troubles and, moreover, were entrusted to crews which had not had sufficient time to become familiar with them. Even more ominously, the Soviets could now secure, at least locally, command of the air over the battlefield. Their aircraft and their aircrews were not yet up to the German standard, but they now appeared in overwhelming numbers.

Thus the northern arm of the German pincer made only small penetrations into the Soviet salient, and at a very high cost. The southern arm, led by Manstein, fared somewhat better. His Fourth Panzer Army overcame the Russian Sixth Army but was then confronted with fresh Soviet tank units brought forward from reserve. Near Prokhorovka converging tank armies began what is regarded as the biggest tank battle of all time. It started on 12 July, and by the end of the next day the Germans seemed to be winning it, although both sides had already lost hundreds of tanks. However, at this point the German effort slackened, although the battle continued for five days longer. A Soviet offensive north of the salient toward Bryansk had altered the situation, and moreover the western Allies were landing in Sicily. Many of the German tanks were dispatched straight to Italy as soon as they were extricated from the Kursk battlefield. With this abandonment of the German offensive the Russians were free to begin their own advance all along the front south of Moscow.

# The Dniepr and Smolensk Battles

In little more than a month after Hitler's abandonment of the Kursk battle, the Soviet front line had been pushed far to the west by a general offensive. The German local commanders were handicapped by the transfer of some of their best units to the Italian front, and in the circumstances their withdrawal was conducted very creditably, never degenerating into a rout and making the best possible use of the geo-

graphical situation. Nevertheless, the Soviets soon captured the two base areas used by the Germans for their pincer movement on Kursk, Orel and its salient in the north, and Kharkov and its salient in the south. In the south, too, Stalino and Taganrog soon fell to the Russians, and Smolensk in the north, all by the autumn. Then, at the beginning of October, three fronts commanded by generals Rokossovsky, Vatutin and Konev forced crossings of the River Dniepr, on which the Germans had been expecting to form their defense line for the winter. Having established their bridgeheads, Soviet troops poured across. Dnepropetrovsk and Melitopol were captured, while Manstein

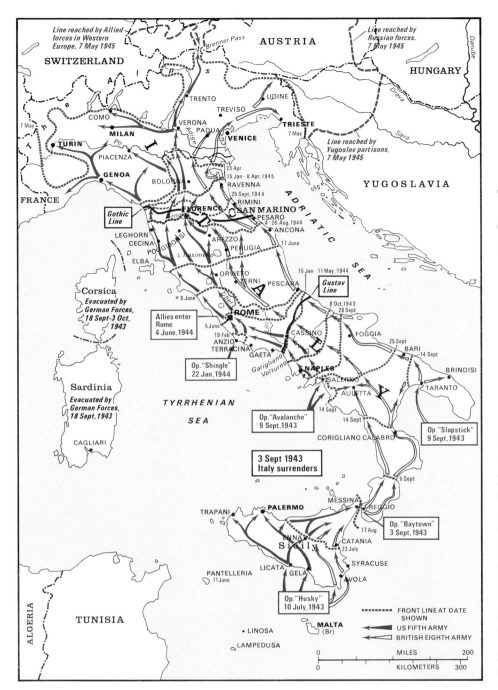

*Line reached by Allied forces in Western Europe, 7 May 1945*

*Line reached by Russian forces, 7 May 1945*

*Line reached by Yugoslav partisans, 7 May 1945*

Gothic Line

Corsica *Evacuated by German Forces, 18 Sept-3 Oct, 1943*

Sardinia *Evacuated by German Forces, 18 Sept, 1943*

Allies enter Rome 4 June, 1944

Op. "Shingle" 22 Jan, 1944

Gustav Line

Op. "Avalanche" 9 Sept, 1943

Op. "Slapstick" 9 Sept, 1943

3 Sept 1943 Italy surrenders

Op. "Baytown" 3 Sept, 1943

Op. "Husky" 10 July, 1943

MALTA (Br)

- - - - - FRONT LINE AT DATE SHOWN
US FIFTH ARMY
BRITISH EIGHTH ARMY

MILES 200
KILOMETERS 300

# The Italian Campaign

By the time the Allied campaign in North Africa was coming to an end it was clear to the Allied leaders that there was no prospect of building up their forces in Britain sufficiently to allow the invasion of northwest Europe to take place in 1943. It had been agreed at the Casablanca conference in January that Sicily should be captured once the campaign in Africa was complete because this would largely free the Mediterranean sea lanes but this comparatively limited objective did not seem to be making full use of the very large Allied forces already in the theater or the massive base organization that had been built up there. The British were strongly in favor of moving on to attack mainland Italy and the Americans too came round to this opinion when Mussolini's government fell in July. Throughout the campaign in Italy the British remained far more ready to press for reinforcements to be sent and an aggressive policy to be followed. The American views prevailed, however, and thus in late 1943 experienced units and commanders were withdrawn to go to England to prepare for D-Day. Again in the summer of 1944, after Rome had been taken, a large proportion of the Allied force was withdrawn to take part in the invasion of southern France.

The campaign in Italy saw some of the fiercest battles of the war. The initial seaborne landings at Salerno and the Anzio attempt to outflank the German Gustav Line were both very vigorously opposed by the Germans because of Hitler's hope that this would deter the Allies from such operations in northwest Europe. Once ashore the Allied forces found themselves facing successive river crossings which were usually overlooked by rugged and dominating hills carefully fortified by the Germans. The most famous of these positions was that at Monte Cassino which defied repeated Allied attacks in the early months of 1944. Even when the Germans were retreating between defense lines demolitions, rear guard actions, booby traps and miserable weather often combined to reduce Allied progress on the few good roads. Only when the Allied attacks were resumed in April 1945, after a long pause, did the German resistance collapse. The German forces in Italy surrendered on 2 May 1945.

tried to find forces for a counterattack to secure a position which he could hold for the winter in the bend of the Dniepr. But his attack, although pressed vigorously, was overwhelmed by the Soviet numerical advantage and he was forced back. Further north Rokossovsky, after crossing the Dniepr, took Kiev and pushed farther in order to cut the vital railroad running north to south from Mogilev to Kazatin. But at Zhitomir his troops were confronted by yet another force assembled by Manstein, and their occupation of that town was very short.

**Right: a Russian tankman points to the damage he has inflicted on a Tiger tank.**

# The Defeat of the U-Boats

By the summer of 1942 the Allies had instituted a comprehensive convoy system off the US East Coast and throughout the Caribbean. The U-Boats' second 'happy time' was therefore at an end. Although the focus of the struggle then began to return to the main North Atlantic convoy routes, several more distant areas still provided important successes for the U-Boats. The convoy system off the American coast was not fully extended south from the Caribbean area to Trinidad until October 1942 and many important oil tankers and other vessels were lost there. The U-Boats also found victims off the Brazilian coast but a particularly audacious run of attacks in August helped bring Brazil into the war, opening new bases to the Allies. A further fruitful area for the U-Boats at this time was off the Cape of Good Hope.

There were several important developments in the Allied effort in the second half of 1942 also. The most important of a number of organizational changes was the the establishment, in September, of the first Support Groups. These were specially trained groups of escort vessels which were to be sent to help hard-pressed convoys or to some other area where there were known to be U-Boats. The support groups were then to stay and hunt the U-Boats to destruction without being distracted by an escort's normal duties. Ideally a group would include a small aircraft carrier, an escort carrier, as well as the surface forces. A further boost to the Allies was a cryptographic breakthrough in December 1942. From then until the end of the war, despite major changes in the German code system introduced in March 1943, the Allied intelligence was normally very accurate and up to date while the equivalent German efforts were frustrated by changes made in June 1943.

Despite the increasing Allied resources the final months of 1942 and the early part of 1943 were the most difficult times of the battle for the Allies. Allied commitments were increased by the Torch invasion of North Africa in November and the newly-formed support groups had to be diverted there. Although a considerable U-Boat force

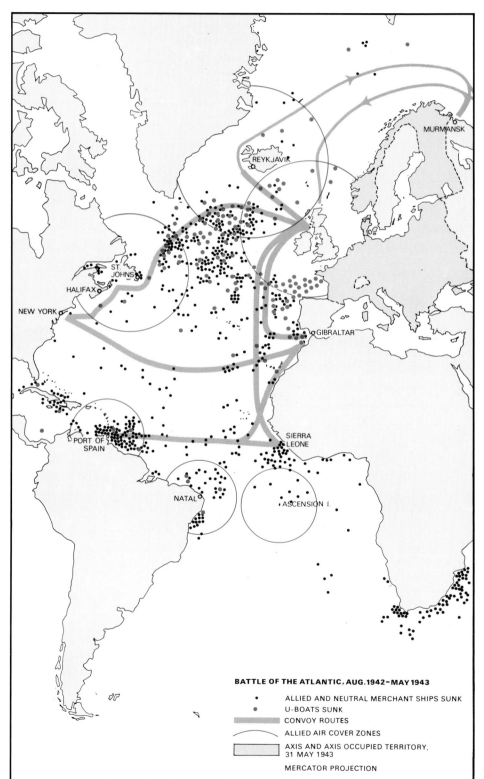

BATTLE OF THE ATLANTIC, AUG. 1942–MAY 1943

- ALLIED AND NEUTRAL MERCHANT SHIPS SUNK
- U-BOATS SUNK
- CONVOY ROUTES
- ALLIED AIR COVER ZONES
- AXIS AND AXIS OCCUPIED TERRITORY, 31 MAY 1943

MERCATOR PROJECTION

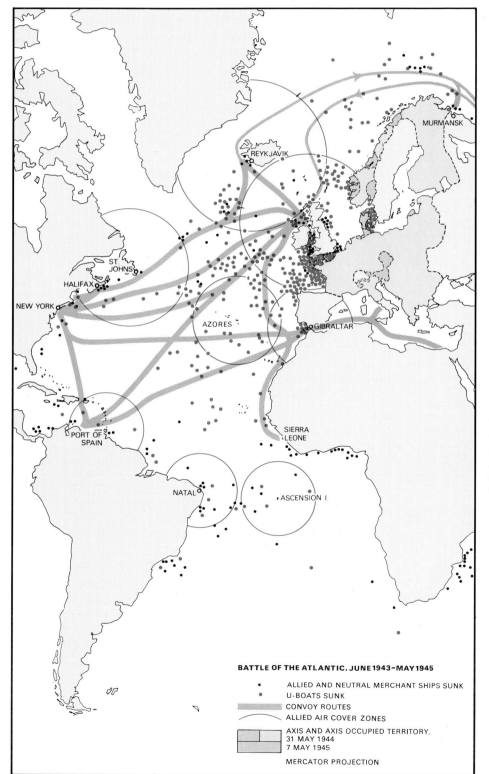

**BATTLE OF THE ATLANTIC, JUNE 1943-MAY 1945**

- · ALLIED AND NEUTRAL MERCHANT SHIPS SUNK
- · U-BOATS SUNK
- CONVOY ROUTES
- ALLIED AIR COVER ZONES
- AXIS AND AXIS OCCUPIED TERRITORY, 31 MAY 1944 7 MAY 1945

MERCATOR PROJECTION

was sent to North Africa also, for little gain, the North Atlantic escort forces remained weakened until March 1943. Losses in these months were very heavy.

The climax of the Battle of the Atlantic came in March 1943. Seventy-three ships were sunk from the North Atlantic convoys out of a total loss of 120 ships of 693,000 tons and for a time it seemed that the Germans were winning the battle. However, as suddenly as the crisis had arisen it was over. The shipping losses in April were much more moderate and in May 41 U-Boats were destroyed while 50 ships were lost to submarine attack. Such losses were insupportable and on 22 May the U-Boats were ordered to withdraw from the North Atlantic. The reasons for this sudden reversal cannot be exactly stated. The United States' industrial effort was beginning to come on stream, particularly in the provision of escort carriers, the support groups returned to the fray in late March and they and the other escorts were more highly trained and experienced while on the technical side improved radar and long-range scout planes helped capitalize on intelligence and radio direction finding information.

As the final map illustrates, the U-Boat offensive continued up to the end of the war but it was never again a serious threat. There was a brief attempt to renew the convoy battles in September-October 1943 after the introduction of new equipment but Allied countermeasures were ready and 25 submarines were lost and only nine merchantmen sunk in this period, although at the time the Germans believed that they had done better. In March 1944 the superiority of the escort forces was recognized when Donitz ordered the U-Boats to disperse from their hunting groups and work singly. In the final months of the war the U-Boats mostly operated in the area close to the British Isles Despite some technical advances they achieved little although there were still some 150 boats operational early in 1945. The Allied victory was won essentially by the co-ordination of all aspects of their effort and it is symbolic that, although German submarine research led the world, bad industrial and scientific management meant that only a handful of the most advanced U-Boats were in service when the Third Reich was finally overrun.

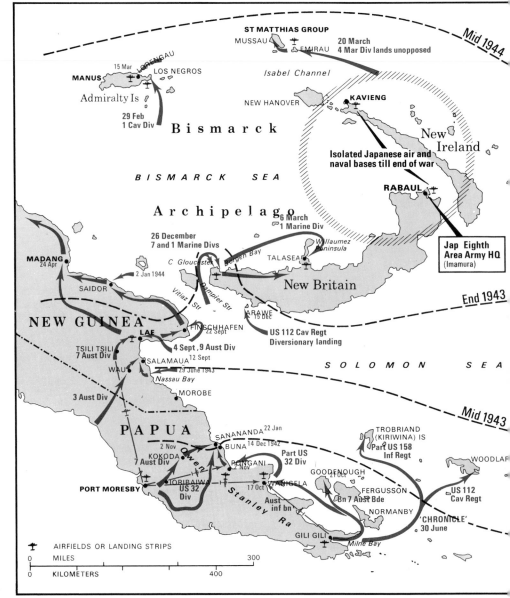

# The Solomons Campaign

Although the Japanese plans to take full control of the Solomons and New Guinea had received a major setback in the Battle of the Coral Sea in May 1942, they made a further attempt to reach Port Moresby by an overland advance from Buna in July–September 1942. This was halted by the defending Australian formations. Australian and American forces had already begun to strike back by building and holding an airstrip at Milne Bay and despite the worst imaginable ground and weather conditions they then succeeded in advancing over the Owen Stanley Range to take Buna and Sanananda. (The later stages of the New Guinea campaign are covered separately.)

The advance in the Solomons, of course, began with the long drawn struggle for Guadalcanal. Once this initial base had been taken the operations took on the soon-to-be-familiar island hopping pattern. Naval and air superiority kept the Japanese guessing about the point of attack and once ashore the Construction Battalions or Seabees quickly built or repaired airstrips for local defense and as a base to provide cover for

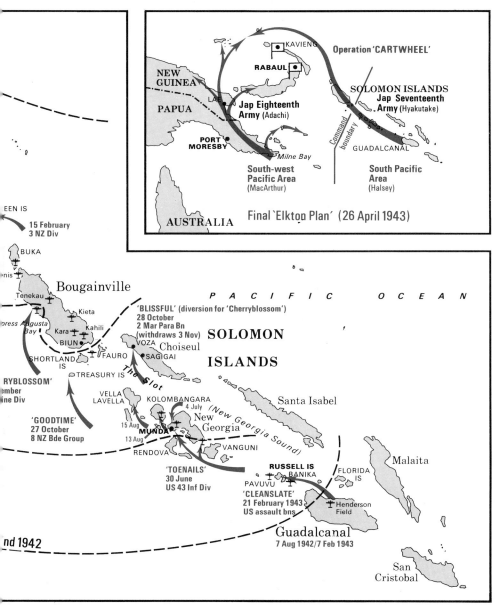

**Final 'Elkton Plan' (26 April 1943)**

Operation 'CARTWHEEL'

KAVIENG

RABAUL

NEW GUINEA

PAPUA

Jap Eighteenth Army (Adachi)

PORT MORESBY

Milne Bay

SOLOMON ISLANDS
Jap Seventeenth Army (Hyakutake)

GUADALCANAL

Command boundary

South-west Pacific Area (MacArthur)

South Pacific Area (Halsey)

AUSTRALIA

---

EEN IS

15 February
3 NZ Div

BUKA

Bougainville

Tenekau

Kieta

press Augusta Bay

Kara    Kahili

BIUN

SHORTLAND IS

RYBLOSSOM'
ember
ine Div

TREASURY IS

'GOODTIME'
27 October
8 NZ Bde Group

nd 1942

P A C I F I C    O C E A N

'BLISSFUL' (diversion for 'Cherryblossom')
28 October
2 Mar Para Bn
(withdraws 3 Nov)

VOZA

Choiseul

SAGIGAI

FAURO

The Slot

SOLOMON ISLANDS

VELLA LAVELLA

KOLOMBANGARA

4 July

New Georgia (New Georgia Sound)

15 Aug

MUNDA

13 Aug

RENDOVA

VANGUNI

'TOENAILS'
30 June
US 43 Inf Div

Santa Isabel

RUSSELL IS

BANIKA

FLORIDA IS

PAVUVU

'CLEANSLATE'
21 February 1943
US assault bns

Henderson Field

Malaita

Guadalcanal
7 Aug 1942/7 Feb 1943

San Cristobal

---

the next step. The technique is perhaps best shown in the landings on Bougainville. This island was defended by about 60,000 Japanese but only a few hundred of these were near Empress Augusta Bay and it was over four months before the Japanese could mount a full-scale attack against the beach-head, by then well defended.

When the plans for the Solomons were first made it seemed clear that it would be necessary to take both the main Japanese bases at Rabaul and Kavieng but in August 1943 it was agreed by bypass Rabaul and in March 1944 it was decided to leave Kavieng also. By that time the harbors and airfields at both bases were largely out of action. Landings in eastern New Britain and the Admiralty and St Matthias groups completed a very economical and effective campaign. The various isolated Japanese garrisons remained in being to the end of the war but could achieve little.

**Below left: destroyer guns blaze during a confused night action which took place off Cape Esperance.**
**Below: an Aichi D3A is shot down directly over the carrier *Enterprise* in the Battle of the Eastern Solomons.**

AMERICAN ATTACKS
JAPANESE COUNTERATTACKS
AND WITHDRAWALS
US DEFENSE PERIMETER 9 AUGUST
US POSITIONS 23 OCTOBER

EARLY DECEMBER, 1 MARINE DIV RELIEVED BY 25 INF, 2 MARINE AND AMERICAL DIVS (XIV CORPS [PATCH])

**Below:** a US Marine stares at a picture of the girl he left behind from his foxhole on Guadalcanal. Note the hand grenades in the foreground.
**Bottom:** tents constructed on a framework of small logs on the New Guinea mainland.

# The Struggle for Guadalcanal

The land and sea battles of the Guadalcanal campaign were the first major steps in the Allied counteroffensive against Japan. Since the American mobilization was only just getting under way and the Japanese were still near the peak of their strength, the forces were finely balanced and the battles were fiercely contested indeed.

The American landings were hurriedly improvised in response to news that the Japanese were beginning to build an airfield on the island. There were, therefore, no formations available for some time to reinforce the assault units from 1st Marine Division. The Japanese Navy made use of its superior torpedo equipment and night fighting training to assert control of the waters round the island at night, winning a number of engagements. They made use of this superiority to land successively stronger forces on the island. The airfield, soon renamed Henderson Field, was quickly put into use by the Marines and planes based there helped give the Americans control of the sea lanes by day. There were two carrier battles, the Battle of the Eastern Solomons in August and the Battle of Santa Cruz in October, in which the Japanese attempted

to dispute this air superiority and cover their supply operations but both of these were indecisive although losses on both sides were heavy.

On land the Japanese mounted three major attacks. The attacks in August and September were not made in sufficient strength because the Japanese had underestimated the size of the American force. Both efforts were defeated after a fierce struggle. By the time the Japanese had again built up their forces the Americans were very well prepared and the badly co-ordinated assaults were thrown back.

By this time also the US Navy had improved its night fighting skills and was making better use of radar. The Japanese night supply operations, known as the Tokyo Express, remained a problem but once the exhausted Marines were relieved in December the battle could only go one way. At the end of the year the Japanese High Command decided to withdraw and this was successfully achieved in February. Naval losses in the campaign were about equal but the Japanese lost far more men on land.

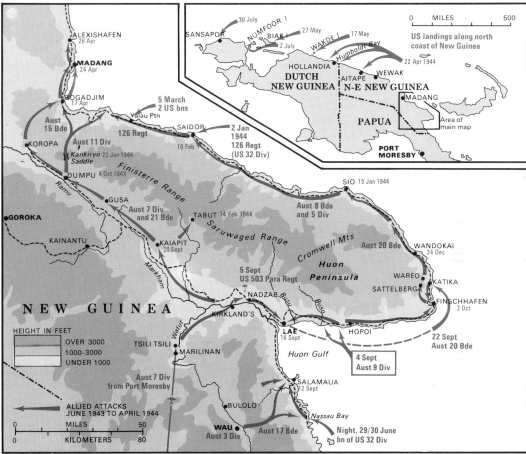

# New Guinea

The Allied campaign in New Guinea was one of the most imaginative and tactically sophisticated of the war. The Allied air forces played a very prominent role in this victory, driving off or sinking Japanese supply ships, transporting large quantities of supplies and dropping paratroop units as well as striking at Japanese ground positions. One little known but vital part of the Allied effort in these and the Solomons battles was the information provided by the Australian coast-watchers, who gave vital warning of many Japanese moves.

The Allied forces, and indeed the Japanese, faced many difficulties nonetheless. The problems of bad weather and tropical disease were acute and difficulties with rugged terrain were compounded by lack of accurate maps and, for landing operations, poor information about tides and reefs. During the Hollandia operation, for example, some units were sent ashore on to totally unsuitable beaches.

The campaign can conveniently be divided into two main phases after the Japanese had been thrown out of Buna at the end of 1942. The first phase, the capture of Lae and the Markham Valley, was made easier by the Japanese forces being cleverly drawn forward by earlier attacks on Salamaua. These successes were followed up by other smaller operations all round the Huon Peninsula. The second major stage brought landings at Hollandia and Aitape. These cut off perhaps 200,000 Japanese troops and civilian workers who were mostly around Wewak. The final landings on Biak and Numfoor and at Sansapor, were designed to take airfields to support Marianas and Philippine operations.

# The Ukraine

Although counterattacks west of Kiev had brought the Germans some breathing space, their forces in the southern Ukraine at the end of 1943 were very vulnerable, particularly in the salient around Krivoy Rog and Nikopol which Hitler insisted was to be held because of the mineral resources situated there. The renewed Soviet offensive began on Christmas Eve with attacks by Vatutin's First Ukraine Front which soon reached into former Polish territory as well as striking to the southwest. The next stage was a limited advance by Konev's troops toward Kirovgrad and this was quickly followed by the elimination of the Nikopol salient and the encirclement of important German formations in a pocket around Korsun. German counterattacks enabled about half the surrounded force to break out.

Despite the difficult conditions imposed by the spring thaw, the Soviet momentum was maintained and on 4 March First and Second Ukraine Fronts led new attacks. Again considerable German forces were threatened with encirclement and some units retreated at a speed which almost approached a rout. Later in March First Ukraine Front moved south, crossed the Dniestr and captured Chernovtsy, thereby severing the last rail link between the Germans in Poland and those in the southern USSR. Farther south Malinovsky's troops captured Odessa in April with hardly a fight, while Tolbukhin took Perekop and cleared the Germans out of the Crimea.

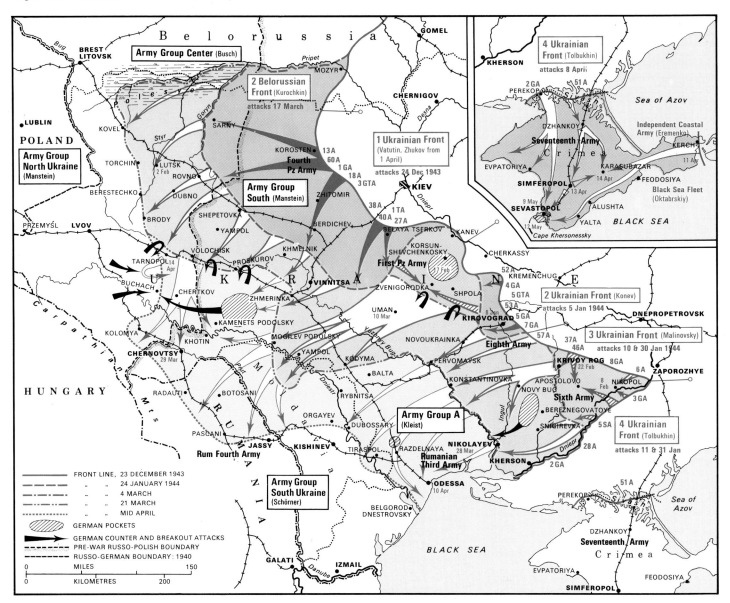

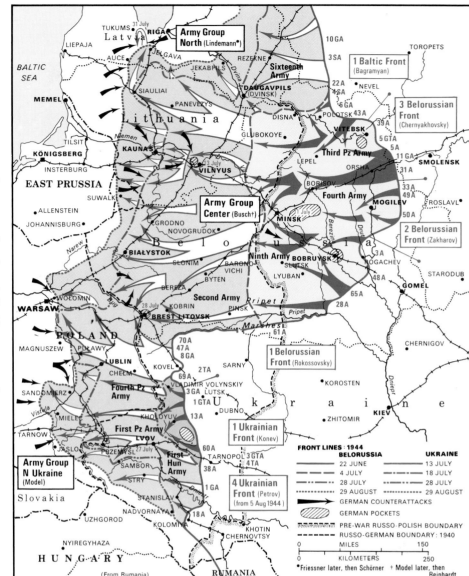

# The Advance into Poland

Intentionally, the Soviet summer offensive of 1944 started just after the western Allies had landed in Normandy. An early success was in the north, where the Russians broke through the Finns' defenses and forced Finland out of the war. Then, at the end of June, a main offensive opened in the central sector, with four fronts advancing with the aim of encircling the German army groups in the Minsk-Vitebsk-Rogachev triangle. Soviet air superiority, and the activities of guerrillas against German supply routes, eased the Red Army's task, although the crossing of the River Berezina was a costly success. Minsk was captured on 3 July and so rapid was the German retreat that Bialystok and Brest Litovsk were taken later the same month. These two towns controlled the approach to Warsaw, and although German counterattacks delayed Rokossovsky's drive against the Polish capital, by 15 August his advanced troops were in the eastern suburbs.

The Soviet approach to Warsaw coincided with a long-planned rising in the capital by the Polish Home Army, a generally anti-communist resistance group owing its allegiance to the exiled Polish government in London. That government wished Warsaw to be liberated by Poles rather than by the Red Army, not only for sentimental reasons but because it would put the Polish government into a stronger bargaining position later. But, contrary to the expectations of the Home Army, Rokossovsky advanced no further; it was not until the following year that the Russians entered Warsaw, and long before then the Germans had ruthlessly destroyed the Home Army and much of Warsaw as well. Subsequently this tragedy was attributed to Soviet malignance, but the Soviet explanation that a consolidation was needed, before embarking on the river crossing needed to enter Warsaw proper, does have some plausibility.

**Right: T-34 tanks moving up for the attack on the Third Belorussian Front in 1944.**

# The Baltic States

By 1944 the Red Army was not only better led than in 1941, but better equipped. Shipments from the western allies had comparatively little effect in the field of weapons, but were quite decisive in transport and other supplies. Not only was the Red Army soldier in 1944 learning to like Spam, but he was travelling on, or at least supplied by, American-built trucks and transport aircraft, the latter very often running on aviation fuel brought to Russia by sea or through Iran. The pace of the Soviet advance in 1944 and 1945 could therefore be fast, depending more on the intensity of German resistance than on problems of supply and communication. This was important not only for the drive through Poland to Berlin, but also for the campaigns in the Balkans and the Baltic States.

The fronts of Eremenko and Maslenikov entered the latter in the summer of 1944. In Estonia, Narva was captured first, while in neighboring Latvia a deep penetration was made. Meanwhile Govorov's Leningrad Front advanced along the coast and captured Tallinn. In October Riga was assaulted and captured by Bagramyan's First Baltic Front, which went on to cut off no fewer than 20 German divisions in Courland. The latter, supplied sporadically by sea, held out right until the end of the war. However, the fall of Riga really marked the end of the war as far as the Baltic states were concerned. Their inhabitants had not welcomed incorporation into the USSR in 1940, and many of them braved the perils of evacuation with the German troops rather than stay behind as citizens of the USSR.

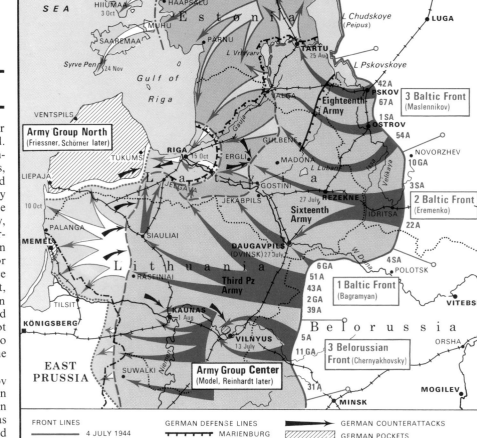

**Right: the KV-1 tank was the principal Soviet heavy tank in the first years of the war. It originally carried a 76mm gun as shown here but later versions had a more powerful 85mm weapon. It was superseded by the JS-series of tanks.**

First Pz and Hun First Armies form Armeegruppe Heinrici
Eighth Army and Rum Fourth Army form Armeegruppe Wöhler
Sixth Army and Rum Third Army form Armeegruppe Dumitrescu

Ⓐ 6TA, 27A, 52A, 53A, 7GA and Cav Mech Group Gorshkov
Ⓑ 37A, 46A, 57A and Cav Mech Group Pliev

4 Ukrainian Front (Petrov)

2 Ukrainian Front (Malinovsky)

3 Ukrainian Front (Tolbukhin)

Army Group South Ukraine (Friessner)

23 August 1944 Rumania surrenders. Declares war on Germany, 25 August

4 September 1944 Bulgaria declares end to state of war with Allies. Declares war on Germany 8 December

Army Group F (Weichs)

Army Group E (Löhr)

**FRONT LINES**

—————— 20 AUGUST 1944
— — — — 29 AUGUST
—·—·—·— 24 SEPTEMBER
—··—··— 12 OCTOBER
·········· 31 JANUARY 1945

RUMANIAN AND BULGARIAN ATTACKS
AXIS COUNTERATTACKS
WITHDRAWAL OF ARMY GROUPS 'E' AND 'F'
GERMAN POCKETS

—·—·—·— INTERNATIONAL BOUNDARIES : 1944
PRE-WAR RUSSO-POLISH BOUNDARY
— — — — RUSSO-GERMAN BOUNDARY : 1940

LAND OVER 1600 FEET

MILES 0 — 300
KILOMETERS 0 — 500

# The Soviet Offensive in the Balkans

Shortly after Finland had withdrawn from the war, Rumania also surrendered. Tolbukhin's Third and Malinovsky's Second Ukrainian Fronts had used bridgeheads on the western side of the River Dniestr to start an advance on 20 August which made rapid progress because the Rumanian soldiers, who had never been enthusiastic fighters, were willing by this stage of the war to surrender or desert as opportunity offered. When the Soviets occupied Iasy the King of Rumania dismissed his pro-German government and initiated negotiations. The Germans in Rumania fought on, but the German Sixth Army was encircled and destroyed near Kishinev. Bucharest was captured by the end of August and this helped to persuade another of Hitler's allies, Bulgaria, to surrender also, on 26 August. Three weeks later Soviet troops entered Sofia, the Bulgarian capital. After these successes the Second Ukrainian Front turned to occupy Transylvania, reaching Arad in September, while Tolbukhin moved north from Bulgaria toward Belgrade, making contact with Tito's Yugoslav partisans in October. Meanwhile, Malinovsky entered Hungary and by mid-November was in sight of Budapest. By the end of March 1945 Hungary was largely cleared of German resistance and the Red Army entered Austria. An energetic counteroffensive around Lake Balaton had been initially successful, but foundered for lack of fuel and in April the Red Army entered Bratislava and Vienna. The Ukrainian fronts ended the war by overrunning Czechoslovakia and linking up with US forces advancing from the west. The last German forces in this area surrendered on 11 May 1945.

# D-Day

The Allied invasion of France on 6 June 1944 was the largest combined land, sea and air operation ever undertaken in war. The planning process and the forces involved were on the largest and most elaborate scale. The Supreme Commander for Operation Overlord was General Eisenhower and he had nearly 3,000,000 men under his control. A massive quantity of equipment, much of it specially designed, had also been assembled. One of the most important aspects of the Allied plan was the preparation of parts for two artificial ports (Mulberry Harbors) which were to be towed across the Channel and sunk or anchored off the Omaha and Gold beaches to enable heavy supplies to be landed easily before a major port had been taken.

Although they had a crushing superiority in fighting aircraft and warships, because of shortages of paratroop-carrying aircraft and naval landing craft and the natural advantages of the defense, the Allied plan relied heavily on elaborate deception schemes and preparatory air attacks to prevent the Germans overwhelming the comparatively limited ground forces deployed initially. The main deception plan was to suggest – by way of reports from double agents, false radio traffic and other means – that a notional First US Army Group was being assembled in southeast England under the command of General Patton ready to invade across the narrowest part of the Channel. The many preparatory air attacks for the real operation were designed mainly to isolate the Normandy area from the rest of France but these were only a proportion of the attacks made and thus the true purpose was concealed and the deception reinforced.

The deception plan contributed greatly to uncertainties in the German command. The German Commander in Chief, West, Field Marshal von Rundstedt believed that beach defenses should come second to the assembly of a strong central reserve to throw the Allied forces back into the sea once they had clearly shown where their main attack was going to be. Rommel, who now commanded the German armies in northern France and the Low Countries, believed that Allied air power would prevent Rundstedt's reserve coming into action

and that the Allies must instead be defeated on the beaches before they could develop their full strength. Hitler insisted on a compromise between these schemes, neither allowing Rommel to strengthen the forces defending the beaches as much as would have been possible, while hamstringing the action of the reserve forces by insisting that they remain under his personal control. On 6 June this arrangement meant among other things that a counterattack by the powerful 21st Panzer Division from the Caen area was delayed for several hours until its effects could only be limited.

As the map shows, the Allies planned landings on five beach areas with paratroop units being dropped on either flank. There was hard fighting on each of the three beaches chosen for the British and Canadian forces but with the aid of specially designed armored vehicles the defenses were overcome and fairly good progress inland was made. The easiest progress of all was in the American area at Utah beach where navigational errors concentrated the landings in sectors that happened to be lightly defended. The other American beach, Omaha, offered a complete contrast. The German defenses were strong and there were important errors in the planning and execution of the attack. As a result, casualties were high but a solid footing had been taken by the end of the day. Many of the airborne troops on either flank were not dropped in the correct areas but nevertheless they achieved most of their objectives in a series of small, hard-fought actions.

By the end of 6 June the Allies had almost 150,000 men ashore and although the first day's objectives had not been reached a strong lodgment had been made. Rommel's plan to win on the beaches had failed and now it was a question of whether the Allied air forces could slow the assembly of German reserves to below the rate at which the Allied armies could be landed and supplied.

**Above right: landing craft arrive at Omaha Beach, where German defenses were well-prepared and casualties high.**
**Right: A scene on Omaha Beach shortly after the first landings.**

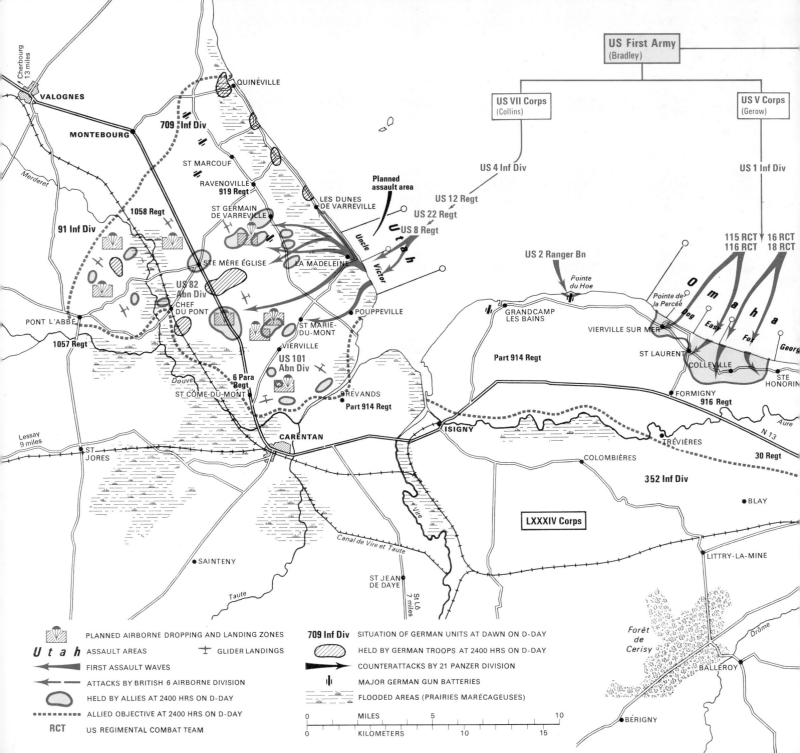

**US First Army**
(Bradley)

**US VII Corps**
(Collins)

**US V Corps**
(Gerow)

US 4 Inf Div

US 1 Inf Div

US 12 Regt

US 22 Regt

US 8 Regt

115 RCT · 16 RCT
116 RCT · 18 RCT

US 2 Ranger Bn

Cherbourg
13 miles

VALOGNES

MONTEBOURG

709 Inf Div

QUINÉVILLE

ST MARCOUF

RAVENOVILLE
919 Regt

1058 Regt

Merderet

91 Inf Div

1057 Regt

PONT L'ABBÉ

ST GERMAIN
DE VARREVILLE

LES DUNES
DE VARREVILLE

Planned assault area

Utah

Uncle

Victor

STE MÈRE ÉGLISE

LA MADELEINE

US 82
Abn Div

CHEF
DU PONT

POUPPEVILLE

ST MARIE-
DU-MONT

VIERVILLE

US 101
Abn Div

Douve

6 Para
Regt

ST CÔME-DU-MONT

BRÉVANDS

Part 914 Regt

Lessay
9 miles

ST JORES

CARENTAN

ISIGNY

Pointe
du Hoe

GRANDCAMP
LES BAINS

Part 914 Regt

Pointe de
la Percée

VIERVILLE SUR MER

Omaha

Dog      East      Fox      George

ST LAURENT

COLLEVILLE

STE
HONORIN

FORMIGNY

916 Regt

TRÉVIÈRES

30 Regt

Aure

N 13

COLOMBIÈRES

352 Inf Div

BLAY

Canal de Vire et Taute

St Lô
7 miles

SAINTENY

ST JEAN
DE DAYE

Taute

Vire

**LXXXIV Corps**

LITTRY-LA-MINE

Forêt
de Cerisy

Drôme

BALLEROY

BÉRIGNY

PLANNED AIRBORNE DROPPING AND LANDING ZONES

**709 Inf Div** SITUATION OF GERMAN UNITS AT DAWN ON D-DAY

*Utah* ASSAULT AREAS

✈ GLIDER LANDINGS

HELD BY GERMAN TROOPS AT 2400 HRS ON D-DAY

FIRST ASSAULT WAVES

COUNTERATTACKS BY 21 PANZER DIVISION

ATTACKS BY BRITISH 6 AIRBORNE DIVISION

MAJOR GERMAN GUN BATTERIES

HELD BY ALLIES AT 2400 HRS ON D-DAY

FLOODED AREAS (PRAIRIES MARÉCAGEUSES)

ALLIED OBJECTIVE AT 2400 HRS ON D-DAY

**RCT** US REGIMENTAL COMBAT TEAM

0          MILES          5          10

0     KILOMETERS     5     10     15

Left: the Allied invasion chiefs at a press conference in Allied Command Headquarters: left to right; Bradley, Ramsay, Tedder, Eisenhower, Mongomery, Leigh-Mallory and Bedell-Smith.
Right: after the D-Day landings, Allied troops pressed inland. A command tank leads a unit of British-manned Sherman tanks.

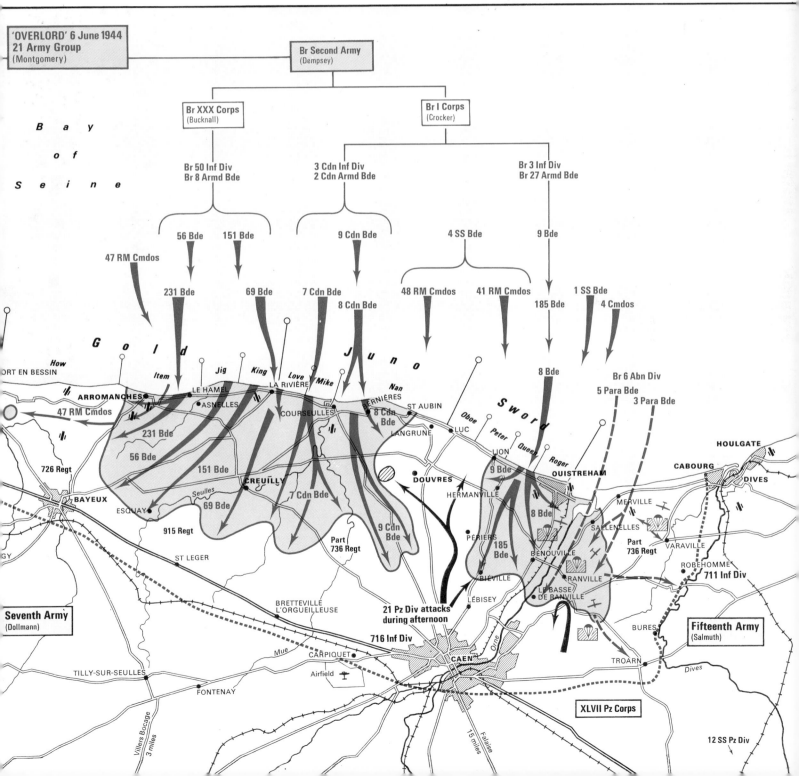

'OVERLORD' 6 June 1944
21 Army Group
(Montgomery)

Br Second Army
(Dempsey)

Br XXX Corps
(Bucknall)

Br I Corps
(Crocker)

Br 50 Inf Div
Br 8 Armd Bde

3 Cdn Inf Div
2 Cdn Armd Bde

Br 3 Inf Div
Br 27 Armd Bde

56 Bde          151 Bde          9 Cdn Bde          4 SS Bde          9 Bde

47 RM Cmdos

231 Bde          69 Bde          7 Cdn Bde          48 RM Cmdos          41 RM Cmdos          1 SS Bde          4 Cmdos

8 Cdn Bde          185 Bde

8 Bde

Br 6 Abn Div
5 Para Bde
3 Para Bde

Bay
of
Seine

Gold

How
ORT EN BESSIN
Item          Jig          King          Love          Mike
Juno
Nan

Sword

HOULGATE

ARROMANCHES
LE HAMEL
ASNELLES
LA RIVIÈRE
COURSEULLES
BERNIÈRES
8 Cdn
Bde
ST AUBIN
LANGRUNE
LUC
Oboe
Peter
Queen
Roger
LION
OUISTREHAM
MERVILLE
CABOURG
DIVES

47 RM Cmdos

726 Regt

231 Bde
56 Bde          151 Bde

BAYEUX

9 Bde
HERMANVILLE
8 Bde
PÉRIERS

SALLENELLES
VARAVILLE

ESQUAY
Seulles
69 Bde
CREUILLY
7 Cdn Bde
9 Cdn Bde
DOUVRES

185
Bde
BENOUVILLE
RANVILLE
LE BASSE
DE BANVILLE

Part 736 Regt

ROBEHOMME
711 Inf Div

915 Regt

ST LEGER
Part
736 Regt
BIEVILLE
LÉBISEY

BURES

Fifteenth Army
(Salmuth)

Seventh Army
(Dollmann)

BRETTEVILLE
L'ORGUEILLEUSE

21 Pz Div attacks
during afternoon

716 Inf Div

Mue
CARPIQUET
Airfield

CAEN

Orne

TROARN
Dives

XLVII Pz Corps

TILLY-SUR-SEULLES

FONTENAY

Villers Bocage
3 miles

Falaise
15 miles

12 SS Pz Div

# Invading Southern France

The Allied plans for landings in the south of France were a cause of much debate and disagreement between the British and American leaders. The Americans, of course, laid overwhelming emphasis on invading northern France and defeating the German forces there. They were somewhat reluctant participants in the Italian campaign, seeing it in a diversionary role rather than as having important strategic objectives in its own right. They believed that landings in southern France would contribute considerably to the initial success of D-Day by drawing off German forces and, by opening the port of Marseilles, would be valuable in the long term. Many of the forces involved were to be drawn from the armies fighting in Italy. The British would have preferred either to maintain them in Italy or to use them to lead a major landing in the Adriatic or even farther east. The Americans refused to countenance this scheme, with support from Stalin who was only too pleased for the western Allies to keep away from the Balkans.

The plan for the landings was originally made under the code name 'Dragoon' but because of fears that this had become known to the Germans 'Anvil' was substituted at a late stage. The original scheme was for the main D-Day invasion and Anvil to be simultaneous but shortages of landing craft dictated a postponement. To opponents of the operation this delay made it seem even more unnecessary. When the landings were made on 15 August resistance was light with only 183 Allied casualties on the first day. Churchill was aboard one of the supporting ships and, from the account in his memoirs, seems to have been bored by the lack of action. General Wiese's German Nineteenth Army had only eight poorly trained and equipped divisions with which to guard the whole of south and southeast France and not surprisingly he was soon compelled to retreat. The Allied force was quickly expanded to become Seventh US and First French Armies and as 6 Army Group took post on the right of the Allied line advancing into Germany.

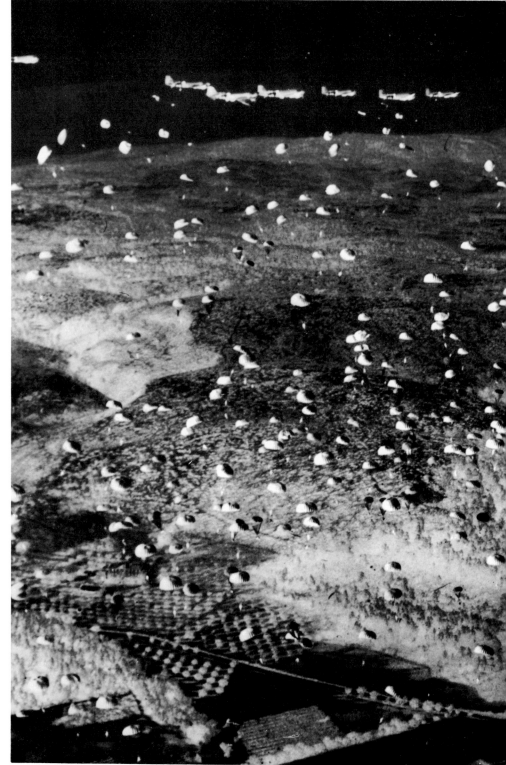

Below: paratroops drop from C-47
transport aircraft to attack behind enemy
lines during the invasion of Southern France
in August 1944.

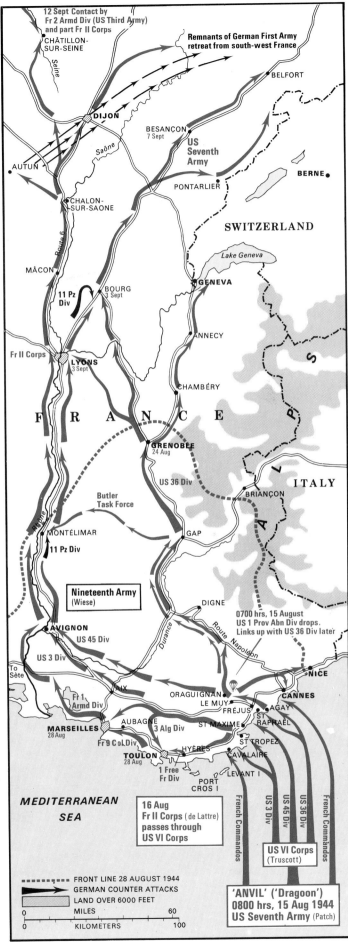

12 Sept Contact by
Fr 2 Armd Div (US Third Army)
and part Fr II Corps

CHÂTILLON-
SUR-SEINE

Remnants of German First Army
retreat from south-west France

BELFORT

DIJON

BESANÇON
7 Sept

US
Seventh
Army

AUTUN

PONTARLIER

BERNE

CHALON-
SUR-SAONE

SWITZERLAND

MÂCON

Lake Geneva

11 Pz
Div

BOURG
3 Sept

GENEVA

Fr II Corps

LYONS
3 Sept

ANNECY

CHAMBÉRY

F R A N C E

GRENOBLE
24 Aug

US 36 Div

BRIANÇON

ITALY

Butler
Task Force

GAP

MONTÉLIMAR

11 Pz Div

DIGNE

Nineteenth Army
(Wiese)

0700 hrs, 15 August
US 1 Prov Abn Div drops.
Links up with US 36 Div later

AVIGNON

US 45 Div

US 3 Div

To
Sète

NICE

AIX

ORAGUIGNAN
LE MUY

CANNES

Fr 1
Armd Div

FRÉJUS
AGAY

MARSEILLES
28 Aug

AUBAGNE

3 Alg Div

ST MAXIME

ST RAPHAËL

Fr 9 Col Div

HYÈRES

ST TROPEZ

CAVALAIRE

TOULON
28 Aug

1 Free
Fr Div

PORT
CROS I

LEVANT I

MEDITERRANEAN
SEA

16 Aug
Fr II Corps (de Lattre)
passes through
US VI Corps

French Commandos

US 3 Div

US 45 Div

US 36 Div

French Commandos

US VI Corps
(Truscott)

FRONT LINE 28 AUGUST 1944
GERMAN COUNTER ATTACKS
LAND OVER 6000 FEET

0        MILES        60
0     KILOMETERS     100

'ANVIL' ('Dragoon')
0800 hrs, 15 Aug 1944
US Seventh Army (Patch)

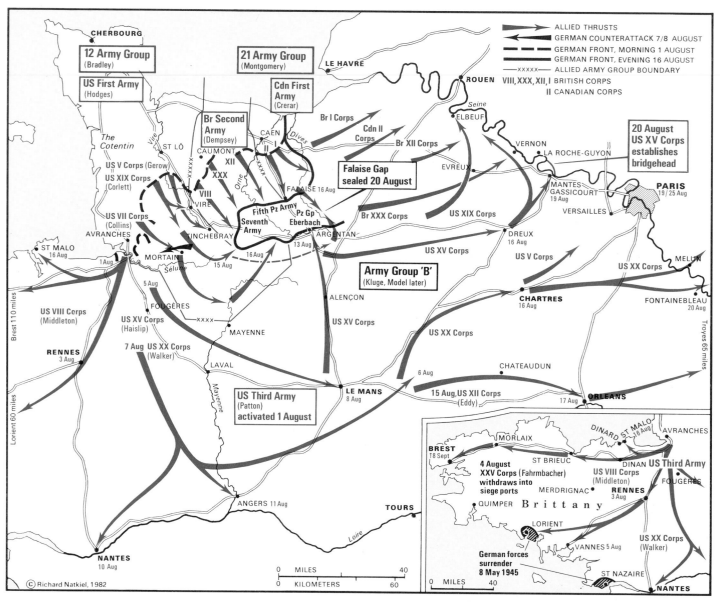

ALLIED THRUSTS
GERMAN COUNTERATTACK 7/8 AUGUST
GERMAN FRONT, MORNING 1 AUGUST
GERMAN FRONT, EVENING 16 AUGUST
XXXXX ALLIED ARMY GROUP BOUNDARY
VIII, XXX, XII, I BRITISH CORPS
II CANADIAN CORPS

CHERBOURG

**12 Army Group** (Bradley)

**21 Army Group** (Montgomery)

**US First Army** (Hodges)

**Cdn First Army** (Crerar)

LE HAVRE

**Br Second Army** (Dempsey)

ROUEN

Seine

ELBEUF

Br I Corps

Cdn II Corps

Br XII Corps

VERNON

LA ROCHE-GUYON

**20 August US XV Corps establishes bridgehead**

The Cotentin

ST LÔ

CAUMONT

XII

XXX

VIII

VIRE

CAEN

Dives

Orne

FALAISE 16 Aug

EVREUX

**Falaise Gap sealed 20 August**

MANTES GASSICOURT 19 Aug

PARIS 19/25 Aug

US V Corps (Gerow)

US XIX Corps (Corlett)

US VII Corps (Collins)

AVRANCHES

TINCHEBRAY

**Fifth Pz Army Seventh Army**

Pz Gp Eberbach

ARGENTAN 13 Aug

Br XXX Corps

US XIX Corps

VERSAILLES

ST MALO 16 Aug

1 Aug

MORTAIN

Sélune

16 Aug

15 Aug

ALENÇON

DREUX 16 Aug

US V Corps

MELUN

US XX Corps

5 Aug

FOUGÈRES

US XV Corps

**Army Group 'B'** (Kluge, Model later)

US VIII Corps (Middleton)

US XV Corps (Haislip)

xxxx

MAYENNE

US XV Corps

CHARTRES 16 Aug

FONTAINEBLEAU 20 Aug

Brest 110 miles

RENNES 3 Aug

7 Aug US XX Corps (Walker)

LAVAL

Mayenne

US XX Corps

6 Aug

CHATEAUDUN

Lorient 60 miles

LE MANS 8 Aug

**US Third Army** (Patton) **activated 1 August**

15 Aug, US XII Corps (Eddy)

ORLEANS

17 Aug

Troyes 65 miles

ANGERS 11 Aug

Loire

TOURS

NANTES 10 Aug

© Richard Natkiel, 1982

0 MILES 40
0 KILOMETERS 60

MORLAIX

DINARD ST MALO 16 Aug

AVRANCHES

**BREST** 18 Sept

ST BRIEUC

DINAN **US Third Army**

**4 August XXV Corps (Fahrmbacher) withdraws into siege ports**

US VIII Corps (Middleton)

MERDRIGNAC

FOUGÈRES

RENNES 3 Aug

QUIMPER

**Brittany**

LORIENT

VANNES 5 Aug

US XX Corps (Walker)

**German forces surrender 8 May 1945**

ST NAZAIRE

NANTES

0 MILES 40

# Allied Breakout from Normandy

Throughout June and July 1944 the Allies gradually extended their initial beachheads inland into Normandy. General Montgomery remained in control of the ground forces and the campaign was fought along the lines which he had first laid down. The plan was for British and Canadian pressure on the Allied left to draw in the strongest German forces and allow American units on the right to advance more rapidly. Montgomery was not well liked by some of the American leaders and did little to improve his position by poor handling of the press but nonetheless his blueprint for the campaign was largely adhered to and brought success.

By the end of July the breakout had begun and newly arrived forces of Patton's Third Army began moving from Avranches into Brittany and east into central France. The other Allied armies also pressed forward. Hitler's response was to order immediate counterattacks from around Mortain to cut off Patton's advances but these were quickly checked by Allied ground and air forces. The German forces involved now found themselves trapped in an exposed salient west of Falaise and Argentan and many were killed or captured in the subsequent Allied attempts to seal off the pocket. The German position was not helped by Hitler's continued insistence on no retreat and his distrust of his generals. Field Marshal von Kluge had replaced both Rundstedt and Rommel early in July and was himself dismissed on 17 August.

While the heavy fighting around the Falaise Gap was coming to an end all the Allied armies joined Third Army in the rapid advance to the Seine. Although some historians believe that the Falaise operations were badly mismanaged by the Allies there is no doubt that the German forces defending Normandy had largely been written off as military formations. Resistance forces began the fight to free Paris on 19 August

and on 20 August the first Allied bridgehead over the Seine was established. The Allies had made far less progress in the June and July battles than their planners had expected but the rapid advances in early August more than restored the original schedule.

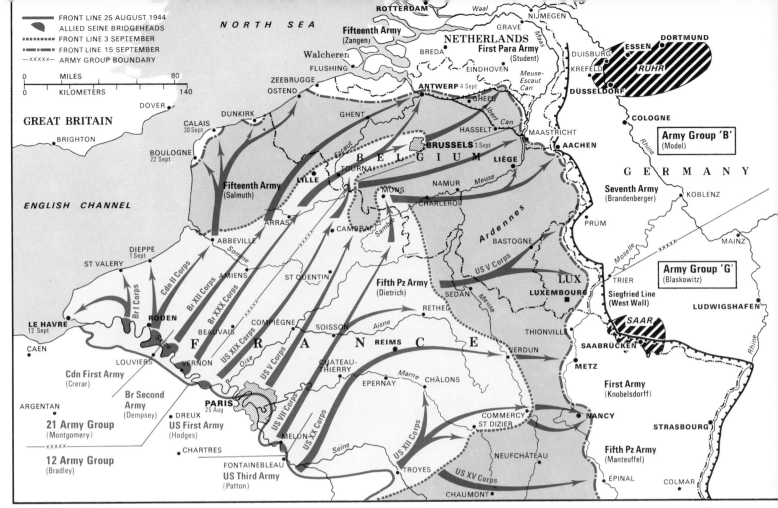

# Advance to Antwerp

As the Allied forces extended their advance north and east of the Seine in late August 1944 their generals were arguing fiercely about the strategy to be adopted. The Allied armies were still almost entirely dependent on supplies landed over the Normandy beaches which were a growing distance behind the front. These supplies were not sufficient to keep every unit advancing at full pace and at full strength. Various generals, of whom Montgomery was the most prominent, proposed that advantage should be taken of the German disorganiza-tion and a proportion of the Allied force given overriding priority in an attempt to support a narrow-front advance into Germany to end the war in 1944. This plan was rejected by General Eisenhower, the Supreme Commander, who took over direct control of the Allied ground forces early in September. Although Eisenhower gave some priority to the British forces for the advance into Belgium and the Arnhem operation that followed, he insisted on a broad front policy in which all the Allied armies would have an equal share of the supplies and the glory attending an advance. There was little possibility of quick success by this method but far less risk of a defeat. Although the narrow-front advance had obvious at-tractions it is by no means clear that it would have been logistically possible even if the German resistance could have been over-come. There can be no doubt that Eisen-hower would have faced considerable politi-cal difficulties if he had tried to halt the advance of Patton's Third Army for example while allowing the British forces to continue their attacks.

The key to solving the whole problem was to alleviate the supply situation. The Canad-ian First Army managed to take several of the French Channel ports in September but these were too small to be of more than limited help. The more important port of Antwerp was seized virtually intact on 4 September but despite the relationship of the vehement strategic debate to the supply problem the importance of Antwerp was not appreciated at first and a series of minor errors and delays allowed the Germans to consolidate their hold on the seaward approaches to the port.

**Left: Corporal Franczalsi hands out the mail to troops recently landed in France. Letters from home played a vital part in maintaining morale.**

# The Advance to the Rhine

The Allied advance in August and early September 1944 had been rapid and successful and in an ambitious effort to retain this momentum General Montgomery devised and had accepted a plan for paratroop landings to seize a series of important river and canal crossings which might otherwise provide serious checks to the advance. A further attraction of the scheme was that the route through Arnhem led into Germany round the north end of the supposedly formidable West Wall defenses. The whole operation had to be planned in a great hurry to fit in with the rapidly developing Allied advance. Although the two US airborne divisions achieved their objectives with the help of the advancing British XXX Corps, shortcomings in the preparation became more apparent with the third part of the operation. It was accepted that the British airborne division dropped at Arnhem would have a difficult task and so it was decided to drop it some way from its objectives to allow for some organization before the attack should go in. The consequent loss of surprise gave the German forces, which were in any case far stronger than Allied intelligence believed, time to recover and the paratroops were not able to reach their objectives in any strength. German resistance to the advance of XXX Corps also increased and after a bitter fight the operation was abandoned. Most of the British paratroops were taken prisoner.

Even as the Arnhem operation was coming to an end British and Canadian troops were beginning a long struggle to clear the Germans away from the Schelde Estuary and open the port of Antwerp. Arguably this operation should have been given higher priority and more of Montgomery's attention than the paratroop plan. The Allies were only able to begin minesweeping to open Antwerp on 4 November after elaborate amphibious attacks and much

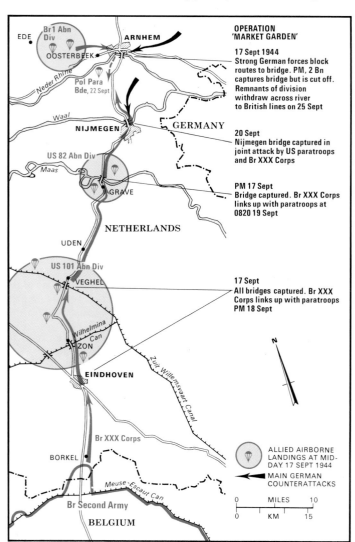

hard fighting in difficult conditions. The first cargoes were landed on 28 November and from then on the supply position for all the Allied armies improved dramatically.

Throughout this period the US forces were gradually pushing forward in a number of sectors but the German resistance was becoming better organized and their defense system more formidable. The battles fought by US First Army around Aachen and Patton's Third Army around Metz were particularly fierce. Hopes of finishing the war in 1944, however, had been abandoned.

**Above: paratroops being dropped during the Arnhem operation.**
**Left: British paratroops move cautiously through a ruined building on the outskirts of Arnhem.**

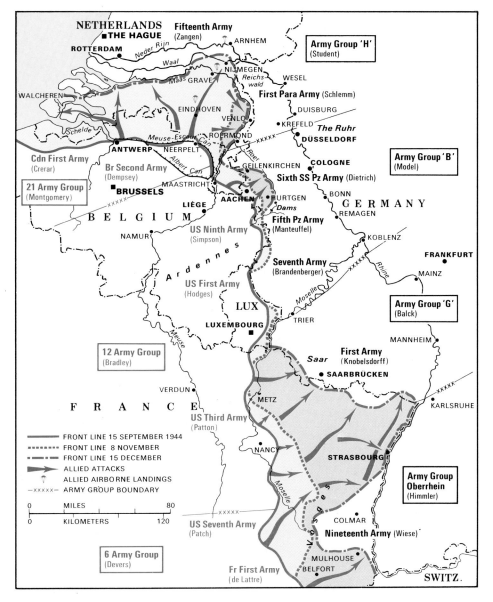

Below: US troops were shot at Malmedy
after they had surrendered to the Germans.
This atrocity did much to stiffen US defense
during the Battle of the Bulge.

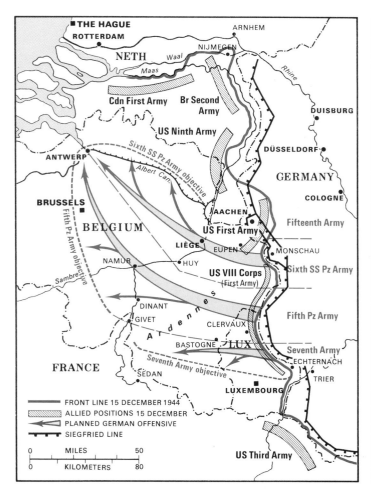

# Planning Germany's Last Offensive

By September 1944 the Western Front had begun to settle down after the fluid operations that followed the Allied breakout from Normandy and although heavy Allied attacks continued in many sectors the German line had been shortened and their forces recovered some strength. The position on the Eastern Front was broadly similar. Hitler and his staff, therefore, began planning for a major counteroffensive using the reserves which this respite would enable them to build. Hitler believed that there was little real cooperation between the British and Americans, that both countries were weary of war and that, at heart, they were

hostile to Soviet communism. Accordingly he decided to attack in the west, convinced that a major success would at worst make Britain sue for peace and America devote her resources to the Pacific while at best there would be changes in the British and American leadership and both countries would join him in the crusade to save European civilization from the Bolsheviks.

The area chosen for the attack was the Ardennes region, where the decisive advance had been made in 1940. The grand aim was to recapture Antwerp, the Allies' most valuable port, and cut the Allied armies in two. Most of the planning was done by Hitler's immediate advisers and when Rundstedt, the Commander in Chief West, and Model, commander of Army Group B were told of the plan, both argued that it was impossibly over-ambitious. They were over-ruled and the preparations continued.

# The Battle of the Bulge

When the German Ardennes offensive began on 16 December 1944 complete tactical and strategic surprise was achieved and the 24 German divisions in the attack were soon making gains at the expense of the six defending divisions of US V and VIII Corps. The Germans employed 10 armored divisions in the advance while most of their infantry was from newly-formed *Volksgrenadier* units. The German preparations had been conducted in extreme secrecy. The assembly of forces had been successfully concealed from Allied reconnaissance while radio traffic had been kept to a minimum, orders being distributed by land line or

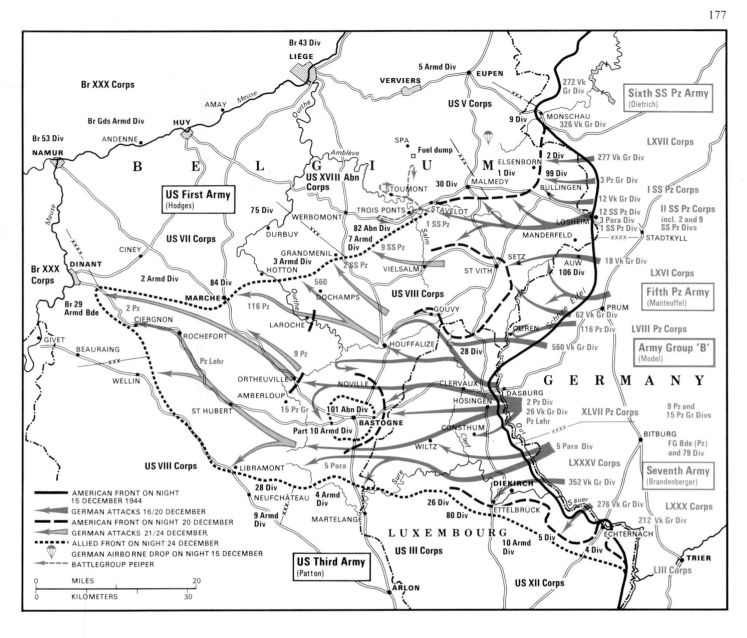

messenger. Although some information had reached the Allies they had become so accustomed to having clear and comprehensive proof of German intentions from their codebreaking services that the scattered hints were ignored.

Several other factors contributed to the initial German success. The overwhelming Allied air support was largely grounded for the first few days of the battle because of bad weather. Special German units, composed of English-speaking troops wearing American uniforms, were sent through the front line on sabotage missions. Although their physical achievements were slight they did succeed in causing considerable confusion. The defending American troops were also an unfortunate mixture of inexperienced newcomers and tired veterans.

The Allied response to the German attack was, however, immediate. Patton's Third Army quickly pulled forces from its front line and rushed them north while the US 82nd and 101st Airborne Divisions were the first of many units to arrive from the main

Allied reserve. On 19 December Eisenhower revised the Allied command arrangements giving Montgomery control of the British and American units north of the Bulge and Bradley charge of the forces to the south. Despite Montgomery's unpopularity with many of the American generals this was an efficient and sensible arrangement.

The Ardennes terrain is dominated by steep wooded hillsides and this places great emphasis on road movement. The decisive points in the battle were, therefore, the junctions at St Vith and Bastogne. Bastogne was successfully defended in an epic struggle by 101st Airborne and 10th Armored Divisions under the command of General McAuliffe. St Vith held out until 22 December by which time so much delay had been inflicted on the advance that all the German commanders wanted the offensive to be abandoned. Hitler insisted that the attacks be continued but by Christmas Eve they had been halted for good. Bastogne was relieved on 26 December as Allied counterattacks got under way. There was hard fighting

throughout January but by the end of the month all the German gains had been retaken. The overall result was a delay of a few weeks in the Allied operations but Germany's last reserve had been dissipated.

178

Right: during the final months of the war the Soviet forces took very large numbers of German prisoners as resistance collapsed. Bottom: Soviet heavy assault guns and trucks in the ruined streets of Königsberg, one of the last German cities to fall.

# Warsaw to the Oder

Having reached the eastern suburbs of Warsaw in the summer of 1944, the Red Army waited until January 1945 before renewing its advance in this sector. The reason for this was partly because the main effort was being made in the Balkans and the Baltic states, partly because the Red Army needed to regroup and re-equip before starting on the final advance to Berlin.

The offensive toward Berlin began on 12 January. While an intense artillery bombardment prevented any German blow from the bridgehead south of Warsaw,

Zhukov advanced past Warsaw, then turned north and threatened the capital from the west, forcing the Germans to evacuate. On 17 January the Russians entered Warsaw and two days later were in Kutno. Konev, meantime, had been advancing through southern Poland and took Krakow on 19 January. In East Prussia, where German forces would have been in a position to threaten the rear of the Russian advance, Rokossovsky crossed the Vistula, passed the site of the Battle of Tannenberg, and reached the Baltic near Elbing. This cut off the Germans in East Prussia, who could be dealt with by Chernyakhovsky's forces, which had broken through the Masurian Lakes defense line farther north.

Only the River Oder now stood between the Red Army and Berlin. In the south, Konev encircled Breslau but postponed its capture while he pushed on to cross the Oder and to halt on the border with Saxony. Zhukov pursued a similar tactic, surrounding Poznan, reaching the Oder, and then occupying East Pomerania to secure his rear. By this time, having captured Danzig, Rokossovsky's troops could join Zhukov's. In preparation for the final stage of the war, Zhukov then forced a crossing of the Oder, establishing two bridgeheads to the north and south of Kustrin. Finally, bringing this phase to a satisfying conclusion, Königsberg surrendered to the Red Army on 9 April, ending German rule in East Prussia.

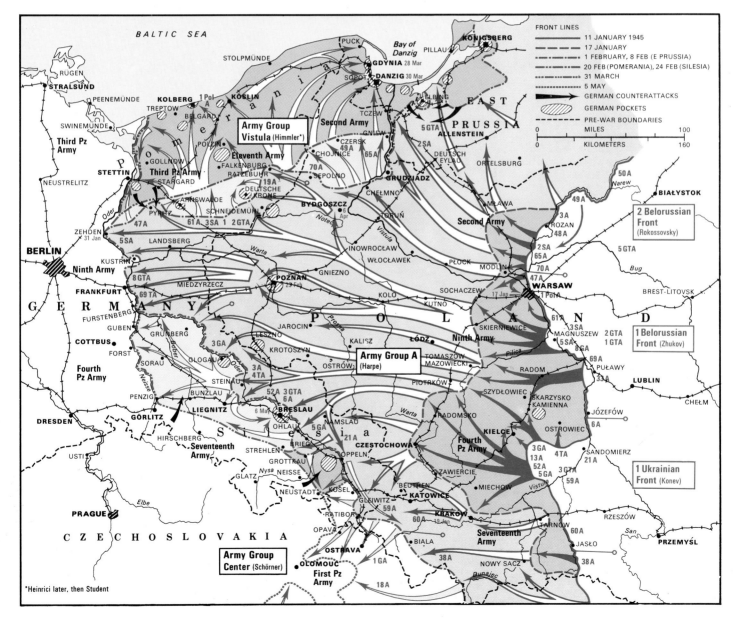

179

Below: US troops and equipment pour
across the Remagen Bridge over the Rhine
and into the heartland of Germany.

# Across the Rhine

By the end of January 1945 the Battle of the
Bulge was over and the German forces were
on the defensive all along the Western Front.

The Allies were ready to resume their
advance to the Rhine. The Allied plan was to
begin their major efforts in the north in
early February where British and Canadian
forces were to advance through the difficult
and heavily defended Reichswald terrain. In
the next phase, from about the middle of the
month, US Ninth and First Armies joined in.
Initially there was fierce German resistance
along the Roer especially at Düren and
Jülich. The German defense was strengthened by use of floodwater from the Schwam-
menauel Dam. By this time Third Army was
also advancing all along its front.

By early March the Allied forces had
reached the Rhine almost everywhere north
of Cologne when the US 9th Armored
Division unexpectedly captured the Ludendorff railroad bridge at Remagen before it
could be destroyed by the retreating
Germans. Although the bridge collapsed on
17 March as a result of German air attacks
and wear and tear from heavy use First Army
was able to seize and consolidate a useful
bridgehead on the right bank.

While this was going on Patton's Third
Army and units of Sixth Army Group were
rushing forward to the Rhine everywhere
between Koblenz and Mannheim and less
obviously 21 Army Group, including Ninth
US Army, was regrouping for a carefully
prepared crossing of the river. They were
forestalled, however, by Patton's Third
Army which sent units across at Nierstein
in a rapidly improvised operation on 22
March. The British and Canadian crossing,
Operation Plunder, got under way successfully on 23 March with the Ninth Army
joining in on the 24th. Units of Third Army
began crossing the Rhine south of Koblenz
on the 25th and Seventh Army took its first
bridgehead near Worms on the 26th. Resistance on the German side was collapsing
accompanied by increasingly strident orders
from Hitler for the institution of a scorched
earth policy.

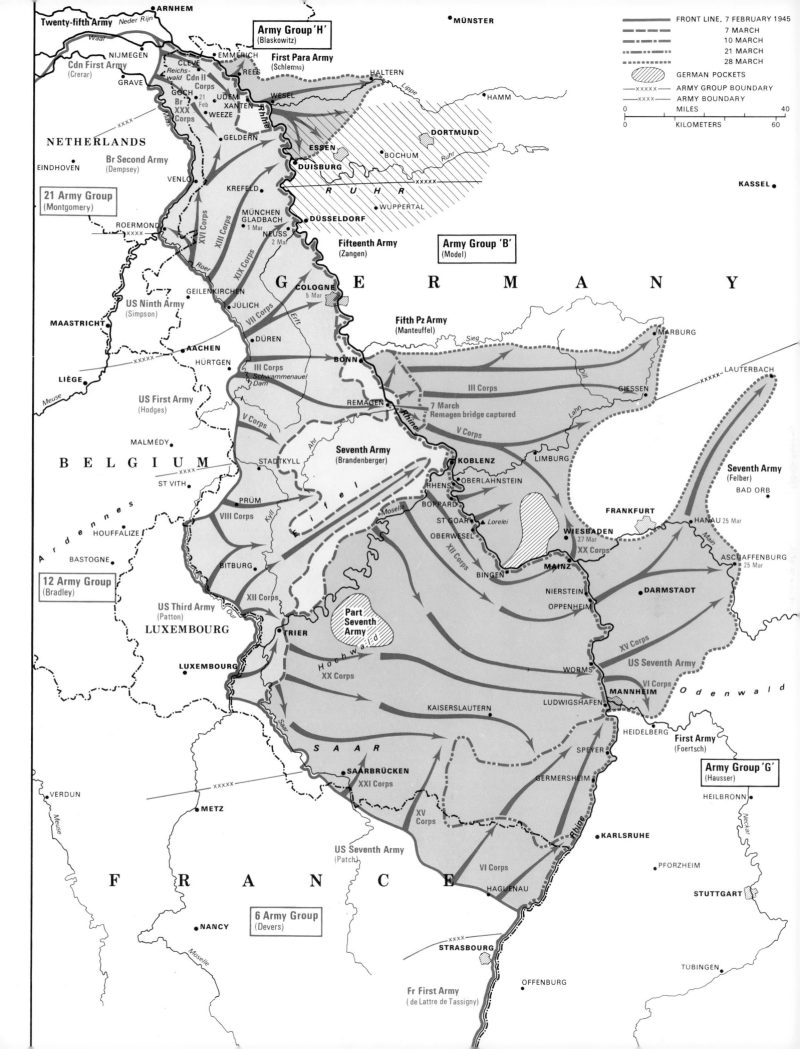

# The Western Advance to the Elbe

By the end of March 1945 the western Allies had established substantial bridgeheads over the Rhine both north and south of the Ruhr industrial area. Although it had previously been his intention to aim his main effort farther north, General Eisenhower, the Supreme Commander, now became concerned by reports that the Germans were fortifying an 'Alpine Redoubt' in the south and were intending to make a last stand there. Eisenhower accordingly decided to switch his main attacks farther south to capitalize on the unexpected ease with which First and Third Armies had crossed the Rhine and forestall retreat by the Germans into such a redoubt. Eisenhower signalled this decision directly to the Soviet High Command. Many of the British leaders felt that this decision was a mistake and that Eisenhower was exceeding his authority by communicating directly with the Soviets without permission from his superiors in Washington and London.

The Allied advance, however, continued as Eisenhower ordered. Although there were occasional stubborn pockets of German resistance most German formations were extremely short of fuel and ammunition and were only too glad to surrender to the western Allies rather than the Russians after a token fight. The Alpine Redoubt proved to be little more than one of Hitler's fantasies. In retrospect, therefore, Eisenhower's decision to concentrate on the military objective of defeating the German Army seems to have been unnecessarily cautious and many would now argue that, although the various Allied occupation zones had already been agreed, it might well have profited the west to advance over the Elbe and farther into Czechoslovakia as would certainly have been possible.

The surrender of the German forces facing the British and Americans was agreed on 4 and 5 May and the formal German surrender was signed on the 7th. Fighting continued for a few days longer in Czechoslovakia. The Allied advances freed many thousands of concentration camp inmates and other victims of the Nazi regime. Although much was already known about Nazi crimes, film and pictures from the camps finally demonstrated the scale and enormity of these to the world.

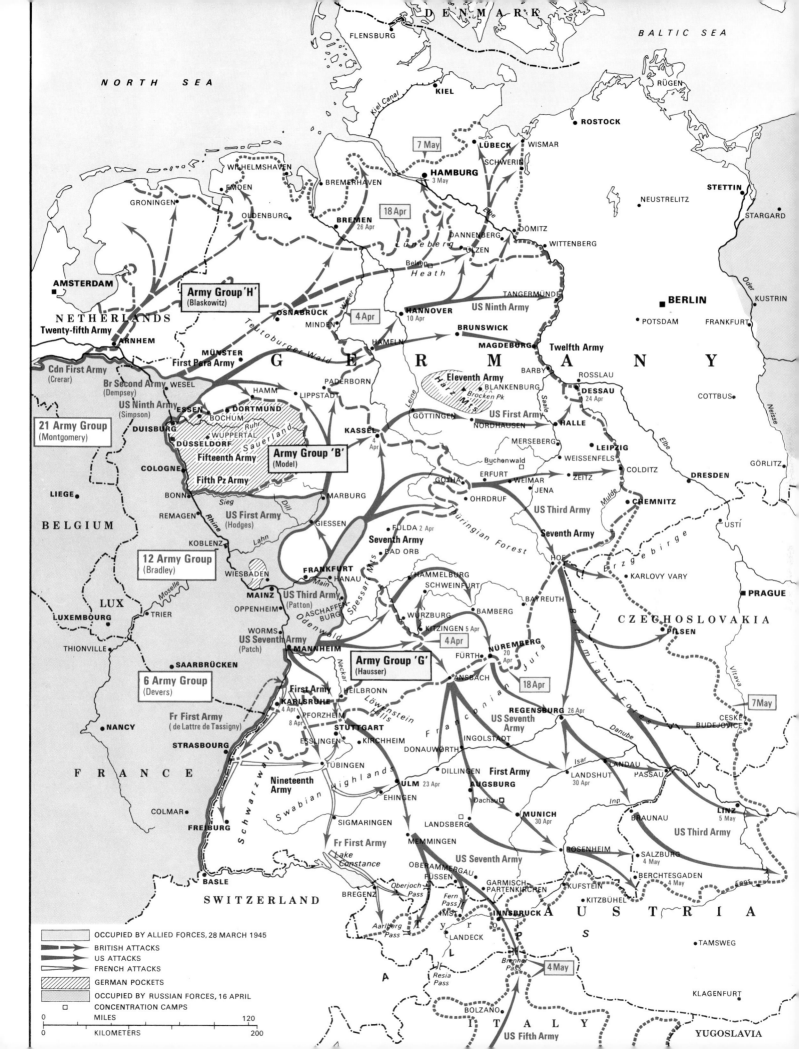

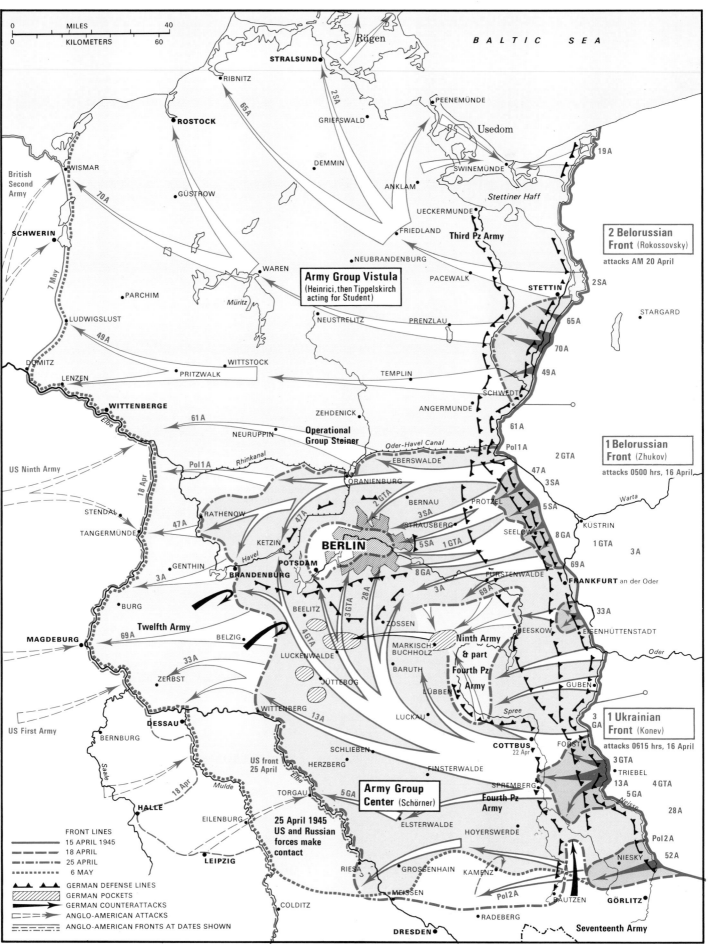

MILES 40
KILOMETERS 60

BALTIC SEA

Rügen

STRALSUND

RIBNITZ

ROSTOCK

PEENEMÜNDE

GRIEFSWALD

Usedom

DEMMIN

SWINEMÜNDE

19A

WISMAR

2SA

British Second Army

ANKLAM

Stettiner Haff

SCHWERIN

WAREN

NEUBRANDENBURG

UECKERMUNDE

65A

70A

Third Pz Army

PARCHIM

Müritz

FRIEDLAND

PACEWALK

STETTIN

2SA

STARGARD

7 May

NEUSTRELITZ

PRENZLAU

2 Belorussian Front (Rokossovsky)

attacks AM 20 April

Army Group Vistula
(Heinrici, then Tippelskirch acting for Student)

LUDWIGSLUST

49A

ZEHDENICK

DÖMITZ

WITTSTOCK

PRITZWALK

TEMPLIN

SCHWEDT

LENZEN

65A

70A

49A

WITTENBERGE

61A

NEURUPPIN

ANGERMÜNDE

61A

Operational Group Steiner

Oder-Havel Canal

Elbe

Rhinkanal

EBERSWALDE

Pol1A

US Ninth Army

Pol1A

2 GTA

1 Belorussian Front (Zhukov)

attacks 0500 hrs, 16 April

18 Apr

47A

ORANIENBURG

2 GTA

BERNAU

PRÖTZEL

47A

3SA

Warta

STENDAL

RATHENOW

47A

3SA

STRAUSBERG

5SA

KÜSTRIN

TANGERMÜNDE

KETZIN

Havel

BERLIN

5SA

1GTA

SEELOW

8 GA

1 GTA

3A

POTSDAM

8 GA

69A

GENTHIN

3A

BRANDENBURG

FÜRSTENWALDE

FRANKFURT an der Oder

BURG

BEELITZ

3GTA

28A

3A

69A

33A

Twelfth Army

BELZIG

ZOSSEN

MÄRKISCH-BUCHHOLZ

Ninth Army & part Fourth Pz Army

BEESKOW

EISENHÜTTENSTADT

MAGDEBURG

69A

LUCKENWALDE

4GTA

BARUTH

Oder

JÜTTEBOG

LÜBBEN

GUBEN

ZERBST

33A

LUCKAU

Spree

1 Ukrainian Front (Konev)

attacks 0615 hrs, 16 April

US First Army

BERNBURG

WITTENBERG

13A

3 GA

COTTBUS
22 Apr

FORST

3GTA

TRIEBEL

Saale

DESSAU

US front 25 April

SCHLIEBEN

HERZBERG

FINSTERWALDE

SPREMBERG

Fourth Pz Army

13A

5 GA

4GTA

Mulde

25 April 1945 US and Russian forces make contact

TORGAU

5 GA

ELSTERWALDE

Neisse

28A

HALLE

EILENBURG

Elbe

Army Group Center (Schörner)

HOYERSWERDE

Pol2A

LEIPZIG

RIESA

GROSSENHAIN

KAMENZ

NIESKY

52A

FRONT LINES
——— 15 APRIL 1945
– – – 18 APRIL
–·–·– 25 APRIL
····· 6 MAY

COLDITZ

MEISSEN

Pol2A

BAUTZEN

GÖRLITZ

GERMAN DEFENSE LINES
GERMAN POCKETS
GERMAN COUNTERATTACKS
ANGLO-AMERICAN ATTACKS
ANGLO-AMERICAN FRONTS AT DATES SHOWN

DRESDEN

RADEBERG

Seventeenth Army

185

Bottom: Soviet tanks advance down a street in Berlin during the closing weeks of the war in Europe.

# The Fall of Berlin

The Red Army's final advance began on 16 April 1945. From his two bridgeheads at Kustrin, Zhukov's troops broke through the German defenses and advanced toward Berlin. His ultimate objective was the River Elbe, beyond Berlin, which was the previously-agreed line where the Anglo-American and Russian occupation zones should meet. South of Zhukov, Konev used bridgeheads on the west bank of the Neisse to start an advance whose left flank was to take Dresden while its right turned north to help surround Berlin. It was Konev's men who, having bypassed Dresden, were the first Russian soldiers to link up with the Americans advancing from the west; this happened at Torgau, on the Elbe, on 25 April.

On 22 April, Zhukov's First Belorussian Front reached the autobahn ringing Berlin, and moved along it to Spandau. With Konev's troops, this effected the complete encirclement of the German capital. Inside Berlin were Hitler and his closest associates, about two million civilians, and 30,000 defenders. On the outskirts, however, were up to one million German troops destined for a last-ditch defense of the city. By this

time the bottom of the German manpower barrel had been scraped, and many of these troops were only half-trained, or of doubtful health, or well below military age. Nevertheless, in the circumstances of a backs-to-the-wall struggle they could be expected to take a heavy toll of the attackers. The latter, with their supporting units, numbered about two and one-half million men, well-trained, well-equipped, experienced, and having the advantage of Soviet command of the air.

In the final assault, Zhukov's Front attacked from the north and Konev's First Ukrainian Front from the south. After two days of fierce fighting Zhukov's tanks reached the northern outskirts on 28 April, by which time Konev's infantry and tanks had fought their way as far as the Tiergarten, which lay close to the center of Berlin. The two Russian fronts were thus only a mile apart, but it took another four days of house-to-house fighting, a Stalingrad in reverse, before they linked up. By this time Hitler, whose bunker lay between these two Russian pincers, had killed himself. The senior surviving German officer, General Krebs, went to negotiate with the Russians and was confronted with a demand for unconditional surrender. By 2 May the red flag was flying from the chancellery and fighting had ceased.

# Battle of the Philippine Sea

After the capture of Kwajalein and Eniwetok in the Marshall Islands the next targets for the US offensive were Saipan, Tinian and Guam in the Marianas. The main US carrier forces began preparatory attacks for the landings on 11 June 1944 and Admiral Toyoda, the Commander in Chief of the Japanese Combined Fleet, prepared for a full-scale battle. The Japanese naval forces came under the direct command of Admiral Ozawa and included five fleet carriers, two light and two seaplane carriers as well as five battleships and numerous supporting vessels. Altogether these ships carried about 470 aircraft and there were about 100 more on Guam which survived the preliminary American attacks to take part in the battle. The Americans had about 950 aircraft on their seven fleet and eight light carriers as well as superior numbers in other classes of ship. Most of the US ships were from Admiral Mitscher's TF.58 but Admiral Spruance, the overall commander of the Marianas invasion, was also present. The US forces were well warned of the

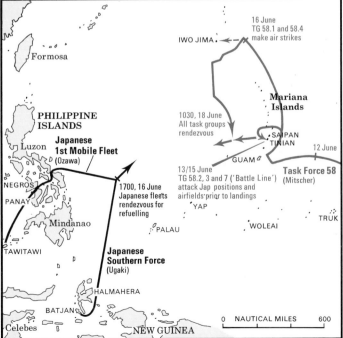

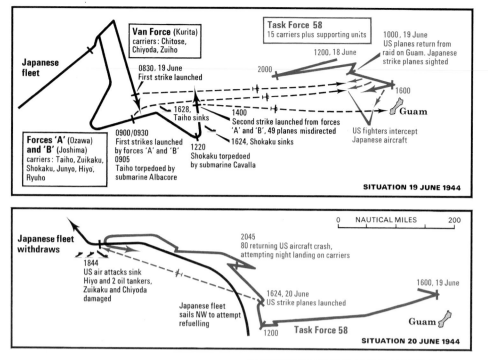

**Japanese fleet**

**Van Force** (Kurita)
carriers: Chitose, Chiyoda, Zuiho

**Task Force 58**
15 carriers plus supporting units

1000, 19 June
US planes return from raid on Guam. Japanese strike planes sighted

1200, 18 June

2000

0830, 19 June
First strike launched

1600

Guam

1628,
Taiho sinks

1400
Second strike launched from forces 'A' and 'B', 49 planes misdirected

US fighters intercept Japanese aircraft

**Forces 'A'** (Ozawa) **and 'B'** (Joshima)
carriers: Taiho, Zuikaku, Shokaku, Junyo, Hiyo, Ryuho

0900/0930
First strikes launched by forces 'A' and 'B'

0905
Taiho torpedoed by submarine Albacore

1220
Shokaku torpedoed by submarine Cavalla

1624, Shokaku sinks

**SITUATION 19 JUNE 1944**

**Japanese fleet withdraws**

0    NAUTICAL MILES    200

2045
80 returning US aircraft crash, attempting night landing on carriers

1844
US air attacks sink Hiyo and 2 oil tankers, Zuikaku and Chiyoda damaged

1600, 19 June

1624, 20 June
US strike planes launched

Japanese fleet sails NW to attempt refuelling

1200

Guam

**Task Force 58**

**SITUATION 20 JUNE 1944**

# The Battles for Leyte

After considerable discussion the Allied High Command decided that, on completion of the Marianas battles and the campaign in New Guinea, the American forces should next begin the reconquest of the Philippines with landings on Leyte Island. General MacArthur's forces from the Southwest Pacific command area combined with Admiral Nimitz's for this operation.

Japanese approach through submarine sightings and a further disadvantage for Ozawa was that the Marianas commanders had failed to inform him how badly hit their air forces had been by the early US attacks. Practically the sole Japanese advantage was that their aircraft generally had a longer range and so they could expect to get in their strikes first.

This in fact they did on 19 June, the first day of the battle. The Americans were content to defend and did so so successfully that their pilots and gunners dubbed the battle the 'Great Marianas Turkey Shoot.' The Americans lost 29 planes and the Japanese about 300 including a number destroyed over Guam. Only one bomb hit an American ship. Two Japanese carriers were sunk by American submarines. On the 20th the Americans pursued and managed to sink a third carrier but lost a number of aircraft.

The Battle of the Philippine Sea dealt a further serious blow to Japanese naval power. Far more than the ships lost, the trained carrier pilots and their aircraft could not be replaced and in the next major naval encounter, the Battle of Leyte Gulf, the Japanese carriers could only find token air groups to embark.

With the US naval forces dominant the ground battles for the Marianas Islands could only go one way despite the ferocious Japanese resistance. There were landings on Saipan on 15 June even before the Philippine Sea Battle, on Guam on 21 July and on Tinian on 24 July. The largest Japanese garrison, 27,000 men, was on Saipan but the last effective resistance there was wiped out on 9 July and the battles for Tinian (garrison 6000) and Guam (10,000) were both concluded by mid-August. Almost all the Japanese defenders on all three islands were killed while the Americans lost over 5000 dead and 20,000 wounded.

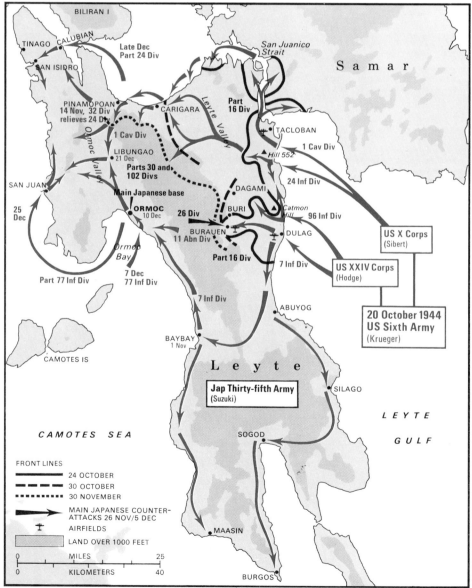

BILIRAN I

TINAGO    CALUBIAN

SAN ISIDRO

Late Dec
Part 24 Div

San Juanico Strait

S a m a r

PINAMOPOAN
14 Nov, 32 Div relieves 24 Div

CARIGARA

Part 16 Div

TACLOBAN

Leyte Valley

1 Cav Div

Hill 552

1 Cav Div

LIBUNGAO
21 Dec

Parts 30 and 102 Divs

DAGAMI

24 Inf Div

SAN JUAN

Main Japanese base

BURI

Catmon Hill

96 Inf Div

25 Dec

ORMOC
10 Dec

26 Div

BURAUEN
11 Abn Div

DULAG

US X Corps
(Sibert)

Ormoc Bay

Part 16 Div

7 Inf Div

US XXIV Corps
(Hodge)

Part 77 Inf Div

7 Dec
77 Inf Div

7 Inf Div

ABUYOG

20 October 1944
US Sixth Army
(Krueger)

BAYBAY
1 Nov

CAMOTES IS

L e y t e

SILAGO

**Jap Thirty-fifth Army**
(Suzuki)

L E Y T E

G U L F

C A M O T E S   S E A

SOGOD

FRONT LINES

———— 24 OCTOBER
– – – – 30 OCTOBER
· · · · · 30 NOVEMBER
——▶ MAIN JAPANESE COUNTER-ATTACKS 26 NOV/5 DEC
✠ AIRFIELDS
▨ LAND OVER 1000 FEET

0    MILES    25
0    KILOMETERS    40

MAASIN

BURGOS

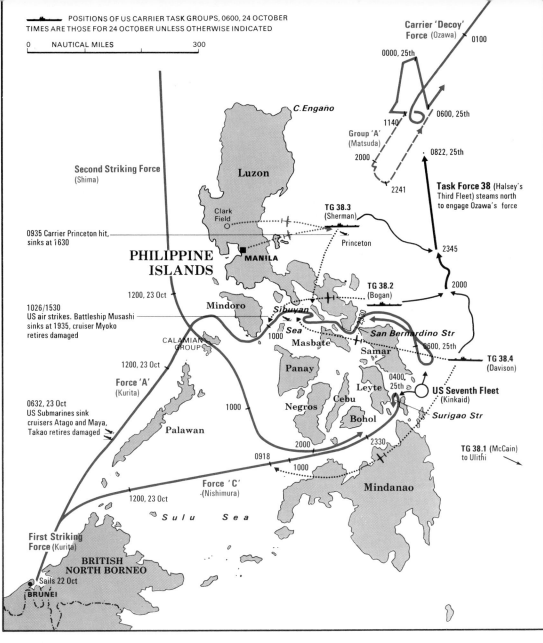

POSITIONS OF US CARRIER TASK GROUPS, 0600, 24 OCTOBER
TIMES ARE THOSE FOR 24 OCTOBER UNLESS OTHERWISE INDICATED

0    NAUTICAL MILES    300

Carrier 'Decoy' Force (Ozawa)    0100

0000, 25th

C. Engano

1140    0600, 25th

Group 'A' (Matsuda)

0822, 25th

2000

2241

Task Force 38 (Halsey's Third Fleet) steams north to engage Ozawa's force

Second Striking Force (Shima)

Luzon

Clark Field

TG 38.3 (Sherman)

0935 Carrier Princeton hit, sinks at 1630

Princeton

PHILIPPINE ISLANDS

MANILA

2345

2000

1200, 23 Oct

Mindoro

TG 38.2 (Bogan)

1026/1530 US air strikes. Battleship Musashi sinks at 1935, cruiser Myoko retires damaged

Sibuyan

Sea

San Bernardino Str

Masbate

0600, 25th

CALAMIAN GROUPS

1000

Samar

TG 38.4 (Davison)

1200, 23 Oct

Panay

Force 'A' (Kurita)

Leyte

0400, 25th

US Seventh Fleet (Kinkaid)

0632, 23 Oct US Submarines sink cruisers Atago and Maya, Takao retires damaged

1000

Negros

Cebu

Bohol

Surigao Str

Palawan

2000

2330

TG 38.1 (McCain) to Ulithi

0918

1000

Force 'C' (Nishimura)

Mindanao

1200, 23 Oct

Sulu    Sea

First Striking Force (Kurita)

BRITISH NORTH BORNEO

Sails 22 Oct

BRUNEI

On land the familiar story of overwhelming American forces gradually wearing down a totally determined defense was repeated. General Krueger's Sixth Army could call on up to 200,000 troops of whom some 130,000 landed on the first day. Initially the Japanese had just over 20,000 men on Leyte and although substantial reinforcements were brought in, these usually took heavy casualties in transit from US air attacks. The Japanese 26th Division, for example, arrived practically bereft of rations and artillery. Although mopping up extended well into 1945 there were few important engagements after Christmas 1944. Japanese casualties have been estimated variously from 50–80,000. The Americans lost 3600 dead.

At sea the Japanese again tried to turn the tide of the war by bringing on a major fleet action. The three-part battle that resulted is known as the Battle of Leyte Gulf. The Japanese naval air arm had lost so many planes and pilots earlier in the war that the remaining aircraft carriers had very few aircraft to embark. It was decided, therefore,

to use the carriers as a decoy while the substantial battleship and cruiser force did the real damage. The strongest squadron, Force A, was to reach the American invasion area via the San Bernardino Strait while two smaller forces advanced by the Surigao Strait.

Force A was detected en route by American submarines and heavily attacked by them and aircraft summed from the main US carrier formation, TF.38. These attacks made Force A turn away. Mistaking this temporary move for a permanent withdrawal, the American carriers then sped north to catch Ozawa's decoy force. Since Force C had also been detected the bombardment support ships of Seventh Fleet were moved to block its approach, in the belief that the San Bernardino Strait was still guarded by TF.38. Nishimura's ships were almost all destroyed in a night battle and Shima turned back after also suffering some losses. The American carriers sank many of Ozawa's ships including the last veteran of Pearl Harbor, the *Zuikaku*. However, Kurita had reversed course and on the morning of

25 October his battleships and cruisers came into gun range of some of the vulnerable and practically unsupported escort carriers of Seventh Fleet. If the Japanese ships had been well and resolutely commanded they might even have penetrated into the American transport fleet and caused untold destruction. Instead they withdrew tamely after only limited success. The Battle of Leyte Gulf was the last important effort of the Japanes Navy.

The task of the Allied naval forces was made more hazardous by the beginning of preplanned suicide attacks by Japanese aircraft. The first ship hit by a Kamikaze attack, on 21 October, was the cruiser *Australia*, one of several Australian ships serving with the American forces.

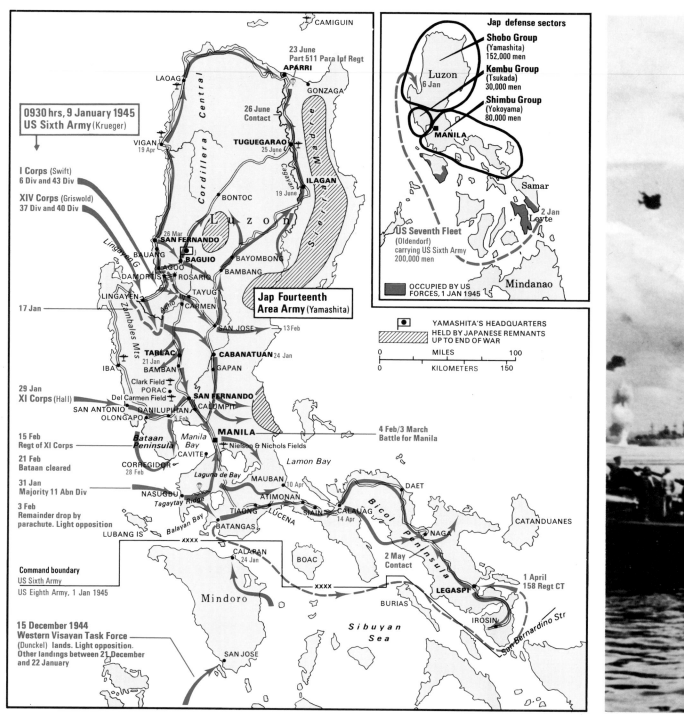

**0930 hrs, 9 January 1945**
**US Sixth Army** (Krueger)

**I Corps** (Swift)
6 Div and 43 Div

**XIV Corps** (Griswold)
37 Div and 40 Div

17 Jan

29 Jan
**XI Corps** (Hall)

15 Feb
Regt of XI Corps

21 Feb
Bataan cleared

31 Jan
Majority 11 Abn Div

3 Feb
Remainder drop by
parachute. Light opposition

**Command boundary**
US Sixth Army
US Eighth Army, 1 Jan 1945

**15 December 1944**
Western Visayan Task Force
(Dunckel) lands. Light opposition.
Other landings between 21 December
and 22 January

**Jap Fourteenth
Area Army** (Yamashita)

**Jap defense sectors**
**Shobo Group**
(Yamashita)
152,000 men
**Kembu Group**
(Tsukada)
30,000 men
**Shimbu Group**
(Yokoyama)
80,000 men

**US Seventh Fleet**
(Oldendorf)
carrying US Sixth Army
200,000 men

OCCUPIED BY US
FORCES, 1 JAN 1945

YAMASHITA'S HEADQUARTERS
HELD BY JAPANESE REMNANTS
UP TO END OF WAR

MILES 100
KILOMETERS 150

# The Capture of Luzon

The Japanese commander responsible for the whole Philippines group, General Yamashita, had been ordered, against his better judgment, to do his utmost to hold Leyte in face of the American attacks. Thus when the Americans quickly moved to invade Luzon as the fighting on Leyte died down, the Japanese forces, though numerically strong, were neither well armed nor well prepared. Kamikaze attacks against the landing fleet were fairly successful in their way for the first few days of the operation but after this almost all the Japanese aircraft were with-

drawn from the Philippines to Formosa or had been destroyed.

After his losses on Leyte Yamashita did not believe that he could repel an American landing and accordingly the beach defenses were only lightly held. Instead Yamashita planned to make his stand in the inland mountain areas for as long as possible and so tie down large American forces. Particularly in north Luzon this was the pattern that the fighting took on. Baguio, where Yamashita had had his HQ, was not taken until 27 April and when he surrendered at the end of the war Yamashita still had some 50,000 fighting men under his command.

Undoubtedly the most bitterly contested part of the campaign was the recapture of

Manila. The city garrison died almost to a man in the defense and the fighting left Manila in ruins. By the end of the war landing operations in cooperation with Filipino guerillas had taken control of most of the other islands of the Philippine group.

**Above: US Navy PT-Boats come under
attack from Japanese bombers during the
reoccupation of the Philippines.**
**Top right: GIs take cover from sniper fire
during the fighting to recapture Clark Field
airbase in the Philippines.**

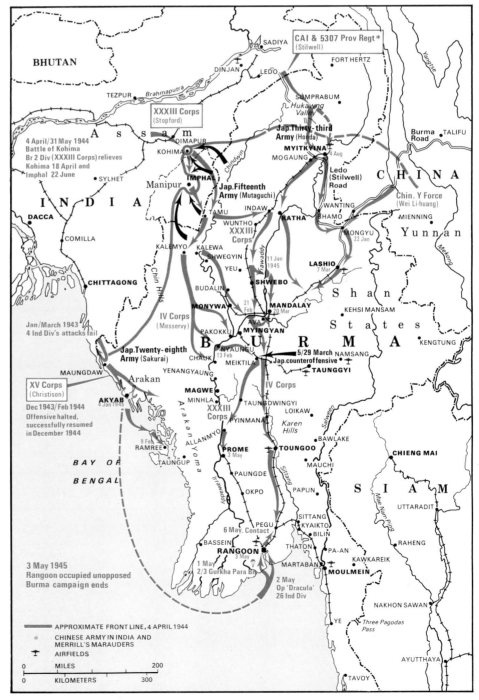

CAI & 5307 Prov Regt *
(Stilwell)

BHUTAN

SADIYA
DINJAN
LEDO
FORT HERTZ
TEZPUR  *Brahmaputra*
SUMPRABUM
*Hukawng Valley*
Burma Road  TALIFU
XXXIII Corps
(Stopford)

4 April/31 May 1944
Battle of Kohima
Br 2 Div (XXXIII Corps) relieves
Kohima 18 April and
Imphal 22 June

A  s  s  a  m
DIMAPUR
KOHIMA
Jap. Thirty-third
Army (Honda)
MYITKYINA  4 Aug
MOGAUNG
Ledo (Stilwell) Road
CHINA

SYLHET
*Chindwin*
IMPHAL
Manipur
Jap. Fifteenth
Army (Mutaguchi)
INDAW
KATHA
BHAMO
WANTING
Chin. Y Force
(Wei Li-huang)
MIENNING
Yunnan

INDIA
TAMU
WUNTHO
XXXIII
Corps
MONGYU  22 Jan

DACCA
YEU
*Irrawaddy*
11 Jan 1945
LASHIO  7 Mar

COMILLA
KALEMYO  KALEWA
SHWEGYIN
BUDALIN
SHWEBO
Shan

CHITTAGONG
*Chin Hills*
MONYWA
21 Feb
MANDALAY  20 Mar
KEHSI MANSAM
States

IV Corps
(Messervy)
AVA
MYINGYAN
PAKOKKU
Jan/March 1943
4 Ind Div's attacks fail
Jap. Twenty-eighth
Army (Sakurai)
NYAUNGU
13 Feb
CHAUK  MEIKTILA
5/29 March  NAMSANG
Jap. counteroffensive
TAUNGGYI
KENGTUNG

MAUNGDAW
Arakan
YENANGYAUNG
B  U  R  M  A

XV Corps
(Christison)
AKYAB
4 Jan 1945
MAGWE
MINHLA
XXXIII
Corps
TAUNGDWINGYI
LOIKAW
*Karen Hills*
IV Corps
*Salween*

Dec 1943/Feb 1944
Offensive halted,
successfully resumed
in December 1944
9 Feb
RAMREE
PYINMANA
BAWLAKE
CHIENG MAI

*Arakan yoma*
ALLANMYO
PROME
3 May
TOUNGOO
MAUCHI

BAY OF
BENGAL
TAUNGUP
PAUNGDE
*Sittang*
PAPUN
S  I  A  M
*Mae Nam Ping*
UTTARADIT

OKPO
RAHENG

3 May 1945
Rangoon occupied unopposed
Burma campaign ends
PEGU
6 May. Contact
SITTANG
KYAIKTO
BILIN
PA-AN
KAWKAREIK

BASSEIN
RANGOON
3 May
THATON
MARTABAN
MOULMEIN
1 May
2/3 Gurkha Para Bn
2 May Op 'Dracula'
26 Ind Div

NAKHON SAWAN

YE
*Three Pagodas Pass*

━━━  APPROXIMATE FRONT LINE, 4 APRIL 1944
  *   CHINESE ARMY IN INDIA AND
       MERRILL'S MARAUDERS
  ✈   AIRFIELDS

0          MILES          200
0        KILOMETERS       300

AYUTTHAYA
TAVOY

# The Burma Campaign

To most of the Allied leaders the Burma theater came very low on the scale of priorities. Even when they agreed that resources could be sent there, the British and Americans rarely agreed on the strategy to be followed. The Americans thought that the main objective should be to reopen land communications with the Chinese Nationalists to help them against the large forces of the Japanese Army which were tied up in China. The British had far less respect for Chiang and the Nationalists (perhaps more realistically) and preferred to plan to recover

190

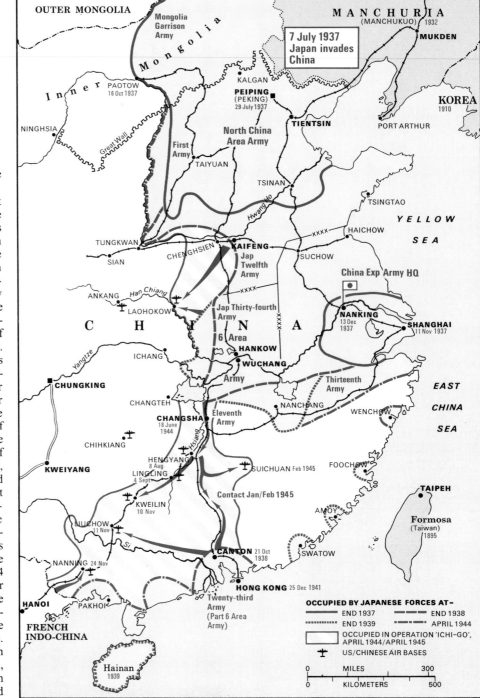

the imperial territories lost to the Japanese in 1942.

Whatever strategy was to be followed it was first necessary to build a respectable fighting force from the shattered remnants that had retreated to the Indian border in April-May 1942. Much work had also to be done to improve communications between India and northern Burma. The first offensive move, an advance in the Arakan in early 1943, was decisively defeated by Japanese infiltration tactics. A new British commander, General Slim, took over at the end of this operation and developed new tactics. He laid down that, in future, encircled units should not retreat to restore their communications but hold out with the help of air supply while reserve units retook the rear areas. A further innovation based on the use of air supply was the establishment of independent units designed to operate behind the Japanese lines. The efforts of these Chindits or their American equivalent, the Maurauders, were not an unqualified military success but they made an important contribution to Allied morale by showing that it was possible to take on the Japanese in the jungle and win. The technique of supplying surrounded formations from the air helped stem a limited Japanese counteroffensive in the Arakan early in 1944 and played a vital part in defeating the major Japanese offensive that followed in the battles of Imphal and Kohima. This campaign was by far the heaviest defeat that the Japanese Army had suffered to that time. The Allied forces resumed their advance on all fronts in late 1944, after the monsoon, and the Japanese were again soundly beaten in the decisive battles around Meiktila and Mandalay. Rangoon was captured by a seaborne landing at the start of May 1945 after virtually all the Japanese forces had been expelled from Burma.

# The War in China

Following Japan's establishment of Manchukuo in 1931–32, there was little fighting between Japan and China until 1937. The Chinese were absorbed in the struggle between the Nationalists and Communists while the Japanese government was opposed to further aggressive moves although it was not always in full control of the army. In July 1937 an incident between Japanese and Nationalist soldiers on the Peking–Tientsin railroad quickly escalated into a major Japanese invasion. There was no declaration of war by either side at this stage. Large areas of China were quickly overrun and Chiang Kai-shek was forced to move his capital to Chungking. Chiang did receive some help from Britain and America but neither country was able or willing to do much at this point.

By 1939 the Japanese advance had been stopped and the Japanese forces were consolidating their gains while it seemed that Chiang had been reduced to being a minor warlord. From then until 1944 the Japanese made no major forward moves apart from occasional 'rice offensives' to seize food supplies, and attacks against the mainly communist guerrilla forces. Chiang's position recovered to some degree with considerable help from the western allies although

Below: American Marines man forward positions on Iwo Jima facing Mount Suribachi. Casualties were very heavy on both sides in this operation.

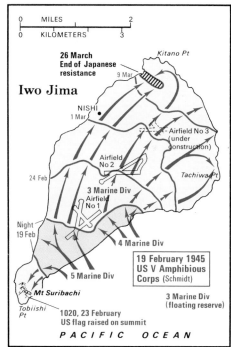

# Iwo Jima

After Saipan and Tinian in the Marianas Islands were taken by the US forces in June and July 1944 huge air bases were constructed there from which B-29 Superfortress bombers could begin an all-out strategic bombing attack on Japan. Although the Japanese air defense system was never as efficient as the German effort to ward off the Allied bomber offensive in Europe, losses were uncomfortably high. A base on Iwo Jima could be used to provide needed fighter support and an emergency landing ground for damaged bombers unable to complete the long journey back to the Marianas. This was the principal reason for the US attack but since it was a part of metropolitan Japan the capture of Iwo Jima would be good for morale too.

From the outset it was clear that a stubborn defense of the island could be expected and a massive preliminary air and naval bombardment was ordered. However, the 21,000-strong Japanese garrison led by General Kuribayashi had constructed an astonishingly elaborate and resilient defense system much of which survived the early attacks. The Japanese plan was to wait until the landings had just begun before showing their hand and opening fire. In the event they held off a little too long and the Marines were able to fight their way off the beaches. By the end of the first day 30,000 US troops were ashore. Although the battle could now have only one result the complex of trenches, tunnels and strongpoints and the fanatical determination of the defenders meant that the US forces had to fight for virtually every yard of the island. Casualties were very high. The US forces lost 6800 dead and 20,000 wounded.

their supply efforts were hampered by the cutting of the Burma Road by the Japanese advance in 1942. From then until January 1945 all supplies to Chiang had to be flown 'Over the Hump' from India. Large quantities were sent, some to General Chennault's Fourteenth US Air Force. Corruption within the Kuomintang and Chiang's preoccupation with building up his forces to meet the Communists, meant that the Kuomintang did not make full use of the supplies against the Japanese.

However, the growing strength and activity of Fourteenth Air Force provoked the Japanese into renewing their attacks. Their initial efforts were by First and Twelfth Armies in April 1944 in the Kaifeng area and, after some regrouping, the attacks were extended south later in the year. In the meantime Superfortress bombers based near Calcutta in India had attacked targets in the Japanese Home Islands using forward airfields in China. Despite the additional incentive this gave to the Japanese attacks the difficult communications and the demands of other areas meant that progress was very slow by early 1945. In the final months of the war the Nationalists recovered some territory near the Indo-China border.

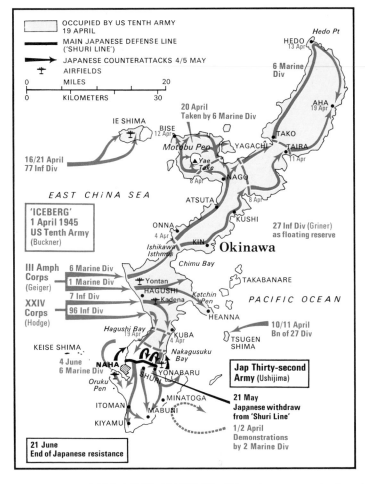

Map legend:

- OCCUPIED BY US TENTH ARMY 19 APRIL
- MAIN JAPANESE DEFENSE LINE ('SHURI LINE')
- JAPANESE COUNTERATTACKS 4/5 MAY
- AIRFIELDS

```
0        MILES        20
0     KILOMETERS      30
```

Hedo Pt
HEDO 13 Apr
6 Marine Div
AHA 19 Apr
TAKO
20 April Taken by 6 Marine Div
IE SHIMA
BISE 12 Apr
Motobu Pen
YAGACHI
TAIRA 11 Apr
16/21 April 77 Inf Div
Yae Take
8 Apr
NAGO
8 Apr
EAST CHINA SEA
ATSUTA

'ICEBERG'
1 April 1945
US Tenth Army
(Buckner)

ONNA
4 Apr
KUSHI
KIN
Okinawa
Ishikawa Isthmus
27 Inf Div (Griner) as floating reserve
Chimu Bay

III Amph Corps (Geiger)    6 Marine Div
                           1 Marine Div    Yontan
XXIV Corps (Hodge)         7 Inf Div       Kadena
                           96 Inf Div
HAGUSHI
Katchin Pen
TAKABANARE
PACIFIC OCEAN
HEANNA
10/11 April Bn of 27 Div
TSUGEN SHIMA
Hagushi Bay 19 Apr
KUBA 4 Apr
Nakagusuku Bay
KEISE SHIMA
Jap Thirty-second Army (Ushijima)
4 June 6 Marine Div
NAHA
SHURI
YONABARU
21 May Japanese withdraw from 'Shuri Line'
Oruku Pen
MINATOGA
ITOMAN
MABUNI
1/2 April Demonstrations by 2 Marine Div
KIYAMU
21 June End of Japanese resistance

# Okinawa

The attack on Okinawa was planned as the last major landing operation before the invasion of the Japanese home islands for which the capture of Okinawa was necessary to provide harbor and air base facilities. As was customary the campaign began with carrier and other air attacks to soften up the local defenses and the supporting air bases on Kyushu. The newly-active British Pacific Fleet joined in these operations. The carrier and bombardment groups continued to give support throughout the battle.

The Japanese Thirty-second Army defending Okinawa under General Ushijima's command was about 130,000 strong and had most of its forces concentrated at the southern end of the island behind a formidable position known as the Shuri Line. There was no intention of resisting the Americans on the beaches and the only heavily defended areas apart from the Shuri position were the Motobu Peninsula and the offshore island of Ie Shima.

The American landings began on 1 April and, as the map shows, most of the island was quickly overrun with little opposition. However, XXIV Corps made little progress once the Shuri Line defenses were met. Despite overwhelming air and bombardment support, gains were few until unsuccessful Japanese attacks in early May had

given away the locations of many of their defensive positions. From that time reinforced attacks by both US corps gradually pushed forward to finish the battle despite difficult ground and weather conditions.

The supporting naval forces had a fierce battle of their own to fight. The kamikaze attacks which had become a feature of Japanese tactics were here developed to their fullest extent. Several thousand Japanese aircraft were destroyed during the Okinawa operation, a great number of them kamikazes. The US and British naval forces had 36 ships sunk and 368 damaged, almost all of them by suicide attacks. Perhaps the most bizarre aspect of the campaign was the employment of the giant battleship *Yamato* which was sent off to Okinawa on what amounted to a suicide mission since too little fuel was carried to make a return journey possible. The *Yamato* was sunk by US carrier planes on 7 April long before she could reach the invasion area and without causing the hoped-for disruption to the American air defense system which would have allowed the simultaneous program of air attacks to achieve important successes.

The casualty lists on both sides were extensive. For the first time a significant number of Japanese troops, over 7000, was taken prisoner, but this still meant that over 120,000 died or committed suicide. In addition there were a great many civilian casualties. Okinawa was fairly densely populated and the local people had been in-

doctrinated with stories of American brutality. The US forces lost 12,500 dead, including the Army Commander General Buckner, and 35,000 wounded. As a rehearsal for the invasion of Japan these casualty totals were frightening to the Americans and could only support the case for bringing the war to an end by other means.

**Left:** Marines from the Sixth Division reach the outskirts of Naha on Okinawa, 6 June 1945.
**Bottom:** F4U Corsair fighters are silhouetted by antiaircraft fire during a Japanese air raid on Yontan airfield, Okinawa, April 1945.
**Right:** Soviet occupying forces in Harbin Manchuria, August 1945.

# Manchuria

After the end of the war in Europe strong Soviet forces were transferred to the Far East to face the Japanese in Manchuria. The USSR declared war on Japan on 8 August 1945 and the Soviet armies attacked on the following day. They employed about 1,500,000 men against the Japanese commander Yamada's 1,000,000 and had far superior tanks and other equipment as well as overwhelming air support. There was little real fighting and Manchuria and northern Korea were quickly overrun.

The possibility of Soviet participation in the Pacific War was first raised seriously at the inter-Allied Teheran conference in December 1943. Stalin promised to join the war against Japan as soon as the war in Europe was over and this promise was confirmed at Yalta in February 1945 in return for some territorial concessions and the promise of Soviet influence in the region being recognized. Roosevelt was the principal architect of these negotiations and he has been criticized for setting aside earlier promises to Chiang Kai-shek to gain this Soviet help. At the time, however, it was generally felt, bearing in mind the very large Japanese forces undefeated in China and the

normal ferocity of Japanese resistance elsewhere in the Pacific, that Soviet participation in the war against Japan would be of vital help.

The Allied leaders met again at Potsdam in July 1945 and issued new calls on the Japanese to surrender. By this time also the atomic bomb had become available and President Truman ordered its use if the Japanese did not respond to the Potsdam Declaration. Although many Japanese leaders wanted peace and had tried to communicate with the Allies through still-neutral Russia, they were unwilling to consider capitulation unless the position of the Emperor was guaranteed and they therefore made no satisfactory reply to the Potsdam message. The first atomic bomb was therefore dropped on Hiroshima on 6 August 1945 and the second on Nagasaki on the 9th as the Soviet attacks began. It has been suggested that the Soviet attacks were started earlier than planned so that advantage could be gained before the bombs

forced the Japanese to surrender. If this was the case then there is evidence that this was misguided since Japanese records lay as much stress on the Soviet attacks as on the atomic bombs as the final cause which brought about the surrender. The western Allies were able to celebrate victory over Japan on 15 August although some fighting continued in Manchuria for a few days longer.

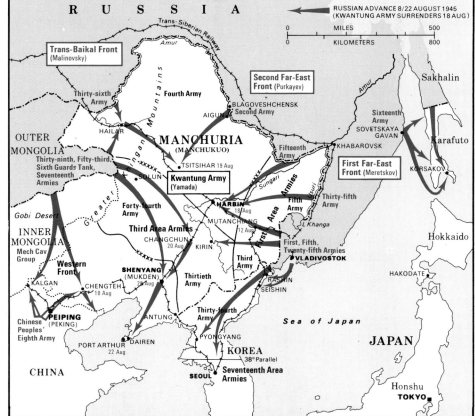

Tanzanian troops advance past a burning Ugandan vehicle during the fighting to depose General Amin in 1978.

# The Postwar World

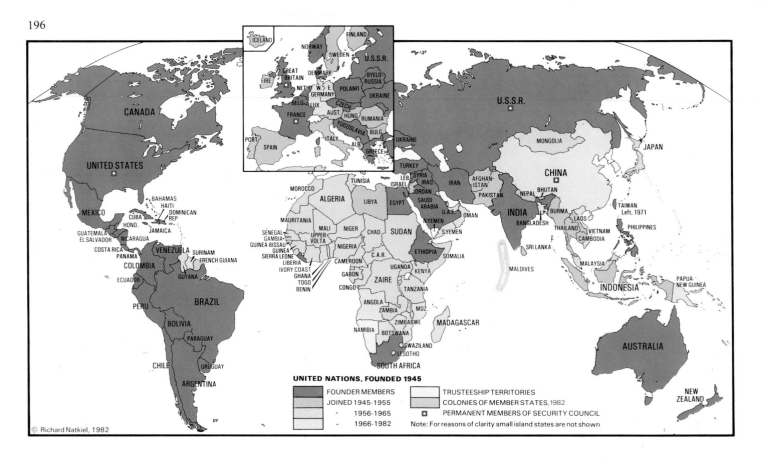

UNITED NATIONS, FOUNDED 1945

FOUNDER MEMBERS
JOINED 1945-1955
"        1956-1965
"        1966-1982

TRUSTEESHIP TERRITORIES
COLONIES OF MEMBER STATES, 1982
□ PERMANENT MEMBERS OF SECURITY COUNCIL
Note: For reasons of clarity small island states are not shown

© Richard Natkiel, 1982

# The United Nations

Looking back at the failures of the League of Nations, the statesmen who in 1945 planned the United Nations Organization laid priority on two precautions: UNO was to have a membership of as near as possible all states, and the great powers had to be among that membership. Secondly, it had to have within itself a small group of powerful states which would not hesitate to act together against a threat to world peace. It was from these considerations that the concept of a General Assembly representing all nations, with a small Security Council as its executive branch, was embodied in the United Nations Charter.

Even though it was only the handful of victorious powers which had the initiative in composing the UN Charter, they could only reach overall agreement at the expense of compromise which weakened the Organization. Thus the concept of one-state-one-vote was weakened when the USSR was granted three seats in the General Assembly; Moscow had argued that if the British dominions each had a seat, so should the constituent republics of the USSR, and after some argument it was agreed that Byelorussia and the Ukraine should have their own representatives. The Security Council was to consist of five permanent members and six (later ten) short-term members. The five permanent members were the victorious powers (USA, USSR, Britain, France, China), each of which had the right to veto a resolution. In practice this

meant that the Council could be paralyzed and, with some exceptions, the peacekeeping activity of UNO depended on the agreement, all too rare, of the permanent members. In practice, therefore, its existence has facilitated rather than compelled conciliation of disputes.

Meanwhile, with decolonization, the number of new states grew and inside the General Assembly a loose alliance of Arab and African states, supported intermittently by the Soviet Bloc, and some Asian and South American states, began to emerge in the 1960s. This alliance could prevent certain questions, notably human rights, being properly discussed. The USA, in particular, resented this situation, especially as it was by far the biggest contributor to UN funds. This, and the increasing use made of the General Assembly not for true debate but for propaganda and counter-propaganda, meant that it did not become quite as respected as its founders had hoped.

# The Partition of Eastern and Central Europe

The post-1945 map of Europe was decided at the three-power wartime conferences of Teheran, Yalta, and Potsdam and at rather more acrimonious post-war foreign ministers' conferences. Poland's frontiers were especially changed by these decisions. It was agreed that Poland should lose to Russia that part of its eastern territory which lay beyond the Curzon Line (a line suggested in 1920, but rejected by the Poles, who had gone on to conquer additional areas of the Ukraine). In exchange, Poland took from Germany the area east of the Oder and Neisse rivers, the southern part of East Prussia (the northern part went to the USSR), plus the international city of Danzig. Yugoslavia received the city of Fiume and its surrounding territory, and some Adriatic islands, from defeated Italy. Italy also sacrificed small parts of its territory to France and Greece.

In the far north Finland ceded Petsamo, and sundry strips along the Soviet-Finnish frontier, to the USSR. The latter was also confirmed in her possession of Northern Bukovina and Bessarabia, taken from Rumania in 1940, and of Estonia, Latvia and Lithuania.

At the close of hostilities in Germany, the Allied troops took up four previously agreed zones of occupation. The Americans were

**Below left:** an RAF Avro York transport aircraft's load brings the total weight of supplies airlifted into Berlin up to one million tons in February 1949.

# Division of Berlin and Berlin Blockade

After the war both the USA and the USSR realized that Germany was pivotal for the control both of west and east Europe, and both feared that the other might take advantage of any concessions in order to strengthen its position there. Thus, although in the sterile debates which took place over two decades both the western Allies and the USSR demanded the reunification of Germany, neither really wanted this except on its own, unobtainable, terms.

In 1947 the western powers took the first steps toward the economic independence of their own zones, and this was cemented early in 1948 by a currency reform which excluded the Russian zone. In the same year, it was decided to establish a German government in the three western zones. The Soviet response was a blockade of Berlin.

Under the post-war arrangement Berlin, which was about 100 miles inside the Soviet

in the south, in Bavaria, Hesse, and Baden Wurtemburg, the British occupied the Ruhr industrial area and North Germany, while the French took the Rhine-Palatinate and the south west. These three zones contained about 45 million residents. Eastern Germany, with a 17 million population, was occupied by the USSR. In Austria, a similar pattern of occupation zones was set up which lasted until the Austrian Peace Treaty was signed in 1955. In Germany the USSR and the Western allies were unable to agree on a peace settlement and, in stages, the western occupation zones were transformed into the German Federal Republic, while the Soviet zone became the German Democratic Republic.

In the late 1940s, pro-Moscow communist regimes took power in Poland, Czechoslovakia, Hungary, Rumania, Albania, Bulgaria, East Germany and, for a time, in Yugoslavia. Soon after the war, therefore, there was a line running from Stettin to Trieste, dividing Soviet-controlled Europe from a western Europe orientated in varying degrees toward the USA. This line became known as the 'Iron Curtain.'

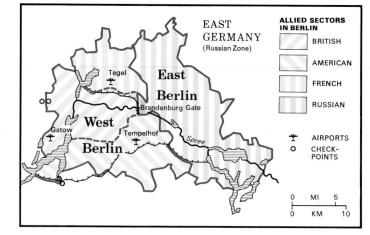

occupation zone, had been divided into four occupation zones, with the British, American and French occupying forces guaranteed road, rail and air access for supply and renewal. The Soviet blockade of Berlin took the form of barring all road and rail traffic to and from the western zones of the city. Its aim was to deprive not only the occupying forces, but also the population, of the necessities of life and thereby force the western powers to make concessions. The western zones of Berlin had about two and one-half million inhabitants and the Soviet government did not think it would be possible for the western powers to supply such a large population by air. On 24 June 1948 the Red Army put up its barricades.

For the western powers either the use of force, which it was feared might precipitate a wider conflict, or a submission to Soviet demands, seemed equally distasteful, so an airlift was the only possible reaction. It was calculated that the aircraft available could fly in 4000 tons of freight each day, on average. This was enough to provide basic rations, and coal for the power stations (but not for any other purpose). In the first weeks a total of 4000 tons was indeed achieved. West Berlin could live, but only in siege conditions. In time, however, larger aircraft became available, and private charter companies gave considerable help. To the original receiving airports (Tempelhof in the US zone and Gatow in the British) was soon added a third, Tegel, in the French zone. A shuttle service was operated, mainly from five airfields in the western zones of Germany proper. The blockade was called off on 12 May 1949.

Soon after, the western zones of Germany were formally united to form the German Federal Republic, while the Russians established the German Democratic Republic in their zone. Both German governments progressively took over the functions previously carried out by the occupying forces, although the latter remained in Germany. While contact between the two Germanies had been sealed off by a highly militarized and mined frontier laid by the Russians, many East German citizens fled to the west through Berlin. This drain of its best citizens persuaded the East German government to erect a high, patrolled, wall to divide its part of Berlin from West Berlin in 1961. However, from the late 1960s, in fits and starts, the very tense relationship between the two Germanies eased to some degree.

# Trieste

The post-war peace treaty with Italy, while it provided for the cession of the Venezia Giulia province to Yugoslavia, did not settle the fate of Trieste. This important port at the head of the Adriatic was demanded by Yugoslavia, but its population was four-fifths Italian. The treaty attempted, unsuccessfully, to solve this problem by assigning the port to neither claimant. Instead Trieste and its immediate surroundings were declared to be a Free Territory, guaranteed by the United Nations Security Council. Most of the non-urban area, having two-thirds of the territory but only a quarter of the population (mainly Slavic) was to be administered by Yugoslavia; this was Zone B. The Americans and British were to look after Zone A, where the bulk of the population, mostly Italian, lived.

Yugoslavia and Italy continued to advance their claims; the former was backed until its defection from the Soviet bloc in 1948, by the USSR. America and Britain supported Italy and in 1948, with France, declared that Trieste should be returned to

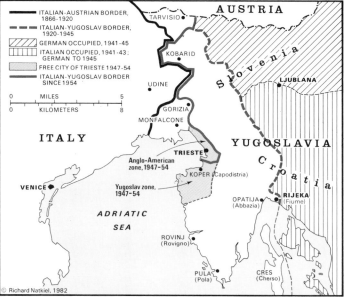

Left: the disputed area of Trieste
bedecked by Yugoslav propaganda in an
attempt to impress the Allied Control
Commission.
Bottom left: Berliners greet a bus which
has driven into the city from Hanover along
the recently reopened land route.

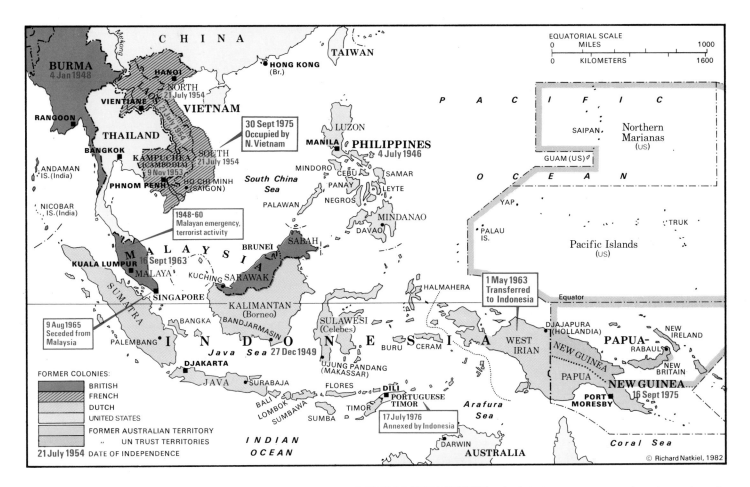

Italy. In Zone A, much of the administration was transferred to Italians. With the relaxation of tension between the West and the USSR, it was possible to reach a final agreement in 1954 which was not wholly to the liking of Yugoslavia. Zone A, less a few square miles around Crevatini, was handed to Italy. Crevatini and Zone B became part of Yugoslavia.

# East Indies Independence

Because of the disturbance caused by Japanese wartime occupation, independence came to most southeast Asian nations sooner than it would otherwise have done. Nowhere was this more evident than in the Dutch East Indies, where strong nationalist guerrilla forces, led by Sukarno, were already in action in 1945, resisting the returning Dutch. The fighting went on for some years, many influential Dutch politicians being convinced, wrongly, that the Netherlands could not survive without the profits of the East Indies. In 1949 the new state of Indonesia was formed as a result of a settlement of this dispute. It comprised all the former Dutch territories except West New Guinea. The latter, much against the will of

its inhabitants, was transferred to Indonesia in 1963. Neighboring East New Guinea, under Australian tutelage, gained independence in 1975.

The federation of Malaysia was formed in 1963 of scattered former British possessions; Malaya, Penang, North Borneo (Sabah), Sarawak, and Singapore (Singapore left in 1965). This federation was not to the liking of Sukarno, who initiated a policy of violent 'confrontation' with Malaysia, until in 1965 the exertions of this policy brought him down himself. The federation was also troubled, although not violently, by the claims of the Philippine Republic (which gained independence from the USA in 1946) to Sabah. This dispute was an embarrassment, though not fatal, to the Association of South-East Asian Nations [ASEAN] organization, formed in 1967 to develop economic cooperation between Indonesia, Malaysia, Singapore, and the Philippines.

200

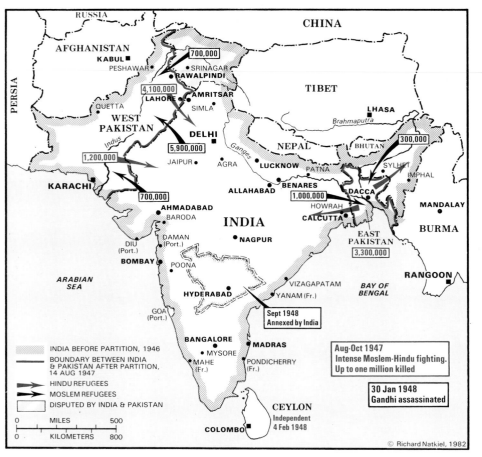

## The Partition of Palestine

# Independence for India and Pakistan

When in 1946 the British government announced its intention to grant complete independence to the Indian sub-continent, the leaders of the large Moslem population were already intent on disengaging themselves from an independent, predominantly Hindu, India and forming their own state, Pakistan. To enable independence to be granted in 1947 the concept of Pakistan was accepted. This Moslem state was in two parts. A large region, West Pakistan, including the port of Karachi and cities such as Lahore and Peshawar, lay between the new India and Afghanistan. Hundreds of miles to the east, across Indian territory, an eastern wing of Pakistan was established for the Moslems of Bengal. The boundary between India and West Pakistan was fixed a few days after independence, and unavoidably divided the Punjab, homeland of the Sikhs. Horrific massacres followed, as Sikhs and Hindus in the East Punjab attacked local Moslems, and Moslems attacked Sikhs in the West Punjab. These massacres were repeated in Delhi and elsewhere. Millions of refugees travelled in both directions across the newly-established Indo-Pakistani frontiers.

Under British rule the Indian princes had been allowed to rule their own states, but by the end of 1948 all except three of the approximately 350 princely states had joined the Indian Union in response to persuasion, concession, and implied threat. Of the three, Junagadh acceded to India after the entry of Indian troops. In Hyderabad, a large state of 17 million inhabitants, the prince was evasive and finally, not without provocation, the Indian government absorbed it by force. In Kashmir, lying uneasily between India and West Pakistan, there was a Hindu ruler, a Hindu majority around Jammu, but a predominantly Moslem population in the Vale of Kashmir. The ruler, alarmed by an incursion of Moslem tribesmen, finally opted for India and saved his capital, Srinagar. But opposing Indian and Pakistani forces were soon in action, and the dispute over the possession of Kashmir was to poison Indo-Pakistani relations for decades.

After World War I Britain had received the League of Nations mandate to rule Palestine. During the 1930s Jewish immigration increased the Jewish population there from 11 per cent of the total in 1922 to 29 per cent in 1939. Local Arabs resented this, so shortly before the outbreak of war Britain restricted immigration.

After 1945 the Jews' wartime experience hardened their resolve to found their own state of Israel, while at the same time world opinion had come to sympathize with them. The British government, realizing that a Jewish state could be created in Palestine only at the cost of antagonizing Arabs all over the Middle East, continued to oppose the large-scale admission of Jewish refugees. Illegal Jewish immigration began, and Jewish terrorists began to prey on Britons in Palestine. In 1947 Britain asked the United Nations to take over the problem. The UN decided to divide Palestine into an Arab state, a Jewish state, and an internationalized city of Jerusalem. This was impossible to put into practice. In December 1947 war started between the Jews and the armed forces of the Arab League, continuing until the spring. In May 1948 the independent state of Israel was proclaimed by the Jews. Jewish troops fought better than the Arabs and won additional territory for Israel, but the Arabs refused to negotiate unless one million Palestinian refugees were returned to their homes.

Left: Lord Mountbatten, the last British Viceroy of India, inspects a guard of honor shortly before independence.
Below: newly independent Israel celebrates Hagana Day to honor the dead freedom fighters, March 1949.

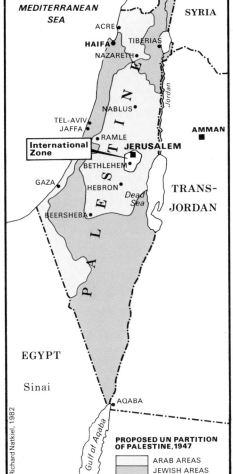

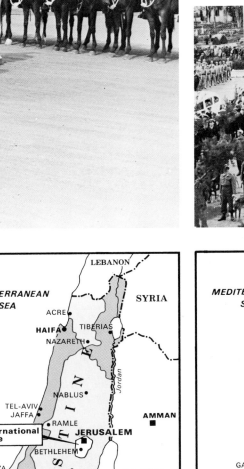

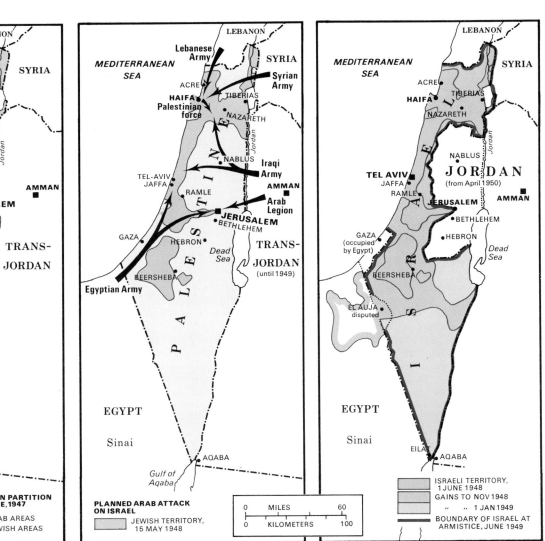

© Richard Natkiel, 1982

**PROPOSED UN PARTITION OF PALESTINE, 1947**
- ARAB AREAS
- JEWISH AREAS

**PLANNED ARAB ATTACK ON ISRAEL**
- JEWISH TERRITORY, 15 MAY 1948

| 0 | MILES | 60 |
|---|---|---|
| 0 | KILOMETERS | 100 |

- ISRAELI TERRITORY, 1 JUNE 1948
- GAINS TO NOV 1948
- " " 1 JAN 1949
- BOUNDARY OF ISRAEL AT ARMISTICE, JUNE 1949

AREAS OCCUPIED BY
COMMUNIST FORCES
- 1934–1945
- 1945–JUNE 1946
- JULY 1946–JUNE 1947
- JULY 1947–JUNE 1948
- JULY 1948–JUNE 1949
- JULY–SEPT 1949

Early-1946
Civil war begins

1 Oct 1949
People's Republic
of China proclaimed

20 Apr 1949
"Amethyst"
incident

Capital
until
1949

Invaded 1950

End-1949
Nationalist
Government
flees to Taiwan

© Richard Natkiel, 1982

| 0 | MILES | 500 |
| 0 | KILOMETERS | 800 |

# The Chinese Revolution

By April 1945 the Chinese communists had about one million men under arms, and looked forward to the post-war struggle for power against the Kuomintang with optimism, because although the latter was receiving American equipment its troops were believed to be of low morale. Stalin did not share this optimism and decided that Russian aid should be given to the communists. Despite the disappointment and resentment which this caused, the communists under Mao Tse-tung took the offensive and by mid-1946 a civil war was raging in Manchuria, where many of the Kuomintang troops deserted and others fought unenthusiastically. By late 1947 the Kuomintang's military superiority had declined from 4:1 to 2:1, and by the end of the civil war two million of the People's Liberation Army's troops were former Kuomintang soldiers. Having taken Manchuria in 1948, the communists drove southward and in 1949 the last remnants of the old regime took refuge in Formosa (Taiwan). There had been little foreign interference, although some British warships on the Yangtze were shelled and one of them,

*Amethyst*, was pinned down by artillery fire for a few days.

Having gained power, the communists set about the transformation of Chinese society. Mao Tse-tung, despite his mistrust of the Russians and the uneasy relations between Moscow and Peking, took a pro-Soviet line in foreign affairs; American policy-makers, who by this time included few who were willing or able to express an informed opinion, believed that China was simply a Soviet satellite, and behaved towards the new republic accordingly. Meanwhile the communist transformation was hampered by the dominance of Mao Tse-tung and his theories. There followed a series of mass campaigns like the Great Leap Forward (for rapid economic development in 1957–59) and the Cultural Revolution (for a replacement of old attitudes by new in 1965–67). These campaigns were accompanied by violence, bloodshed, and blind and exaggerated adherence to centrally laid-down theories; their results reflected the Chinese saying, 'They drained the pond to catch a fish.'

# The Korean War

When Japan surrendered in 1945, the Red Army occupied the northern and less populous part of Korea and the US Army the southern. By previous agreement the division was made at the 38th Parallel, but there was a loose understanding that the two halves would soon be reunited, and elections held. However, the United Nations commission sent to arrange a reunion of the two Koreas could make no progress because the Russians and Americans had very different concepts of what they meant by free elections. In the end, the elections were held only in the South, whose new government was recognized by the United Nations. In reply, the Russians established a communist government in North Korea and, unlike the Americans in the South, ensured that it had a large and well-equipped army.

In 1949, partly because the Republic of Korea (ROK) seemed secure, the US troops left South Korea. In early 1950 several US leaders seemed to express doubts as to whether it would be practicable for the USA to defend South Korea if the latter should be attacked. Perhaps with this encouragement, on 25 June 1950 the North Korean army invaded South Korea at several points and made a rapid advance. While efforts, soon successful, were made to obtain the UN Security Council's recommendation that member states should aid South Korea, American troops were sent from Japan to stem the rout. The troops were only partially successful, both they and the surviving ROK divisions ending their retreat inside a perimeter enclosing a small area in the south which, however, included the vital port of Pusan.

More American troops, fighting under the United Nations flag, soon began to arrive, joined afterward by units from other countries, of which Britain sent the largest contingent. The US Commander in Chief, MacArthur, against the advice of almost all his colleagues, decided to turn the tide with an amphibious assault at Inchon, on the west coast not far from the 38th Parallel. Despite extensive mudbanks and difficult tides, this operation was a complete success and the North Koreans, with their supply lines threatened, began to withdraw. Soon the American and ROK forces recaptured the South Korean capital of Seoul,

Below: a tank goes into action in support of infantry fighting in Korea during the second winter of the war, January 1952. Bottom left: President Harry S Truman proved to be a tough and uncompromising war leader during the Korean War.

FRONT LINES
4 JULY 1950
14 JULY
25 JULY
5 AUG
26 AUG
10 SEP
PUSAN PERIMETER, 10-15 SEPT
NORTH KOREAN ATTACKS

25 June 1950 Korean attack begins

© Richard Natkiel, 1982

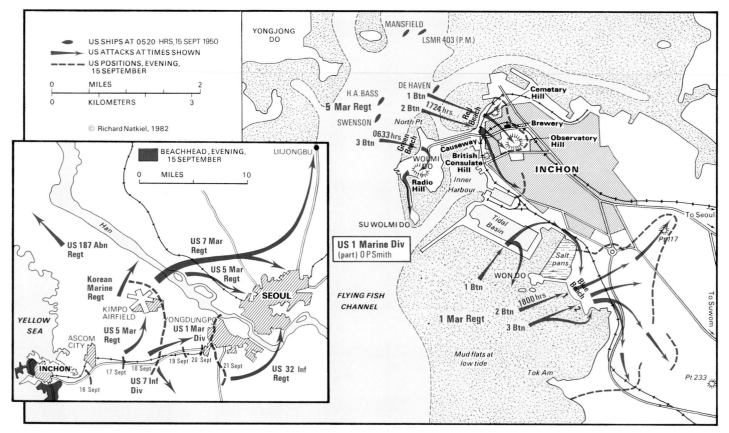

US SHIPS AT 0520 HRS, 15 SEPT 1950
US ATTACKS AT TIMES SHOWN
US POSITIONS, EVENING, 15 SEPTEMBER

MILES 0 — 2
KILOMETERS 0 — 3

© Richard Natkiel, 1982

BEACHHEAD, EVENING, 15 SEPTEMBER
MILES 0 — 10

YONGJONG DO
MANSFIELD
LSMR 403 (P.M.)

H.A. BASS
5 Mar Regt
SWENSON
DE HAVEN
1 Btn
2 Btn    1724 hrs.
Relief Beach
Cemetary Hill
Brewery
Observatory Hill
North Pt
0633 hrs
3 Btn
Green Beach
Causeway
British Consulate Hill
INCHON
WOUMI DO
Radio Hill
Inner Harbour
SU WOLMI DO

US 1 Marine Div (part) O P Smith

FLYING FISH CHANNEL

Tidal Basin
Salt pans
Blue Beach
Pt 117
To Seoul
WON DO
1 Btn
1 Mar Regt
2 Btn    1800 hrs
3 Btn
Mud flats at low tide
Tok Am
To Suwom
Pt 233

UIJONGBU
Han
US 187 Abn Regt
US 7 Mar Regt
US 5 Mar Regt
SEOUL
Korean Marine Regt
KIMPO AIRFIELD
YELLOW SEA
YONGDUNGPO
US 5 Mar Regt
US 1 Mar Div
ASCOM CITY
INCHON
16 Sept   17 Sept   18 Sept   19 Sept   20 Sept   21 Sept
US 7 Inf Div
US 32 Inf Regt

and pushed on to the 38th Parallel. Here a decision had to be made whether to pursue the invaders inside North Korea itself. MacArthur was among those who favored this, despite a warning from Communist China that if the UN forces approached closer to the River Yalu, the China-Korea frontier, they would intervene. By this time there were about 50,000 US troops in Korea, and more were on their way.

Having linked up with the forces that had broken out northward from the Pusan perimeter and with authorization from Washington, on 27 September MacArthur moved his troops across the 38th Parallel. In October the North Korean capital, Pyongyang, was captured. Many North Korean soldiers began to desert or surrender, and on 26 October ROK forces reached the Yalu, but were soon confronted by massed Chinese troops who crossed the Yalu and routed the outnumbered UN forces. The Chinese moved south along the high ground, enabling them to take UN units from the flank or rear; a great advantage. The Americans, in particular, were dependent on road transport and made easy targets as they moved along the valley highways. By the end of the year the UN forces had withdrawn behind the 38th Parallel, and Seoul was lost. However, in early 1951 the UN command launched a series of counter offensives. Because the Americans had command of the air, and the Chinese troops had long supply lines, these offensives were immediately successful, Seoul being recaptured in March. A final Chinese effort was made in April, at the Imjin River, but this had limited success and it was clear to the Chinese that this war, if continued, would be very costly. An armistice commission had its first meeting in July 1951, but, largely because of Chinese stalling tactics, it was not until 27 July 1953 that an armistice was actually signed. In the intervening period hostilities continued, although at a lower level and in conditions of trench warfare as each side tried to improve its defensive line. After the armistice things continued much the same as they had before, with the two Koreas developing separately and in mutual dislike and distrust.

**Left: General MacArthur inspects the Inchon bridgehead following the successful amphibious assault in September 1950. Right: landing craft head in for the sea wall at Inchon.**

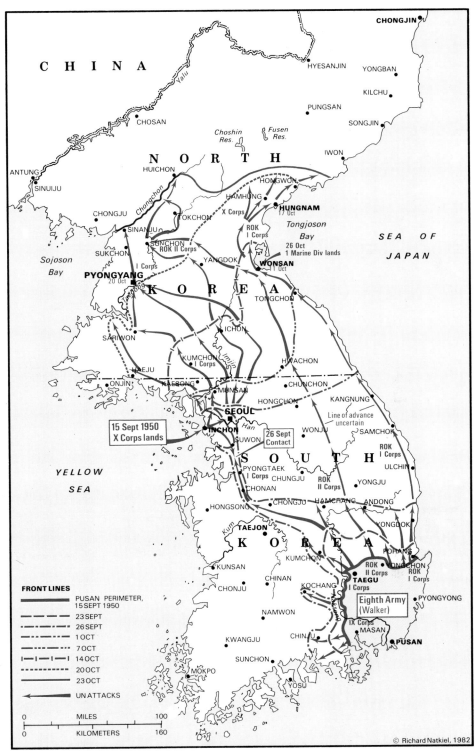

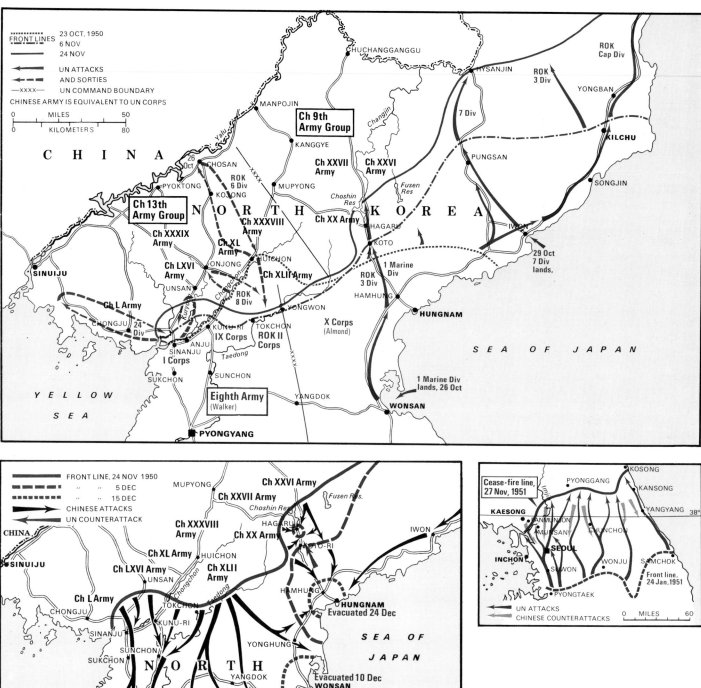

**Above right:** Vietnamese peasants during road building operations near Dien Bien Phu.
**Right:** the Hwachon Dam is attacked by US Navy Skyraider aircraft with torpedoes. The aim of the attack was to release floodwater which would disrupt enemy positions downstream.

© Richard Natkiel, 1982

# Revolution in Indo-China

In 1945 the first Allied troops to arrive in French Indo-China were British. In Saigon they encountered confusion, as nationalist groups tried to take advantage of the situation to assert their own control, and Free French detachments arrived to support the French settlers. At one point the British were using, to maintain order, the same Japanese troops whose surrender they had come to accept.

By the end of 1946 the French seemed to have re-established themselves although, realizing the strength of national feeling, they had agreed in principle to the establishment of an independent Vietnam in a proposed Indo-Chinese Federation within the French Union. The leader of the most powerful nationalist organization, the Viet Minh, was the communist Ho Chi Minh, whose status had risen during the war, partly because of US support; the Americans had no love for French colonialism. But by the end of 1946 Ho Chi Minh, with his military commander, the former schoolmaster Giap, had realized that the French were determined to hold on to what they had, and retired to the mountains to develop guerrilla activities. In the following two years the French sent more troops to Vietnam, and

instituted a native but highly-supervised government under the titular Emperor, Bao Dai.

The victory of the Chinese communists in 1949 changed the situation, because Viet Minh forces could now obtain supplies over a friendly frontier. Giap began a campaign of attacks, usually successful, on isolated French garrisons and on the relief columns sent to help them. The French responded with the use of mobile columns and parachute troops. In 1950 Ho Chi Minh claimed to be the head of the true Vietnam government, and was recognized by China and the USSR. The USA, deciding that communism was worse than colonialism, granted Bao Dai military aid to fight the Viet Minh. Nevertheless, Giap was in sufficient strength to force the French to abandon most of the Red River Delta in October 1950. By this stage Giap had progressed beyond guerrilla warfare and possessed full-scale and properly equipped regular divisions. Overconfident, he made attacks on French strongholds at Vinh Yen, Mao Khe, and Phat Diem which were unsuccessful and costly. Guerrilla warfare continued throughout 1951–53.

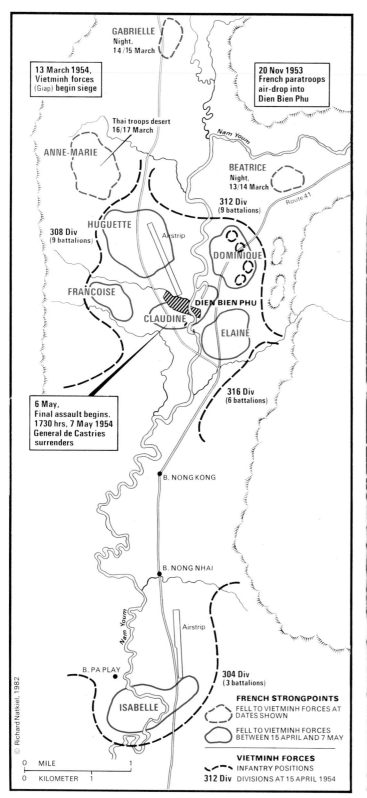

GABRIELLE
Night,
14/15 March

13 March 1954,
Vietminh forces
(Giap) begin siege

20 Nov 1953
French paratroops
air-drop into
Dien Bien Phu

Thai troops desert
16/17 March

ANNE-MARIE

Nam Youm

BEATRICE
Night,
13/14 March

312 Div
(9 battalions)

Route 41

HUGUETTE

308 Div
(9 battalions)

Airstrip

DOMINIQUE

FRANÇOISE

DIEN BIEN PHU

CLAUDINE

ELAINE

316 Div
(6 battalions)

6 May,
Final assault begins.
1730 hrs, 7 May 1954
General de Castries
surrenders

B. NONG KONG

B. NONG NHAI

Nam Youm

Airstrip

B. PA PLAY

304 Div
(3 battalions)

ISABELLE

© Richard Natkiel, 1982

FRENCH STRONGPOINTS
FELL TO VIETMINH FORCES AT
DATES SHOWN

FELL TO VIETMINH FORCES
BETWEEN 15 APRIL AND 7 MAY

VIETMINH FORCES
INFANTRY POSITIONS
312 Div   DIVISIONS AT 15 APRIL 1954

0   MILE   1
0   KILOMETER   1

# Dien Bien Phu

The war between the French and the communist-led Viet Minh in French Indo China took a new turn in April 1953 when Giap's forces, instead of pursuing the war in Vietnam, invaded another French territory, Laos. French reinforcements poured in and Giap withdrew, having demonstrated that he had the French on the run. Later in the year the French decided to block Giap's expected renewal of the attack in Laos. The settlement of Dien Bien Phu was selected as a French defensive strongpoint, rudimentary fortifications were built there, and fresh troops flown in. When the Viet Minh did attack, in March 1954, it had about 18,000 defenders, of whom about 3,000 were French and the rest colonial troops. But Giap had an overwhelming numerical superiority, and was well-supplied with artillery, including anti-aircraft guns supplied by China. When the encirclement closed in, the airstrip could no longer be used: supplies could be parachuted in, at some risk, but wounded could not be moved out. The defense was genuinely heroic, and ended only when the Viet Minh divisions broke into the center of the position.

When Dien Bien Phu fell the conference to end this war was already in progress at

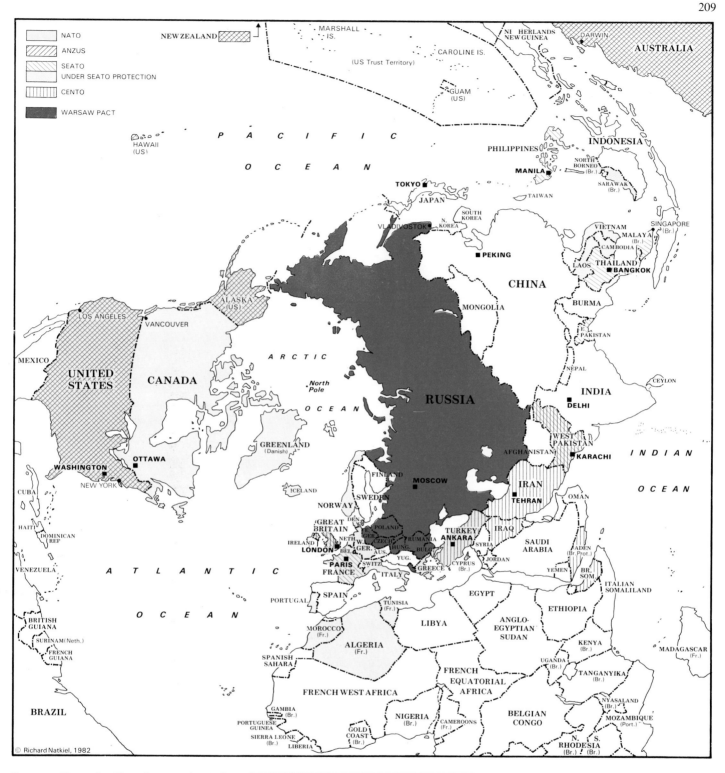

NATO
ANZUS
SEATO
UNDER SEATO PROTECTION
CENTO
WARSAW PACT

NEW ZEALAND

Geneva. Here the French agreed to the provisional formation of a Viet Minh North Vietnam and a French-orientated South Vietnam, with internationally supervised elections in both within two years. The independence of Cambodia and Laos, formerly parts of French Indo-China, was also recognized.

**Above left: Vietnamese porters carry supplies to the front by bicycle during the build-up to Dien Bien Phu.**

# Encirclement of the USSR in 1955

Soviet expansion into Eastern Europe in 1945 was virtually completed by the absorption of Czechoslovakia into the Soviet bloc in 1948. The establishment of the North Atlantic Treaty Organization (NATO) in 1949 was a direct response to the Berlin blockade and the Czech coup. The ANZUS Pact (Australia, New Zealand, USA) in

1951, which accompanied the peace treaty with Japan, as well as the US-Philippine treaty signed at the same time, linked these three countries with the United States.

Eisenhower's Secretary of State, John Foster Dulles, sought to respond to the collapse of French Indochina and the end of the Korean War by forming the South East Asia Treaty Organization in 1954. SEATO's basic weakness lay in the fact that most of its membership was already linked to the United States in the Alliance already, and the treaty called for no automatic response to overt Communist aggression, unlike

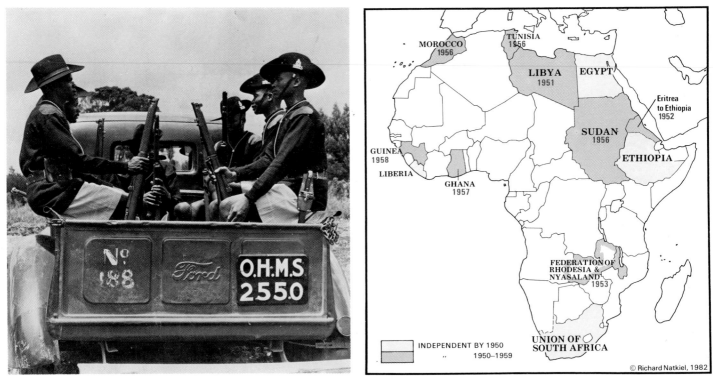

## Africa in 1950s

## Algeria

NATO. Pakistan and Thailand were the only two new states added, as Malaya, British North Borneo, Brunei and Sarawak were still parts of the British Empire in 1954. The so-called protocol states of South Vietnam, Laos and Cambodia, were not in fact members of SEATO, but were able to call upon the aid of SEATO in case of overt Communist aggression. This never was done because SEATO required unanimity among its members, and usually France or Pakistan was unwilling to be committed to the defense of Southeast Asia. Therefore SEATO, unlike NATO, was a weak reed in the bundle of American alliances meant to surround the Communist bloc.

The Central Treaty Organization (CENTO) was originally known as the Baghdad Pact. Its lynchpin was Great Britain, the only member of all the alliances, and it included Turkey, Iraq, Iran and Pakistan. The United States was only an observer in the Baghdad Pact. Since Turkey was a NATO member as was Britain, Pakistan was included only because she was a member of SEATO. Iraq was a reluctant member of the alliance and dropped out of it after the assassination of King Faisal, and therefore CENTO was based on Iran.

Although appearing formidable on such a map as this, the strength of the encirclement policy lay in NATO, the ANZUS Pact, and in the bilateral treaties the United States had with Japan, the Philippines and South Korea. Nonetheless, from a Soviet perspective, these encircling alliances and the United States' great nuclear superiority, must have seemed formidable indeed. It is not surprising therefore that the suspicious attitudes of the Cold War and the concurrent arms race were the dominant factors in US-Soviet relations.

In the mid-1950s four-fifths of the African population lived under some kind of European rule, genuinely independent native governments being found only in Egypt, Libya, Ethiopia and Liberia. But all over the continent the scene was being set for upheavals that would, within a decade, mean that four-fifths of the Africans would have their own independent states. Already, in 1956, the French relinquished Tunisia. In 1958 another French colony, Guinea, became the next part of French West and Equatorial Africa to gain independence, the other parts reaching that stage in 1960. In the English-speaking parts, the Gold Coast ceased to be a crown colony and became independent Ghana in 1957.

**Top left: armed native police set out in their truck to search a Kenyan village for Mau Mau terrorists. The colonial authorities defeated the terrorist campaign. Top right. French troops during an advance against Algerian rebel forces in the course of the Challe offensive in August 1959. Right: troops patrol the European quarter of Algiers in March 1962 to guard against terrorism.**

In response to developing nationalism, in 1947 the French government introduced a constitution for Algeria which gave all residents French citizenship. But the European minority had as many seats in the legislative assembly as the native majority, and the nationalists' drive was hardly weakened. However, until 1954 the different nationalist groups attacked each other as much as they attacked the French. In that year, the terrorist FLN (National Libration Front) was formed.

The terrorists' bombing campaign caused many casualties and brought a strong French reaction. Soon there were half a million French troops, with aircraft, attempting to control a population which was becoming increasingly hostile in response to reprisals, particularly in Algiers. European settlers, fearing that the French government might negotiate with the rebels, staged, in collusion with army officers, a coup which so discredited the government that de Gaulle returned to power. At first intent on defeating the Algerian terrorists, de Gaulle in 1959 acknowledged that Algerians had the right to choose their future. This caused the settlers to rebel again in January 1960 but, lacking army support this time, they were dispersed. Negotiations between France and the FLN were long and intermittent and in April 1961 four French generals, fearing a 'sell-out,' tried to seize power in Algiers; this unsuccessful coup was organized by the OAS (Secret Army Organization). Nevertheless, after a referendum in Algeria, de Gaulle proclaimed Algerian independence on 3 July 1962.

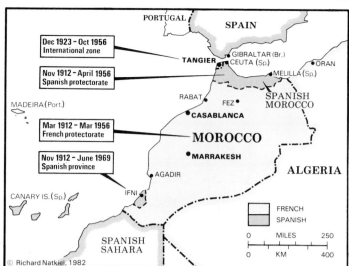

Dec 1923 – Oct 1956
International zone

Nov 1912 – April 1956
Spanish protectorate

Mar 1912 – Mar 1956
French protectorate

Nov 1912 – June 1969
Spanish province

FRENCH
SPANISH

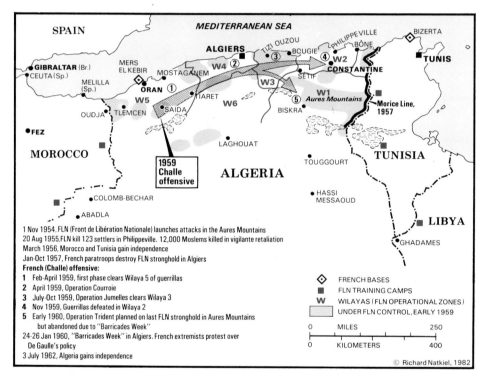

1 Nov 1954, FLN (Front de Libération Nationale) launches attacks in the Aures Mountains
20 Aug 1955, FLN kill 123 settlers in Philippeville. 12,000 Moslems killed in vigilante retaliation
March 1956, Morocco and Tunisia gain independence
Jan-Oct 1957, French paratroops destroy FLN stronghold in Algiers
**French (Challe) offensive:**
1  Feb-April 1959, first phase clears Wilaya 5 of guerrillas
2  April 1959, Operation Courroie
3  July-Oct 1959, Operation Jumelles clears Wilaya 3
4  Nov 1959, Guerrillas defeated in Wilaya 2
5  Early 1960, Operation Trident planned on last FLN stronghold in Aures Mountains
    but abandoned due to "Barricades Week"
24-26 Jan 1960, "Barricades Week" in Algiers. French extremists protest over
De Gaulle's policy
3 July 1962, Algeria gains independence

◆  FRENCH BASES
■  FLN TRAINING CAMPS
**W**  WILAYAS (FLN OPERATIONAL ZONES)
    UNDER FLN CONTROL, EARLY 1959

# Morocco

At the beginning of the century Morocco seemed a tempting object for French colonial expansion and in 1904, France and Spain settled on an eventual partition of the country between themselves. Britain and France were by then aligned in the *Entente Cordiale* and Britain recognized French interest in Morocco in return for acceptance of British pre-eminence in Egypt and the Sudan. In an effort to weaken the Entente the Germans twice, in 1905–06 and 1911, disputed the French influence in Morocco but although they gained some concessions from the French in Equatorial Africa the French hold on Morocco was maintained. This was followed, in 1912, by most of Morocco becoming a French protectorate, with Spanish territories in the north and south. Marshal Lyautey, the first Resident-General, brought large areas under French control fairly quickly.

In the mid-50s nationalist groups began violent resistance to French rule. The French were preoccupied by Algerian problems and rather than add to these France recognized Moroccan independence in 1956. Tangier, which the great powers had 'international-ized' in 1923, was returned to Morocco in the same year. The new state, a monarchy, soon laid claim to the Spanish Sahara, the Spanish enclave of Ifni, Spanish Morocco, Mauritania, and parts of southwest Algeria. At Independence Spain had agreed to hand over Spanish Morocco, excluding the two cities of Cueta and Melilla and, after skirmishes Spain agreed to give up most of her southern territories too, with the exception of Ifni and most of the Spanish Sahara. In 1962 Moroccan troops crossed the undemarcated frontier with southern Algeria but a ceasefire in 1963 brought this conflict to an end although Algerian-Moroccan relations remained poor. Ifni was ceded by Spain in 1969 and in the same year the claims to the now-independent Mauritania were abandoned.

# The Middle East, 1956

After the Arab-Israeli War of 1948–49 border battles, guerrilla activity, and terrorism continued. In 1955 President Nasser of Egypt, having earlier secured by agreement the evacuation of British troops from the Suez Canal Zone, announced that the Canal would be closed to Israeli commerce. Soon the Egyptian government also announced that ships using the Israeli port of Eilat might be shelled by guns commanding the Tiran Strait, and a British steamer was indeed hit by Egyptian shells. All this persuaded the Israeli government that some counterstroke was necessary.

Nasser, meantime, had projects both for a new Aswan dam on the Nile and for rearmament. Britain and the USA had expressed willingness to help with the dam but not with arms. Nasser therefore turned to the eastern block for arms, which so alarmed Washington and London that they announced that they would no longer help with the Aswan Dam. In retaliation, Nasser announced the nationlization of the Suez Canal. This action, while directly affecting France and Britain, the principal shareholders, was also a threat to international commerce, or so it was thought. Since international support for the Anglo-French rights over the Canal was more vocal than substantial, the US government being especially lukewarm, Britain, France and Israel evolved a plan for the invasion of Sinai and the Canal Zone. Israel commenced

hostilities on 29 October 1956, and Britain and France then announced that they were going to occupy, forcibly, the Canal Zone in order to protect it from the damage it might suffer in the course of Israeli-Egyptian hostilities.

The Anglo-French invading forces had little difficulty in getting ashore near Port Said and advancing down the Canal; Egyptian forces had already been demoralized by defeats inflicted by Israel in the Sinai Desert. However, pressure exerted by the USA, and in the United Nations, persuaded Britain and France to halt their advance and soon, in December, to begin a withdrawal. The situation returned to normal, except that the Canal, blocked by Nasser, took several months to clear. British and French prestige had been irreparably damaged in the Middle East.

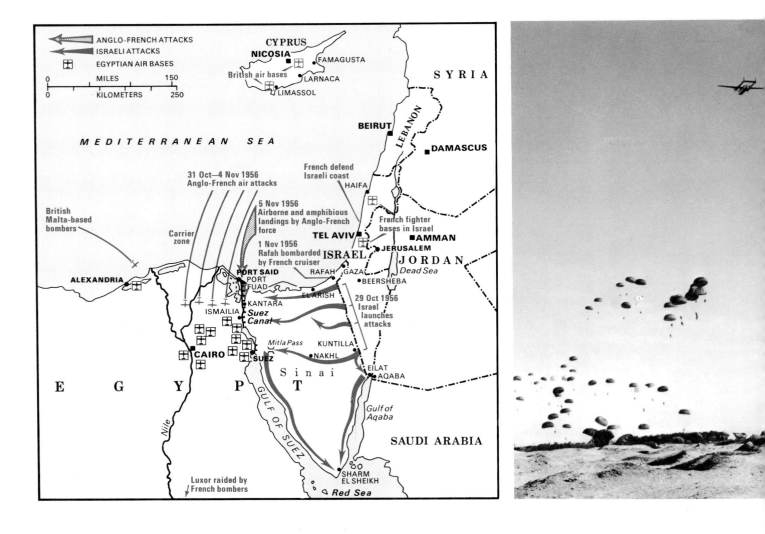

213

Right: this Soviet-built tank of the Egyptian army was captured by Israeli forces in Sinai.
Below: British troops of the 3rd Battalion the Parachute Regiment assault El Gamil airfield, near Port Said on 5 November 1956.
Bottom: French Noratlas transport aircraft drop paras on Fuad during the Suez operation, November 1956.

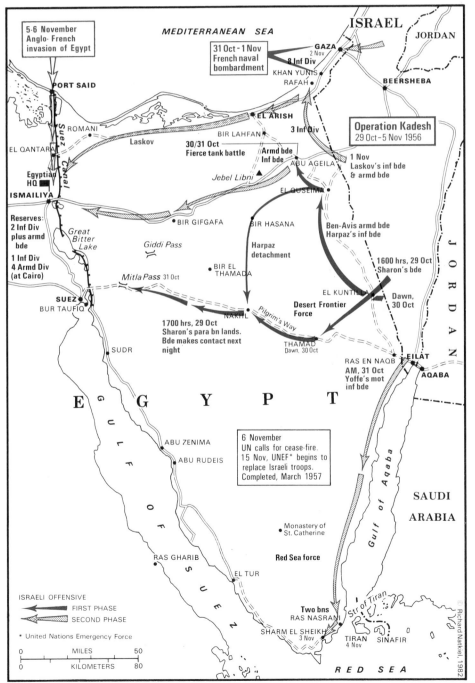

# Africa in 1960s

It was not until the 1960s that big changes were made in Africa south of the Sahara. In 1960 the French and Belgian Congos became independent, as well as Nigeria and Tanganyika, the latter uniting with the island of Zanzibar to become Tanzania in 1964. Also in 1960 independent Somalia was created from British and Italian Somaliland. In Kenya, independence was delayed until 1963, the Mau-Mau guerrilla and terrorist movement of 1952–55 having soured the atmosphere. Uganda, which became independent in 1962, kept its tribal monarchies until 1967, but that did not solve its tribal problems. After the failure of the short-lived Rhodesian Federation, former Northern Rhodesia became independent Zambia, while Nyasaland became Malawi. These were both states in which the predominant, black, population provided the government. In neighboring Southern Rhodesia, however, the white minority did not relish the prospect of majority (that is, black) government, and made a 'unilateral declaration of independence' which resulted in the *de facto*

end of colonial status and the preservation of a white government.

By the end of the 1960s European rule had been confined to South Africa and Rhodesia, together with the Portuguese colonies, principally Angola and Mozambique, the Spanish Sahara, and French Djibouti. Meanwhile in 1963 the Organization of African Unity was established. This had a general council in which each non-European African government was represented. One of its most intelligent decisions was to agree that the colonial frontiers, unsatisfactory though they were, should be regarded as fixed, thereby sterilizing many potential disputes. The OAU also helped to solve conflicts between Algeria and Morocco, and between Somalia and its neighbors Ethiopia and Kenya, but the Nigerian Civil War was too much for it, although it tried hard.

**Below right: Jomo Kenyatta became president of newly-independent Kenya in 1964.**

# The Congo

In 1960 the Belgian Congo gained its independence and a new government headed by the nationalist Lumumba took office in the capital Leopoldville (later Kinshasa). An army mutiny led to general disorder and at the request of the government a UN force was sent, but in the confusion a prominent member of the Lunda tribe, Tshombe, with the help of Belgian residents and of Anglo-Belgian companies, declared the mineral-rich province of Katanga to be an independent state. Tshombe hired white mercenary troops to block any attempt by UN forces to subdue him, while Lumumba, despairing of obtaining real UN help to eject Tshombe, appealed to the USSR for aid. But the UN did secure Tshombe's agreement to the entry of UN forces into Katanga. Meanwhile, the confusion in the Congo was reflected in political life at Leopoldville, where Prime Minister Lumumba and President Kasavubu dismissed each other. Kasavubu prevailed with support from the army led by Colonel Mobutu. Lumumba was later murdered, in February 1961, probably by Katangan

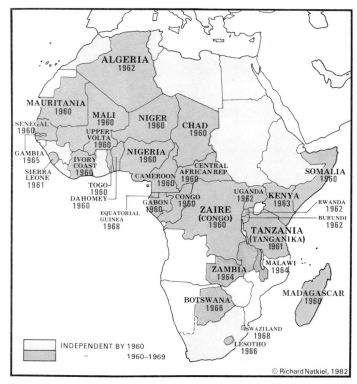

© Richard Natkiel, 1982

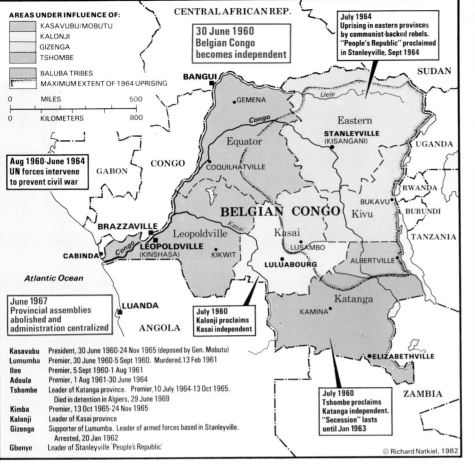

AREAS UNDER INFLUENCE OF:
KASAVUBU/MOBUTU
KALONJI
GIZENGA
TSHOMBE
BALUBA TRIBES
MAXIMUM EXTENT OF 1964 UPRISING

0 MILES 500
0 KILOMETERS 800

30 June 1960
Belgian Congo
becomes independent

July 1964
Uprising in eastern provinces
by communist-backed rebels.
"People's Republic" proclaimed
in Stanleyville, Sept 1964

Aug 1960-June 1964
UN forces intervene
to prevent civil war

June 1967
Provincial assemblies
abolished and
administration centralized

July 1960
Kalonji proclaims
Kasai independent

July 1960
Tshombe proclaims
Katanga independent.
"Secession" lasts
until Jan 1963

Kasavubu   President, 30 June 1960-24 Nov 1965 (deposed by Gen. Mobutu)
Lumumba    Premier, 30 June 1960-5 Sept 1960. Murdered, 13 Feb 1961
Ileo       Premier, 5 Sept 1960-1 Aug 1961
Adoula     Premier, 1 Aug 1961-30 June 1964
Tshombe    Leader of Katanga province. Premier, 10 July 1964-13 Oct 1965.
           Died in detention in Algiers, 29 June 1969
Kimba      Premier, 13 Oct 1965-24 Nov 1965
Kalonji    Leader of Kasai province
Gizenga    Supporter of Lumumba. Leader of armed forces based in Stanleyville.
           Arrested, 20 Jan 1962
Gbenye     Leader of Stanleyville 'People's Republic'

© Richard Natkiel, 1982

**Below: President Tshombe of the Congo inspects a guard of honor at Stanleyville airport after the suppression of the 'People's Republic.'**
**Bottom: President Kasavubu's Congolese troops parade through Leopoldville in 1961.**

mercenaries. Following Lumumba's fall his supporter Gizenga began a rising based on Stanleyville which was, however, put down in January 1962 after periods of fighting and negotiation. The province of Kasai had also been declared independent under the leadership of Kalonji but he was reconciled to the Kasavubu-Ileo government in 1961.

The Katanga problem remained unresolved and after negotiations had failed, there was fighting in September 1961 between the Katanga army and the UN forces. The fighting was resumed in December 1961 and again in October 1962 after the failure of talks. However, in January 1963 Tshombe agreed to end the secession, going into exile a few months later.

As the last UN troops were leaving the country in mid-1964 communist-supported rebel forces gained increasing strength in the eastern provinces. Tshombe returned in July to become premier of a compromise government and, with western help and the use of mercenaries, suppressed the Stanleyville 'People's Republic' in late 1964.

Political troubles continued until November 1965 when General Mobutu led a further coup and himself took over the presidency. Mobutu was almost ousted by the mercenaries in his turn but his rule survived. Though the new government was neither incorrupt nor wholly efficient it did enable the Congo to settle down to solve its pressing economic and social problems. In 1971 the name of the state was changed to Zaire.

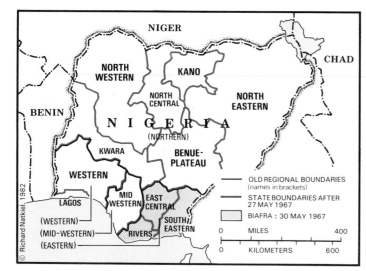

# Biafra

Before the British colony of Nigeria obtained its independence in October 1960, a federal constitution was evolved which, with its three largely autonomous regions (North, West and East), attempted to balance the conflicting interests of the various groups and tribes. These groups were already represented by their own political parties. The NCNC Party represented the better-educated East, and especially the Ibo people. The NPC was the party of the Moslem North, which was the most populous but less educated region, while the Action Group represented the West, and especially the Yoruba people. With party divisions repeating regional and hence tribal divisions, electoral democracy failed to produce governments which were both effective and respected, and in 1966 junior army officers staged a coup, killing the Prime Minister and various North and West leaders. Senior army officers intervened and installed a military government under Major General Ironsi.

The Ironsi regime was at first popular, but its use of Ibo civil servants all over the country helped to provoke discontent in the West and North. Oil, meanwhile, had been discovered in the East, which promised to become the richest region. After thousands of Ibo professionals in the North and West were killed in disorders, the East, under Lieutenant Colonel Ojukwu, announced its secession. By this time Lieutenant General Gowon headed the Federal Government, and he proposed a re-division of the country into 12 regions (plus the federal territory of Lagos). But this did not remove the East's fears of northern domination. Civil War broke out in July 1967, the East calling itself the state of Biafra, with its capital at Enugu.

The fighting went well for the Biafran forces at first but a Nigerian counter-offensive soon seized Enugu. Nigerian gains continued with the capture of the important base at Port Harcourt and the Biafrans be-

came confined to a small embattled enclave. Food supplies in Biafra had become very short and a dreadful famine ensued. Nonetheless, the Biafrans held out until January 1970. The peace settlement was not ungenerous but the old problems remained and provoked a series of coups throughout the 1970s.

**Above right: Nigerian Federal troops stop and search a car on the road to Onitsha.
Right: an RAF Hercules transport aircraft prepares to fly medical supplies to Nigeria in the closing days of the war.
Below right: an apprehensive Biafran officer is interrogated by Federal troops.**

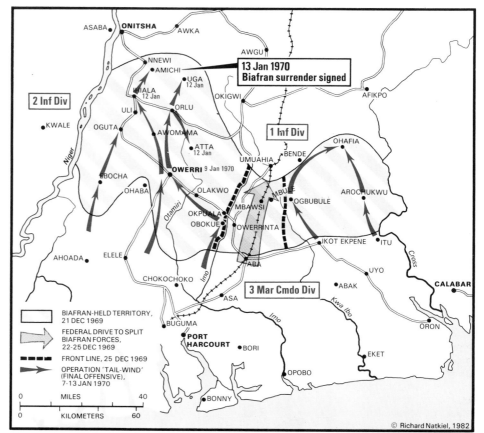

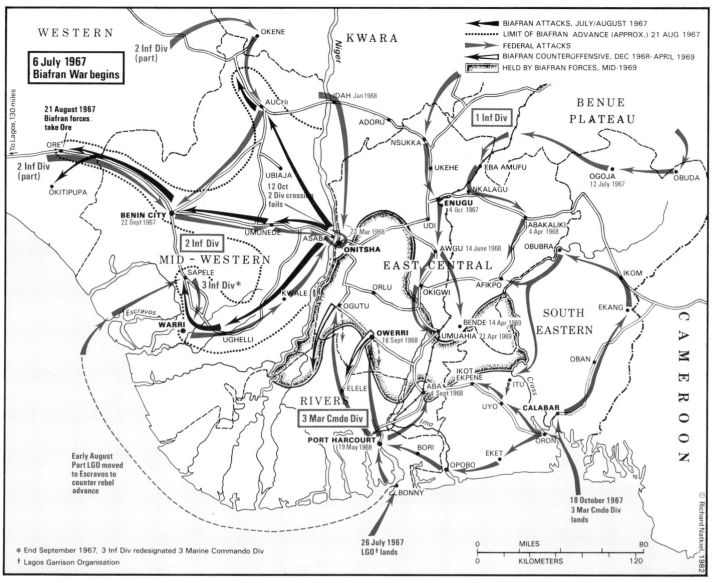

WESTERN

2 Inf Div
(part)

**6 July 1967**
**Biafran War begins**

To Lagos, 130 miles

**21 August 1967**
Biafran forces
take Ore

ORE

2 Inf Div
(part)

OKITIPUPA

OKENE

KWARA

Niger

AUCHI

IDAH Jan 1968

ADORU

NSUKKA

UKEHE

UBIAJA

12 Oct
2 Div crossing
fails

**BENIN CITY**
22 Sept 1967

UMUNEDE

ASABA

23 Mar 1968

**MID - WESTERN**

**2 Inf Div**

SAPELE

**3 Inf Div** *

KWALE

ORLU

WARRI

ESCRAVOS

UGHELLI

OGUTU

**OWERRI**
16 Sept 1968

**RIVERS**

ELELE

**3 Mar Cmdo Div**

**PORT HARCOURT**
(19 May 1968)

Early August
Part LGO moved
to Escravos to
counter rebel
advance

BONNY

BORI

OPOBO

BIAFRAN ATTACKS, JULY/AUGUST 1967
LIMIT OF BIAFRAN ADVANCE (APPROX.) 21 AUG 1967
FEDERAL ATTACKS
BIAFRAN COUNTEROFFENSIVE, DEC 1968- APRIL 1969
HELD BY BIAFRAN FORCES, MID-1969

**1 Inf Div**

**BENUE**
**PLATEAU**

EBA AMUFU

NKALAGU

OGOJA
12 July 1967

OBUDA

**ENUGU**
14 Oct 1967

UDI

ABAKALIKI
4 Apr 1968

OBUBRA

**EAST CENTRAL**

AWGU 14 June 1968

**ONITSHA**

OKIGWI

AFIKPO

IKOM

EKANG

BENDE 14 Apr 1969

**SOUTH**
**EASTERN**

UMUAHIA 22 Apr 1969

OBAN

IKOT
EKPENE

ABA
4 Sept 1968

ITU

Cross

UYO

**CALABAR**

EKET

ORON

**C**
**A**
**M**
**E**
**R**
**O**
**O**
**N**

Imo

26 July 1967
LGO† lands

18 October 1967
3 Mar Cmdo Div
lands

0        MILES        80
0    KILOMETERS    120

© Richard Natkiel, 1982

* End September 1967, 3 Inf Div redesignated 3 Marine Commando Div
† Lagos Garrison Organisation

# China-India Border Disputes

In colonial times the frontier between China and India had been fixed sufficiently for most purposes by the MacMahon Line, which ran through largely uninhabited terrain and was not precisely delineated, nor really accepted by the Chinese. In the 1950s the Indians' readiness to discuss certain obvious frontier difficulties was dampened by the Chinese insistence on reopening the question of the entire frontier. Moreover, when, after a revolt of Tibetans against the Chinese, the Dalai Lama was offered refuge in India, the Chinese began to doubt Indian goodwill. In 1960, however, the Chinese offered to accept the MacMahon Line in its entirety if the Indians would accept that the existing Chinese occupation of Aksai Chin was legitimate and permanent. Nehru, the Indian prime minister, would have agreed to this, but a powerful press campaign in India so aroused public opinion against the proposal that he was unable to pursue it.

Meanwhile, the Indian Army's request for re-equipment to enable it to match the Chinese was refused, and the generals were told by the defense minister, Menon, that a Chinese attack was out of the question and should not even be discussed. However, after continuing reports of a Chinese build-up around Dho La, Nehru incautiously said that the Indian Army would throw them out. He said this on 13 October 1962, and eight

days later the Chinese army attacked. Indian troops were poorly prepared, many units being sent into battle before they were properly acclimatized for mountain warfare. An Indian withdrawal was inevitable, even though some of the regular mountain troops acquitted themselves creditably. Having gained ground in the Ladakh area and defeated the Indians in the eastern part of the frontier, threatening the Brahmaputra the Chinese withdrew, implying that the Indians had been taught a lesson.

After this the Indian army chief of staff lost his job, but the real culprit, Menon, was unable to withstand popular outrage and was soon dismissed. The frontier question remained unsettled.

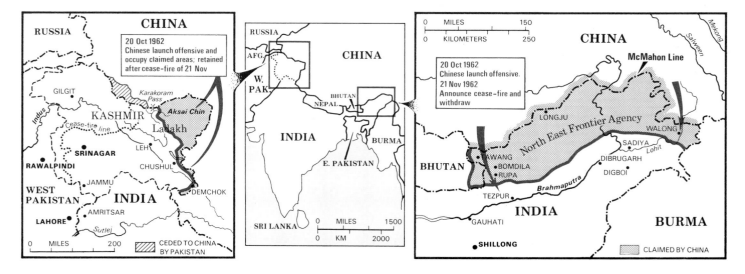

© Richard Natkiel, 1982

5 September, 1965
Cross-border skirmishes
develop into full scale war

········· CEASE-FIRE LINE

| 0 | MILES | 200 |
| 0 | KMS | 300 |

| 1 | 5 Aug 1965 | : 5 Pakistanis killed in clash with Indian police | 7 | 1 Sept | : Pakistani brigade launches major attack in Chhamb/Jammu Sector |
| 2 | 9 Aug | : Widespread clashes along cease-fire line | 8 | 6 Sept | : Indian forces cross border towards Lahore and Sialkot |
| 3 | 14-15 Aug | : Pakistani battalion attacks near Chhamb | 9 | 8 Sept | : India launches attack on Gadra |
| 4 | 16 Aug | : Indian troops take two Pakistani outposts | | 10-19 Sept | : Fighting fades into stalemate |
| 5 | 25 Aug | : Indian forces take outposts in Tithwal area | | 20 Sept | : UN Security Council calls for cease-fire |
| 6 | 26-30 Aug | : Indian attack on the Uri-Poonch salient | | | |

# The Kashmir Dispute, 1965

The relations between India and Pakistan had been soured, above all, by their dispute over the ownership of Kashmir. In pursuing this quarrel both had allowed themselves to be drawn into the affairs of the great powers in order, especially, to obtain modern arms. Pakistan had become a member of the US-sponsored Central Treaty Organization (CENTO) and had also drawn closer to China. India had moved closer to the Soviet orbit. In a brief campaign in the Himalayas, fought over a disputed frontier, Indian forces had been clearly beaten by the Chinese in 1962, and this encouraged the Pakistani forces in their belief that, although outnumbered, they could defeat India.

The war which broke out in January 1965 between the two countries had no real aims. Both sides simply thought it was a good time to have a battle. The ostensible cause was a minor infringement of a poorly demarcated frontier in the barren Rann of Kutch. This occurred in January, and by April the resulting skirmishes had developed into large-scale warfare. Hostilities were interrupted by an agreement made in June.

Independently of the Rann of Kutch dispute there was increasing unrest in Kashmir from May following the arrest of a Moslem leader. Throughout the succeeding weeks there were various incidents in the Indian held part of Kashmir and along the border in which Pakistani and irregular forces were involved. To prevent infiltration over the cease-fire line the Indians, who had three divisions in Kashmir, advanced in late August to capture the Haji Pir Pass, threatening Muzafarabad, the capital of Pakistan-Kashmir. On 1 September Pakistan made a diversionary offensive around Chhamb and Bhimbar which threatened Indian communications with Srinagar. The conflict now escalated into a full-scale war and the Pakistani threat was countered with an Indian attack toward Lahore which was strongly held. When this petered out the Indians launched another attack toward Sialkot, and after a big tank battle they remained in well-defended positions close to that town.

Meanwhile both sides were coming to the end of their resources. The USA and Britain had stopped arms supplies to both sides, and although the USSR had not taken this step, it also was in favor of peace. A cease fire was imposed on 23 September and in January 1966 both governments agreed to return to their pre-August positions.

220

# The Caribbean

The political situation of the Caribbean, and indeed of the Americas, was transformed in 1959, when revolutionaries led by Fidel Castro won a long guerrilla war against the US-supported Batista regime in Cuba. Soon Castro declared himself a Marxist, and by the early 1960s Cuba was part of the Soviet bloc. In 1961 a US-supported landing by Cuban exiles at the Bay of Pigs was a pathetic failure, but the following year the US emerged from the Cuban Missile Crisis with restored prestige, having obliged the USSR to forswear the installation of medium-range nuclear-armed missiles on Cuban soil.

Meanwhile decolonization, especially by the British, resulted in many Caribbean islands becoming independent states. Britain had hoped, in the late 1950s, that these would join in the West Indian Federation, but soon Jamaica, Trinidad and Tobago and

Barbados left this, robbing it of any significance. Of the smaller newly-independent islands, Anguilla was the scene in 1969 of a revolt against its government, and similar disturbances followed over the years in neighboring islands. One of the last British colonies to be decolonized was British Honduras, whose independence was granted late because of Guatemalan claims on its territory. British Guyana, part of which was claimed by Venezuela, did, however, receive independence in 1970 despite the mutual fears dividing its black and Indian population.

From time to time the USA, usually quietly, intervened in the interests of stability, especially in Haiti and the Dominican Republic. Puerto Rico became a part of the USA, while in 1979 the long dispute over the ownership of the Panama Canal Zone was settled in a compromise treaty between the USA and Panama. US fears of communist subversion continued and in the early 1980s led to support for the troubled government of El Salvador.

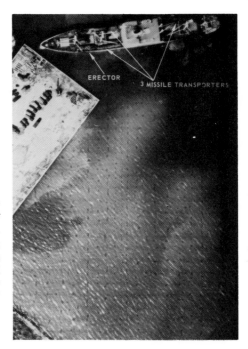

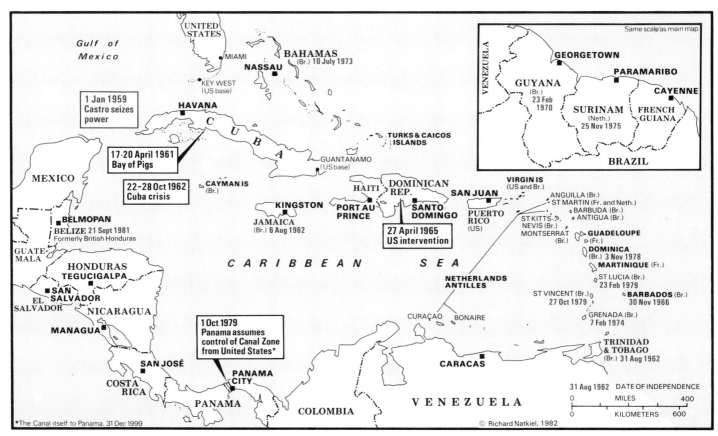

**Below left: missile-carrying Soviet cargo ships were photographed at the Cuban port of Mariel by USAF reconnaissance aircraft. Right: Soviet ballistic missiles were established in Cuba in October 1962, leading to a serious international crisis.**

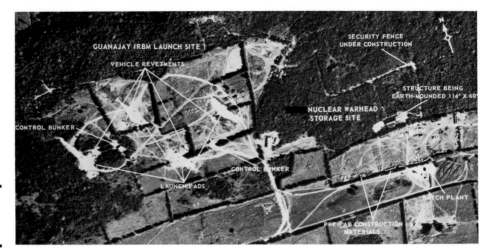

# The Six-Day War, 1967

The Suez War of 1956 had seen Israeli military successes in Sinai but her strategic position did not improve, despite the presence of a United Nations peacekeeping force in the buffer zone of the Sinai Desert. A new Iraqi regime quit the Western-sponsored Baghdad Pact in 1959 and allied itself with Egypt, while Egypt and other Arab countries began to receive armaments from the Soviet Union, as well as more diplomatic support. The Suez Canal was still blocked to Israeli commerce, and the Gulf of Aqaba was covered by Egyptian artillery, while the Palestinian refugees remained unsettled and presented a threat to Israel's security. Israel's frontier with Syria was especially troubled. Here, the Syrians' possession of the Golan Heights facilitated frequent bombardment of Israeli settlements close to the border.

In May 1967 Egypt, claiming that Israel was about to launch a reprisal attack against Syria, deployed its army on the frontier with Israel and at Sharm el Sheikh, meanwhile requesting the United Nations to remove its 3,000-strong peacekeeping force from Sinai. The UN, because it had no authority to station troops on Egyptian soil without Egyptian consent, complied with this demand. Statements by Egyptian and other Arab leaders seemed to indicate that another attack on Israel was imminent. Israel appealed to the United Nations and to various powers but did not obtain the reassurances which she requested. Moreover, on 25 May, Iraq, Jordan, Syria and Saudi Arabia deployed their forces along Israel's frontiers. The Strait of Tiran was declared by Egypt to be closed to Israeli shipping on 22 May.

By the beginning of June Israeli leaders calculated that they were outnumbered on the frontiers by about three to one and that they could be invaded any moment. Rather than wait for this to happen, they had planned a pre-emptive attack, and this was launched on the morning of 5 June, when Egyptian air bases, some as far distant as Cairo and even Luxor, were the victims of destructive surprise attacks by the Israeli air force. These attacks were well-planned and well-executed and resulted in the virtual removal of the Egyptian air force from the

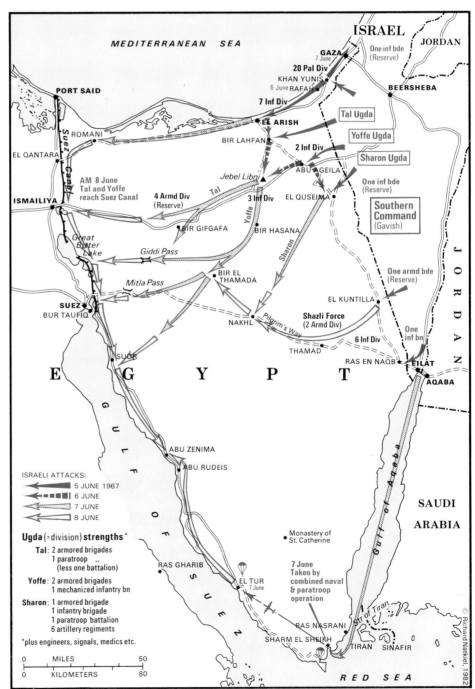

222

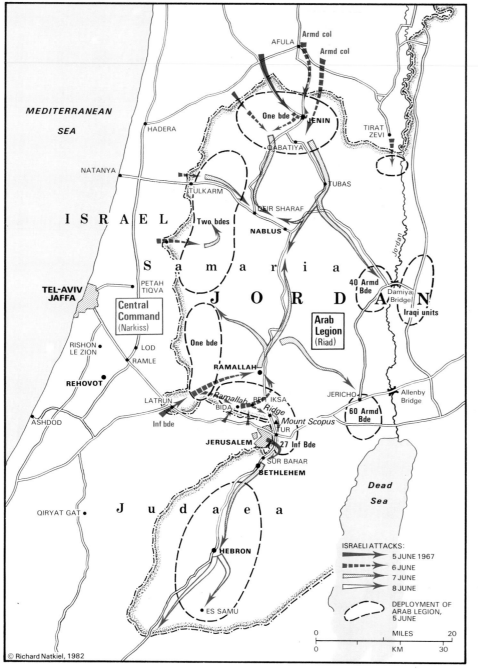

ISRAELI ATTACKS:
5 JUNE 1967
6 JUNE
7 JUNE
8 JUNE
DEPLOYMENT OF
ARAB LEGION,
5 JUNE

0       MILES      20
0      KM       30

**Below:** Egyptian prisoners under guard at El Arish on the second day of the 1967 Arab-Israeli War.
**Bottom:** the Israeli army advances to the outskirts of Suez.
**Right:** an Israeli armored column advances into the Sinai Desert.
**Bottom right:** an Arab soldier surrenders to Israeli forces in Sinai.

following days' hostilities. Having won command of the air, the rout of the Egyptian army in Sinai followed almost automatically. On 9 June the Syrian Golan Heights were assaulted by Israeli forces, and after a day's fighting were captured. Israeli troops entered Kuneitra. Meanwhile, Israeli forces were also throwing back the Jordanians from west of the Jordan and in Jerusalem.

In these victorious circumstances, Israel was able to obtain ceasefire agreements within a week of the commencement of hostilities. As a result of this 'Six-Day War,' the whole of Sinai remained in Israeli hands, as well as the 'West Bank' (Jordan's territory west of the River Jordan) and the Golan Heights. Thus Israel had gained new frontiers which were more easily defensible than the old but the basic causes of hostility remained.

223

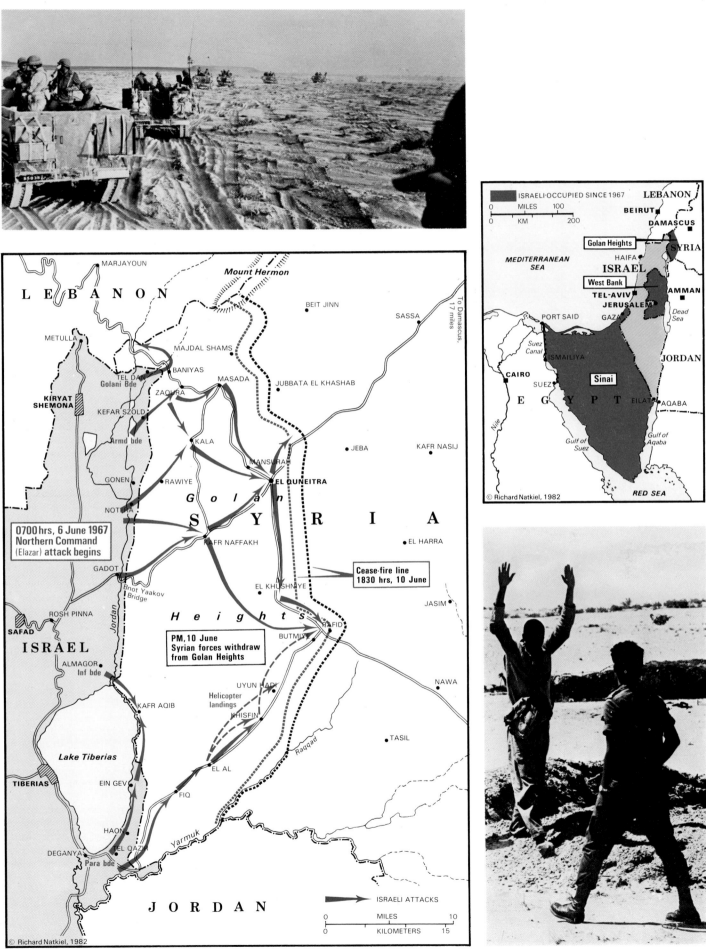

ISRAELI-OCCUPIED SINCE 1967

MILES 100

KM 200

LEBANON

BEIRUT

DAMASCUS

Golan Heights

SYRIA

MEDITERRANEAN SEA

HAIFA

ISRAEL

West Bank

TEL-AVIV

JERUSALEM

AMMAN

PORT SAID

GAZA

Dead Sea

Suez Canal

ISMAILIYA

JORDAN

CAIRO

SUEZ

Sinai

EGYPT

EILAT

AQABA

Nile

Gulf of Suez

Gulf of Aqaba

RED SEA

© Richard Natkiel, 1982

LEBANON

Mount Hermon

MARJAYOUN

BEIT JINN

SASSA

To Damascus, 17 miles

METULLA

MAJDAL SHAMS

BANIYAS

TEL DAN

Golani Bde

MASADA

JUBBATA EL KHASHAB

KIRYAT SHEMONA

ZAQURA

KEFAR SZOLD

Armd bde

KALA

JEBA

KAFR NASIJ

GONEN

RAWIYE

MANSURAH

Golan

SYRIA

NOTERA

EL QUNEITRA

0700 hrs, 6 June 1967
Northern Command
(Elazar) attack begins

KAFR NAFFAKH

EL HARRA

GADOT

Bnot Yaakov Bridge

Cease-fire line
1830 hrs, 10 June

ROSH PINNA

Jordan

Heights

EL KHUSHNIYE

JASIM

SAFAD

ISRAEL

RAFID

ALMAGOR

PM, 10 June
Syrian forces withdraw
from Golan Heights

BUTMIYE

Inf bde

NAWA

KAFR AQIB

UYUN HADI

Helicopter landings

KHISFIN

Lake Tiberias

TASIL

TIBERIAS

EIN GEV

EL AL

Raqqad

FIQ

HAON

TEL QAZIR

Yarmuk

DEGANYA

Para bde

ISRAELI ATTACKS

JORDAN

MILES 10

KILOMETERS 15

© Richard Natkiel, 1982

Bottom: Egyptian air force MiG-17s
attack an Israeli truck convoy in the
vicinity of the Suez Canal.
Bottom right: Soviet border guards take up
a defensive position on the disputed
Sino-Soviet frontier in 1969.

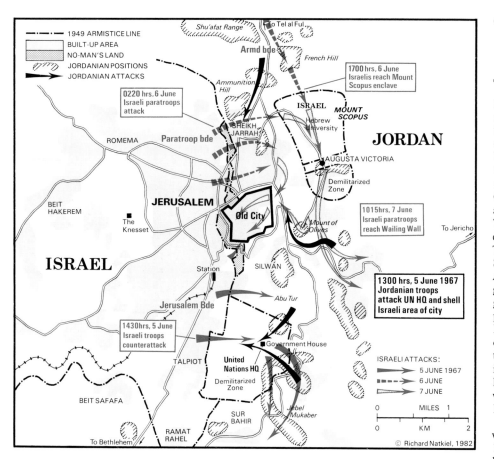

# Sino-Soviet Border Disputes

From the end of the 1950s Soviet-Chinese relations, which had been close ever since the Chinese communists gained power, deteriorated. China, among other responses, began to demand revision of the 'unfair' treaties in which a weak Chinese Empire had ceded territory to tsarist Russia. In 1858 China had ceded the north bank of the Amur and in 1860 the east bank of the Ussuri. Taken together, this was an enormous expanse, forming a new Russian province. Then, in 1864, in the far west, much of Sinkiang became part of tsarist Turkestan. After the Bolshevik revolution the Soviet government had steadily advanced in Mongolia, annexing part of it and sponsoring a pro-Soviet government in the remainder. In the 1930s, when the Japanese were occupying north China, they tried to 'rectify' the frontiers by force, but were beaten back, in large-scale battles, by the Red Army. The heaviest fighting was in the summer of 1939 when the Soviet forces were led by the future Marshal Zhukov.

In the 1960s, as tension mounted, there were numerous frontier incidents, and in 1969 this culminated in quite serious fighting between the frontier troops of the two powers. Frontier negotiations were begun, but their progress was intermittent, and in 1978 there was another serious incident on the Ussuri River.

Although navigation rights on the Amur and Ussuri were peacefully negotiated, agreement on the main issues seemed unobtainable, so long as there was no general improvement in Soviet-Chinese relations. Soon after the break with the USSR, the Chinese government placed the USSR and the USA together as aggressive superpowers and claimed leadership of the Third World countries against the domination of these two. By the mid-1970s, however, Chinese-American relations had been much improved. In the early 1980s, although there were occasional hints of a reconciliation, the Soviet-Chinese relationship was as unfriendly as ever and strong forces remained in position on both sides. That underpopulated Siberia was so close to well-populated China was one cause of Soviet mistrust.

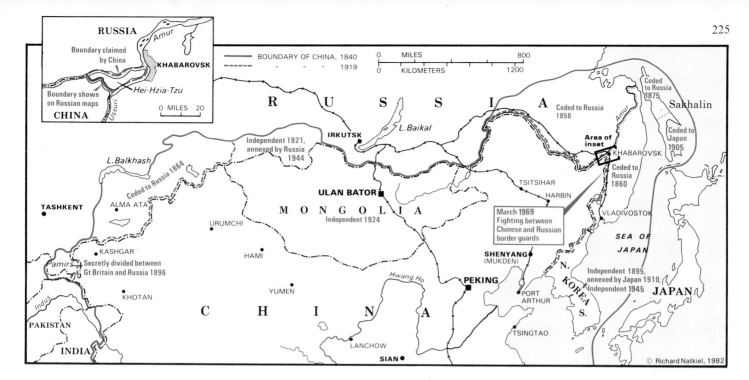

**Right: South Vietnamese refugees are escorted across the flight deck of USS *Hancock* during Operation Frequent Wind, the evacuation of Saigon.**

# Vietnam: the Tet Offensive

After the French disengagement from Vietnam, the Americans tried to encourage the development of a local Vietnamese government which would have the support of its people and thereby be in a position to defend the country against the communists. The American government considered that the elections, promised by the Geneva agreements for 1956, would produce a communist victory, and therefore had no intention of holding them until a date far in the future. But, step by step, the USA found itself drawn into the conflict in Vietnam.

In the late 1950s, while the Vietcong movement in South Vietnam gradually extended its control to almost all the country areas, the US-backed governments proved ineffective, unpopular, and often corrupt. Coups and the occasional assassination did remove the most-disliked government leaders, but each seemed to be followed by a man who was no better. American aid, including advisers, began to create an army for South Vietnam (the ARVN), but at first this was no match for the increasingly large Vietcong formations. In 1959 North Vietnam took control of the anti-government operations in South Vietnam, but it was not until 1964, after incidents in the Gulf of Tonkin, that the US president obtained congressional authority for committing large numbers of US troops to Vietnam. In December of that year Vietcong attacks intensified, and some US air bases were struck. The US Air Force began to bomb North Vietnam and in January 1965 the North Vietnamese Army was committed to action inside South Vietnam.

By 1967 about half a million American troops were in Vietnam, and the ARVN was becoming an effective force. At the end of the year a painstaking operation was begun, aimed at totally eliminating Vietcong from a limited area around Saigon. Extension of this drive, however, was interrupted by the Vietcong's Tet Offensive. This took the form of attacks on cities and towns by small formations which, using infiltration tactics, launched assaults on key government buildings. Although these tactics worked, the attackers were in due course thrown out with very heavy losses.

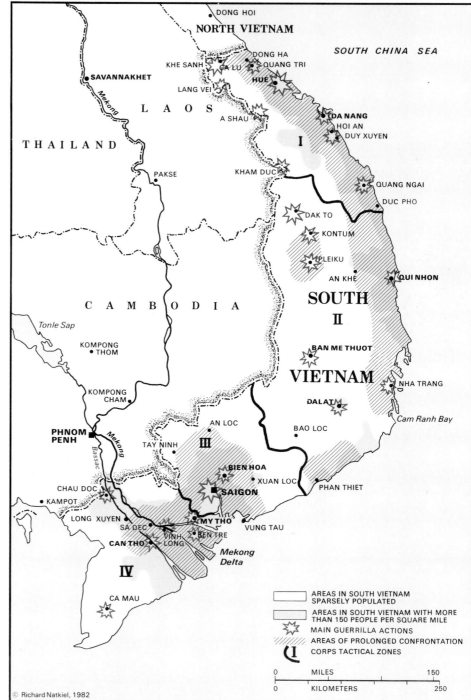

© Richard Natkiel, 1982

☐ AREAS IN SOUTH VIETNAM
SPARSELY POPULATED

▨ AREAS IN SOUTH VIETNAM WITH MORE
THAN 150 PEOPLE PER SQUARE MILE

✶ MAIN GUERRILLA ACTIONS

▨ AREAS OF PROLONGED CONFRONTATION

Ⓘ CORPS TACTICAL ZONES

| 0 | MILES | 150 |
| 0 | KILOMETERS | 250 |

# Vietnam: the Fall of Saigon

The Tet Offensive was victory concealed in a failure. Although beaten militarily, the Vietcong had made a great impression in the USA. Americans asked themselves how it was that, after so much American blood and money had been spent, the enemy could install himself for a few hours or days in almost all the towns and cities. The key town of Hué had been held by the Vietcong for 25 days, and they had even penetrated into the US Embassy in Saigon. Also, as a preliminary to the Tet Offensive, North Vietnamese divisions had heavily attacked Khe Sanh, defended by American Marines. Although it had held out, it was a reminder

of the great fear in Washington that the USA, too, could suffer a Dien Bien Phu. It was from this time, January 1968, that the American government, and perhaps most Americans, came to believe that this was a war they could not win and the best thing to do was to get out in as dignified a manner as possible. The request by the American commander in Vietnam, Westmoreland, for reinforcements to exploit what he rightly saw as the enemy's failure during the Tet Offensive, was unsuccessful. Only a few thousand troops were sent, while at the same time American bombing was limited to the enemy's supply routes through Laos and a small part of North Vietnam close to the border.

The morale of American troops was deteriorating, and they began to be progressively withdrawn from 1969 as the US government sought to extricate itself from

Vietnam by negotiation. But in the end the terms it wanted were unobtainable, despite periodic flurries of activity including a US invasion of Cambodia and a renewal of bombing attacks on Hanoi. In January 1973 the US signed an agreement by which its troops finally quit Vietnam, and in exchange North Vietnam merely agreed to release US prisoners of war. The ARVN was left to fight on alone. In late 1974 the North Vietnamese Army began an offensive in the Mekong Delta, followed in January 1975 by another in the Central Highlands. Meanwhile the ARVN had to deal with a successful revolt in Cambodia by the Khmer Rouge revolutionaries. It could not cope with so many crises, and was soon making its last stand before Saigon. This did not last long. At the end of April Saigon fell, bringing the 30-year struggle to a close.

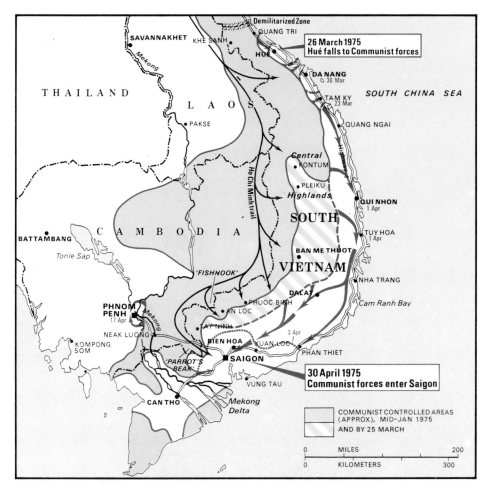

228

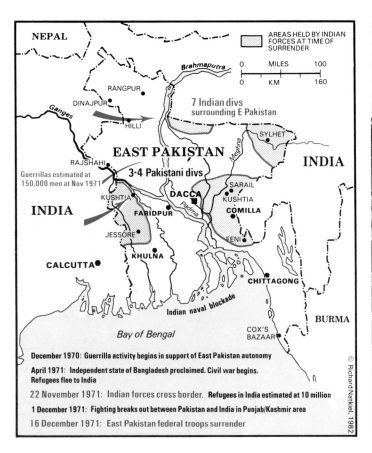

Map annotations:
NEPAL

AREAS HELD BY INDIAN
FORCES AT TIME OF
SURRENDER

0 MILES 100
0 KM 160

Brahmaputra

RANGPUR
DINAJPUR
Ganges
HILLI

7 Indian divs
surrounding E Pakistan

SYLHET

EAST PAKISTAN
RAJSHAHI
Guerrillas estimated at
150,000 men at Nov 1971

INDIA

3-4 Pakistani divs

DACCA
KUSHTIA
FARIDPUR
Padma

SARAIL
KUSHTIA
COMILLA

INDIA

JESSORE
FENI

CALCUTTA
KHULNA

CHITTAGONG

Indian naval blockade

BURMA

Bay of Bengal
COX'S
BAZAAR

© Richard Natkiel, 1982

December 1970: Guerrilla activity begins in support of East Pakistan autonomy

April 1971: Independent state of Bangladesh proclaimed. Civil war begins.
Refugees flee to India

22 November 1971: Indian forces cross border. Refugees in India estimated at 10 million

1 December 1971: Fighting breaks out between Pakistan and India in Punjab/Kashmir area

16 December 1971: East Pakistan federal troops surrender

# The Creation of Bangladesh

The Bengali population of East Pakistan had become steadily disenchanted with its political situation because, although nominally equal with the West as a constituent of the state of Pakistan, in reality the East was dominated by numerically inferior West Pakistan. In 1970 the East's Awami League, which demanded greater independence for the East, won an overwhelming election victory, giving it a considerable majority in the all-Pakistan Assembly. Faced with this, the leader of the next largest, and mainly West Pakistan, party, Bhutto, decided to boycott the Assembly. There were protest demonstrations in East Pakistan. Bit by bit, the army took up the role of an oppressive army of occupation while the Awami League strengthened its resistance movement, the Mukti Bahini.

The Mukti Bahini began conventional terrorist and guerrilla activity, concentrated near the frontier with India, which was becoming increasingly cooperative. Meanwhile the flow of refugees from East Pakistan to India grew to perhaps 15 million, or no fewer than one in five of the population. In November, in a further step toward open war, the Indian and Pakistan governments announced that their troops were authorized to cross the frontiers in case of need.

On 3 December an excuse to go to war was provided by Pakistan, which began to make attacks on Indian positions in the west and in Kashmir. These attacks were small, and presumably intended as warnings; Pakistan was ruled by a general, Yahia Khan, whose political understanding was unsophisticated. The Indian forces destined for East Pakistan were given extra complements of engineering troops in order to speed the crossing of the many rivers and streams of the region, the plan being to make quickly for the towns and railroad junctions, relying on the Mukti Bahini to

hold down the Pakistanis' defensive positions. One Indian corps attacked from the west, around Hilli, while another made three thrusts from the east to capture the capital Dacca and cut off Chittagong. The third corps attacked from the southwest to capture Jessore and reach the Padma River. On 6 December India recognized the independence of the new state of Bangladesh, and ten days later Indian troops reached Dacca, bringing the war to a close and guaranteeing independence. Internal political problems and recurrent famine continued to unsettle Bangladesh throughout the 1970s and beyond.

# EEC, EFTA, and COMECON

The success of the European Coal and Steel Community, established in 1951 to coordinate coal and metallurgical industries and also to bring France and Germany, enemies for decades, into a healthier relationship, led to the European Economic Community (EEC). There was a growing opinion that the west European states, in order to survive in a difficult world economy, needed to join together in mutual support. But, initially, its main effect was the elimination of tariffs and other trade barriers between its members, which is why it became known as the Common Market. However, it steadily developed many other functions; its main bodies are the EEC Commission, the Council of Ministers, the Court of Justice, the European Parliament, and the Economic and Social Committee. The six original members which signed the 1958 Treaty of Rome were the members of the Iron and Steel Community; that is, France, West Germany, Italy and the Benelux trio (BElgium, the NEtherlands, LUXembourg).

Neighboring European states, led by Britain, formed another free trade organization, largely as protection against tariff barriers and other restrictions which were expected to limit trade between themselves and EEC countries. This new organization, the European Free Trade Area (EFTA) comprised Britain, Sweden, Switzerland, Austria, Norway, Denmark, and Portugal. These agreed to remove trade barriers between themselves but to maintain them against other nations. For Britain, EFTA had the advantage that it could maintain its preferential trading arrangements with Commonwealth countries. But when Britain's links with the Commonwealth were seen to be weakening in any case, her government decided to ask for membership of the EEC. At first rebuffed, Britain later succeeded, and became a member in 1973, together with Denmark and Ireland. The other EFTA nations continued with the existing free trade agreement.

In communist Europe there had existed since 1949 a Council for Mutual Economic Assistance, later known in the west as COMECON. Originally intended to oversee the sovietization and the exploitation of

the economies of communist eastern Europe, it was later developed to coordinate the communist bloc economies, with some specialization of production so that, for example, Czechoslovakia supplies streetcars to the whole bloc while the USSR provides oil. In course of time extra-European members were admitted, although the entry of Vietnam was resented by some of the original members as it seemed to be part of the struggle between the USSR and China for influence in that new state.

**Right: the opening of the 1972 Common Market summit conference in Paris.**

| | | | | | | |
|---|---|---|---|---|---|---|
| **EEC** | | **EFTA** | | **COMECON** | | |
| APPLICATION PENDING | | ASSOCIATE MEMBER | | AFFILIATED | | |

**DATE OF JOINING AND POPULATION IN 1979 (MILLIONS)**

| | | | | | | | | | |
|---|---|---|---|---|---|---|---|---|---|
| West Germany | 1958 | 61.34 | Portugal | 1960 | 9.87 | Russia | 1949 | 264.11 |
| Italy | 1958 | 56.91 | Sweden | 1960 | 8.29 | Poland | 1949 | 35.23 |
| France | 1958 | 53.48 | Austria | 1960 | 7.50 | Rumania | 1949 | 22.05 |
| Netherlands | 1958 | 14.03 | Switzerland | 1960 | 6.36 | Czechoslovakia | 1949 | 15.25 |
| Belgium | 1958 | 9.85 | Norway | 1960 | 4.07 | Hungary | 1949 | 10.70 |
| Luxembourg | 1958 | 0.36 | Iceland | 1960 | 0.23 | Bulgaria | 1949 | 8.98 |
| Britain | 1973 | 55.88 | | | | Albania (Left 1961) | 1949 | 2.67 |
| Denmark | 1973 | 5.12 | Finland | 1961 | 4.76 | East Germany | 1950 | 16.75 |
| Ireland | 1973 | 3.37 | | | | Mongolia | 1962 | 1.62 |
| Greece | 1981 | 9.44 | | | | Cuba | 1972 | 9.78 |
| | | | | | | Vietnam | 1978 | 51.08 |
| Turkey | | 44.31 | | | | | | |
| Spain | | 37.18 | | | | Yugoslavia | 1964 | 22.16 |
| Portugal | | 9.87 | | | | | | |

© Richard Natkiel, 1982

# OPEC

The Organization of Petroleum Exporting Countries (OPEC) was formed in 1960 by five founder-members (Iran, Saudi Arabia, Iraq, Kuwait, Venezuela). At the time, its purpose was to slow and perhaps halt the decline in oil prices which the international oil companies had been powerful enough to impose. Thanks to the accession of new members, it did consolidate itself as a strong bargaining body and by 1970, aided by increased world demand, was able to obtain somewhat higher prices.

The very sharp price rises which OPEC enforced in 1973 had a damaging effect not only on the western economies, but throughout the world. Eastern Europe, for example, although mainly supplied by a non-OPEC member, the USSR, found itself faced with price increases as the USSR brought its oil prices closer to world prices. Third World countries in the early stages of economic growth were faced with enormously inflated

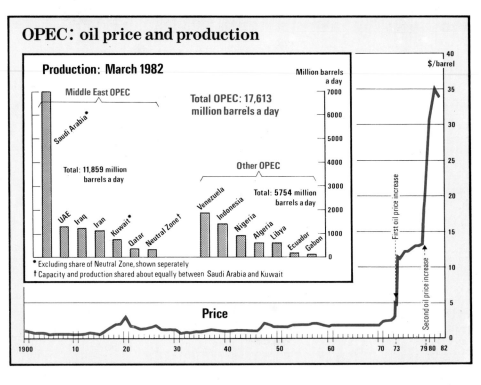

import expenditures; OPEC did establish a special fund in 1976 to help them, but it was only a palliative.

In the advanced economies the immediate effect of the 1973 and subsequent price rises was an increase in the general price level, since most production depended directly or indirectly on energy. These higher prices were accompanied by a decline of output in specific sectors. There was, therefore a general decline of growth rates and

this entailed a decline of oil imports. The exploitation by the energy-consuming nations of alternative fuels, including oil deposits outside the OPEC countries, and various energy-saving measures, led to a further diminution of oil imports and a situation where several OPEC members preferred to lower prices in order to increase their exports rather than maintain high prices which could result in their oils losing a market.

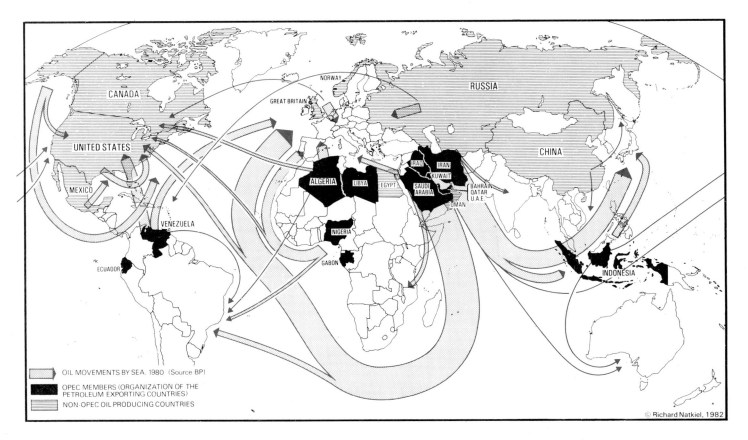

OIL MOVEMENTS BY SEA, 1980 (Source BP)

OPEC MEMBERS (ORGANIZATION OF THE PETROLEUM EXPORTING COUNTRIES)

NON-OPEC OIL PRODUCING COUNTRIES

© Richard Natkiel, 1982

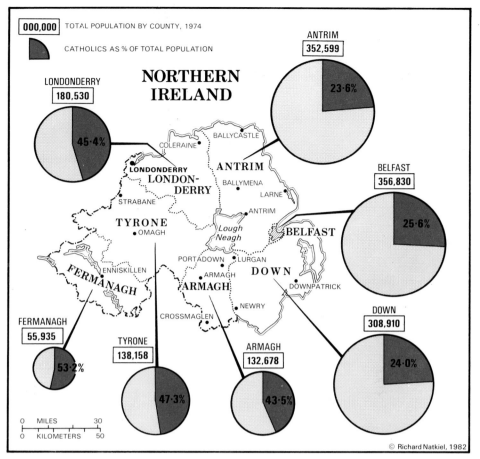

000,000 TOTAL POPULATION BY COUNTY, 1974

CATHOLICS AS % OF TOTAL POPULATION

NORTHERN IRELAND

ANTRIM
352,599
23·6%

LONDONDERRY
180,530
45·4%

BELFAST
356,830
25·6%

FERMANAGH
55,935
53·2%

TYRONE
138,158
47·3%

ARMAGH
132,678
43·5%

DOWN
308,910
24·0%

© Richard Natkiel, 1982

# Northern Ireland

In Ulster the Catholic population has usually not exceeded a third of the total, largely because so many Catholics emigrate. Hence the Protestants, helped by careful manipulation of electoral boundaries, retained control of the Ulster government and were able to discriminate against Catholics in the allocation of cheap public housing, in jobs and in other areas.

Londonderry was a city where these grievances of the Catholics were most intense, and in 1968 a civil rights march there, banned by the authorities, nevertheless took place, and was violently dispersed. In August 1969 the traditional Protestant, and provocative, Apprentice Boys' march was not banned, and was followed by rioting by the inhabitants of Londonderry's Bogside quarter. Rioting spread through the Province, violently countered and sometimes provoked by the Protestant police reservists, the B Specials, and British troops were sent in. The British government promised that reforms would be introduced, and soon established 'direct rule' from London.

The August riots led to a split in the Irish Republican Army [IRA], an underground organization, with those of its members who favored violent tactics leaving to form the Provisional IRA, or Provos. Gradually the British army lost the confidence of the Catholic population, which had initially welcomed its protection, and in February 1971 the first soldier was killed by the Provos. The leader of the Protestant ruling party, the Unionists, despite internal opposition, intro-

duced limited 'power-sharing,' in which two other parties, wholly or partly representing Catholic interests, could take part. In the face of increasing terrorism, and much to the indignation of an aroused Catholic population, he also introduced internment. This was the arrest, all too often bungled, of known IRA members. In 1972 a London-sponsored proposal for a Council of Ireland, in which Dublin, London, and the Northern Ireland Executive would work together, at first seemed likely to succeed, but failed to receive enough support from Unionist politicians, and foundered. Attempts of the powersharing Northern Ireland Executive to govern the Province came to an end when a strike staged by Protestant organizations brought ordinary life to a halt. The British government's weakness in allowing the

Protestants to thereby put an end to any hope of compromise was later severely criticized. In the following years, various political initiatives failed, although attempts to improve conditions by the encouragement of new industries in the Province were partly successful. Killings continued, by Provos, by a new Irish National Liberation Army, and by Protestant, or 'Loyalist,' groups. The political temperature was further raised in 1981 by the deaths of Provo hunger-strikers in Northern Ireland prisons, and at the end of that year a solution was still not in sight. The level of violence had declined from its peak in the early 1970s and improved relations between the London and Dublin governments offered some prospects for the future although such contacts with the Irish Republic were anathema to Loyalist leaders.

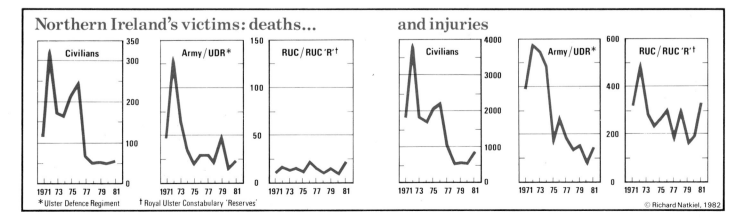

# Northern Ireland's victims: deaths...            and injuries

Civilians

Army / UDR*

RUC / RUC 'R'†

Civilians

Army / UDR*

RUC / RUC 'R'†

* Ulster Defence Regiment    † Royal Ulster Constabulary 'Reserves'

© Richard Natkiel, 1982

Left: a remotely-controlled bomb-disposal apparatus goes into action in Belfast.
Below: rioters pelt British troops with stones as they attempt to control the mob in the Bogside area of Londonderry in April 1971.
Bottom: Turkish occupation forces in position near Famagusta, Cyprus, August 1974.

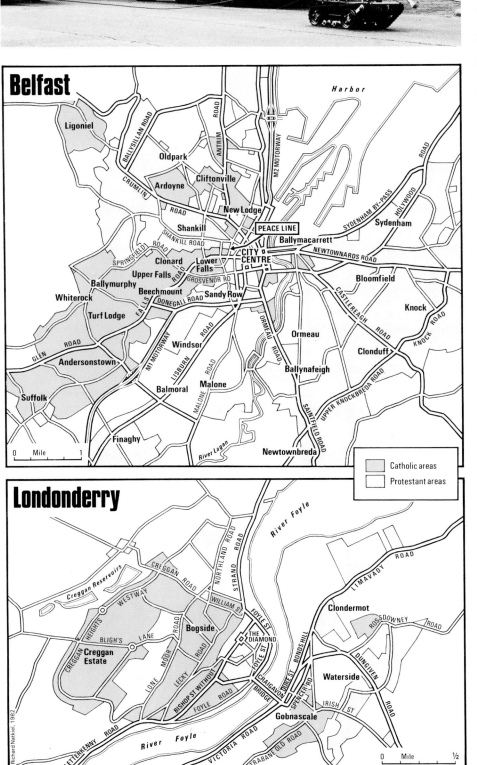

# Belfast

Ligoniel
Oldpark
Ardoyne
Cliftonville
Shankill
New Lodge
PEACE LINE
Ballymacarrett
Sydenham
Clonard
Lower Falls
CITY CENTRE
Upper Falls
GROSVENOR RD
Ballymurphy
Beechmount
Sandy Row
Bloomfield
Whiterock
Knock
Turf Lodge
Ormeau
Clonduff
Windsor
Andersonstown
Ballynafeigh
Suffolk
Malone
Balmoral
Finaghy
Newtownbreda

Harbor

Catholic areas
Protestant areas

0  Mile  1

# Londonderry

River Foyle

Creggan Reservoirs
Creggan Heights
Westway
Bligh's Lane
Creggan Estate
Bogside
THE DIAMOND
Clondermot
Rossdowney
Waterside
Gobnascale

River Foyle

0  Mile  ½

# Cyprus

After World War II in the British colony of Cyprus the patriarch of the Orthodox Church, Archbishop Makarios III, became the moral leader of the *Enosis* movement, which sought union with Greece. However, it was the local Greek terrorist organization, EOKA, instigator of murderous attacks on British servicemen and colonial officials, which had the main effect on British policy. In 1957 negotiations were begun which led to a 1959 agreement granting the island independence. Thirty percent of key positions were reserved for Turks, who amounted to 18 percent of the population. Any suggestion of union with Greece was rejected, and Britain retained sovereign rights in two military base areas.

Makarios, retaining religious authority as Archbishop and having won secular authority as President, proved less enthusiastic for *Enosis* than expected, so EOKA made a new start, abetted by the Greek government. Some pro-Greece bishops attempted to depose Makarios from his archbishopric, but were outmaneuvered and unfrocked. More serious were the several unsuccessful attempts to assassinate Makarios. Then, on 15 July 1974, a coup organized by *Enosis* and EOKA elements was successful, and Nikos Sampson, a local Greek Cypriot, was placed in the presidency. In response, and surprisingly promptly,

Turkey dispatched an invasion force to Cyprus, which landed near Kyrenia on 20 July and steadily moved inland. The covert but plain-to-all involvement of the Greek government as instigator of this new international crisis led to the dismissal of the Greek cabinet on 23 July and Sampson, after a week of fame, was deposed by the Cyprus National Guard. The three guarantor-powers of the Republic of Cyprus (Britain, Turkey, Greece) met at Geneva, but a lasting ceasefire was obtained only on 16 August. This left the Turkish Army in control of the northern third of the island, mainly inhabited by Turks. Late in 1974 Makarios returned to the presidency in the capital, Nicosia, but he had no authority in the Turkish zone, which became increasingly linked with the Turkish mainland. A UN peacekeeping force patrolled a buffer zone between the two parts, and there were sporadic attempts to arrive at a settlement under UN auspices. Talks between Turkish Cypriot and Greek Cypriot leaders were successful in avoiding further violence but unsuccessful in ending the *de facto* partition of the island. Makarios died in 1977, and five years later the 'Cyprus Problem' was still unsolved.

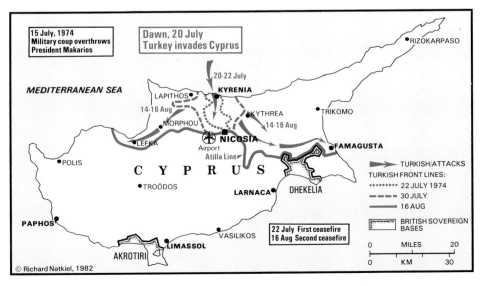

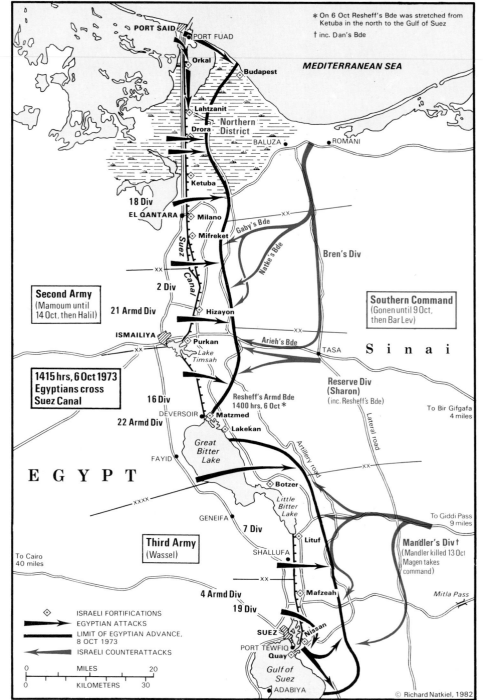

# The October War, 1973

The ceasefire after the Six-Day War of 1967 was followed by six years of tension in the Middle East. Arabs and Israelis resorted to terrorism and counter-terrorism, with the occasional air battle punctuating the situation, as the Arab states bordering Israel continued to demand a restoration of the pre-1967 frontiers. By 1973 President Sadat of Egypt had enhanced, with Soviet help, the battleworthiness of his army, but he had then invited the Soviet military specialists to leave, thereby freeing himself from a possible restraining Soviet influence over his military ambitions.

On the Jewish Day of Atonement (*Yom Kippur*), 6 October 1973, Egyptian and Syrian forces launched a coordinated surprise attack on Israel, with the stated intention of regaining the 1967 frontiers. The Egyptian crossing of the Suez Canal, thanks to the surprise achieved, was successful, and the Israeli forces defending Sinai were put into disarray. In the north, too, the Israelis were thrown back, losing much of the Golan Heights. Help for both sides soon began to arrive. Iraq sent tanks to help the Syrians, and so did Jordan, while Kuwait and Saudi Arabia sent token forces to the same front. Egypt received some aircraft from Iraq, while Moroccan and Algerian troops arrived to release more Egyptian troops for the front. Meanwhile, the USA airlifted military supplies to Israel, while Soviet aid was sent by air and by sea to

Left: the ceasefire line in the town of Suez at the end of the Yom Kippur War, October 1973.
Top right: Israeli troops cross the Suez Canal over a temporary causeway.
Right: Israeli soldiers relax during a lull in the fighting in Sinai.

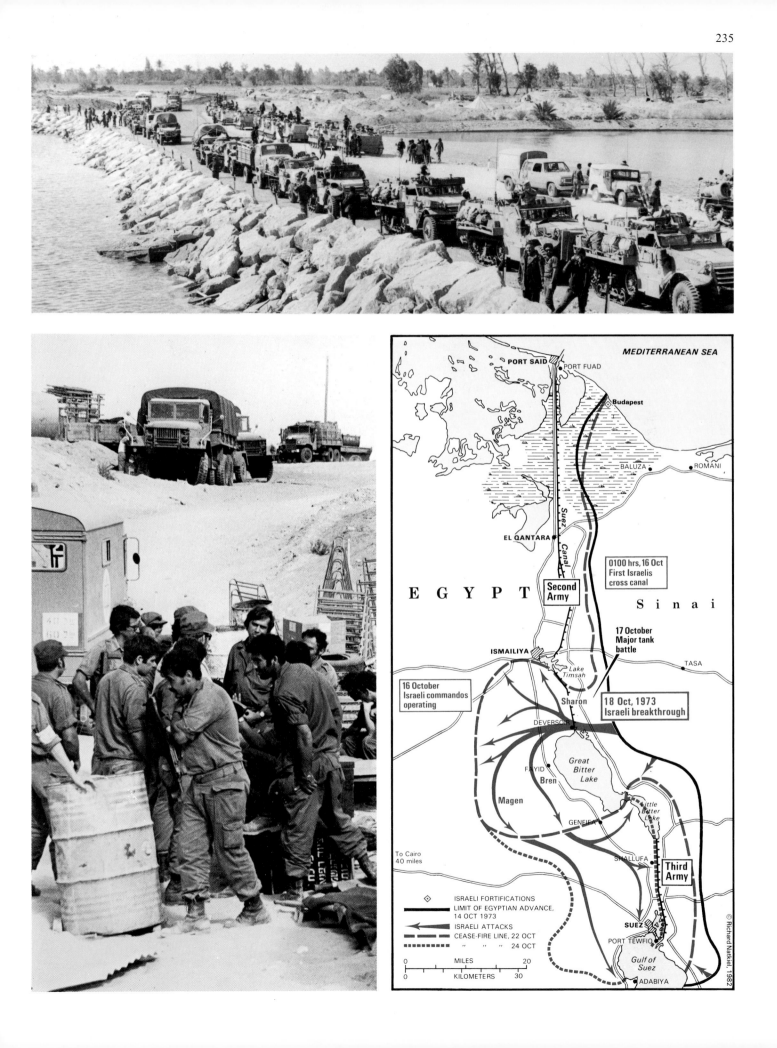

MEDITERRANEAN SEA

PORT SAID
PORT FUAD
Budapest
BALUZA
ROMANI
EL QANTARA

**EGYPT**

Sinai

Second
Army

0100 hrs, 16 Oct
First Israelis
cross canal

ISMAILIYA

17 October
Major tank
battle

Lake
Timsah

TASA

16 October
Israeli commandos
operating

Sharon

18 Oct, 1973
Israeli breakthrough

DEVERSOIR

FAYID
Bren

Great
Bitter
Lake

Little
Bitter
Lake

Magen

GENEIFA

To Cairo
40 miles

SHALLUFA

Third
Army

◇    ISRAELI FORTIFICATIONS
──    LIMIT OF EGYPTIAN ADVANCE,
        14 OCT 1973
◄─    ISRAELI ATTACKS
─ ─    CEASE-FIRE LINE, 22 OCT
·····    "    "    "    24 OCT

SUEZ

PORT TEWFIQ

Gulf
of
Suez

ADABIYA

0 ─── MILES ─── 20
0 ─── KILOMETERS ─── 30

© Richard Natkiel, 1982

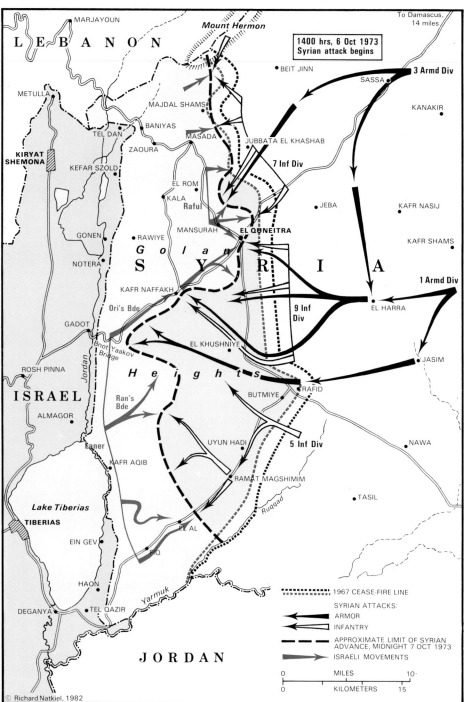

**1400 hrs, 6 Oct 1973 Syrian attack begins**

To Damascus, 14 miles

LEBANON

Mount Hermon

MARJAYOUN

METULLA

MAJDAL SHAMS

BANIYAS

TEL DAN

ZAOURA

MASADA

BEIT JINN

SASSA

3 Armd Div

KANAKIR

JUBBATA EL KHASHAB

KIRYAT SHEMONA

KEFAR SZOLD

EL ROM

KALA

Raful

7 Inf Div

JEBA

KAFR NASIJ

GONEN

RAWIYE

MANSURAH

EL QUNEITRA

KAFR SHAMS

NOTERA

*Golan*

S Y R I A

KAFR NAFFAKH

Ori's Bde

1 Armd Div

9 Inf Div

EL HARRA

GADOT

Bnot Yaakov Bridge

EL KHUSHNIYE

*Heights*

JASIM

ROSH PINNA

Jordan

Ran's Bde

RAFID

BUTMIYE

ISRAEL

ALMAGOR

Baner

KAFR AQIB

UYUN HADI

5 Inf Div

NAWA

Lake Tiberias

TIBERIAS

RAMAT MAGSHIMIM

*Ruqqad*

TASIL

EIN GEV

EL AL

HAON

BIQ

DEGANYA

TEL QAZIR

*Yarmuk*

JORDAN

........ 1967 CEASE-FIRE LINE

SYRIAN ATTACKS:
◄──── ARMOR
◄──── INFANTRY

- - - - APPROXIMATE LIMIT OF SYRIAN ADVANCE, MIDNIGHT 7 OCT 1973
──► ISRAELI MOVEMENTS

0 — MILES — 10
0 — KILOMETERS — 15

© Richard Natkiel, 1982

Egypt and Syria. Israel was again out-numbered, having about 300,000 troops against Egypt's 650,000 and Syria's 150,000.

By 10 October the Israelis had beaten back the Syrians in the north, and were just holding the Egyptians in Sinai. Israeli air-craft, which had been vulnerable to Soviet-made missiles while attacking the Suez Canal bridges and the Syrian and Egyptian troops, were now free to deal with their opponents' own air forces. A strong counter-offensive was launched against the Syrians, whose defense line was pushed back. A threat to Damascus was avoided as this, it was feared, might have brought the USSR into the war in support of her protégé Syria. Having weakened the Syrian position, the Israelis concentrated their next effort on the Suez Front. Egyptian tanks, attempting to push eastward and especially toward the vital Mitla Pass, were routed in an enormous tank battle by Israeli armor and aircraft. This victory encouraged the Israeli generals, who were rarely in agreement with each other, to launch a decisive counterblow. The aim was to cross the Suez Canal in the area of the Great Bitter Lake, and thereby trans-form the situation. Despite some difficulty, when unexpectedly strong Egyptian action was encountered east of the Canal, a bridge-head was established and this was progres-sively enlarged until the Egyptian Third Army found itself almost cut off. A USSR delegation to Cairo realized that Egypt was facing total defeat, and with US and Soviet help the United Nations Security Council arranged a ceasefire, effective from 24 October.

Although Israel had emerged triumphant from this new ordeal, the war had shown

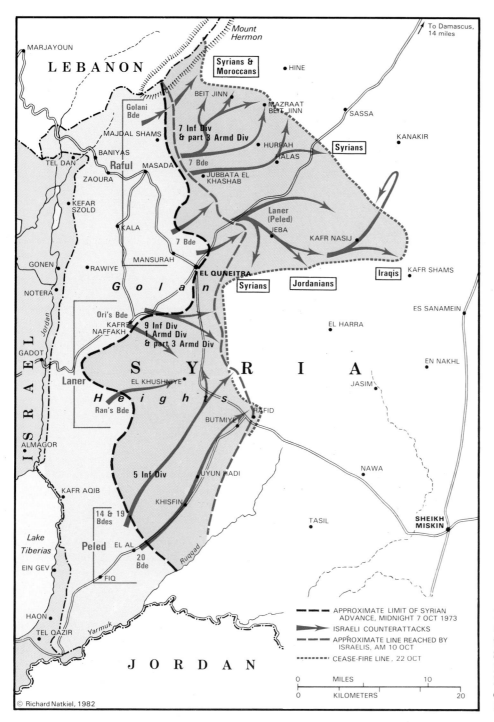

that the Egyptian Army was more battle-worthy than had been believed, and that Israel was more vulnerable to surprise attack than had been thought. UN forces were sent to Sinai, while Israeli forces were withdrawn east of the passes. Egyptian forces remained on the right bank of the Canal, but the UN force separating the two armies was equipped to issue early warning of troop movements to both sides.

**Below left:** Egyptian troops load supplies aboard amphibious craft, which were used to ferry food and ammunition across the Suez Canal to the encircled Third Army. **Below:** these Palestinian terrorists were killed when the explosives they were carrying into Israel across the Golan Heights accidentally detonated.

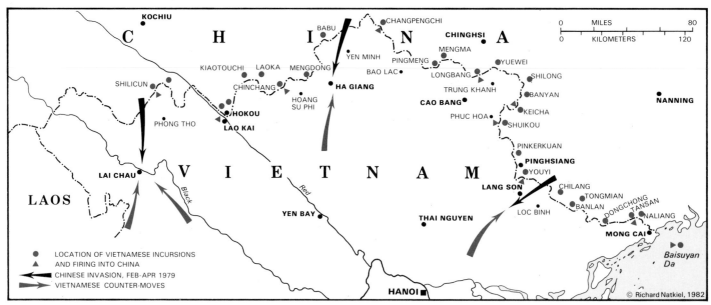

CHINA

KOCHIU

BABU  CHANGPENGCHI

CHINGHSI

YEN MINH

MENGMA

PINGMENG

YUEWEI

KIAOTOUCHI  LAOKA  MENGDONG

BAO LAC

LONGBANG

SHILONG

SHILICUN

CHINCHANG

HA GIANG

TRUNG KHANH

BANYAN

HOANG
SU PHI

CAO BANG

KEICHA

HOKOU

NANNING

PHONG THO

LAO KAI

PHUC HOA

SHUIKOU

PINKERKUAN

LAOS

VIETNAM

LAI CHAU

Black

Red

PINGHSIANG

YOUYI

LANG SON

CHILANG

TONGMIAN

BANLAN

DONGCHONG

TANSAN

YEN BAY

THAI NGUYEN

LOC BINH

NALIANG

MONG CAI

Baisuyan
Da

0  MILES  80
0  KILOMETERS  120

© Richard Natkiel, 1982

● LOCATION OF VIETNAMESE INCURSIONS
▲ AND FIRING INTO CHINA
◀━ CHINESE INVASION, FEB-APR 1979
➤ VIETNAMESE COUNTER-MOVES

HANOI

# Vietnam versus China

After the establishment of the Socialist
Republic of Vietnam, following the overrunning of South Vietnam in 1975, the
new state had serious policy differences with
China. The Vietnamese wished to draw the
neighboring states of Kampuchea (Cambodia) and Laos into close association,
whereas China wished them to be independent and orientated toward Peking. In 1977
Vietnamese forces invaded Kampuchea and,
despite Chinese help for the Cambodian
government, captured the capital, Phnom
Penh, and installed a new, friendly government, which agreed to the stationing of
Vietnamese troops on its territory.

Meanwhile the tough socialist measures
introduced in newly-conquered south Vietnam affected Chinese residents especially,
since they were the trading and managerial
class. In the summer of 1978 up to 200,000
fled into the Chinese provinces across the
frontier. Chinese technical and economic
aid to Vietnam was cut off. For this and other
reasons Vietnam drew closer to the USSR,
raising the possibility of Soviet bases close
to China inside Vietnam. In early 1979 there
were clashes on the Chinese-Vietnamese
frontier and on 17 February the Chinese
Army invaded in considerable strength. The
town of Lang Son was captured; this opened
the direct route to Hanoi, across flat country,
but the Chinese, who had not, and did not
wish, to deploy their full strength, called a
halt and began to withdraw, claiming that
they had done enough to 'teach Vietnam a
lesson.' Although they had gained ground,
and no doubt alarmed the Vietnamese
government, their casualties had been heavy,
the month's fighting having been quite fierce.
In April negotiations began, and in May the
two sides began to exchange prisoners.
However, Vietnam continued to treat its
Chinese citizens with hostility.

Page 239

**Below left: Vietnamese gunners bombard Chinese invading forces in 1979. The fine fighting qualities of the Vietnamese troops more than compensated for the numerical strength of the Chinese.**

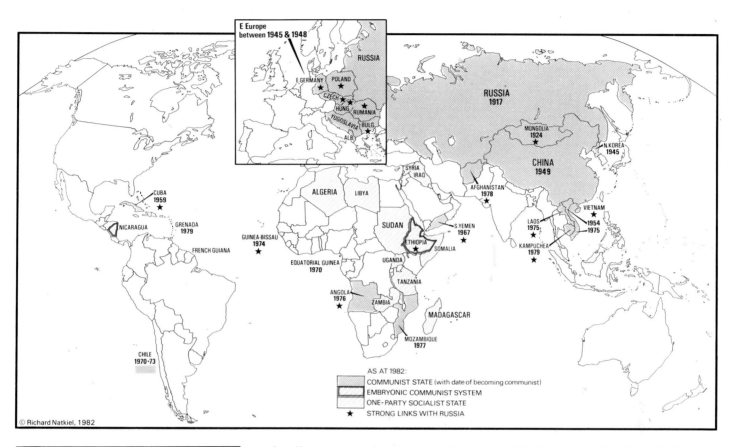

© Richard Natkiel, 1982

AS AT 1982:
COMMUNIST STATE (with date of becoming communist)
EMBRYONIC COMMUNIST SYSTEM
ONE-PARTY SOCIALIST STATE
★ STRONG LINKS WITH RUSSIA

# The Spread of Communist Influence

After 1945 the spread of Moscow's influence was largely a matter of consolidating control of the newly-established people's democracies. Elsewhere the policy was to help local communist parties, while ensuring that they did not deviate from the Moscow line which, briefly, was that the Russian way to communism was the only possible way and that Moscow was and would remain the ideological and inspirational centre of the communist world. In France and Italy there were very large communist parties, and in the late 1940s these staged disturbances, which included sabotage, but were unable to create the revolutionary opportunity for which Moscow had hoped. However, the communist victory in China seemed a great success.

This situation changed after the mid-1950s, when a new policy of supporting, and thereby influencing, non-communist nationalist movements in overseas territories was adopted, even though this meant Soviet support for newly-installed 'bourgeois' regimes in the Third World. In some cases these devices worked well. In Cuba, especially, Soviet help for Castro's revolutionary regime soon created a Soviet-orientated communist government in that island. In other cases, however, Soviet hopes were dramatically disappointed. Egypt, for example, at the time it was receiving substantial Soviet economic aid, had no hesitation in keeping its local communists safely in gaol, and later invited Soviet military advisers to leave. Almost always, Third World governments were skilled in obtaining what they wanted by playing off east against west while making irrevocable concessions to neither. The USSR did establish shore facilities for its navy in several countries, a vital need for a country intent on becoming a world naval power, but these bases were dependent on local goodwill which was not always long-lived.

Meanwhile the strong communist parties in Italy, France and Spain steadily moved from a position of servility to one of open hostility in their relationship with Moscow, while the emergence of China as an ideological and political opponent of the USSR made it easier for the smaller communist states to act more independently. Suppression of popular movements in eastern Europe further lowered Moscow's prestige, while the establishment of loyal communist regimes in Cuba and, later, Afghanistan, involved a heavy economic drain which was resented by Soviet citizens still living in conditions of scarcity. In general, western attempts to halt Soviet expansion by backing unpopular regimes which happened to be anti-communist were self-defeating, and certainly less important than local nationalisms and the provision of economic and technical aid to governments which, without necessarily being anti-communist, did not sympathize with Russian aspirations.

# Africa in the 1970s

During the 1970s there was a growing tendency for the independent African states to take a stronger attitude toward the richer, industrialized, countries. This change became evident at a Commonwealth conference of 1971, in which Zambia, Tanzania, and Uganda threatened to impose economic penalties on Britain if the latter should export substantial arms and munitions to South Africa. The South African issue dominated the continent's outlook, as it was evident that the South African government not only intended to continue its restrictive attitude toward its black inhabitants at home, but also would interfere in its neighbors' affairs; South Africa's continued blocking of a majority-rule solution for Namibia, its incursions into Angola, and its aid to the rebel white regime of Rhodesia were regarded as examples of this. An informal alliance developed in which Arab states declared their hostility to South Africa in return for African states breaking off relations with Israel. However, South Africa continued on its course despite the attainment of black rule in Angola and Mozambique and, in 1980, in Zimbabwe (formerly Rhodesia).

In East Africa the situation was disturbed as the new Marxist regime in Ethiopia sought to consolidate its position and beat off the hostility of Eritrean nationalists and Somalia. There were several regional economic cooperation schemes but an old one, the East African Community, broke up because of animosity between its members, Kenya, Uganda and Tanzania. Here and there hostilities over border issues, or civil wars, broke out. At the beginning of the decade there were about seven million Africans under arms, but this soon increased. At the same time, of the world's 25 poorest nations, 18 were in Africa. Many Africans blamed the power of big international companies for their slow economic development and it seemed likely that, with the process of decolonization almost complete, the stronger states, like Nigeria, would begin to assert their economic independence.

**Right: a UNITA soldier seen in Lobito during the civil war in Angola.**
**Below: UNITA forces on the attack in Southern Angola, February 1977.**

# Angola

In the 1950s and 1960s three competing organizations opposed the Portuguese administration in Angola. They all aimed at independence, but had different philosophies and different foreign backers. The MPLA (The Popular Movement) represented revolutionary nationalism and was Marxist. The FNLA (The National Front) defended the interests of northern tribes and had the tacit sympathy of the USA and Belgium. Curiously, the UNITA movement in the south depended on Portuguese tolerance; such tolerance was forthcoming because UNITA seemed likely to cause more damage to the MPLA than to the Portuguese.

When, in 1974, an army coup in Portugal made an opening for political parties which were willing to grant independence to the colonies, the MPLA, FNLA and UNITA continued their fight against each other. City-dwellers, especially in the capital Luanda, were largely in favor of the MPLA. This gave the latter an advantage, but FNLA and UNITA received much support from and through Zaire. Moreover, in August 1975 South African forces advanced into south Angola, where their effect was to strengthen the UNITA movement. But by July the MPLA had succeeded in gaining control of Luanda, through which military supplies were received from eastern Europe, helping the MPLA to

control 12 of the 16 Angolan districts. However, in October South African units advanced and helped FNLA and UNITA forces to capture Moçâmedes, Sá da Bandeira, Benguela, Lobito and Novo Redondo. But troops sent by Cuba were now arriving and these helped the MPLA to regain the initiative, and in February 1976 to proclaim Angolan independence and form a government.

**Right: an MPLA soldier mounts guard at the Cuanda River, near the town of Dondo, Angola 1976.**

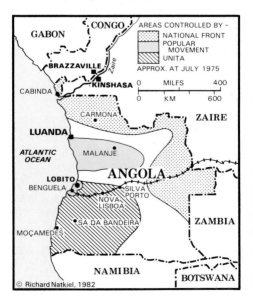

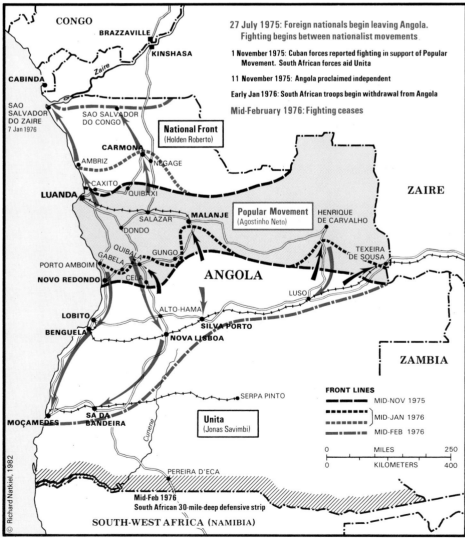

27 July 1975: Foreign nationals begin leaving Angola. Fighting begins between nationalist movements

1 November 1975: Cuban forces reported fighting in support of Popular Movement. South African forces aid Unita

11 November 1975: Angola proclaimed independent

Early Jan 1976: South African troops begin withdrawal from Angola

Mid-February 1976: Fighting ceases

National Front (Holden Roberto)

Popular Movement (Agostinho Neto)

Unita (Jonas Savimbi)

FRONT LINES
MID-NOV 1975
MID-JAN 1976
MID-FEB 1976

Mid-Feb 1976
South African 30-mile-deep defensive strip

SOUTH-WEST AFRICA (NAMIBIA)

AREAS CONTROLLED BY –
NATIONAL FRONT
POPULAR MOVEMENT
UNITA
APPROX. AT JULY 1975

242

Below: Captured Somali guns and a Soviet-made T-54 tank at an army camp in Ethiopia.

# Eritrea, the Ogaden, and Ethiopia

In 1950 the United Nations Assembly approved the federation of the former Italian colony of Eritrea with Ethiopia. Eritrea had a mainly Moslem population, whereas Ethiopia was Christian, and this, with Ethiopia's 1962 termination of Eritrea's federal status, gave edge to Eritrean resistance. Farther south, in 1960 the former British and Italian Somaliland colonies were united, becoming independent Somalia with its capital at Mogadishu. However, the colonial frontiers were such that many Somalians remained outside, in Kenya and Ethiopia. After a few unsettled years, frontier agreements were made with Ethiopia and Kenya, but Somalia did not obtain the Somali-speaking area of the Ogaden, in southern Ethiopia.

Eritrean nationalist guerrillas received much support from Arab countries, and the Ethiopian Army was still fighting them, unsuccessfully, when a revolution deposed Haile Sellassie and installed a Marxist government in Addis Ababa in 1974. Profiting by the confusion, the Eritrean Liberation Front, (ELF) almost captured the Eritrean capital Asmara. By 1977 the Ethiopians were being pursued by the ELF, and by the Eritrean People's Liberation Front (EPLF) in the north. Disunity between these two movements, and the rebuilding of the Ethiopian Army with Soviet help, helped the Ethiopians to regain the initiative in 1978 and relieve Asmara and Massawa. But, reduced to a small area of difficult country, the ELF continued to hold out, as did the EPLF in the far north.

Meanwhile from 1973, the Western Somali Liberation Front (WSLF) was active in the Ogaden, and from July 1977 was supported by regular Somali forces. The USSR, previously supporting Somalia, switched its support to Ethiopia and, with the help of Cuban troops, saved the Ethiopian Army from rout. The Somali Army withdrew from the conflict while its government turned to the USA for help. Somalian guerrillas remained active in the Ogaden, while Somalia continued to demand a frontier revision, and remained, technically at least, in a state of war.

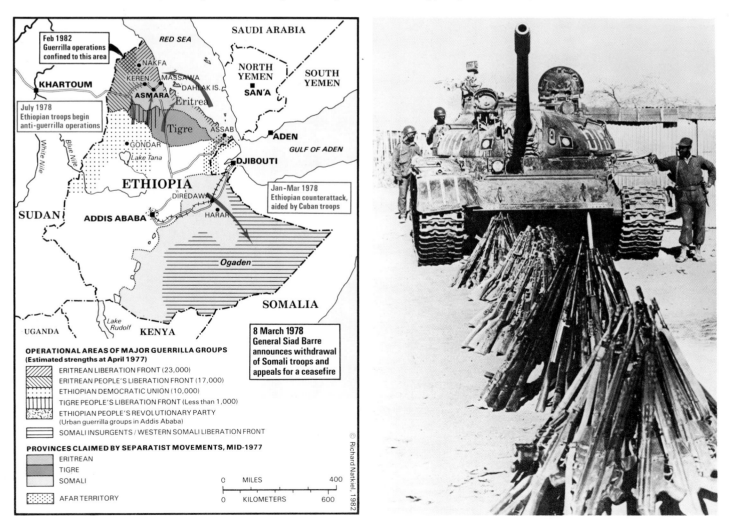

# The Western Sahara

By the early 1970s it was clear that Spain was unlikely to maintain her hold on the Spanish Sahara for long. Morocco, Mauritania and Algeria each had interests in the colony. Algeria supported the Polisario movement (formed in 1973) which was nationalist and Marxist oriented whereas in October 1974 Morocco and Mauritania secretly agreed to partition the country between themselves. This they duly did when Spain withdrew and were immediately opposed by Polisario guerrillas.

From May 1976 the Polisario attacks were concentrated on Mauritania, very much poorer and weaker than Morocco, and despite the presence of Moroccan troops, a coup in Mauritania in July 1978 led to an agreement between Polisario and Mauritania in 1979. Mauritania then withdrew from the occupied territory. The fighting between Polisario and Morocco continued into the 1980s and was a heavy burden on the Moroccan economy. Although Algeria became less active in support of Polisario after the death of President Boumedienne in 1978 Polisario did receive arms from Libya and formal recognition from a number of other countries.

**Right: a display of weapons which Ethiopian soldiers were carrying when they fled across the border into Sudan following fighting with the ELF in 1977.**
**Above right: Enthusiastic WSLF guerrillas on their way to the front, November 1977.**

244

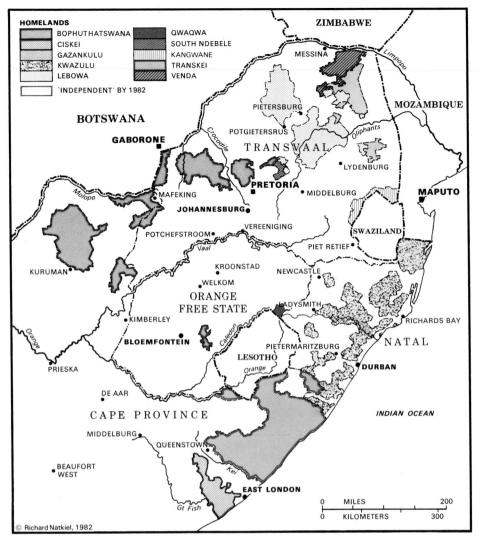

© Richard Natkiel, 1982

# The South African Homelands

In 1948 in the Union of South Africa the hitherto minority Nationalist Party won an electoral majority, which it gradually increased over the following three decades. Thus the Union (since 1960 the Republic) found itself ruled by an Afrikaner ('Boer') party, advocating *apartheid*. *Apartheid*, or separation, implied that each race should have its own homeland where it could develop economically and culturally in accord with its own desires and capabilities. *Apartheid* also implied the concept of 'white supremacy,' although this term was later avoided, 'separate development' being favored instead.

In theory, the African majority was to live in its own homelands, while the white minority would occupy other parts of the territory. The first of the homelands, the Transkei, was granted internal self-government in 1963 and, with support from the Republic's government, Chief Matanzima became its first prime minister. Other homelands were subsequently given their own

legislative assemblies. In addition, earlier British colonial policy had created the independent black states of Swaziland and Lesotho; these were not part of the South African homelands strategy, but because of their geography had close connections with it. A further step was taken in 1976, when the South African government declared the Transkei to be independent, followed by Venda (1979), Bophuthatswana (1977) the Ciskei (1981), and others.

Most countries did not recognize the independence of these new so-called states, claiming that they were not truly independent. Criticis emphasized that the planned homelands could not possibly support the entire African population, while the forcible removal of many Africans from the white areas to the homelands aroused international criticism. The homelands possessed no ports and no industry and had few economic resources. In practice, they seemed to serve as reservoirs of cheap migrant labor for use by the white economy.

# South America

Most countries of South America experienced accelerated industrial development during the two world wars and some, in the interwar years, strove to attain self-sufficiency in oil production. The exploitation of Mexican oil had led to over-rapid development and the 1910 Mexican revolution, but Venezuela became a major oil exporter and avoided this situation. Nevertheless the growth of the middle and working classes in many South American countries, together with the Mexican example, meant that changes of government by traditional coups sometimes developed into real revolutions seeking to change the social balance. Uruguay's constitutional revolution of 1919, the post-1945 Peronist movement in Argentina, and the Bolivian revolution of 1952 (that country's 179th), had much in common. In most cases these revolutions lost impetus, as did moves toward democracy,

NETH. ANTILLES

PANAMA
PANAMA CITY
CARACAS
TRINIDAD & TOBAGO
VENEZUELA
ATLANTIC OCEAN
1903 Gained independence from Colombia
GEORGETOWN
GUYANA
PARAMARIBO
CAYENNE
BOGOTA
COLOMBIA
1922 To Colombia from Ecuador
SURINAM
FRENCH GUIANA
1900 To Brazil from French Guiana
QUITO
ECUADOR *
1904-05 To Brazil
Negro
Amazon
1942 To Peru from Ecuador
Amazon
1903 To Brazil from Bolivia
PERU
BRAZIL
Tocantins
São Francisco
LIMA
1909 To Peru from Bolivia
1902 To Peru from Bolivia
1927 To Brazil from Bolivia
1929 To Peru from Chile
BOLIVIA
LA PAZ
1938 To Paraguay from Bolivia
1960 New capital founded
BRASILIA
Paraguay
PACIFIC OCEAN
PARAGUAY
ASUNCION
Paraná
SAO PAULO
RIO DE JANEIRO
CHILE
Paraná
Uruguay
URUGUAY
SANTIAGO
BUENOS AIRES
MONTEVIDEO
ARGENTINA
ATLANTIC OCEAN
1899-1902 Disputed by Chile and Argentina
Claimed by Argentina
FALKLAND IS. (Brit.)
*Ecuador boundary disputed by Colombia and Peru prior to 1942
0 MILES 500
0 KILOMETERS 800
© Richard Natkiel, 1982
Disputed by Chile and Argentina

and in the early 1980s most South Americans lived under military regimes, or governments under military influence. Population continued to increase in the twentieth century, although this was less a result of continued immigration (especially from Italy, Spain and Portugal) than of improved public health. By the 1960s Brazil seemed set to be the future economic giant of the continent, a development symbolized by the construction of an expensive new capital at Brasilia.

The nineteenth century struggles for independence had left many indefinite frontiers, and disputes over these continued to plague the continent. The Chaco War (1932–1935) between Paraguay and Bolivia was the most destructive of these disputes, and resulted in Bolivia losing most of the Chaco territory. In the early 1980s Venezuela still had a territorial claim on Guyana (formerly British Guiana) and Argentina remained bellicosely dissatisfied with an arbitration award which confirmed Chilean possession of three islands in the Beagle Channel.

246

# Uganda

The former British colony of Uganda had great difficulty in reconciling its new independent style of government with the strong tribal loyalties of its peoples. In 1971 the army commander, Idi Amin, in a coup which was largely tribal in its aspirations, deposed and then succeeded President Obote. Amin's eight-year rule was characterized by the elevation of his cronies to high office, the imprisonment, torture and murder not only of his enemies, real or suspected, but of any Ugandan who had the courage to criticize, the expulsion of the large Asian community and the takeover of the Asian-run businesses by Amin's supporters, the alienation of almost all Uganda's friends, including fellow-members of the British Commonwealth and of the Organization for African Unity, and a general run-down of the economy. Lacking other friends outside the country, and increasingly distrustful of his compatriots, Amin began to rely increasingly on Libya and Palestinians.

Having achieved all this, Amin declared 1978 to be a year of peace and reconciliation. But this proved to be wishful thinking for in July the army, hitherto cossetted by Amin in return for its support, staged a mutiny which was suppressed only by Palestinians flown in from Libya. In October Amin accused Tanzania of invading southwestern Uganda and dispatched three battalions, with tanks and artillery, to cross the frontier into Tanzania. Within a few days, however, Tanzanian troops and Ugandan exiles were advancing in south Uganda toward the capital, Kampala, which fell in April.

# The Falklands Crisis

Although the Argentine invasion of the Falkland Islands on 2 April 1982 came as a complete surprise to the people of Britain and the rest of the world, the status of the islands had long been a source of dispute between Britain and Argentina. Despite the British military victory which ultimately ensued most Argentinians were and remain convinced that the islands, which they know as the Malvinas, ought rightfully to be part of Argentina. In negotiations over many years Britain had gone some way toward recognizing this claim. One suggestion had been to transfer sovereignty over the islands to Argentina but for Britain to continue to administer them on a 'lease-back' arrangement giving them a similar status as Hong Kong vis-à-vis China. However, Britain was unwilling to enforce such a deal against the wishes of the islanders who vehemently insisted that they wanted to remain British.

Negotiations in early 1982 made no new progress and, presumably after careful preparation, the invasion of the Falkland Islands and South Georgia followed. It has been suggested that a major motive for the Argentine military junta's decision was a desire to distract the Argentinian people from the country's appalling economic problems. The Argentinians were certainly surprised by the speed and anger of the British response. Britain was able to mobilize extensive diplomatic support in the UN and among her EEC partners who joined in imposing economic sanctions on Argentina. The USA at first remained neutral in the

dispute and tried to mediate but after Secretary Haig's diplomatic efforts had failed America also condemned the Argentine aggression. The UN Secretary General also attempted to resolve the dispute but he too was unsuccessful.

While the diplomatic efforts were continuing the British task force was making its way to the South Atlantic. As well as sending warships the British government also requisitioned a number of merchant vessels, including luxury liners, to carry troops and supplies and act as hospital

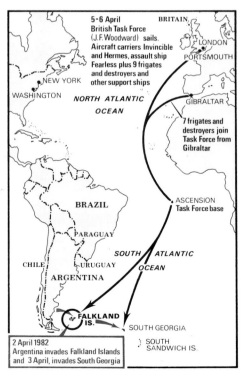

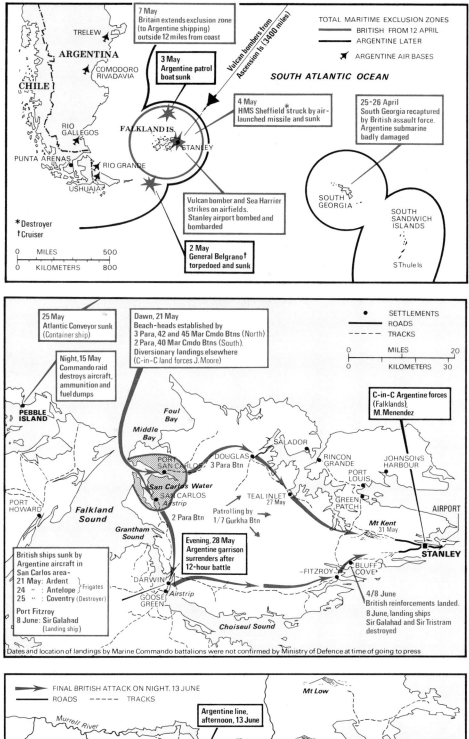

**7 May**
Britain extends exclusion zone (to Argentine shipping) outside 12 miles from coast

TRELEW

ARGENTINA

COMODORO
RIVADAVIA

CHILE

**3 May**
Argentine patrol boat sunk

Vulcan bombers from
Ascension is (3400 miles)

TOTAL MARITIME EXCLUSION ZONES
—— BRITISH FROM 12 APRIL
—— ARGENTINE LATER
✈ ARGENTINE AIR BASES

SOUTH ATLANTIC OCEAN

RIO
GALLEGOS

**4 May**
HMS Sheffield* struck by air-launched missile and sunk

**25-26 April**
South Georgia recaptured by British assault force. Argentine submarine badly damaged

PUNTA ARENAS

RIO GRANDE

FALKLAND IS.

STANLEY

USHUAIA

*Destroyer
†Cruiser

Vulcan bomber and Sea Harrier strikes on airfields. Stanley airport bombed and bombarded

SOUTH
GEORGIA

SOUTH
SANDWICH
ISLANDS

0 MILES 500
0 KILOMETERS 800

**2 May**
General Belgrano† torpedoed and sunk

S Thule Is

Far left: a portrait of Idi Amin, former president of Uganda, lies smashed on the floor of his residence in Kampala.
Below: loading a Tigerfish torpedo on the British nuclear submarine *Conqueror*. The *General Belgrano* was sunk by two of these weapons fired from *Conqueror*.

**25 May**
Atlantic Conveyor sunk (Container ship)

**Dawn, 21 May**
Beach-heads established by 3 Para, 42 and 45 Mar Cmdo Btns (North) 2 Para, 40 Mar Cmdo Btns (South). Diversionary landings elsewhere (C-in-C land forces J. Moore)

● SETTLEMENTS
—— ROADS
--- TRACKS

0 MILES 20
0 KILOMETERS 30

**Night, 15 May**
Commando raid destroys aircraft, ammunition and fuel dumps

PEBBLE
ISLAND

Foul
Bay

Middle
Bay

**C-in-C Argentine forces (Falklands), M. Menendez**

SALADOR

DOUGLAS
3 Para Btn

RINCON
GRANDE

JOHNSONS
HARBOUR

PORT
SAN CARLOS

PORT
LOUIS

PORT
HOWARD

San Carlos Water

SAN CARLOS
Airstrip

TEAL INLET
27 May

GREEN
PATCH

AIRPORT

Falkland
Sound

Patrolling by 1/7 Gurkha Btn

Mt Kent
31 May

2 Para Btn

**Evening, 28 May**
Argentine garrison surrenders after 12-hour battle

STANLEY

Grantham
Sound

**British ships sunk by Argentine aircraft in San Carlos area -**
21 May: Ardent ⎫ Frigates
24 " : Antelope ⎬
25 " : Coventry (Destroyer)
Port Fitzroy
8 June : Sir Galahad (Landing ship)

DARWIN

GOOSE
GREEN

Airstrip

-FITZROY

BLUFF
COVE

**4/8 June**
British reinforcements landed. 8 June, landing ships Sir Galahad and Sir Tristram destroyed

Choiseul Sound

Dates and location of landings by Marine Commando battalions were not confirmed by Ministry of Defence at time of going to press

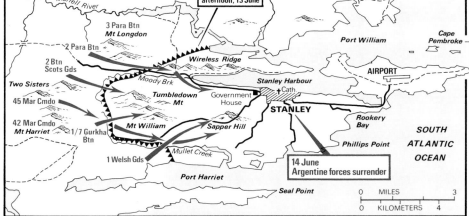

➤ FINAL BRITISH ATTACK ON NIGHT, 13 JUNE
—— ROADS --- TRACKS

Mt Low

Murrell River

**Argentine line, afternoon, 13 June**

3 Para Btn
Mt Longdon

2 Para Btn

Port William

Cape
Pembroke

2 Btn
Scots Gds

Wireless Ridge

AIRPORT

Two Sisters

Moody Brk

Stanley Harbour

45 Mar Cmdo

Tumbledown
Mt

Government
House

Cath

42 Mar Cmdo
Mt Harriet

Mt William

1/7 Gurkha
Btn

STANLEY

Sapper Hill

Rookery
Bay

SOUTH
ATLANTIC
OCEAN

1 Welsh Gds

Mullet Creek

Phillips Point

**14 June**
Argentine forces surrender

Port Harriet

Seal Point

0 MILES 3
0 KILOMETERS 4

ships. The principal military problem for the British was in the air where the few Harrier aircraft carried by the two small aircraft carriers had, with help from missiles from the ships, to hold off the whole Argentine Air Force and support the troops in any landing. Although the Argentinian pilots fought very bravely and gained a number of successes as the maps show, they were unable, despite their own heavy losses, seriously to hinder the British operations. The Argentinian Navy had little chance to make any positive contribution and must have been deterred by the sinking of the cruiser *General Belgrano* by a British nuclear submarine.

South Georgia was quickly and easily recaptured by the British forces soon after they arrived but there then followed a delay, punctuated by air attacks by both sides before the main British landings at San Carlos. The first British formation to land was made up of elite Royal Marine and Parachute Regiment troops. Goose Green was captured after a hard fight and the British, reinforced by Ghurka and Guards units, pushed forward to surround, and eventually accept the surrender of Port Stanley. Although the Argentinian forces were numerically at least as strong as the British many of them were young conscripts, no match for the British regulars in morale or training.

In the aftermath of the surrender President Galtieri of Argentina was forced to resign but with the British seemingly more than ever determined to keep the islands any final settlement of the dispute remained unlikely.

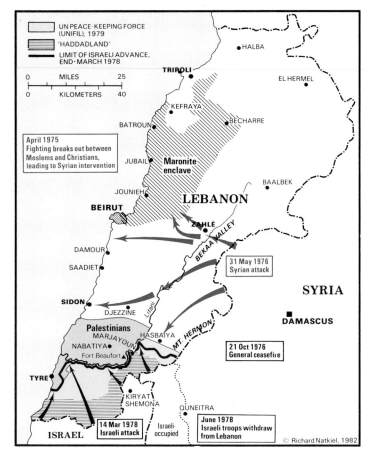

# The Lebanon

Once part of the Ottoman Empire, and under French administration between the wars, the Lebanon emerged as an independent state after World War II. Socially it was finely balanced, for its population was divided between Moslems and Christians of various denominations, the delicacy of this situation being reflected in the practice of appointing a Maronite (Christian) president to balance the Moslem prime minister. Friction, however, was exacerbated by the presence of camps for Palestine refugees from Israel. These refugee camps provided both recruits and sanctuary for anti-Israeli guerrillas.

It became almost an Israeli custom to stage air attacks, military incursions, and assassinations in the Lebanon as reprisals for terrorist attacks on Israelis anywhere in the world. Against its will, therefore, the Lebanon became a battlefield in the Israeli-Arab struggle, and the resulting stress soon brought inter-communal violence; right-wing Christians began by attacking Palestinians but soon found themselves fighting their Moslem fellow-citizens. Syria intervened, at first quietly but finally, in summer 1976, with a full-scale invasion. Even after this officially ended in October, Syrian troops remained in a peace-keeping role which, by and large, was sincerely if clumsily executed.

In March 1978, in reprisal for continuing Palestinian guerrilla attacks, Israeli troops occupied the south part of the Lebanon. A United Nations force was sent as part of a peace settlement, but when the Israelis withdrew they handed over their positions to a friendly right-wing Christian Lebanese militia. In April 1979 this militia, under Major Haddad, declared the area to be 'Independent Free Lebanon.' Meanwhile, farther north, the Syrian peacekeeping troops were fighting Christian militia forces around Beirut, and besieging Zahlé. The alliances and alignments of the Syrians seemed highly flexible, but one constant factor were the Israeli raids. In summer 1981 a general war on Lebanese soil between Syria and Israel seemed imminent, but US mediation postponed the crisis. It was sometimes difficult to discern whether the activities of Palestinian guerrillas were a justification or merely a pretext for these incursions. Israeli pressure in the south intensified early in 1982. The Israelis mounted a full-scale invasion in June 1982 and there was renewed fierce fighting involving Syrian and Palestinian forces. The Israeli forces again had the best of the fighting and, although the Palestinians lost very heavily, it remained uncertain whether the Israelis would obtain their objective of settling with the Palestinians once and for all.

# The Soviet Invasion of Afghanistan

In 1973 the King of Afghanistan was overthrown by Mohammed Daoud, who accepted Soviet military as well as economic assistance. Military help was required to back up Afghanistan's claim to territory on the Pakistan side of the frontier, provocatively called by the Afghans Paktoonistan. But in 1978, after attempting to limit Soviet influence, Daoud was overthrown in a Marxist coup and the new leaders were largely Soviet-trained army officers. The new government of Mohammed Taraki depended heavily on Soviet advisers, while the two wings (Parcham and Khalq) of the ruling communist party, the People's Democratic Party, remained in ideological and often violent conflict. In 1979 Taraki died in mysterious circumstances and the prime minister, Amin, became president and continued his hard-line policies. The latter aroused much resentment among the Afghans, many of whom had been arrested or had relatives arrested or executed. Amin pushed ahead with an attempt to transform social and economic life, but his attempt to end traditional feudal practices by land reforms, attacks on the priesthood and on landlords, abolition of the veil and dowries, intensified opposition. Rebels became bolder, and Amin called on Soviet-armed

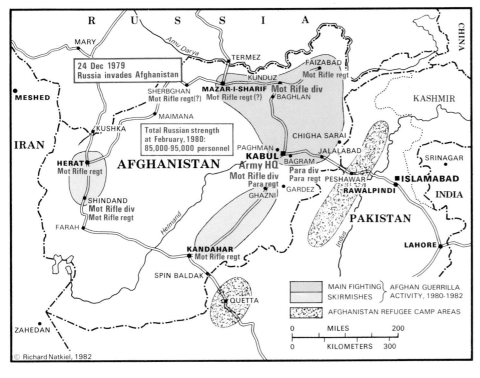

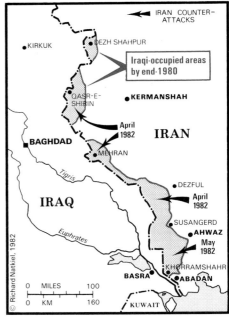

helicopters to bombard villages said to be harboring rebels. Armed conflict between rebels and government forces was marked by the ferocity employed by both sides.

Amin's presidency lasted only three months. His reliance on ever-increasing numbers of Soviet troops and advisers made it easy for the USSR to arrange a coup in which he was replaced by Babrak Karmal, a man regarded by the Soviets as a reliable communist who would tread more softly. This coup took place in December 1979, but did not bring peace. By the next summer former ministers who belonged to the Khalq faction had been executed, and the Red Army and Red Air Force were operating in Afghanistan in ever larger numbers. Only the capital Kabul, and cities like Jalabad, Herat, and Kandahar, could be considered safe by the government. The Afghan Army was demoralized, and large scale desertion made it ineffective. In the countryside the rebels were dominant, becoming quiet only when a Soviet punitive expedition was sent to the particular locality. The Soviet forces, which numbered as many as 100,000, used helicopters and armored vehicles, but were handicapped by the lack of roads. Raids by helicopter gunships and ground-support aircraft on rebellious villages produced little effect even though the rebels had no way of opposing them. Meanwhile refugees poured over the frontiers; about a million crossed to Pakistan in 1980, settling around Peshawar. Another half-million went to Iran. By 1981 one in every seven Afghans had fled his country. In 1982 the military situation was still a stalemate, with Soviet troops making the cities safe for the regime but holding little sway in the countryside. In this inhospitable environment the Karmal government was still attempting to introduce social reforms based on Marxist principles.

# The Gulf War

In April 1969, when the Shah of Iran enjoyed US backing and possessed powerful forces, he decided to abrogate a 1937 treaty defining the Iran-Iraq frontier in which the waterway known as the Shatt-el-Arab was entirely allocated to Iraq. Iran sent ships, flying the national flag, along this waterway, but this show of strength was followed by armed clashes in the area and in January 1970 the two countries severed diplomatic relations. However, relations were restored in 1973, and in 1975 the two countries declared themselves back on a brotherly footing, with an agreement that their frontier would pass along the center of the deepest main shipping channel of the waterway. Iran also

agreed to stop helping the Kurds of Iraq, who had been fighting Iraqi government forces in the hope of establishing their own independent state. The Shah's annexation of the Persian Gulf islands of Abu Musa and the Greater and Lesser Tumbs, which had occurred in 1971, by threat in the first place and by invasion in the second, was, however, still resented by Iraq and other Gulf states. The Shah regarded these islands, command-

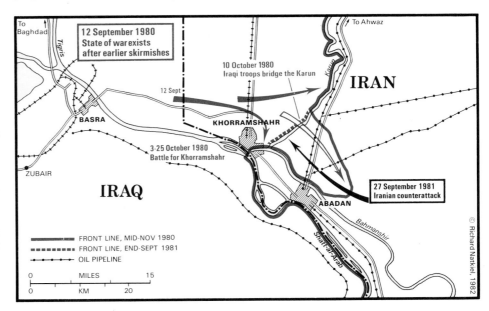

ing strategically-important straits, as vital and had lost no time in taking them after Britain's withdrawal from this region.

To Iraq's wish to regain control of the entire Shatt-el-Arab and to secure the withdrawal of Iranian forces from the Musa and Tumb islands, was added fear of Shi'ite Moslem influence. After the fall of the Shah and his replacement in Iran by a priestly (Shi'ite) government it seemed quite likely that the latter might encourage resistance of the Shi'ite majority in Iraq against the established Sunni leadership. In the meantime, Iraq had supported Arab demands that Iran should give autonomy to its Arabian territory of Khuzestan.

The Iranian revolution, its antagonizing of the USA by its detention of the US Embassy staff in Teheran, the murderous purge of the Iranian officer class, all suggested by mid-1980 that Iran was militarily weak. There were small frontier skirmishes, and on 22 September, following Iran's refusal to accept Iraq's demand that Iranian forces should be withdrawn from

one disputed area, the Iraqi Army crossed the frontier on a 300-mile front. Iraq had announced its abrogation of the Shatt-el-Arab agreement on 16 September.

Iran's resistance proved stronger than expected. Its first response was to bomb not only the advancing Iraqis, but also the port of Basra. The hostile capitals, Baghdad and Teheran, also came under air attack in September. By the end of that month the Iraqi army was besieging the ports of Abadan and Khorramshahr and the town of Susangerd. But Iraq was unable to capture these objectives before winter.

Mediation attempts failed during the winter and after the rains ceased in April 1981 full-scale warfare recommenced. In early June the Iranians fought some bloody battles to regain parts of their lost territory. But at the close of the dry season in 1981 the campaign was still a stalemate, although the vigor of Iranian counterattacks on the Iraqi salient toward Abadan suggested that time was not on Baghdad's side. Iranian attacks in 1982 made important gains.

# The Antarctic

After Captain Cook became the first European to cross the South Polar Circle, scientific curiosity, love of adventure, and the quest for national prestige ensured that there would be a succession of expeditions to the Antarctic. Meanwhile seal-hunters and others who made their living from the seas visited and explored the coasts. The late nineteenth century and the early twentieth was a period of heroism and rivalry. Expeditions were mounted as much for the prestige of planting national flags in virgin territory as for the purpose of scientific discovery. Nevertheless, and perhaps because the Antarctic is the land most remote from the great powers, in recent decades it has become the scene of international harmony rarely encountered elsewhere in the world.

The age of rivalry, which was really the age of colonization, resulted in several territorial claims being staked out in Antarctica. Such claims were based on exploration or on propinquity, the nearness of a sector of the Antarctic to a claimant state. Claims of the latter type, made by Chile and Argentine, have brought them into dispute with Britain, which claims the same territory by right of exploration and discovery. Norway and France also have claims based on exploration, while New Zealand and Australia defend their claim to other sectors of the continent on both counts.

Apart from the investigation of Antarctica itself, scientific research conducted there has made very useful contributions to studies of the world's climate. Realizing that scientific research would progress more rewardingly in an atmosphere of cooperation, free of territorial acrimony, the different nations began to associate more closely and in the International Geophysical Year of 1957–58 ten nations set up coordinated research bases in the continent. From this cooperation was developed the Antarctic Treaty of 1961 in which a dozen states agreed that the continent should be used only for peaceful purposes, and that every part would be open to observers from all countries to ensure that this agreement was not being violated. The Treaty carefully sidestepped the subject of various nations' claims to sovereignty: it neigher recognized nor questioned any of these claims, either directly or implicitly.

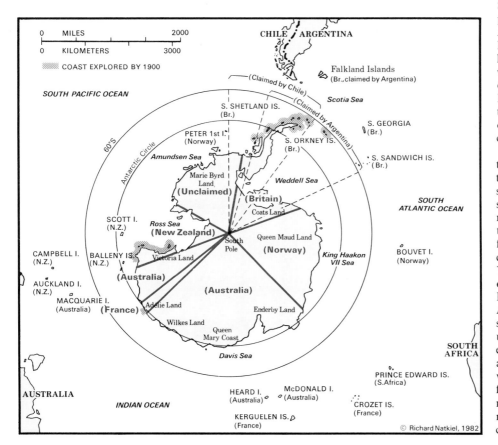

© Richard Natkiel, 1982

# The Formation of Senegambia

In colonial times, The Gambia was a British crown colony while Senegal, which surrounded it on three sides, was part of the French Empire, sending a deputy to the French parliament from 1848. Geographically, both countries are really one unit, with a common economic interest in the Gambia River, but politically they were split by accidents of the colonization process. The Gambia, with a population of only about 600,000, is simply two narrow strips on either side of the river, with a small port, Banjul, which is also the capital. Although it is about 200 miles long, it is only about twenty miles wide. Senegal is much bigger and has the largest port in West Africa, Dakar.

Both Senegal and The Gambia encountered social and economic problems following independence. Senegal at first joined with French Sudan, in 1959, to form the Mali Federation, but a year later seceded. Economic difficulties led to social unrest which in 1968 came to a head in strikes and demonstrations which, however, were quelled by a show of military force. French capital saved the economy from collapse but did little to help it become economically independent. Meanwhile, The Gambia was attempting in the 1970s to rescue its economy by the creation of a big tourist industry, but the signs were that this was creating many problems.

In June 1981 a left-wing coup just failed to overthrow the Gambian president, the situation being saved by the intervention of the Senegalese Army. Some of these troops stayed in Gambia, and this may have helped persuade the president of Gambia to accept the merger of Senegal and The Gambia, which had been sporadically discussed for at least 20 years. On 7 September 1981 it was announced that the merger would take place on 1 January 1982, and that the new state would call itself Senegambia.

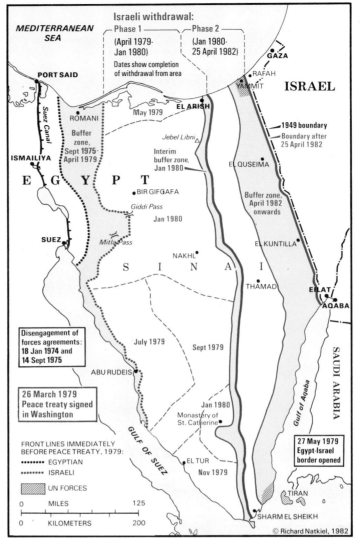

# Israeli Withdrawal from Sinai

In November 1977 President Sadat of Egypt unexpectedly visited Israel and addressed the *Knesset* and almost a year later the leaders of Israel and Egypt, hitherto uncompromisingly hostile, signed what became known as the Camp David Agreements in the USA. The first of the two agreements envisioned a five-year transitional period in which the inhabitants of two territories, occupied by Israel during the Arab-Israeli conflict, would be granted self-government and autonomy. These were the Gaza Strip and the West Bank, hotly disputed areas, and in the years since the agreement there has been little sign of progress toward their promised liberation. The second agreement arranged for a peace treaty between Israel and Egypt (signed in 1979, much to the distaste of other Arab governments) and for an Israeli withdrawal from Sinai. This, which did go according to plan, was to be made in several stages.

A strip alongside the Suez Canal had been recaptured by Egypt in the 1973 war, and this was bordered on the east by a wide buffer zone, which was Israeli territory occupied by the UN Peacekeeping Force. The first stages of the new Israeli withdrawal were from the latter zone, the withdrawal being not so much military as civil. By the end of January 1980 rather more than half of Sinai had been handed over, the boundary running almost directly north to south from east of El Arish to the southern tip of Sinai. For Israel, these withdrawals meant, among other things, the relinquishment of oilfields in southwest Sinai. The final stage was to a frontier stretching from just west of Rafah, in the north, to a point west of the Israeli port of Eilat at the head of the Gulf of Aqaba. In early 1982, as the final evacuation drew nearer, Israeli settlers in Sinai began to resist the withdrawal, but the Israeli Army controlled the situation and the process was completed by May.

# The World Today

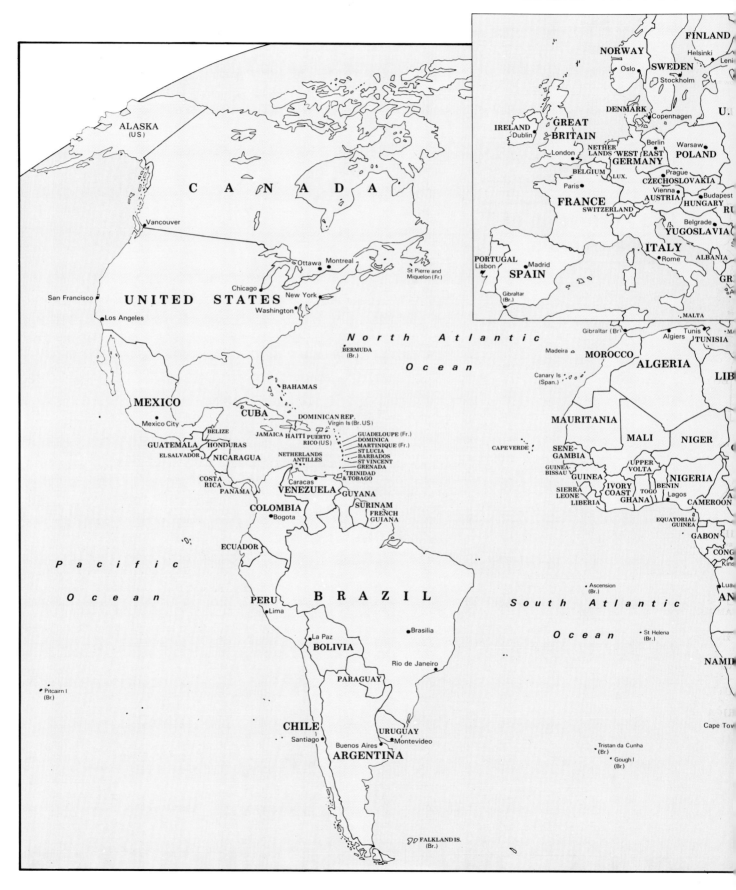

ALASKA
(US)

C A N A D A

Vancouver

Ottawa  Montreal

Chicago  St Pierre and
Miquelon (Fr.)

San Francisco  UNITED STATES  New York

Los Angeles  Washington

North Atlantic

Ocean

BERMUDA
(Br.)

MEXICO

BAHAMAS

Mexico City  CUBA

BELIZE  DOMINICAN REP.

Virgin Is (Br. US)

JAMAICA HAITI PUERTO
RICO (US)

GUATEMALA  HONDURAS

EL SALVADOR  NICARAGUA  GUADELOUPE (Fr.)
DOMINICA
MARTINIQUE (Fr.)
ST LUCIA
BARBADOS
ST VINCENT
GRENADA

NETHERLANDS
ANTILLES  TRINIDAD
& TOBAGO

COSTA
RICA

PANAMA  Caracas

VENEZUELA  GUYANA

COLOMBIA  SURINAM
FRENCH
GUIANA

Bogota

ECUADOR

Pacific

Ocean

PERU  B R A Z I L

Lima

Brasilia

La Paz

BOLIVIA

Rio de Janeiro

PARAGUAY

Pitcairn I
(Br)

CHILE  URUGUAY

Santiago  Buenos Aires  Montevideo

ARGENTINA

FALKLAND IS.
(Br.)

CAPE VERDE

Ascension
(Br.)

South Atlantic

Ocean  St Helena
(Br.)

Tristan da Cunha
(Br.)

Gough I
(Br)

NORWAY  FINLAND

Helsinki

Oslo  SWEDEN  Leni

Stockholm

IRELAND  DENMARK  Copenhagen  U.

GREAT

Dublin  BRITAIN  Berlin  Warsaw

London  NETHER-  WEST  EAST  POLAND
LANDS  GERMANY

BELGIUM  Prague

LUX.  CZECHOSLOVAKIA

Paris  Vienna  Budapest

FRANCE  AUSTRIA  HUNGARY

SWITZERLAND

Belgrade  RU

YUGOSLAVIA

PORTUGAL  Madrid  ITALY
Lisbon  SPAIN  Rome  ALBANIA

GR

Gibraltar
(Br.)

MALTA

Gibraltar (Br)  Tunis

Madeira  Algiers  TUNISIA

MOROCCO

Canary Is  ALGERIA
(Span.)  LIB

MAURITANIA

MALI  NIGER

SENE-
GAMBIA

GUINEA-  UPPER
BISSAU  GUINEA  VOLTA  NIGERIA

SIERRA  IVORY  BENIN
LEONE  COAST  TOGO  Lagos

LIBERIA  GHANA  CAMEROON

EQUATORIAL
GUINEA

GABON

CONG
Kins

Lua

AN

NAMI

Cape Tow

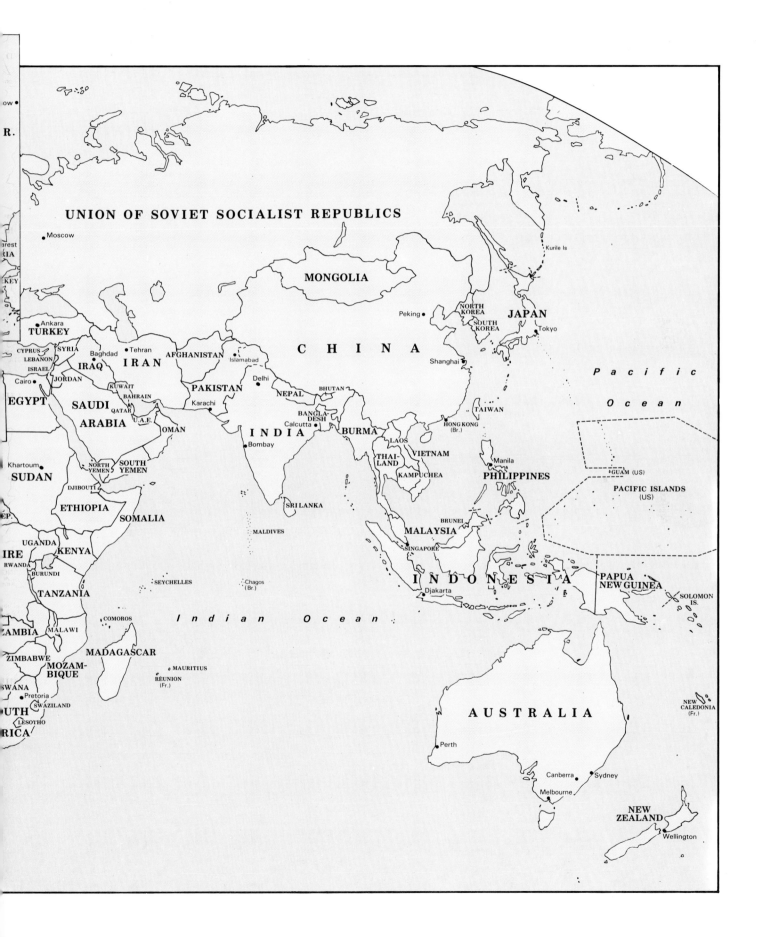

UNION OF SOVIET SOCIALIST REPUBLICS

R.

ow •

arest

RIA

KEY

• Moscow

MONGOLIA

Kurile Is

Ankara
TURKEY

CYPRUS
LEBANON     SYRIA
ISRAEL

Baghdad    • Tehran

Cairo •

JORDAN

IRAQ        IRAN

AFGHANISTAN

Islamabad

NORTH
KOREA
SOUTH
KOREA

JAPAN

Peking •

Tokyo •

C H I N A

Shanghai •

EGYPT

KUWAIT

SAUDI

BAHRAIN

QATAR

ARABIA

U.A.E.

OMAN

PAKISTAN

Delhi •

NEPAL

BHUTAN

BANGLA-
DESH

Karachi •

I N D I A

Calcutta •

BURMA

Khartoum •

NORTH
YEMEN

SOUTH
YEMEN

Bombay •

TAIWAN

HONG KONG
(Br.)

P a c i f i c

O c e a n

LAOS

SUDAN

DJIBOUTI

THAI-
LAND

VIETNAM

Manila •

ETHIOPIA

SOMALIA

SRI LANKA

KAMPUCHEA

PHILIPPINES

GUAM (US)

IRE

UGANDA     KENYA

RWANDA

BURUNDI

MALDIVES

BRUNEI

MALAYSIA

PACIFIC ISLANDS
(US)

TANZANIA

SEYCHELLES

Chagos
(Br.)

SINGAPORE

I N D O N E S I A

PAPUA
NEW GUINEA

SOLOMON
IS.

ZAMBIA    MALAWI

COMOROS

Djakarta •

ZIMBABWE

MOZAM-
BIQUE

MADAGASCAR

I n d i a n      O c e a n

SWANA

Pretoria •

MAURITIUS

RÉUNION
(Fr.)

NEW
CALEDONIA
(Fr.)

UTH

SWAZILAND

A U S T R A L I A

RICA

LESOTHO

Perth •

Canberra •    • Sydney

Melbourne •

NEW
ZEALAND

Wellington

# Index

## General Index

*Page numbers in italics refer to illustrations*

## Acknowledgments

The publishers would like to thank David Eldred who designed this book and Ron Watson who prepared the index. The following agencies kindly supplied the illustrations.

**BBC Hulton Picture Library** p 109
**Bildarchiv Preussischer Kulturbesitz** p177
**Bison Picture Library** pp 17 (top), 85, 101, 102 (top), 136, 152, 174
**Bundesarchiv** pp 29 (top), 67, 68–69, 98, 99, 104, 107, 116, 117 (both), 129 (both), 140
**Camerapix** pp 243, 246
**Charter Consolidated** p 244
**ECP Armées/Mars** p 212
**Fujiphoto/Mars** p 135 (bottom)
**Heeresgeschichtlichen Museum, Vienna** p 51
**Robert Hunt** pp 18, 44, 47, 59, 73, 74, 75, 96–97, 112, 114 (both), 115, 120, 121 (both), 123, 148 (top), 149, 207 (both), 208, 222 (top), 223 (top), 233 (top)
**Imperial War Museum** pp 31 (top), 32, 110, 125 (both), 169
**Imperial War Museum/Mars** pp 26–27, 31 (both), 33, 34, 35, 37 (both), 39 (both), 40, 42, 43 (both), 46–47, 48 (both), 49 (top), 50, 54, 55, 64 (left), 65, 148 (bottom), 151, 312 (left)
**Imperial War Museum/Faces** pp 1, 62 (both)
**Keystone Press Agency** pp 4–5, 194–95, 198 (top), 200, 201, 210, 211 (both), 213 (right), 214, 215 (both), 216 (both), 217, 218, 219 (both), 222 (bottom), 223 (bottom), 224, 225, 228, 229, 233 (bottom), 234, 235 (both), 236, 237, 238, 240 (both), 241, 242, 243 (both), 245, 246, 248
**Mansell Collection** pp 25, 60 (both), 71, 72
**Military Archive and Research Services** p 102 (bottom)
**Ministry of Defence/Mars** p 232 (top left)
**National Archives** pp 78–79, 130, 139, 146 (top), 158, 159, 167 (both), 188, 203 (bottom), 204, 206, 207 (top)
**National Army Museum/Mars** p 14–15
**Novosti Press Agency** pp 12–13, 17 (bottom), 125, 142, 143, 144, 146 (bottom), 154, 155, 163, 164, 178, 179, 185
**Panama Canal Co./Mars** pp 20 (top), 21
**Personality Picture Library** p 49 (bottom)
**Popperphoto** pp 23, 24
**SADO** p 129 (top)
**Ted Stone** p 128
**Ullstein Bilderdienst** pp 76 (both), 100 (both), 197, 198 (bottom)
**United Nations/Mars** p 70
**US Air Force** pp 160 (below), 175, 189, 220, 221
**US Air Force/Mars** p 170
**US Army** pp 6, 80, 95, 135 (top), 168, 173, 176, 180, 203 (top)
**US Marine Corps** pp 160 (top), 191, 192 (both), 205, 226, 227
**US Marine Corps/Mars** p 20 (bottom)
**US Navy** pp 2–3, 91, 93, 132, 138